PERFORMANCE MEASUREMENT & MANAGEMENT

PERFORMANCE MEASUREMENT & MANAGEMENT

A STRATEGIC APPROACH TO MANAGEMENT ACCOUNTING

Malcolm Smith

⑤SAGE Publications
London • Thousand Oaks • New Delhi

First published 2005

SAGE Publications Ltd
1 Oliver's Yard
55 City Road
London EC1Y 1SP

SAGE Publications Inc.
2455 Teller Road
Thousand Oaks, California 91320

SAGE Publications India Pvt Ltd
B-42, Panchsheel Enclave
Post Box 4109
New Delhi 110 017

British Library Cataloguing in Publication data

A catalogue record for this book is available from the British Library

ISBN 1-4129-0763-2
ISBN 1-4129-0764-0 (pbk)

Library of Congress Control Number: 2004116097

Typeset by Selective Minds Infotech Pvt Ltd, Mohali, India
Printed and bound in Great Britain by Cromwell Press Ltd, Trowbridge, Wiltshire

Contents

Preface

Accounting journals abound in a variety of three-letter acronyms, each describing the very latest innovative tool or technique which purports to be the solution to all our ills. The content and presentation of these terms often seem to be designed to intimidate the unwary user, both by their apparent complexity and by the suggestion that our current ways are outdated and must be mended. The proponents of such views suggest, often with vested interests, that the new developments are both original and must completely supplant our traditional ways of doing things. The adoption of such ideas is potentially disastrous, since most of the techniques are not suitable to all commercial circumstances. Far from being 'original', some of the developments are merely repackaged and remarketed versions of accepted concepts. They represent a revised approach or the integration of existing methods already in use in accounting, or stolen from other disciplines.

The examples of activity-based costing (ABC), the balanced scorecard and business process re-engineering (BPR) most readily spring to mind. Numerous examples of failed implementations of such schemes are to be found in the practitioner literature, often when the powers of persuasion of the consultant have overcome the evidence available from the information base. We are concerned here with the strategic advantage that might accrue to our businesses from the adoption of the latest management accounting tools and from the non-adoption of the latest fads.

By burrowing beneath the surface of the accounting jargon, this book identifies the underlying themes and integrates common messages. By seeing what is new and what is useful, we can achieve a fresh awareness of the way in which we currently operate and observe how innovations can complement existing methods by improving on current practice. Measurement practices, current and possible, pervade all of these issues, and we are closely concerned with improvements in performance measurement and all its implications. We accept that we cannot manage what we cannot measure, but also that managers and supervisors may only respond to what is being measured and reported. The onus is therefore on us to get the measurement framework right so that dysfunctional activity is discouraged.

This book analyses developments with respect to five key themes:

1 strategic goals:
    (a) strategic management accounting,
    (b) strength, weaknesses, opportunities and threats (SWOT) analysis,
    (c) resource-based view of the firm;

2 customer focus:
    (a) total quality management (TQM),
    (b) target costing,
    (c) customer profitability analysis;

3 employee creativity:
    (a) total employee involvement (TEI),
    (b) lateral thinking,
    (c) employee empowerment;

4 processes:
   (a) activity-based costing,
   (b) activity-based management (ABM),
   (c) value-added management (VAM),
   (d) just-in-time scheduling (JIT),
   (e) theory of constraints (TOC),
   (f) business process re-engineering,
   (g) supply-chain management;

5 information:
   (a) non-financial indicators (NFI),
   (b) balanced scorecard,
   (c) performance measurement,
   (d) risk measurement;
   (e) predictive modelling.

By increasing our awareness of new developments, we are forced to question the appropriateness of existing systems and measures, and to consider the relevance of management initiatives for doing things better. Throughout the text we recognize that we are working in a dynamic process; just as globalization has changed the nature of business, so too what was once acceptable in accounting research may no longer be so because of a more appropriate emphasis on research ethics. Many journals remain very conservative in the type of research they will publish, often on the grounds that it is difficult to demonstrate that 'new' methods constitute 'good' research in the same way as is possible with traditional methods. But thankfully this situation is changing gradually, and the wider opportunities for publishing case-based research in recent years provide evidence of this. Similarly, the timeliness and relevance of much of the content of the refereed literature does little more than suggest that it is written by academics for academics!

If dynamism has not impacted on all refereed journals, the same cannot be said of the professional journals: there were once two such journals called *Management Accounting*, but now there are none, the US version becoming *Strategic Finance* and the UK one *Financial Management*. These changes both reflect the need suggested, among others, by Otley (2001) for there to be more 'management' in 'management accounting' – so that a move towards strategic management and recognition of the wider financial implications is much appreciated. This dynamism parallels that between 'accounting system change' and 'performance measurement innovation'. While the incidence of management accounting system change is both low and slow, the same cannot be said of performance measurement frameworks, where initiatives are embraced more readily.

Thus it is appropriate that throughout we are concerned with measurable improvements in performance that address the interests of all stakeholders of the organization, especially where those benefits result from embracing accounting change.

Professor Malcolm Smith
Leicester Business School

October 2004

Acknowledgements

The helpful comments of academics and management accounting practitioners have been essential to the successful completion of this volume. Special mention must be made of Peter Phillips of Alcoa Australia; Shane Dikolli of the University of Texas at Austin; Richard Taffler, of the Cranfield School of Management; Keith Houghton, of the Australian National University in Canberra; Bev Schutt, Paul Martin, Chris Graves, Basil Tucker, Bruce Gurd and Chen Chang of the University of South Australia; John Cullen of Sheffield Hallam University and John Darlington.

Grateful acknowledgement is made to the following sources for permission to reproduce material in this book:

Smith, Malcolm (2002) 'Benjamin Greygoose: Survival in the Death Industry', *Accounting Education: An International Journal*, 11(3): 283–93. Reprinted with permission of Taylor & Francis (www.tandf.co.uk).

Smith, Malcolm (2002) 'Deane-Draper Stores: Employee Empowerment in a Retail Environment', *Accounting Education: An International Journal*, 11(2): 199–206. Reprinted with permission of Taylor & Francis (www.tandf.co.uk/journals).

Smith, Malcolm and Graves, Christopher (2002) 'Cunningham Construction: Bonus Schemes and Participant Behaviour', *Journal of Accounting Case Research*, 7(1): 1–6. Permission to use has been granted by Captus Press Inc. and the Accounting Education Resource Centre of the University of Lethbridge (www.captus.com).

1 Introduction

Manufacturers in general recognize the importance of a knowledge of the cost of their product, yet but few of them have a cost system on which they are willing to rely under all conditions.

While it is possible to get quite accurate the amount of materials and labor used directly in the production of an article, and several systems have been devised which accomplish this result, there does not yet seem to have been devised any system of distributing that portion of the expenses, known variously as indirect expense, burden or overhead, in such a manner as to make us have any real confidence that it has been done properly.

As an illustration, I may cite a case which recently came to my attention. A man found that a cost on a certain article was 30 cents. When he found that he could buy it for 26 cents, he gave orders to stop manufacturing and to buy it, saying he did not understand how his competitor could sell at that price. He seemed to realize that there was a flaw somewhere but he could not locate it. I then asked him what his expense consisted of. His reply was labor 10 cents, material 8 cents, and overhead 12 cents.

The next question that suggested itself was how the 12 cents overhead would be paid if the article was bought. The obvious answer was that it would have to be distributed over the product still being made, and thereby increase its cost. In such a case it would probably be found that some other article was costing more than it could be bought for, and, if the same policy were pursued the second article should be bought, which would cause the remaining product to bear a still higher operating expense rate.

If this policy were carried to its logical conclusion, the manufacturer would be buying everything before long, and be obliged to give up manufacturing entirely.

People as a whole will finally discard theories which conflict with common sense, and, when their cost figures indicate an absurd conclusion, most of them will repudiate the figures. A cost system, however, which fails us when we need it most, is of but little value and it is imperative for us to devise a theory of costs that will not fail in use.

Wise words indeed, and on a subject which clearly requires more in-depth analysis. But this misses the point, which is not to re-enter the 'make versus buy' debate, but to highlight the source of the citation. These extracts were part of a speech identifying the inadequacy of our cost accounting systems, delivered in 1915 by H.L. Gantt (see Gantt, 1994: 4), the father of Gantt charts, and a contemporary of F.W. Taylor. Yet such is the rate of progress in cost accounting research over the past 90 years, that such views would not be out of place in the pages of a current issue of a management accounting journal. With such progress it is unsurprising that many view accountancy as more art than science, a view that this volume will attempt to rectify.

The fact that the problems identified by Gantt (i.e., allocation of overheads, performance measurement) are the same ones that still occupy us now is a clear indication that we are looking in the wrong places for answers and travelling down too many blind alleys. By taking a cue from Mr Gantt and ensuring that we develop management accounting principles which facilitate relevant, common-sense solutions, a goal-oriented approach will surely emerge.

Too often, while the stated goal of an organization may be to increase its corporate wealth, the basis of measurement is short-term profit rather than a longer-term or share-priced-related indicator. It is not always clear that current actions are wholly consistent with overriding corporate goals.

Increasing the wealth of the organization through its trading activities demands that we generate and act upon management information which facilitates optimum business decisions in terms of wealth generation. To do so, we need to get back to basics by focusing on fundamental accounting information; paying less attention to such as standard costing and materials requirements planning, and more to our wealth-creation goal.

Accounting information can be quantitative or qualitative, financial or non-financial. Traditional methods of processing information are biased towards the use of quantitative financial information, often to the exclusion of all else. As a consequence, decision-making models in accounting usually focus on financial ratio combinations and make little use of non-financial indicators or non-traditional information sources.

Figure 1.1 shows the range of alternatives, with the left-hand side of the diagram very much the focus of attention. In some instances financial ratio models work extremely well (in, for example, the early-warning models of distress among competitors or suppliers, considered in Chapter 9); in others they are less than useful. In such instances we must ensure that we use relevant information and, where that information is not currently available, we should institute procedures to collect it. The importance of fundamental analysis of the appropriate data in order to improve our decision-making capabilities and generate a competitive edge is central to the message of this book.

Recent developments in management accounting have, however, not revolved around *techniques* of data analysis. These remain pretty much at the stage they reached in the 1950s, although advances in computer hardware and software have improved the speed and efficiency of operations. Instead, recent work has focused on the availability of traditional data from on-line sources, new data from non-traditional sources, and on changing attitudes towards the interpretation of data and the implementation of change.

Figure 1.2 illustrates the diverse range of management accounting activities in the planning and control framework. Traditional management accounting teaching, and most textbooks, still follow the right-hand route through this diagram, focusing on the use of accounting information to

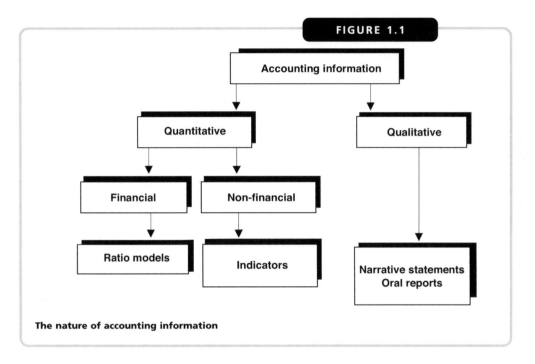

FIGURE 1.1

The nature of accounting information

institute managerial and operational control and management reporting, based on traditional accounting systems. The new management accounting tools recognize the relevance of the traditional methods, where appropriate, but change the emphasis towards the left-hand side of the diagram. The focus is then on a decision support system (leaning on disciplines outside the traditional realm of accounting) in order to facilitate decisions congruent with stated corporate goals. Behavioural, cultural and attitudinal changes in both management and the workforce at large are necessary if such systems are to work properly, and many of the latest developments are designed to reinforce such changes.

The need for a revised focus stems from the failure of financial accounting to satisfy our need for timely, decision-useful information. Financial accounting information focuses on compliance, with the adherence to standards, rules and procedures being paramount. The information requirements and processing differences of users and the communication of such information is, at best, a secondary consideration. Thus, while we finish with accurate, consistent, reliable and replicable historic information with which to pursue a stewardship function, the information is hardly timely and the opportunities for legal manipulation are plentiful; see Griffiths (1986), Smith (1992), Clarke et al. (1997) and Fox (2004) for a multitude of examples.

Management surveys have repeatedly shown that financial accounting numbers are used as the basis for strategic decisions despite the inappropriate assumptions they embrace. Management accounting is *present-* and *future*-oriented and historic information is often of limited, though significant, usefulness.

Cost accounting systems fail to address the causes of overhead costs and the use of one cost system for several alternative purposes inevitably causes problems. It is no surprise, then, that misleading numbers are generated when we attempt to use the same accounts for inventory valuation, product costing and process control.

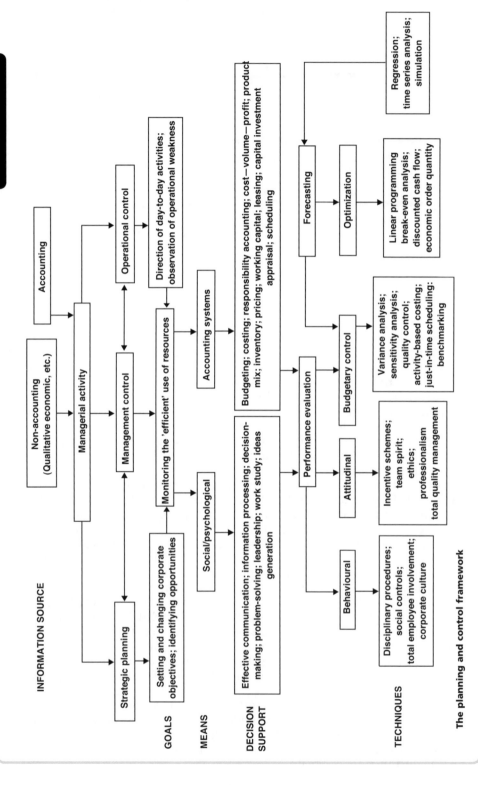

FIGURE 1.2

The planning and control framework

The solution lies in the innovative use of new information sources, predictions and estimates, and of non-financial data. Close enough may indeed be good enough when it comes to management accounting decision-making, because, in an uncertain environment, information must be timely even if it is imprecise. Opportunities for the manipulation of information still exist, but the source of that manipulation is largely behavioural, rather than lying in non-compliance with accounting standards. Potentially decision-useful information may be biased by individuals acting in their own interests rather than those of the company, plant or division. New initiatives aim to improve the decision-usefulness of information by increasing goal congruence; that is, by changing the attitudes and work practices of individuals so that they pursue goals which are in the long-term interests of the enterprise of which they are a part.

Figure 1.3 illustrates how easily goal conflict can occur through misperceptions and over-reliance on short-term financial accounting numbers. In case 1, short-term profit is the stated corporate goal, presumably based on strategic considerations. However, actions at lower levels of the organization may not be consistent with such a goal. At the operational level the time span on which employees focus may be a month, week, day or even shift. Performance measurement may be based on time envelopes of eight hours (or less), making it easy to lose track of longer-term objectives. Productivity measures are frequently employed to monitor the use of resources and, where supervisors' performance is based on productivity achievements, it is hardly surprising that they focus on idle time and slack for both labour and equipment. The consequences of keeping everyone and everything busy all the time include:

- high levels of work in process;
- high inventory costs;
- work carried out and costs incurred before necessary; and
- increased machine maintenance and downtime.

In an absorption costing environment all of these practices will increase short-term profit but produce outcomes inconsistent with the corporate goal. Goals must be communicated clearly down through the corporate structure and performance measures devised which produce behaviour congruent with them.

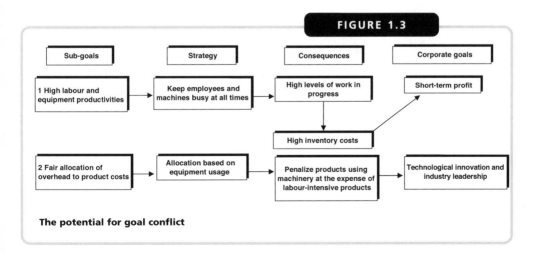

FIGURE 1.3

Sub-goals	Strategy	Consequences	Corporate goals
1 High labour and equipment productivities	Keep employees and machines busy at all times	High levels of work in progress	Short-term profit
		High inventory costs	
2 Fair allocation of overhead to product costs	Allocation based on equipment usage	Penalize products using machinery at the expense of labour-intensive products	Technological innovation and industry leadership

The potential for goal conflict

Case 2 stems from the financial accounting stipulation that overhead costs be allocated to product costs in a 'fair' manner. In practice this usually means on the basis of direct labour hours or direct machine hours. An inappropriate choice of allocation method could be detrimental to the achievement of corporate goals. If the company is pursuing one of the niche strategies outlined by Porter (1980) – industry leadership via technological innovation – then the use of direct machine hours will penalize those products using machinery and benefit those that remain labour-intensive; an outcome contrary to that required. In this context, Hiromoto (1988) recommends allocation on the basis of strategic goals, ignoring ideas of 'correctness' or 'fairness' by deliberately penalizing those operations whose activities are not congruent with corporate goals. In Chapter 5, a wider consideration of cost drivers within the context of activity-based costing presents us with many more opportunities for implementing strategies consistent with stated goals.

SUMMARY

In this chapter we have identified some of the deficiencies commonly apparent in management accounting systems and performance measurement frameworks, together with their potential implications. In Chapter 2, we turn to a consideration of the development of management accounting techniques, so paving the way for the detailed discussion of a practical approach to performance measurement and the implementation of strategic management accounting in Chapter 3. The associated issues raise a number of current concerns, and suggest alternative methods, which then provide the focus for the remaining chapters.

2   Emerging Issues

INTRODUCTION

Robert Kaplan's tongue-in-cheek comment on the evolution of management accounting from the early years of the twentieth century suggests that nothing has changed much, especially where teaching and textbooks are concerned:

> Despite considerable changes in the nature of organisations and the dimensions of competition during the past 60 years, there has been little innovation in the design and implementation of cost accounting and management control systems. Virtually all of the practices employed by firms today had been developed by 1925. (Kaplan, 1984: 390)

Like most rash generalizations, the statement contains an element of truth, and in this chapter we examine both what has, and has not, changed, together with the developments in management accounting research. We conclude by speculating on the future direction of such activity.

HISTORICAL DEVELOPMENT

The traditional basis of management accounting was firmly established by the 1920s, as Table 2.1 demonstrates. The industrial revolution, particularly in the UK and USA, drove the implementation of managerial controls in the 1890s, and generated scientific approaches to optimizing the use of physical and material resources. Thus, internal administrative processes were established to co-ordinate multiple production activities; operating statistics were generated to evaluate performance, and elaborate cost reporting mechanisms were devised, particularly for the use of direct labour and raw materials.

By the 1920s, normal managerial practice embraced both a centralized accounting system on the one hand and a decentralized functional organization on the other. Such a distinction allows management to finance

TABLE 2.1

The historical development of management accounting

Development	Date
Cost and management control information	1890
Scientific management	1901
Break-even charts	1903
Standard costing and variance analysis	1908
Centralized accounting systems with decentralized functional organization	1900
Capital and operating budgets	1910
Centralized control and decentralized responsibility	1920
Separation of financial and cost accounting	1923

capital requirements and allocate investments appropriately between competing activities while allowing time for the development of specialist managers and freeing senior management from operational responsibilities sufficiently to allow them to adopt strategic and planning roles.

The decentralization of responsibilities into divisional entities necessitates annual forecasting to co-ordinate operations and performance monitoring for the early detection of budget variances. The efficient allocation of resources demands uniform performance criteria embracing the use of sophisticated, market-based transfer pricing mechanisms.

The recognition of the importance of non-accounting disciplines – notably mathematics, statistics, sociology, psychology, management and marketing – in the identification and modelling of factors influencing infor-mation processing and decision-making has changed the direction of management accounting practice and research. Table 2.2 details the major developments in management accounting since 1940, many of them the result of the adaptation of methods already established in other disciplines.

As Lothian (1987) observes, the factors critical to corporate success now bear little resemblance to those applicable in the 1920s . Neely et al. (2003: 8) echo the remark by emphasizing the extent to which globalization has changed the nature of business. Changes in technology and the manufacturing environment mean that world-class manufacturers must now focus on:

- quality of output;
- zero defects in supplies;
- minimum inventory levels made possible by just-in-time deliveries;
- flexible manufacturing systems; and
- goal-oriented programmes for the workforce.

The investigation of the role of management accounting information in complex operations has focused on the interaction of disciplines in actual practice and the formalization and correction of deficiencies. This is par-ticularly applicable to the pioneering work of Cooper, Johnson and Kaplan in the development of activity-based costing (ABC) since the mid-1980s, and of Kaplan and Norton in the development of the balanced scorecard since the mid-1990s. Although the great majority of published examples have so far been based on production and assembly operations, there is

TABLE 2.2

Post-1925 developments

Development	Date
Residual income method	1940
Simplex method for linear programming	1944
Discounted cash flows	1950
Total quality management	1950s
Cusum charts	1954
Optimum transfer pricing	1957
Computer technology	1960
Opportunity cost budgeting	1966
Zero-base budgeting	1969
Information economics and agency theory	1970s
Just-in-time scheduling	1970s
Activity-based costing	1980s
Target costing	1980s
Value-added management	1980s
Theory of constraints	1980s
Business process re-engineering	1990s
Balanced scorecard	1990s
Economic value added	1990s

now sufficient evidence to suggest that the basic principles will also apply to the small business and service sectors.

MANAGEMENT ACCOUNTING RESEARCH

The published findings of academic research in management accounting have frequently been criticized for lacking both relevance and timeliness. Both characteristics remain important issues:

- The most recent survey evidence suggests that there is still a sizeable gap between the topics that academics write about and those that managers want to hear about.
- The rigorous refereeing requirements of the top academic journals mean that the time lags prior to publication are excessive – perhaps three years from project to publication for the 'best' journals – so we must still look to the professional and practitioner literature, and to the *Harvard Business Review*, for the latest ideas.

The requirement for relevance has seen a trend towards field studies and the use of case study research, reflecting both internal and market requirements in determining the development of management accounting information systems, but difficulties remain. Over 15 years ago, Bromwich and Bhimani (1989) identifed five persistent weaknesses in management accounting practice that required further research:

- the subservience of management accounting to external financial accounting requirements;
- the lack of strategic considerations in management accounting and project appraisal;
- the reliance of management accounting on redundant assumptions concerning manufacturing processes;
- the maintenance of traditional assumptions in performance evaluation; and
- the continued short-term orientation of performance measurement.

Their research findings were instructive in providing indications of the likely direction of research. In particular, they identifed:

- the overwhelming need to identify *cost drivers* which link processes to the costs of output;
- the need to measure *activity-based costs* where these are meaningful and can lead to significant benefits;
- the benefits of *non-financial* accounting information in different manufacturing environments;
- the opportunity to incorporate both *qualitative* and non-financial, quantitative information into management accounting information systems; and
- the increasing relevance of a *strategic* approach to management accounting.

Each of these areas provided fruitful research avenues: ABC issues dominated the literature for the next decade, and cost allocations and capacity considerations remain at the forefront of concern and have generated renewed, and welcome, interest in operations management issues. More recently, cost drivers and activity-based costing have lost their prominence, initially to a fleeting flirtation with the theory of constraints and throughput issues, but latterly through the balanced scorecard, which has become a focus for the study of non-financial measures. However, it would be fair to say that 'strategic' approaches and 'qualitative' measures have remained under-researched.

A number of subsequent studies report the conduct of up-to-date literature views and speculate on the future direction of management accounting research. It is instructive to compare these 'expectations' with outcomes over the period to identify those topics which remain under-researched, from both an academic and a practitioner perspective.

Atkinson et al. (1997a), in a study that included contributors from around the world, established three broad areas which might attract management accounting researchers:

- the role of management accounting in organizational change;
- the interaction between accounting and organizational structure; and
- the role of accounting information in supporting decision-making.

They (like Shields, 1997) recommended the adoption of a multi-method approach to research in these three broad areas, and provide more specific guidance with the following structure.

1 Change:
  - the effect of management accounting on organizational change;

- organizational change as an impetus for management accounting change; and
- the process of change.

2 Structure:
- at the micro level – for example, the impact of empowered work groups on decision-making and performance evaluation;
- at the macro level – for example, the adaptability of management accounting to both centralized and decentralized organizational structures; and
- linkages within control systems in, for example, the balanced scorecard.

3 Decision-making:
- strategic decisions and the design of management control systems;
- resource-based views of the organization;
- non-profit organizations; and
- tactical decision-making.

Two important literature reviews, by Shields (1997) in the USA, and by Scapens and Bromwich (2001) in the UK, detail what was being published in the top tier of academic literature in management accounting in the final years of the twentieth century. Management accounting practice, management accounting change and cost accounting techniques (including ABC) dominate the lists. Shields (1997) identified six key areas for future research:

- management accounting change;
- supply and value chains;
- strategy accounting;
- virtual accounting; and
- multiple research methods.

Foster and Young (1997), in another US study, argue that an important source of research topics is the view of management, often gleaned from the press or from practitioner journals. But such topics might be deemed to be too 'new' or too 'different' for them to be published in the most prestigious academic journals. Foster and Young (1997) identified five topic areas of relevance to organizations which they deem to be 'under-researched':

- customer profitability and satisfaction;
- cost management and cost control;
- quality;
- growth; and
- profitability.

Otley (2001) suggests that management accounting research has become misdirected: too focused on 'accounting' and consequently with too little attention directed towards 'management' issues. He suggests that as a result we see a widening gap between academic research and management accounting practice. Jazayeri and Cuthbert (2004) investigate the nature and extent of this 'gap' by comparing practitioner requirements with the output of the leading academic journals in the field. They note some change in publishing practices since the Shields (1997) and Scapens and Bromwich (2001) papers, with an observed movement from 'cost reporting and analysis' towards a more future-oriented approach to cost management. More important, they detail what is *not* being published, especially where there is a clear difference with the requirements of decision-makers. High on the list of manager preferences in the Jazayeri and Cuthbert study were 'change management', 'technological impact', 'regulatory impact' and, most importantly, 'staff-related issues'. Indeed, research into human resources aspects of management was consistently the top requirement of decision-makers in organizations of all sizes – while such studies rarely, if ever, grace the pages of the top management accounting journals.

Interestingly, some of the topics identified by Shields (1997) and Foster and Young (1997) in the USA, and by Atkinson et al. (1997a), did not rate highly in the preferences apparent in the UK survey conducted by Jazayeri and Cuthbert (2004). While 'cost control' accounted for 12.6% of responses, 'customer retention' was responsible for a miserly 1.1%! However, there is some common ground and the highest-rated issues in the manager survey have clear implications for management accounting research. These issues are:

1 Staff-related (HRM) issues. While the major concerns might embrace the mainstream management/psychology literature (e.g., leadership, motivation, staff and customer retention) the accounting implications revolve around our ability to create value from these attributes. The focus therefore moves to intangible assets and our ability to link these to financial performance. The issues of customer relationship management, for example, are examined in more detail in Chapter 4; there we see the conflicting nature of the existing empirical evidence, very little of which has appeared in the accounting literature.
2 Impact of legislation on competitiveness. For the UK this would embrace issues concerned with the enlargement of the European Union, for example, including currency issues, transfer pricing and cross-border performance comparisons. It would also include globalization and cultural issues, particularly where these impact on issues of costs and managerial control.
3 Change management. The key issue in Shields' (1997) listing and a prominent topic, particularly in the practitioner literature.
4 Value and supply chain management. Second in the Shields (1997) list but still highly under-researched, perhaps because of its association with lengthy and expensive in-depth field studies.
5 New product development. A topic which reflects the relative neglect in the academic management accounting literature of start-up issues, and of issues related to small and medium-sized enterprises generally.

It is perhaps appropriate to finish this section with mention of the balanced scorecard from a research perspective. We will return to the scorecard and its implications for practice at several other points in this volume. Despite the numerous criticisms of the balanced scorecard (e.g., Atkinson et al., 1997b; Norreklit, 2000; Otley, 2001), it remains the management accounting innovation that has had the biggest impact on practice in the last decade. It is therefore deserving of more research attention than it has had to date. Otley (2001) identifies five specific areas where research into the balanced scorecard and its implementation would make a notable contribution:

• the benefits of a scorecard *per se*, rather than of its constituent measures;
• procedures for the mapping of the causal relationships implicit in the scorecard;

- the role of target setting;
- links with reward structures; and
- the establishment of information systems and feedback loops.

Empirical evidence in some of these areas is already beginning to emerge – for example, Ittner et al. (2003b), in suggesting that the existence of a scorecard in its own right has no positive impact on financial performance. We might anticipate progress in each of these five areas.

The words of Hayes and Abernathy (1980) have become sadly prophetic in that the outcomes they suggested were likely from financial accounting manipulation, and reward structures to match, have indeed come to fruition with the likes of Enron, Worldcom (in the USA), Parmalat (in Europe), and no doubt others. What Maltz et al. (2003) describe as 'asset restructuring and balance sheet wizardry in lieu of key investments' have serious implications for management accounting if they are to ensure that appropriate internal control procedures are in place. Wallin (2004) emphasizes the role of the finance professional in providing the reliable internal governance systems required by the Sarbannes–Oxley Act (2002). She draws parallels with total quality management systems in that quality has to be designed and built up from the *inside*, rather than inspected (or audited) from the outside. We might therefore anticipate future research that will highlight the role of the *accountant*, rather than accounting, so that the focus is more on the ethics, values and motivations of the individual, and the way in which these interact with the incidence of internal control.

SUMMARY

Recognition of the expanded scope of management accounting has yielded, and will continue to yield, great benefits. A strategic approach, recognition of the importance of the market and the impact of other disciplines has been paramount. The focus on value-added management and the use of shareholder value-type measures have highlighted weaknesses in our traditional financial accounting measures and have provided useful additions to the management accountant's armoury. Perhaps the greatest current opportunity lies in the recognition of the importance of a global approach. Globalization has changed the nature of business over the last ten years, increasing the levels of both complexity and uncertainty. We now have more external competitors, many of them 'virtual', and an expanded number of stakeholders (many of them with conflicting interests). Awareness of international trends and recognition of inter-country approaches and cross-cultural differences should all foster research into differences between individual management decision-makers associated with culture, gender and information processing styles. The implications for performance measurement and management control will be similarly pervasive.

3 Performance Measurement and Analysis

INTRODUCTION

Executive decisions rely on information from many sources, not all of which is accounting information. The various sources might be described simply as:

- accounting/non-accounting;
- qualitative/quantitative;
- financial/non-financial; and
- internal/external.

Non-financials are becoming increasingly important in management accounting, but the major source of information is still currently the internal–quantitative–financial–accounting combination. Systems to provide this information embrace the planning and control of activities and the costing of products. Such systems would gather information from the control and monitoring mechanisms in place – inventory control, working capital management, budgeting and variance analysis. The systems in place must be seen as *relevant*, having been based around the operation of the different processes of the organization and providing information appropriate for support and reporting. They should not have the potential to mislead by distorting the true picture (see Cooper and Kaplan, 1988). Lack of relevance – which would normally include lack of timeliness – is perhaps the greatest potential deficiency of any management accounting information system. The nature of the systems will differ between organizations, generally being simpler when there is process manufacturing and when there are only minor fluctuations in work-in-progress inventories.

In this chapter we explore alternative measurement systems, with the emphasis on providing a strategic perspective which embraces the interests of all stakeholders of the organization.

STRATEGIC MANAGEMENT ACCOUNTING

Strategic management accounting (SMA) is an integral part of the establishment of a decision-support system providing information to decision-makers. Decision-makers use accounting information and systems to pursue the goals of an enterprise, so that five key factors pull in the same direction and facilitate the achievement of corporate goals. Those factors are:

- mission statement;
- goals;
- objectives;
- operational strategies; and
- performance measurement.

Strategic decisions may be required in a variety of areas:

- *Corporate strategy*. What business should we be in?
- *Competitive strategy*. How do we compete?
- *Operational strategy*. How do we organize internally to pursue corporate goals?

For any organization the choice of an optimum set of non-financial indicators (NFIs) is inextricably linked to its goals. A given set of NFIs must provide measures consistent with the achievement of corporate goals. Where the goals change, the optimum set of NFIs will change too, and a system should be in place which is sufficiently robust to reflect these changes over time. Figure 3.1 illustrates just such a system.

The various processes of the operation are designated A1, A2, ..., A7. An initial evaluation allows their classification into value-adding (A1, A3, A4, A5, A7) and non-value-adding (A2, and A6) activities, immediately highlighting the importance of eliminating, or at least restricting, the latter where they do not constitute essential control procedures.

For each activity there is an associated group of cost drivers – a sequence of events or actions which cause costs to be incurred within that activity. For simplicity these are numbered C1, C2, ..., C21, and arbitrarily allocated on a proportional basis to activities. In practice, the number of cost drivers and their allocation will be dependent on the complexity of the activities.

For each cost driver we will have alternative measures of performance, usually NFIs, designated F1, F2, ... There will, therefore, be a multiplicity of A–C–F combinations representing particular measures of particular cost drivers for particular activities; in practice, too many to measure and monitor on a regular basis. We need to identify a subset of indicators (A–C–F combinations) and associated targets the achievement of which is most closely congruent with corporate goals – as few as five or six such combinations

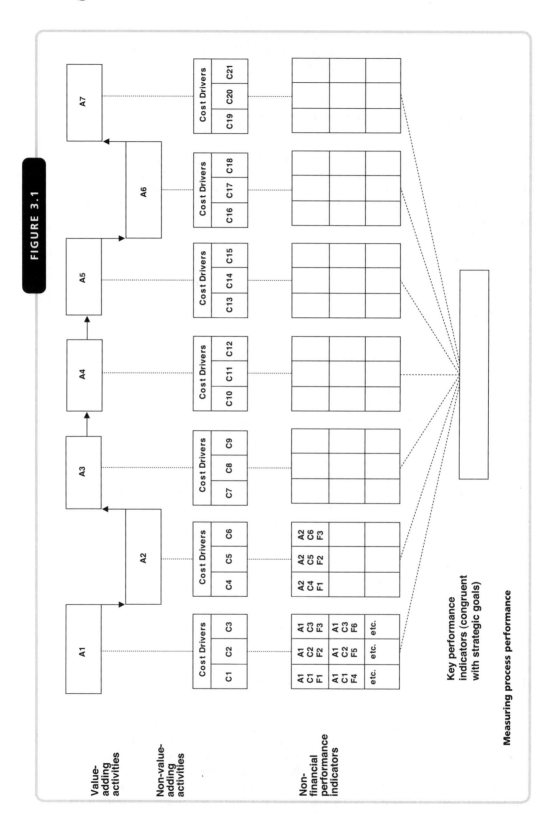

FIGURE 3.1

may be enough. These must be monitored to measure trends in performance, and the constituent combinations changed when corporate goals change.

Figure 3.2 shows the stages that must be considered in adopting a strategic approach to management accounting. It is worth examining each of these stages in some detail, and the remaining sections of this chapter do just that.

John Harvey-Jones reveals a systematic approach to managerial problem-solving in practice which corresponds closely with the SMA approach of Figure 3.2 (see Harvey-Jones and Massey, 1990; Harvey-Jones, 1992). He adopts a five-stage analytical process:

- *The published accounts.* Scrutiny of five years of published accounts, looking for trends, patterns and exceptional items. Focusing on the key numbers allows a clear picture to emerge of overall financial performance.
- *The 'top man'.* A face-to-face meeting with the top man (there were no 'top women' in his sample) highlights his personal values and the vision that he has for the future of the enterprise. A statement of the perceived problems provides a basis for analysis and a standard against which the 'real' problems can be measured.
- *The shop floor.* A visit to the shop floor, observation of systems and processes, and apparently idle chatter with employees reveals a great deal about the efficiency of operations, the competence of senior management and workplace morale. A smooth, unhurried product flow, the latest technology, a 'smiley' workforce and managers who 'know their numbers' are paramount.

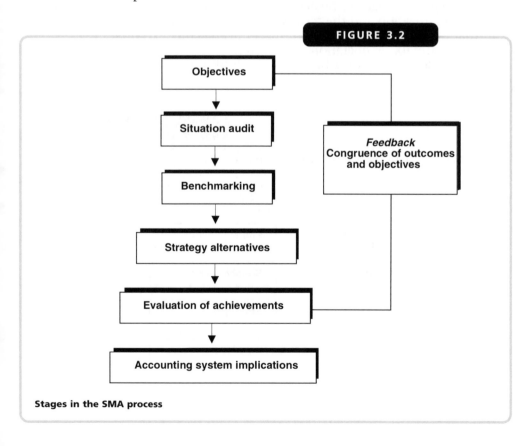

FIGURE 3.2

Stages in the SMA process

- *Testing hypotheses*. The real problem, rather than that perceived by the chief executive, is formulated by reference to theory, practice elsewhere and expert opinion. Alternative solutions and implementation strategies are developed.
- *Implementing solutions*. The optimum solution must be sold to the company. The directors are the decision-makers and have to believe that the chosen solution is consistent with the objectives of the organization. The alternatives are established and the realities of the financial situation laid bare. In practice, many of the alternatives will be unpalatable; they imply criticism of senior managers, tackle the 'wrong' problem from their perspective and/or convey a different message than what the executive had expected/wanted to hear.

Enlightened management listens and implements the solution, with appropriate modifications to meet a hidden agenda – or, more likely, the implementation does not take place, because the executives do not want to hear the hard truth or they rationalize to explain why the 'troubleshooter' reached the wrong conclusion.

If we link Figure 3.2 to the five-stage Harvey-Jones approach, we can draw the parallels of Figure 3.3. Thus, *the published accounts* and *the shop floor* stages constitute a situation audit, whereby an examination of the historic data (accounting or otherwise) and reference to current practice allow us to appraise current performance and speculate on likely future direction, if unchecked. The implications of a 'do nothing' strategy quickly become apparent.

The *top man* stage establishes corporate goals, the long-term objectives of the organization and the means deemed acceptable to meet those goals, in that they suit the values and mindset of the chief executive.

A benchmarking operation is consistent with seeking expert opinion in order to identify industry best practice. It allows us to compare our own

---

FIGURE 3.3

• The published accounts	Historic data
• The 'top man'	Goals
• The shop floor	Situation audit
• Testing hypotheses	Benchmarking
	Strategies
• Implementing solutions	Solutions

The Harvey-Jones approach to problem-solving

performance with that of others and provides a link from the situation audit to the formulation of hypotheses. The development of strategy alternatives follows, which must be weighed against each other as part of the *testing hypotheses* stage.

The final stage of *implementing solutions* is common to both processes; the optimum alternative is sold and the strategy implemented. Evaluation of achievements follows in order to measure the benefits resulting from the new strategy and to determine whether these benefits exceed the costs of implementation and meet the expectations of the participants.

The feedback loop in Figure 3.2, 'congruence of outcomes and objectives', parallels the 'acceptability' criteria, for both solutions and achievements, apparent from the personal values of the chief executive. Goals are being met in a manner consistent with the moral and ethical guidelines set by the chief executive, or the managing family group. The monitoring of outcomes for consistency with strategic goals has choice implications for the accounting methods employed. A failure to match the two may necessitate the adoption of innovative management accounting techniques to ensure that there is a closer correspondence.

Far from being haphazard, the whole process is a systematic one which leans heavily on the interpersonal skills of the analyst. Information must be gleaned in an efficient, even devious manner, analysed appropriately and realistic alternatives formulated. Customer focus is paramount throughout the whole process, but no more so than at the solutions stage, where decisions must be made. The decision-maker is the 'customer' for the strategic alternatives and recommendations for action, and he/she likes nothing less than being told what to do with his/her own business. There must be alternatives and the decision-maker must be allowed to choose.

OBJECTIVES

Once they have been developed, we should resolve to achieve our objectives without compromise. The communication of objectives should come from the top, together with a commitment to monitor their achievement at all levels. It is helpful to identify separate management and leadership executive roles and to distinguish between planning and control functions. Table 3.1 details a matrix of management activities allowing the development of different objectives to be actioned by different personnel.

It is important to take a holistic view of objectives, to ensure that they are consistent and that they are tightly linked to operating processes and associated measures of process performance. Putting goals and objectives into operation across all the processes of the organization should highlight their precise impact on customers and employees. Japanese management accounting emphasizes the direct link between strategic corporate goals and management accounting practices, so that a productive approach is taken in developing a management accounting system which positively supports, rather than tacitly monitors, operational performance.

For example, the process of setting objectives is taken to a second level by the Japanese technique of 'target costing' – a technique devised for high-tech assembly industries but which has now been modified for use in

TABLE 3.1

Management activity by role

	Planning	Control
Management	Setting budgets and standards Revising estimates Organization and staffing	Corrective action Performance appraisal Resource allocation

Leadership	Forecasting
	Setting objectives
	Changing direction
	Strengths, weaknesses,
	    opportunities and threats
	    (SWOT) analysis
	Resource-based
	    view (RBV)
		Motivation
		Group alignment
		Goal congruency

process-oriented industries too (see Chapter 6 for a more detailed discussion of target costing).

SITUATION AUDIT (SWOT ANALYSIS)

Central to the development of strategic approaches for the future is a detailed awareness of the current situation. This will include a detailed assessment of organizational effectiveness:

- compared to last year;
- compared to our competitors; and
- compared to the industry as a whole.

Figure 3.4 provides a skeleton for a full strengths, weaknesses, opportunities and threats (SWOT) analysis to determine the potential and the vulnerability of the enterprise across different spheres of activity. Again, the importance of the database to the successful completion of the analysis cannot be stressed sufficiently. It is likely that most organizations will need to collect more data, especially relating to future projections and the intentions of competitors, to make the most of the analysis. Overall, the analysis attempts to provide answers to a number of specific questions:

1 What is our current position?
2 Where would we like to be?
3 Where might we be if we *do not* react to the current situation?
4 What strategies must we adopt:
  (a) to achieve 2?
  (b) to avoid 3?

A fundamental industry analysis (following Porter, 1980) of each sphere of activity provides one means for us to be fully aware of the existence of

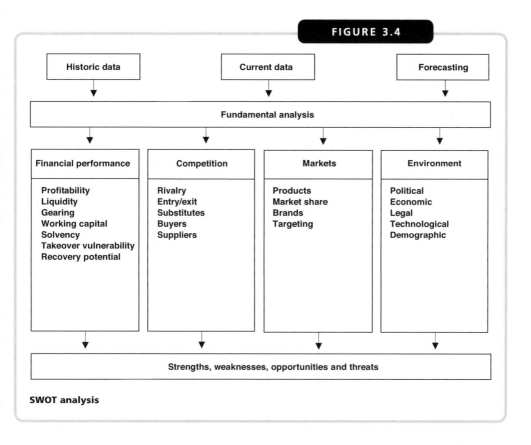

FIGURE 3.4

SWOT analysis

opportunities and threats. (An alternative approach, the resource-based view, is discussed later in the chapter.) Each activity merits detailed consideration, allowing us to identify and measure the multitude of variables which indicate how well we are doing.

Financial performance SWOT analysis

Performance appraisal based on historical financial data is fraught with danger because of the doubts surrounding the timeliness of historical information and the comparability of different time periods and companies. Despite these difficulties, and the opportunities for 'creative accounting' and 'window dressing' within generally accepted accounting principles, this fundamental financial analysis must be performed. Such analyses can be extremely powerful and can offer real predictive power, provided that they use:

- the right financial variables;
- the appropriate weighting for importance; and
- the best mathematical combination to integrate the variables.

We must be prepared to perform this analysis both for ourselves and for all companies with which we are associated. These include:

- competitors;
- customers;
- suppliers;
- joint-venture partners; and
- subsidiaries.

Failure, takeover or obvious weakness among any of these businesses is likely to have a significant impact on the outcomes of our business.

Small businesses, particularly those led by entrepreneurs in business for the first time, frequently fail because of an absence of basic business acumen. Shortage of working capital and the lack of proper books and records, with which to exercise control, merely exacerbate the situation.

Argenti (1976) offers five kinds of symptoms of failure, still relevant today, each impacting upon the financial performance of the enterprise:

- financial accounting;
- over-optimism;
- mistakes;
- defects; and
- external signs.

Financial accounting symptoms are readily apparent from poor profitability, heavy indebtedness (and the associated burden of loan interest) together with cash flow problems reflected in difficulty in meeting commitments, paying bills or finding working capital to fund change.

Over-optimism is frequently evident in encouraging public statements issued in the persistent hope that the present adverse conditions will turn around. A web of secrecy will often hide the true situation from banks, creditors and even the enterprise itself. Creative accounting involving the exploitation of woolly accounting standards relating to the recognition and realization of assets and liabilities may be employed to inflate income figures and to massage balance sheet ratios. Management fraud may be adopted as a short-term defensive manoeuvre while the economic upturn is awaited. Dividends are frequently maintained at levels higher than financial analysts believe to be prudent.

Mistakes may be so serious as to alter the status of the company. These are apparent in single large projects – potentially profitable but so risky that they make the survival of the enterprise precarious – and in attempts to grow too fast, over-trading, so that sales levels are greater than the working capital base can support.

Defects in board structure, internal organization or accounting systems may not be apparent as weaknesses when a company is profitable and growing. But when things start going wrong, lack of financial leadership and management depth, especially coupled with an autocratic chief executive and weak board, are often terminal. Young companies will often have no business plans, no budgeting or inventory control and no costing systems, making them inadequately equipped to deal with any change or crisis.

External signs, evident from a visit to the plant or office, often highlight the difficulties under which a company is operating. Physical deterioration of the plant reflects the lack of maintenance expenditure and is frequently coupled with the absence of senior management through illness. Staff turnover will be high because of salary cuts, a lack of promotion opportunities, low morale and lack of long-term employment opportunities. Product quality and service are low, with no money available to fund the development of new products.

Despite the undoubted value of these indicators, many are, however, difficult to quantify. The development of a decision-useful model is further hampered by the requirement of first-hand knowledge of the enterprise. Fortunately, models constructed on the basis of publicly available financial information can perform extremely well.

Four key financial areas can be identified:

1 *Profitability*. The ability to generate earnings.
2 *Gearing*. The degree of dependence on external borrowings.
3 *Liquidity*. The ability to generate suitable cash flows.
4 *Working capital*. The ability to generate sufficient resources to promote future growth.

The combination of these factors can provide an excellent indication of financial risk and a measure of solvency and relative financial performance. The major problem is one of constructing an optimum model of financial performance (a question considered in more detail in Chapter 9, with the development of linear discriminant models). Three questions need to be answered:

1 Which financial variables best represent each of the key financial areas?
2 What weighting should be assigned to each of the variables?
3 What mathematical function best describes the relationship?

The first of these questions is the most difficult to answer, since the 'best' single ratio may not necessarily be the one that is statistically most useful within a combination of such ratios. For example:

$$\frac{\text{Profit before interest and tax}}{\text{Total assets}}$$

is a sensible and widely-used ratio measuring profitability, but in practice it is usually outperformed by the more obscure

$$\frac{\text{Profit before tax}}{\text{Current liabilities}}$$

for the purpose of model building. The reasons for this are difficult to explain in the absence of a widely accepted theory of business failure, but may be connected with the ease with which the constituent items can be manipulated.

Optimum variable weightings are determined by computer software, and linear models have been shown to work extremely well. A suitable model would therefore be of the form:

$$Z = f(\text{probability, gearing, liquidity, working capital})$$

which transforms to the following, when employing representative weightings:

$$Z = a + b\frac{PBT}{CL} + c\frac{TL}{NW} + d\frac{QA}{CL} + e\frac{WC}{NCE}.$$

Here a is a constant; b, c, d and e are the weightings for the ratios. PBT is profit before tax, CL is current liabilities and PBT/CL represents profitability. TL is total liabilities, NW is net worth and TL/NW represents gearing. QA is quick assets, and QA/CL represents liquidity. Finally, WC represents working capital after division by net capital employed. Z is the overall measure of financial risk, with a negative value indicating a company currently exhibiting signs of financial distress, in that it has a financial profile similar to previous failures.

Such models can be intimidating and formidable to construct. Even so, very simple, unit-weighted models can be incredibly robust and give a clear indication of overall performance. For example, the three-variable combination

$$\frac{PBT}{CL} + \frac{QA}{CL} - \frac{TL}{NW} < 0$$

gives a very quick, simple indicator of a company likely to be financially distressed – better still if a composite industry average score can be used as the standard for comparison, rather than zero. Such comparisons are extremely useful rules of thumb before more detailed analyses are conducted.

The commercial Z-score model due to Taffler (1983), for the UK manufacturing sector, detailed all companies with a distressed profile, as reflected by their negative score. The model was the most successful predictive model of its type in the UK, but the equation parameters were unknown until published in Agarwal and Taffler (2003), so facilitating the calculation of overall financial performance scores for all UK manufacturing companies based on their published accounting numbers. The model is detailed below:

$$Z = 3.2 + 12.18X_1 + 2.5X_2 - 10.68X_3 + 0.0289X_4.$$

Here X_1 is profit before tax divided by average current liabilities, contributing 53% of the explanatory power of the model; X_2 is current assets divided by total liabilities, contributing 13%; X_3 is current liabilities divided by total assets, contributing 18%; and X_4 is the no-credit interval (NCI), contributing 16%. The NCI indicates the number of days the company can continue to trade when it can no longer generate revenues. It may be calculated as

$$NCI = \frac{\text{Defensive assets} - \text{actual liabilities}}{\text{Projected daily expenditure}}$$

$$= \frac{\text{Current assets} - \text{inventory} - \text{current liabilities} \times 365}{\text{Sales} - \text{profit before tax} + \text{depreciation}}.$$

The major problem with models of this type, as emphasized in Morris (1998), is that they deliberately overstate the possibilities of failure.

In identifying 'distressed' companies they ensure that they do not miss any potential failures, so that many companies who will in fact continue to trade successfully over a number of years will be deemed to be in danger. At any one time, about 25% of all listed companies will be designated as 'distressed', but only a third of these will actually fail. The remainder will either:

- be taken over before they are allowed to fail;
- effect a full recovery as a result of the adoption of appropriate managerial turnaround strategies; or
- continue to trade while remaining distressed in the short term.

This over-prediction is a cause for concern in all failure prediction models. The inclusion in the 'distressed' set of those companies who might effect a financial recovery if they implement appropriate turnaround strategies provides a positive angle for early-warning models, in that it identifies some cases in need of remedial action. Slatter (1984: 105) identifies a number of generic recovery strategies that might be adopted, depending on the cause of the 'distressed' state. He specifies seven major causes of decline and potential failure:

- poor management;
- inadequate financial control;
- high cost structure;
- lack of marketing effort;
- competitive weaknesses;
- financial policy; and
- ill-advised acquisitions and projects.

Each of these is associated with a particular set of generic recovery strategies.

Poor management he associates with autocratic leadership, an ineffective board, the neglect of core businesses and lack of management depth. Appropriate remedial action would require new blood in the management team, organizational change and decentralization.

Inadequate financial control is associated with a poorly designed accounting system, misuse of information, the distortion of costs through misallocation of overheads and an organizational structure which hinders rather than facilitates control. This would be improved by new management and decentralization if accompanied by tighter financial controls.

High cost structure is associated with operational inefficiencies, competitor control of raw materials and proprietary knowledge, low-scale economies and high labour costs. Cost reduction strategies and a revised product-market focus are appropriate for recovery. The former would be directed towards:

- raw material costs – aimed at improved buying practices, better utilization and the possible substitution of materials;
- unit labour costs – aimed at increasing productivity and reducing headcount;
- overhead costs – targeting manufacturing, marketing and distribution.

Lack of marketing effort is associated with inadequate or inflexible response to changing patterns of demand and product obsolescence. Improved marketing pursues a revenue-generating strategy embracing:

- changed prices;
- more selling effort;
- rationalizing of the product line;
- focused promotion; and
- a closer focus on customer needs.

Competitive weakness is reflected by lack of strength in both price and product competition and an absent product-market focus. A reliance on old products will be apparent, with inadequate differentiation and no new product ideas on the horizon. Cost, marketing and product weaknesses must be addressed, with growth via acquisition considered as a means of overcoming deficiencies in the product-market area.

Financial policy weakness is characterized by high debt–equity ratios, expensive sources of funding and conservative financial policies. A new financial strategy will likely include debt-restructuring and revenue-generating policies.

Failed acquisitions are characterized by the purchase of losers at a price which is set too high. Poor post-acquisition management often results in a quick resale. Ill-advised big projects, which threaten the company's survival, are associated with start-up difficulties, the loss of major contracts and the underestimation of capital requirements and market entry costs.

Asset reduction is the most appropriate recovery strategy in the circumstances, embracing:

- reducing fixed assets – through divesting operating units and specific assets, management buyouts, and sale and leaseback arrangements.
- reducing working capital – through extending creditors and reducing both inventories and debtors. This would include cancelling orders, returning goods, the sale of surplus raw materials, tighter credit and possibly factoring arrangements for debtors.

The extent to which these strategies are appropriate will also be determined by the severity of the crisis and peculiar industry characteristics. Where short-term survival is threatened we might anticipate a recovery strategy comprising four strands:

- cash generation;
- asset reduction;
- debt restructuring; and
- very tight financial control, embracing cash management, cost reduction, product refocus and improved marketing.

Research continues in order to improve existing failure prediction models so that they are better able to distinguish between 'failed' companies and those capable of recovery. Several interesting avenues are being pursued, including the better utilization of evidence of the deliberate adoption of income-increasing accounting policies and procedures (see Smith et al., 2001), of narrative evidence of changed management priorities and strategies (see Smith and Gunalan, 1996), and increased attention to variables suggested by the management literature (see Smith and Graves, 2005).

Porter's work on competitive structure is grounded in industrial eco-nomics and has been very influential in the analysis of current and future strategic positions (e.g., Porter, 1980). One of the weaknesses of models designed to identify takeover victims among distressed enterprises, evident from the previous section, is the focus on financial variables to the exclu-sion of organizational factors. We might speculate that such models would be improved by reference to data relating to potential competitors and takeover predators, notably:

- their ability to overcome barriers to entry to a new industry;
- their potential for achieving synergy through takeover;
- opportunities for the extension of an existing strategy to new companies or industries;
- opportunities for backward vertical integration to seek control of raw material suppliers; and
- opportunities for forward vertical integration to seek control of retail outlets.

Porter identifies three generic strategies in the thwarting of competitors. There is considerable empirical support to suggest that successful firms can attribute their short-term advantage to one or more of them. Those firms aim to:

1 achieve overall cost leadership
    (a) by pursuing technological change to maintain an innovative edge, and
    (b) by adopting a strict cost-conscious approach, observing high labour and equipment productivities;

2 differentiate and promote the product
    (a) by pursuing brand loyalty rather than price competition,
    (b) by product promotion which makes successful imitators unlikely,
    (c) by stimulating demand from particular customer types; and

3 target a particular market niche
    (a) by identifying distinct sub-markets, and
    (b) by responding to specific customer needs.

These strategies are consistent with measures which reduce short-term vulnerability and provide the base from which to build long-term success, namely:

- large-scale production economies, and associated low prices and quality product (consistent with industry leadership);
- product differentiation and associated high prices and quality (consistent with brand promotion); and
- short-term objectives in which the strategic target may be cost or quality (consistent with niche marketing).

Each of the strategies is still vulnerable to outside influences, notably from international competition and market fragmentation but the pursuit of specific goals considerably reduces that vulnerability. Depending on the nature of the industry, competition between participants may take one of a number of forms:

- *Threat of entry by newcomers.* Overcome by the deliberate creation of market barriers or by retaliatory action against new entrants to force them out of business.
- *Threat of substitute products.* Necessitating investment in new technology and industry leadership to ensure an awareness of potential advances to which the company is vulnerable.
- *Buyer power.* Dictated by size and market share, which can effectively allow buyers to dictate price and quality to suppliers.
- *Seller power.* Again determined by size and a quasi-monopoly position, allowing sellers to dictate price and quality to potential buyers.
- *Intensity of rivalry.* Determined by growth and cost structures and the difficulty of extricating oneself from a business. In the worst-case scenario, sponsorship or the easy availability of funding may make entry easy, but low margins, specialized assets, negligible liquidation values and high closure and redundancy costs may make exit difficult.

The choice of generic strategy will often dictate the *operational strategy* necessary to meet consumer demand. Capacity planning offers three alternatives:

- *demand matching* (i.e., production = demand), with a consequent impact on the efficient use of resources, equipment and labour;
- *operation smoothing* (i.e., production = average demand), with a consequent impact on the inventory holding necessary to meet variations;
- *subcontracting* (i.e., buy not make), with a consequent impact on the power the company exerts to control its own destiny.

The focus on capacity considerations highlights the importance of product cycle time, bottlenecks and delivery reliability, and the consequent need for innovative measures of operating performance. The intricacies of job scheduling and the time variations inherent in production set-ups and operations sequences foreshadow complexities which may lead to substantial operating delays and outcomes inconsistent with corporate strategy. The research literature addressing throughput issues and the theory of constraints have been particularly influential here (e.g., Darlington et al., 1992; Coughlan and Darlington, 1993).

The 'cost leadership' strategy has popularized strategic cost analysis, with its identification of a value chain between raw materials and end user and the specification of cost drivers and cost reduction opportunities for each activity of the chain. The implications of this for accounting information requirements in order to effect appropriate internal management have been explored by Shank and Govindarajan (1992), and provide the basis for the discussion in the *Cambridge Business Conferences* case study which follows. Importantly, despite the cost focus, one of Porter's six stages of strategic cost analysis calls for the impact of cost reduction strategies on the alternative 'product differentiation' and 'niche marketing' strategies to be carefully monitored. The implications for SMA are clear: a goal focus for each activity, internal and external measurement across a whole range of variables and continuous benchmarking of performance against that of competitors.

CASE STUDY

Cambridge Business Conferences: A case study of strategic cost analysis

Cambridge Business Conferences (CBC) is a company skilled in the organization and running of conferences and seminars. It normally runs six or seven events per year and is currently planning a two-day conference to take place at the University Arms Hotel in August 2004. The conference will be entitled 'Information Technology in the 21st Century' and will present 12 speakers of international reputation, five from UK, three from western Europe and two each from Australia and the USA. The booking of the venue has already incurred the payment of a non-returnable deposit of £2000. The conference organizer, Alice Tan, estimates the following costs to be applicable:

- A daily delegate rate of £30 per head on each day of the conference, to cover tea/coffee and use of all hotel facilities.
- Meals charged at a standard rate – breakfast £12, lunch £18, dinner £28.
- Overnight rate of £49.50 for a double room.
- Stationery and conference papers costing £10 per delegate pack.
- Conference speakers are to be paid a combination of fee plus expenses, and will be offered meals and overnight accommodation at the company's expense.

The following fees have been agreed (and must be paid even in the event of the prior cancellation of the conference): three speakers are to be paid £500; two £600; two £100; one A$2500; and one US$2800. The remaining speakers have either offered their services free or are prevented from charging a fee (i.e., government departments and foreign embassies). Expenses (estimated at £100 out-of-pocket expenses plus travelling expenses per person) are only payable after they have been incurred.

    An advertising budget of £1500 has been agreed for the period from March to June. The major marketing thrust will be via mailshot. An initial print run of 5000 brochures has been agreed for distribution by post. Envelopes and covering letters can be reckoned to make the total cost of the mail-out 55p per addressee. Printing costs can be calculated at £500 set-up plus 15p per brochure. Confirmation letters will be sent to those delegates making firm bookings by post at a further cost of 50p per addressee. Administration costs and the costs of word-processing mailing lists are estimated to amount to £7000.

    Turning to revenues, pilot testing reveals that delegates will be prepared to pay a conference fee of around £700, the rate to include overnight accommodation between the days of the conference and inclusive of all meals between lunch on day 1 and lunch on day 2. Any delegates requiring overnight accommodation prior to day 1 will be billed separately. The venue can accommodate a maximum

CASE STUDY (cont.)

of 150 delegates in theatre style, or 90 delegates in seminar style, over each of the two days of the conference. Alice is actively seeking other means of raising additional conference-related revenue.

The directors are currently evaluating the viability of this conference in order to make recommendations consistent with the short- and long-term goals of CBC. The analysis should embrace break-even and sensitivity analyses associated with the financial aspects of the proposed event, together with an exploration of the critical non-financial factors.

CASE ANALYSIS

Cambridge Business Conferences is apparently in the conference organization business in the long run, so the single event under consideration cannot be viewed in isolation. The key issues of the case appear to be:

- a company with goals of survival and long-term profitability;
- a single event, 'Information Technology in the 21st Century', which may or may not contribute to company profitability;
- the strategic importance of this event to the long-term viability of the company; and
- the financial impact of the success/failure of this event.

Clearly the company would like this event to make a contribution to profitability and will take pains to ensure that it does so. But its long-term reputation may be more important, so that strategic decisions may be necessary to cope with loss-making contingencies.

A formal SWOT analysis could be conducted here, but would be of limited use in this particular case because very little information is provided on the 'group', its staffing or its alternative 'products'. The calculations are the simplest starting point because they will answer some of our unknowns regarding this particular event. However, we must remain fully aware that the financials – whatever message they give – may be peripheral to the strategic actions eventually undertaken.

Sketching out the relationships reveals that a fixed–variable cost division does not work particularly well, nor does a sunk–discretionary cost division. The focus is clearly on relevant costs and the conference activity, as well as its timing, reveals a possible avenue of analysis.

A simple break-even analysis requires that we establish precise relationships for costs and revenues. Our first assumptions require the formulation of linear relationships:

$$C = a + bq,$$

and

$$R = pq,$$

CASE STUDY (cont.)

where C is total costs, R is total revenues, a is up-front conference-related costs fixed costs, b is variable costs per unit (related to q, the number of delegates) and p is the price to delegates, assumed to be fixed and, therefore, initially eliminating the prospect of discounting. Break-even occurs where $R = C$, that is,

$$pq = a + bq$$

or

$$q = \frac{a}{p - b}.$$

We can similarly express break-even output, q_1, as

$$q_1 = \frac{\text{Fixed costs}}{\text{Price} - \text{variable cost per unit}}.$$

In order to allocate costs appropriately, realistic assumptions need to be made, but there is no single 'right' answer.

Table 3.2 shows a number of areas of uncertainty which require a sensitivity analysis to determine their impact:

• How do we treat the £2000 non-returnable deposit? It may constitute an up-front booking cost or a deposit which is lost only in the event of cancellation. In the latter instance it may be used to offset other conference-related costs, and not constitute additional expense, should the conference go ahead.

TABLE 3.2

Costs and revenues for Cambridge Business Conferences

Cost per delegate	£	Up-front pre-conference costs	£
Delegate rate	60	Speakers fees	2,900
(2 @ 30)		AUD$2500	1,000
Meals: 2 @ 18;		US$2800	2,000
1 @ 12; 1 @ 28	76		5,900
		Deposit	2,000
Room rate	49.50		
		Advertising	1,500
Stationery	10		
		Mailshot: set-up	500
Confirmation letter	0.50	5,000 @ 0.70	3,500
Total	196.00		
		Administration	7,000
		Total	20,400
		Conference-related fixed costs	
		Speaker expenses	1,200
		Speaker travel (economy)	10,800
		Total	12,000

CASE STUDY (cont.)

- The standard combination of meals is assumed to comprise two lunches, one breakfast and one evening meal.
- Double rooms are provided, but it is unrealistic that we can assign two strangers to share one room.
- Speakers' fees (and travel costs) require assumptions about the level of exchange rates.
- Speakers' travel costs require assumptions regarding the likelihood of having to meet first-class/business/economy modes of travel.

Earlier assumptions yield:

Total fixed costs $= £20,400 + £12,000 = £32,400 = a$

Variable cost per unit $= £196 = b$

Price per unit $= £700 = p$

So that the break-even no. of delegates is

$$\frac{a}{p-b} = \frac{32,400}{700-196} = 65.$$

This figure would be marginally higher were we to include the costs of accommodating and feeding the speakers too!

Given that the venue can only accommodate 90 delegates in seminar style, the 65 delegate break-even is high, severely limiting the potential profitability of the event (i.e., a maximum profit of less than £13,000 with all seats filled). Theatre style, increasing the accommodation to 150 possible delegates, at least provides the opportunity for expanding the viability of profit levels.

A detailed sensitivity analysis reveals that this solution is relatively robust to uncertainties – except for the necessity of paying first-class airfares for pivotal conference speakers. This could cause a blow-out in travel-related expenses. Costings based on economy-rate fares are probably unrealistic for all but academics! CBC might expect to pay first-class fares for several and business-class for the remainder of the speakers, seven in all, flying to the venue. Conference-related fixed costs might easily double to £24,000, increasing the break-even figure to 88 delegates.

Up-front expenses of £20,400, with no matching revenues, will put pressure on the overdraft facility. With realistic assumptions we cannot make a profit with a seminar-style presentation. Even with a theatre-style format we need well over 100 delegates to make it a viable proposition.

There is a distinct possibility that we will not manage to attract delegates in these numbers at a fixed fee of £700. These factors increase the risk attached to this conference, so that other contingencies have to be examined, one of which is the cancellation option.

If we have already incurred the up-front pre-conference expenses (approximately £20,400) then these can be considered as sunk costs and unrecoverable. Of more concern is our ability to recover those costs incurred in the actual running of the event, and if possible to make a contribution which alleviates the sunk cost burden. Either way the event will result in a loss, but one which might be smaller than it otherwise would have been. To justify continuing to run the conference at all, on financial grounds, we must cover the fixed costs element of speaker expenses and travel: on the economy fare assumption

$$\frac{12{,}000}{700-196} = 24 \text{ delegates,}$$

or on the first/business class fare assumption

$$\frac{24{,}000}{700-196} = 48 \text{ delegates.}$$

The latter result suggests that we may be struggling to justify the non-cancellation of the event on financial grounds, in that the extent of the losses may be extended past the initial £20,400 by doing so. The numerical analysis here is a great help in heightening our awareness of problems and facilitating the examination of non-financial factors.

It is possible that the survival of the whole company might be endangered by this one event. Early cancellation would cut short the haemorrhage of funds, but at what cost to the company's reputation? If we wish to continue to be regarded as conference professionals we may have to bear the loss of this one event, making it crucial that such losses are minimized. This is the only real problem facing CBC; it is pointless going into great detail on peripheral issues (e.g., sensitivity analysis of obscure items) if these will matter little to the final outcome.

Although conference cancellation may be the best (or even only) option on financial grounds, from a strategic point of view it may be a non-starter. Cancellation of an event at a late stage will inevitably incur short-term financial costs and long-term, perhaps even insuperable, damage to reputation. The problem is, therefore, to run the event at a minimum loss, both to profit and loss account and professional reputation. We, therefore, need to develop alternative approaches to:

- increasing the number of paying delegates (to increase revenue);
- increasing the number of non-paying delegates (to improve ambience and reputation);
- seeking other sources of revenue;
- reducing costs (fixed and variable); and
- adopting accounting procedures which alleviate the impact of the losses incurred.

Each of these issues is worthy of more detailed consideration.

CASE STUDY (cont.)

We might *increase the number of paying delegates* by marketing the two days of the conference or the individual sessions separately. Discounts might be offered for early payment and for the second and subsequent delegates from the same organization. Price discrimination might be practised in favour of local delegates approached at the last minute.

As to *increasing the number of non-paying delegates*, the reputation of the company will depend on the ambience of the conference venue and the 'feel' of the event. If there are very few paying delegates then the conference room must not look empty; a return to a seminar style, with tables, chairs and static flower displays, will reduce the extent of spare space. The number of attendees may only be increased by providing free places (e.g., to colleagues, academics, friends, spouses, etc.). It may even be necessary to 'pay' for free places by providing lunch and afternoon tea. This strategy might backfire if the newcomers are differentiated from the paying delegates (e.g., through age or dress code) and do not conceal the circumstances of their presence.

There may be a number of *alternative sources of revenue*:

- Sponsorship of the event, in whole or parts. Small-scale sponsorship of meals and cocktail parties by firms wishing to advertise their name will be relatively easy to come by and will, at least, reduce the costs to CBC of meals. Major sponsors, with acknowledgement in all literature, and with an opportunity to speak to delegates at opening or plenary sessions, should also be sought, particularly from among members of the hardware and software industry.
- Selling space in thoroughfares of the venue to book publishers and computer companies to provide sales opportunities for them with interested delegates. Prime selling space adjacent to tea/coffee areas would command premium fees.
- Selling collected conference proceedings immediately after the event in the form of books, CDs and/or DVDs/videos. A high price, though significantly discounted from the conference fee, might be charged at the outset to those unable to attend as delegates. The computer and information technology industries and financial institutions might then be targeted for the sales of collected proceedings, but this must commence immediately because the material will age quickly.

Reducing costs may be difficult because quality must not be sacrificed in return for a few pence. Most delegates remember the venue, food, drink and contacts from a conference and not the content of the presentations! It is important that we do not skimp on the quality of, for example, meals; better to try to reduce long-term costs by coming to some single-venue agreement with the hotel for future events.

Turning, finally, to *alternative accounting procedures*, it is doubtful whether all of the fixed costs identified earlier are specific to this

CASE STUDY (cont.)

conference. It could be that at least part of the following expenditures are attributable to other events or to the company as a whole:

- advertising (£1500) – may include flyers for future events;
- administration (£7000) – will include the establishment of a database of names/addresses for use in targeting delegates of future conferences.

Part of these could, arguably, be treated as depreciable assets rather than being expensed directly and attributed to this particular conference activity.

The going-concern assumption relative to CBC incorporates a commitment to running this conference once it has been promoted. Any financial losses incurred must be borne in the cause of furthering the reputation of the company. All of the suggestions above which involve increasing revenue, increasing the number of delegates and seeking new sources for both should be explored. Great care should be addressed in cost-cutting, and accounting procedural manipulation attempted only if it is essential that the financial outcome of this particular conference 'looks' better; for the company as a whole it may well represent wasted effort.

The message from the foregoing analysis is clear. Although the focus on the financials highlights the problems therein, it is the non-financial and the intangible factors which assume the highest priority. Ultimately long-term measures of customer satisfaction, loyalty, credibility and reputation are of greater importance than short-term profitability.

The framework of Figure 3.5 establishes the focus for SMA so that we are able to address both financial and non-financial factors in a flexible manner. Just as the focus moves from company analysis in Porter (1980) to globalization in Porter (1990), there is also a paradigm shift – one which shifts the emphasis to innovation and the impact on competitiveness, but returns to focus on industries rather than economies.

The traditional sources of competitive advantage are entrenched in the economics literature:

- *macroeconomic factors* – advantageous interest and exchange rates, low rates of inflation;
- *government intervention* – to achieve the above through appropriate monetary policies, and to stimulate particular industries through grants/ subsidies;
- *economies of scale* – large-scale production and technological leadership which minimize both cost per unit and vulnerability to competition;
- *low labour costs* – contributing to competitiveness through a low cost per unit.
- *management policies* – associated with increased productivity and quality, and reduced inventory holdings and set-up times.

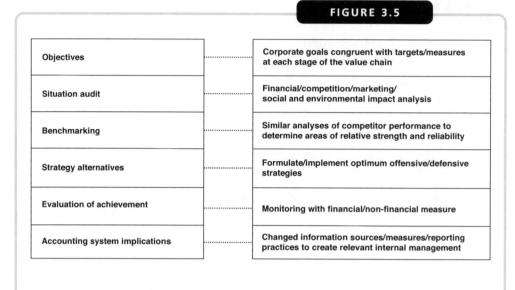

Framework for strategic management accounting

Although anecdotal evidence exists to support any one of these factors in particular circumstances, the sum total is lacking. Competitive industries exist which do not combine any of these characteristics, suggesting that some explanatory factors are missing. Porter cites the Italian shoe industry as an example: a world leader which combines low technology and high wages, in small family-run companies free from government intervention. The roots of their competitive advantage lie elsewhere, in their ability to innovate and not in the traditional sources above.

Porter (1990) identifies four interrelated key factors (termed the 'diamond') which appear to facilitate innovation and competitive advantage:

- *Factor availability* – not in terms of the usual infrastructure and workforce requirements, which are necessary but insufficient conditions for competitiveness, but access to required specialized and scarce resources. A shortage of required resources may even be a positive factor because it will drive innovations to correct the shortage – for example, space-saving devices in Japan, and labour-saving devices in the USA.
- *Home market* – the size of the home market is less important than its sophistication. Demanding and knowledgeable customers will create the conditions which drive improvement and innovation. Home-market saturation in its turn drives globalization and international innovation.
- *Support industries* – these provide a network for co-operation in problem-solving and information flows relating to new developments and common difficulties. The existence of strong suppliers servicing a cluster of similar industries will mean the suppliers know the business and its problems, facilitating innovative solutions.
- *Rivalry* – local competition will promote aggressive investment under like environmental conditions. The geographic concentrations of competitors will create pressures to succeed through cost reduction and new

model introduction. There are no excuses for failure, as there might be with overseas competitors.

Competitiveness arises out of the pressure which forces continuous progress, and local pressures, far from providing adverse conditions, appear to be beneficial to innovation by establishing a breeding ground for the development of global competitive advantage. We would anticipate the top innovators combining each of these four factors competing in a cluster of industries, in a tight geographical area, with strong common suppliers and a demanding local market. Factor availability in the particular local circumstances drives the precise nature of the innovation. Chance, too, will always play its part; we may be in the right place at the right time or appropriately positioned to take advantage of changes in government policy.

Market SWOT analysis

Competitor analysis embraces the evaluation of the nature of competition and of the potential competitors, and a consideration of the likely actions and reactions of competitors in the market. A similar analysis can be conducted in assessing potential takeover predators or victims relative to market shares, share prices and the structure of shareholdings.

Competition in the market takes five major forms:

- price cutting – often retaliatory in nature, and with the potential to damage the market;
- advertising and promotion – likely to expand the whole market as well as that for individual branded products;
- introduction of new products;
- improved customer service; and
- entry of new companies.

An analysis of one's own position and that of competitors with respect to these forms of competition should reflect:

1 offensive predictability, including
   (a) the level of satisfaction with the current situation, and
   (b) the likelihood of shifts in strategy; and

2 defensive capability, including
   (a) areas of vulnerability and
   (b) areas likely to provoke retaliation.

The entry of new competitors is, potentially, particularly problematical because the resultant increase in capacity is likely to lead to in-fighting in a bid to maintain market share. New entrants may be completely new companies but are more likely to be existing companies which are diversifying or which are acquired by competitors.

Porter's generic strategies provide ready-made barriers to the entry of competitors in the form of large-scale production economies, product differentiation and access to niche distribution channels (Porter, 1980). However, even they may not be sufficient to deter a large, determined bidder.

Diversification can take a number of alterative forms depending on the nature of the industry. These are illustrated in Figure 3.6. Horizontal and vertical integration within existing or related markets are often associated

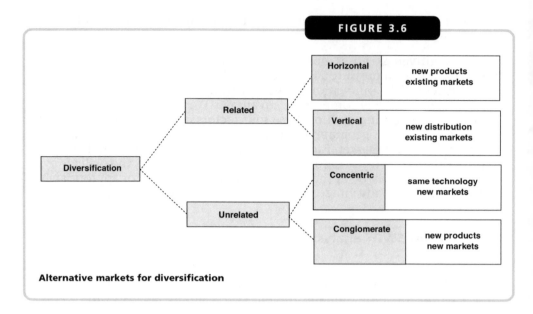

FIGURE 3.6

Alternative markets for diversification

with defensive strategies leading to large-scale production economies and eventual industry leadership.

Conglomerate diversification is the riskiest strategy in terms of the likely outcome, but with the potential to reap great rewards and market penetration. In particular:

- risks are spread, but so is management strength over diverse interests;
- it opens up new and exciting markets, but ones in which the company may have no experience or expertise, and which may be alien to the corporate culture; and
- while acquired assets may be underperforming, with the potential to improve, they may need the attention of specialists to effect recovery or turnaround.

In the worst-case scenario, a company without market share, capital investment or strength of purpose would be incapable of seeking overall cost leadership. The absence of marketing resources would also make it unable to differentiate products or target specific niche customers. The poor strategic position relative to competitive forces will make it impossible for such a company to pursue any of Porter's three generic strategies with a reasonable hope of success. As a result, the company will sacrifice profitability and high-volume customers because costs and selling prices are too high, and the high-margin, high-quality niche business will be lost to firms which are more appropriately targeted and differentiated.

The *product life cycle* provides a useful framework for the consideration of alternative product strategies and for alerting management to the dynamics of the market and the consequences of inaction. Figure 3.7 illustrates the five stages of the basic cycle.

The cycle begins, appropriately enough, with an *introduction* stage. Some new products diffuse very slowly into their potential market while others virtually ignore this stage, using it as a swift trajectory into rapid growth.

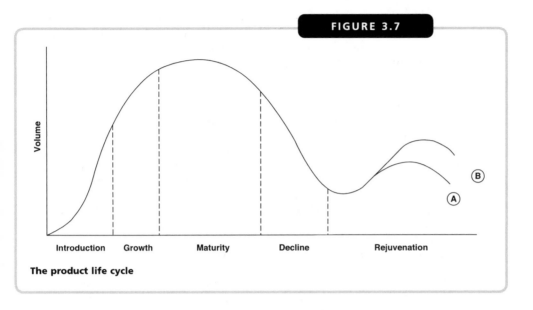

FIGURE 3.7

The product life cycle

A number of factors can contribute to a slow product take-up:

- lack of comparative advantage on price or quality with existing products;
- uncertainty about the longevity of the product, such that consumers perceive a potential risk of, say, failure or technical obsolescence; and
- lack of availability of product information or the product itself.

Producers must invest in promotion (to improve consumer awareness) and distribution (to ensure that the product is on the shelf and available for trial). Warranties and demonstrable after-sales service will reduce the perceived risk of purchase, but may not eliminate it in areas of rapid technological advancement.

The transition to rapid *growth* will be characterized by one or more of three factors:

- a changed relationship with substitute products so that consumers perceive the existence of distinct price and/or quality advantages;
- reduced uncertainty surrounding the likely success of the product so that it gains widespread acceptance and imitators attempt to enter the market; and
- repeat buyers as an element of brand loyalty develops.

Producers must invest in increased capacity to meet demand, expanding both distribution channels and inventory holdings. Product extensions might be added to the basic line.

At the *maturity* stage the growth rate will slow as the target market reaches saturation point. Producers will seek to attract new users while retaining their existing ones. As products become more familiar buyers become more price sensitive and less responsive to advertising, so that producers must focus on quality continuity and competitive pricing, at a time when competitors are likely to be reacting in a similar manner.

The onset of *decline* may be rapid especially if attributable to changes in fashion, or may be more gradual if it results from technological change. Producers will attempt to slow down the decline by focusing on subgroups of customers and by restricting the product line, aiming to stabilize sales at a level which, though below the original, is still acceptable. The rate of decline will depend on the comparative price/quality advantages of emerging products.

After the decline stage comes *rejuvenation*. Producers will attempt to prolong the life cycle through product and user innovation, corresponding to positions A and B in Figure 3.7. One rejuvenation strategy may involve major product improvements and repositioning the product with regard to customer perception (position A). Another could be to seek new distribution outlets, possibly through exports, and to establish new uses for the same product (position B). Only when rejuvenation strategies have failed to arrest the decline and the product is no longer profitable should product withdrawal be contemplated.

The major problem of applying the product life cycle in practice is the difficulty of establishing exactly what stage product development has reached. The position will be product and industry dependent and cannot be forecast simply on the basis of past sales. A product may be designated 'mature' when in practice it has reached only a temporary plateau midway through the 'growth' stage.

The same kind of market analysis conducted for individual products can also be attempted for companies and individual company subsidiaries. The performance and importance of the subsidiary relative to the parent company can be evaluated to determine the likely strategy of the parent. A number of key questions arise:

• Is financial performance below group expectations?
• Is the subsidiary peripheral, expendable or of strategic importance to the group?
• Does the degree of economic interrelationship within the group make the subsidiary an essential element of the company portfolio?
• Is the product strategy consistent with that for the overall group?
• Is the subsidiary starved of funds because of the competing capital requirements of other subsidiaries?

The Boston Consulting Group (BCG) portfolio matrix provides a framework with which to categorize subsidiaries within a group, or even products within a company. It then facilitates the specification of the strategies to be employed in the promotion or demotion of individual companies and products. At its inception (Henderson, 1970) the BCG model revolutionized strategic planning, and facilitated the development of alternative portfolio planning methods (e.g., Miles and Snow, 1978; Covin, 1991) helping management to understand how each of its businesses contributes to the whole and clarifying the overall picture. They have provided an information source to formalize the identification of weak businesses and shift resources into those with more promise. Overall they have provided the data to improve the level of analysis in the strategic planning process, with the potential for eliminating observed weakness.

The BCG portfolio matrix provides a useful framework for the analysis of a 'whole' into the sum of its component parts, to determine the extent of the synergy existing in the 'whole'. By allocating

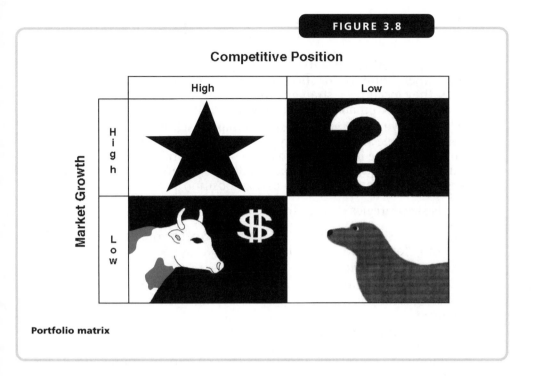

FIGURE 3.8

Competitive Position

Portfolio matrix

subsidiaries/products/customers to distinct categories we can clarify overall group strategies or highlight the impact of changes in the product or customer mix.

Figure 3.8 illustrates the BCG matrix, mapping industry leadership and associated competitive position against market growth. On the vertical axis the market growth rate provides a measure of market attractiveness, while on the horizontal, relative market share measures the competitive strength in the market.

A market growth rate in the range 0–20% would be normal. A market growth rate for any individual product/company in excess of 10% is high, and 10% is, therefore, normally used as the cut-off point between the upper and lower quadrants. The relative market share measures the company's strength relative to that of the largest competitor. A log scale is normally used on this horizontal axis so that equal distances represent the same percentage increases. A value of 1.0 is used as the divider of the quadrants into left-and right-hand sides. Values less than one (right-hand side) demonstrate low market share, while those greater than one (left-hand side) identify market leaders.

By positioning subsidiary companies on a map graphing competitive position against market growth we can classify them as follows:

- *Cash cows.* In a mature market in which they are strongly positioned so that few investment resources are needed but consistent cash outflows are generated. Cash cows are market leaders, despite an annual market growth rate below 10%. They enjoy economies of scale and high profit, but these might be drained by supporting the rest of the group.
- *Stars.* The market leaders in the portfolio; profitable and high-growth businesses but still requiring extensive injections of investment and

promotional expenditures to maintain their position and reputation. Eventually their growth will slow and they will be turned into 'cash cows'.

- *Dogs*. Uncompetitive in static markets. No further promotional or investment expenditure is justified and elimination might be considered unless they occupy a strategic role in the portfolio. They may earn sufficient cash to maintain themselves, but little more.
- '*?*' Competitive operations but still to make a significant market impact. Barely profitable at present, they have the potential to become 'stars' but require large-scale investment to do so. A question mark hangs over their future such that if their market penetration is insufficient to justify further investment they will decline to a 'dog' position.

Four basic strategies emerge from the matrix:

- Build – increase market share, even at the expense of short-term profits, by turning 'question marks' into 'stars'.
- Hold – preserve market share.
- Harvest – increase short-term cash flow, perhaps without adequate regard to its long-term effects, for example by using 'cash cows' to fund other businesses.
- Divest – eliminate those businesses whose use of resources is inefficient and which are sufficiently peripheral to the rest of the group to merit abandonment. These will usually be the underperforming 'dogs' and 'question marks'.

A group managing its subsidiaries, or a company managing its products, must aim for a balanced portfolio. This means a combination of market leaders, new ideas and cash generators. An unbalanced portfolio would have too many 'dogs' and 'question marks', and too few 'stars' and 'cash cows'. Too often, in practice, a company or group portfolio is entirely in the 'question mark' sector, with no funds to promote success, or entirely in the 'dog' sector, with no new products on the horizon and very little by way of future optimism.

To illustrate this method, consider the position of Thorn EMI. Based in the UK, Thorn EMI once manufactured and distributed its products throughout the world and comprised a number of well-known subsidiaries in diverse markets. We will consider their position as it stood in 1986, since it is no longer commercially sensitive. The products and market areas of interest might be positioned in the grid as indicated in Figure 3.9. Identifying the subsidiary companies, we find a plethora of once household names.

An ideal strategy is delightfully simple:

- divestment of unprofitable 'dogs', notably in the white goods and brown goods area;
- employment of funds from the 'cash cows' to promote high-technology stars and new developments with 'star' potential; and
- use of film stocks, music rights and the entertainment structure to provide software for success in the cable TV and satellite broadcasting spheres.

Unfortunately, in practice, the company had far too few high-yielding 'cash cows' and too much debt to provide the funding for such a diverse portfolio. Despite the divestments and a rights issue, a blow-out of costs and delays

FIGURE 3.9

Defence	• Software Sciences Datasolve Inmos; THORN EMI Electronics	Satellite broadcasting	• BSkyB
		Music	• Film library; Cinema Chain
Music	• EMI Records; Capitol Industries; HMV	Entertainment	• Elstree studios Thames TV; Screen
STAR		**?**	
TV rental	• DER; Multibroadcast; Radio Rentals	Electrical	• Rumbelows • Ferguson Television
		White goods	• Cookers/fridges/ washing machines
		Lighting	• Thorn Lighting
		Heating	• Radiators
CASH COW		**DOG**	

Thorn EMI portfolio matrix

in implementation in the satellite broadcasting arm spread available funds too thin. Screen Entertainment and most film distribution rights were sold in April 1986. Thorn EMI was forced to withdraw and focus on the core records and rentals businesses, largely abandoning an imaginative and potentially successful growth strategy. The bulb division was sold to General Electric (US) in 1990, and the heating operations to Blue Circle in the same year; the rest of the lighting division was the subject of a management buy-out in 1993. The Rumbelows electrical chain closed in 1995, and in 1996 Thorn EMI demerged, with the music (EMI Group) and rentals (Thorn) businesses becoming two separate entities. HMV Retail was spun off as a separate business in 1998, then subsequently sold in 2002. EMI's restructuring has continued into 2003/4 with the outsourcing of CD and DVD manufacture, and, like most other music companies, EMI has suffered both from the downturn in music sales and the impact of piracy.

In general terms, we would expect an optimum strategy to fit that described by Figure 3.10. The adoption of a group perspective to the matrix would seek a balanced portfolio by shifting funds between the component companies:

- Use of funds made available by the 'cash cows' to promote both the 'star' performers and those with the potential to become 'stars'.
- Management of 'dogs' to ensure that they are not a cash drain; unless they generate even marginal positive cash flows, divestment must be considered an option.

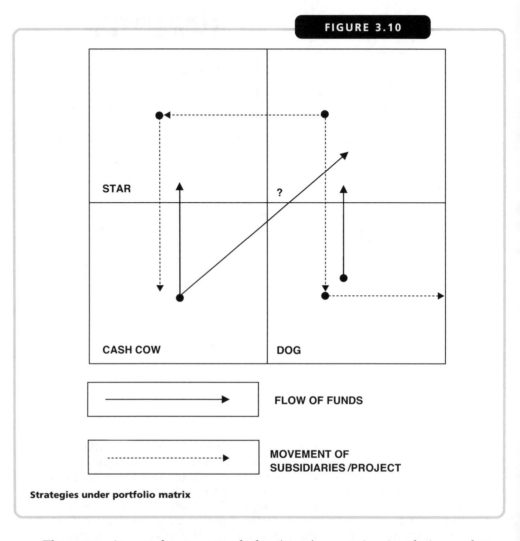

FIGURE 3.10

FLOW OF FUNDS

MOVEMENT OF SUBSIDIARIES /PROJECT

Strategies under portfolio matrix

- The nurturing and support of the 'stars' to maintain their market prominence may eventually be rewarded with 'cash cow' status – market leadership in a mature sector.
- The portfolio must always have its '?' quadrant as a feeder for the future. 'Star' performers will emerge here but will require careful management and an eye for the strategic withdrawal if the profits and market penetration required do not arise.

The main priority of 'star' companies or products will be to maintain their competitive position in order to be able to assume 'cash cow' status when the market eventually matures and growth slows. Both 'cash cows' and 'dogs' must be managed in a way which avoids major investment and promotes cash flow. The balanced portfolio will provide both cash-generation potential and plentiful growth opportunities. The most difficult decisions arise with regard to the 'question marks', in judging the extent to which they should be funded while the market is maturing and the advisability of a strategic withdrawal if the required growth does not eventuate. It is unsurprising, therefore, that they are often referred to as 'problem children', in need of constant and often painful attention if they are to reach their full potential!

Such models are not without their limitations. They can be costly and time-consuming to construct and implement. Data collection may be difficult and subject to manipulation so that the assignment of companies to cells is somewhat arbitrary. They focus on the present rather than the future, so that managerial judgement is still required to make innovations and resource movements. A blinkered approach to the development of a 'balanced portfolio' based on market-share growth may have unfortunate consequences, especially if the group decides to:

- diversify into areas/industries of which it has no experience or expertise;
- over-milk 'cash cows' to finance the rest of the business, so that they are unable to maintain market leadership without reinvestment;
- abandon healthy mature businesses still capable of recovery or of continuing to make a positive contribution to the group;
- neglect the management of current businesses;
- neglect inter-business relationships, so that each business is appraised separately without reference to the services it provides to other parts of the business;
- invest unwisely in 'dogs' in the hope of securing recovery in what are hopeless causes; and
- maintain too many 'question marks' in the portfolio, so that it is impossible to fund them all adequately.

The BCG portfolio matrix is simple – perhaps too simple – in design. We may have to make assumptions about the classification of some components. Their precise positioning in the matrix will be even more difficult since it requires some quantification and ranking. But despite the difficulties, the BCG matrix does facilitate an overview of group activities and avoids a blinkered focus on individual components. The strictest interpretation of the BCG matrix suggests that organizations involved in the portfolio planning process are internally self-financing, and that there is no close relationship between any of the participating organizations. These limitations, among others, have led to the BCG matrix becoming much less popular than it once was, though the contribution made from recognition of different positioning in the matrix, and hence different treatment, remains powerful. Though its resource allocation role has become unfashionable, the matrix can still be useful in addressing strategic issues.

Social and environmental SWOT analysis

The SWOT analysis must extend to social and environmental factors (in a triple bottom-line approach) in order to be able to predict and, if possible, to quantify changes on the company and its products. Among the factors that should be considered are:

1 *Economic.* These include:
   (a) the growth rate of the economy;
   (b) changes in interest rates;
   (c) changes in exchange rates;

(d) the rate of inflation; and

(e) the impact of inflationary or deflationary economic policies.

2 *Political*. These include:

(a) the effects of environmental pressure groups;

(b) the effects of changes of government (for local or overseas trading partners);

(c) the effects of particular political policies; and

(d) the impact of regulations, codes and guidelines.

3 *Legal*. These include:

(a) the issuing of new patents and licences;

(b) product liabilities; and

(c) health, safety and employment law.

4 *Technological*. These include:

(a) trends in related products and manufacturing capability;

(b) impact on markets;

(c) impact on production capacity; and

(d) impact on individual products.

5 *Demographic*. These include:

(a) effects of climatic variation;

(b) availability of natural resources;

(c) changing age distribution of the population and consequent variation in consumer demand and social expectations; and

(d) growth in population.

Companies should be able to predict and, wherever possible quantify the impact of social and environmental changes on their products and markets. It is instructive to consider each of these five factors in more detail, focusing on the economic and political factors to investigate environmental models developed to assist management decision-making.

Economic factors

Companies must be aware of the extent to which the key economic indicators will impact on their business and the likelihood of their direction of change in the future. Changes in interest rates will impact quickly on those in the construction industry and all companies reliant on short-term debt; changes in exchange rates will impact on those trading in overseas export markets or who rely on overseas raw material or component sources; the rate of inflation and the growth rate of the economy will impact heavily on the spending power of consumers. Changes in government policy, particularly the use of deflationary policies will have a similarly negative effect on the availability of discretionary expenditures.

For companies highly exposed overseas and whose export markets and investments are vulnerable to changed economic circumstances, economic risk analysis is vital in the evaluation of trading partners. Commercially available economic risk indicators monitor the risks associated with doing business overseas, and are particularly useful when the trading partners are less developed countries or unstable political regimes. The economic risks of concern would include the following (many of which cannot be divorced from political factors):

- deteriorating trading conditions;
- lack of demand through a shortage of foreign exchange;

- imposition of import controls or tariff barriers;
- default on payment;
- punitive measures for foreign investors; and
- restrictions on the repatriation of profits.

Publicly available information can give a good indication of trading partners whose economies are not sufficiently robust to ward off short-term difficulties. These are frequently those associated with:

- susceptibility to adverse climatic conditions;
- vulnerability to swings in basic commodity prices;
- single-commodity export economies;
- countries with a single export target, increasing vulnerability to protectionism; and
- incidence of political unrest.

Close monitoring of the balance of payments situation and the foreign debt position over time can be very revealing. Taffler and Abassi (1984) detail a discriminant model measuring economic risk, in terms of likelihood of debt rescheduling, as a function of wealth, external indebtedness, rate of price inflation and monetary policy. They suggest the model

$$Z = a + bX_1 + cX_2 + dX_3 + eX_4,$$

where $Z < 0$ indicates an economy exhibiting signs of distress through a profile resembling previous cases of debt rescheduling; X_1 is the ratio of debt to exports, X_2 the ratio of loan commitment to population, X_3 the consumer price index, and X_4 the ratio of domestic credit to gross domestic product. The model works well, particularly for less well-developed countries (though less well than the equivalent models based on company failure detailed elsewhere). They do not reflect instability due to either political unrest or single-commodity economies, and we might speculate on their being improved by the inclusion of political risk analysis variables.

Political factors

Companies need to be aware of the impact a change of government or political policy would have on their products or customers, as well as the more indirect impact of the machinations of environmental pressure groups. The imposition of new regulations (e.g., exhaust gases for motor manufacturers, or CFC emissions for refrigeration and air-conditioning producers), and changed acceptability of smokestack pollution resulting from well-orchestrated protests, will change both product and customer attitudes. For companies highly exposed to export markets or with overseas subsidiaries, governmental changes have the potential to threaten foreign investments and disrupt income streams. Many of the political changes at home, and their environmental consequences, are predictable, but it is important that the social ramifications are deemed to be acceptable. Those changes taking place overseas might present nasty surprises unless some form of political risk analysis is undertaken.

The modelling of political outcomes on the basis of alternative risk scenarios is well established commercially and indicates the level of risk associated with particular overseas trading partners. If political developments are not taken into account they can bear heavily on a company's ability to conclude a contract on time and in profit. Political or social conflict can lead to political instability and politically motivated violence directed against personnel and/or facilities. These might include acts of destruction, bomb extortion or product contamination (targeting physical assets) or kidnap and intimidation (targeting key personnel). Such acts may be perpetrated to prevent contracts being completed, impacting upon all those who are part of the investment cycle.

While it is difficult to make absolute predictions about eventualities, it is possible to assess the probabilities of change and their likely impact on a business. The evaluation and forecasting of investment decisions in dangerous locations must include the risk of adverse political actions. In this way the analysis of political risks ensures that managers make decisions in the full knowledge of their potential consequences.

Legal factors

Companies must closely monitor trends in legislation worldwide to give an early indication of likely changes, so that their impact on the business can be gauged in time to take appropriate action. Some products may have to conform to national legislation while also following international guidelines. Regulations which protect consumers (e.g., product liability and misleading advertising) will constrain the way a product is made and sold; regulations which protect employees (e.g., health and safety, employment law) will impact on the profitability of the workplace; regulations which protect companies from each other (e.g., patents, licences, anti-trust legislation) may impact on a company's acquisition or diversification strategy; and regulations which protect society (e.g., heritage listings) may force companies to take a longer-term perspective than would otherwise be the case. Changes in any of these areas could have a critical effect on product planning and business survival.

Technological factors

Companies must be aware of technological changes regarding their own and related products so that they can respond appropriately and eliminate, or at least alleviate, their impact on markets. They must not focus on technological wizardry to the exclusion of all else, when it is not the major factor determining customer purchase patterns. For example, Sony's Betamax may have been technically the more advanced video-recorder, but the superior marketing efforts of JVC ensured that VHS became the industry standard; similarly, Kodak's slow reaction to the advent of digital technology in cameras threatened the prosperity of the enterprise. Now the growth of DVD technology for playing and burning recorded information, and the availability of this material both over the internet and through digital TV providers, will threaten the livelihoods of many in the entertainment sector, most immediately in the retail sale and rental of pre-recorded material.

Technical advances in machine tools and operating technology will impact on manufacturing capability with the potential to create instant obsolescence. The advances in computer-aided manufacturing and design through, for instance, desktop publishing have changed the face of the print and newspaper industries. Those companies unable to foreshadow and respond to the changes have departed from the scene.

Technological change increases customer expectations in individual products (e.g., safety features in motor vehicles) so that producers have to be flexible enough to respond to remain competitive. Companies that fail to respond to such changes will soon find their product outdated and will miss new product opportunities.

Demographic factors

Population changes will be of interest to all companies and a vital feature of any marketing plan. The density, location, age, gender, race, ethnic diversity and occupation of target consumer groups will determine both the nature of the product, the public's attitude towards the product and the manner in which it is marketed. The ageing of the population, attributable to declining birth rates since the 1960s and greater life expectancy, has brought a response from companies in different marketing strategies and new products to cater for a changed lifestyle. The 'baby boom' population group ceased to be the most dominant group at the turn of the century and companies must be flexible enough to respond to the increased geographical mobility, earning potential, unrealized product preferences and social awareness of the new dominant groups – Generations X and Y.

There has been only limited success in the development of environmental prediction models, with the most successful being those in the economic and political areas. Even these have been relatively weak compared to their financial counterparts, because they lean on scenarios which are highly interdisciplinary and which require data inputs from many alternative sources.

Despite these difficulties, a sound appreciation of the direction of change and the lead time before newly imposed environmental factors have a significant impact can be gauged from parallels in other countries. Estimates of the quantitative effects on particular countries can then be made on a best-case, worst-case or most likely basis.

The following case concerns the development of a strategic direction for a family company which simultaneously faces problems of succession. It provides an opportunity for identifying the strengths and weaknesses of the firm's current position, diversification opportunities and threats to its survival.

CASE STUDY

Westlake Printing: A SWOT case study

Tony Belton founded his printing company over 30 years ago and has proudly maintained the family ownership since. Now he is in ill health and knows that he must soon release the reins of the company he so cherishes. Worse, none of his three children shows the slightest interest in involvement in the business so that it seems his successor must be an 'outsider'. He recognizes that the problem is of his own making because his autocratic control, decision-making without consultation and refusal to take on debt to fund the growth of the company have not endeared him to senior management.

Nevertheless, the workforce idolize him and most are on first-name terms. Many have been with him for over 20 years and have seen the business grow to the largest in the North-West of England. Their loyalty is not in question, and neither is the technical

CASE STUDY (cont.)

competence of senior management – but they have rarely had the opportunity to 'manage' in any real sense.

The relative isolation of a Cumbria-based enterprise has always aided the growth of the company because competition has been negligible. Now the situation is reversed because continued growth and diversification are largely dependent upon increased penetration of the bigger markets in South-East England and East Anglia.

Tony is well aware of the challenges and opportunities currently facing the company (e.g., the environmental edge possible with recycling and diversification into computer software) and of likely threats to its stability (e.g., the spread of street-corner 'cowboy' franchises, wayward internal communications, the need to import expensive new technology to stay competitive and, worse, the possibility of government intervention if market share is perceived to be too great).

Latterly he has begun to pay more attention to internal efficiency and improving the bottom line even if sales growth proves impossible. He has focused on four key areas of internal efficiency:

- *Process improvement* – by balancing cost and quality in determining optimum machine speed; by eliminating non-productive downtime.
- *Plant layout* – by seeking a more efficient design.
- *Information systems* – by computerizing the primitive manual operations control for costing and scheduling so that quotations can be nearer the mark both on cost and time.
- *Client education* – by establishing a 'quality' goal which makes the inferior product and service of competitors unsatisfactory.

Performance appraisal is currently undertaken with the help of a set of financial and non-financial indicators. The financial indictors are profitability (return on assets), sales revenue, gross margins, gearing, and the number of days debtors are outstanding. The non-financial indicators are customer complaints (registered and resolved), spoilage rates, percentage of quotations successful, direct labour productivity, and percentage cost variation (actual versus quotation). Despite the availability of existing control data, Tony feels that much of the management effort is misdirected and that new initiatives are essential if meaningful improvements are to be achieved. He wishes to identify alternative strategies for the future direction of Westlake Printing, which capitalize on priority improvement opportunities while reducing its vulnerability to outside influences.

CASE ANALYSIS

SWOT analysis is a useful starting point in highlighting the critical factors impacting on Westlake Printing. Reference to Table 3.3 suggests that the correction of current weaknesses and the pursuit of diversification opportunities represent the priority targets for Westlake.

CASE STUDY (cont.)

TABLE 3.3

SWOT analysis for Westlake Printing

Strengths	Weaknesses
• Secured markets	• Lack of empowerment
• Superior product	• Manual management
• Committed and competent	information systems
employees	• Inefficient plant layout
• Absence of debt financing	• Process inefficiencies

Opportunities	Threats
• Larger markets in the East and	• Low entry barriers
South East	• Wayward internal
• Environmental edge	communications
• Computer software diversification	• Technology requirements
• Debt financing	• Government intervention

A focus on *weaknesses* yields internal improvement opportunities to address clear deficiencies:

- Quality improvements – establish quality standards and ensure compliance.
- Process improvements – eliminate non-value-added activities and improve plant layout. Both will contribute towards improving the quality of the final printed product.
- Information and technology improvements – establish a costing system that will produce accurate numbers in which management have faith. Consider using activity-based costing, depending on the extent of overheads and product diversity.
- Product differentiation improvements – invest in the resources required to exploit their environmental edge.
- Communication improvements – empower managers with appropriate authority to facilitate two-way communication of information useful for strategic decision-making at upper levels of management, and operational decision-making at the shop-floor level of personnel.
- Management accounting information systems clearly need addressing, through the provision of performance indicators to improve management control. Those indicators related to the printing process would include: downtime as a percentage of total available machine time; time between machine failures; time between overhauls; time spent on repeat work; average time to effect repairs; total time in backlog jobs; number of final units lost through maintenance; number of repeat jobs; number of backlog jobs; percentage of failed jobs; preventative maintenance, corrective maintenance and breakdown maintenance, each as a percentage of total maintenance; cost of lost production; overtime hours

CASE STUDY (cont.)

as a percentage of total hours; overtime costs as a percentage of payroll; throughput time (time taken from start to finish of job); set-up time; number of component parts per printing job (to determine product complexity); space occupied by printing activities; and distance materials moved. Those related to the final product would include: percentage completion of units (actual versus target); percentage of stock-outs (materials not in stock); cost of quality; percentage dependence on post-inspection; and percentage conformance to quality standards. Those related to market would include: percentage local volume; percentage South East volume; percentage of expenditure devoted to research and development; percentage new product innovation; percentage increase in market share; new customers as a percentage of total customers; index of competitive value; and index of vulnerability to competition. Those related to employees would include: index of educational attainment; cost of recruitment error; percentage training costs; percentage of staff turnover lost to competitors; percentage absenteeism; cost of employee downtime; index of leadership impact (e.g., percentage of cancelled meetings); new employees as a percentage of total employees; and employee productivity (i.e., standard hours achieved as a percentage of direct and indirect labour hours worked). Finally, those related to customers would be: percentage approval rating; percentage repeat orders; number of overdue deliveries; and average delivery delay.

Which of these additional measures Westlake choose to collect, analyse and disseminate will depend on the perceived cost-benefits attaching to their use. A number of opportunities exist for Westlake to change the strategic direction of the business, many of them consistent with Porter's generic strategies of seeking cost leadership, differentiating the product, and targeting new sectors of the market:

- expansion into the South East and East Anglia at a time of financial strength;
- use of existing liquid resources to diversify into new areas by buying appropriate companies;
- use of the existing capability to move into the writing and marketing of software programs;
- seeking industry leadership by purchasing the most up-to-date equipment available, and exploiting economies of large-scale operation;
- differentiating the existing product to gain a significant competitive advantage – this might embrace an expansion of the current product range to include colour copying and book publishing;
- exploiting the advantages associated with non-financial factors, notably quick, dependable, efficient and high-quality service; and
- expanding the existing market for recycled products and provide an accompanying professional service to exploit public recognition as the source of acknowledged expertise.

The weaknesses/opportunities identified above will provide a suitable starting point for the implementation of a systematic process (similar to that developed in Chapter 7) for prioritization of issues and the development of implementation strategies.

BENCHMARKING

A number of articles (e.g., McNair and Leibfried, 1993; Barber, 2003) have argued the benefits that can be achieved by benchmarking without providing hard evidence which justifies the time and expense involved. This section gives an indication of the practical improvements in management accounting information systems that can be achieved, using evidence from the author's involvement in the implementation of the benchmarking procedure within a large Australian manufacturing enterprise.

That we can benefit from sharing the experiences of others has never been in doubt. Benchmarking provides the opportunity of comparing performance across sites and between companies to give an indication of current best practice. Provided that the exchange is restricted to non-confidential information, the transaction is potentially rewarding. The realization that others do something better than oneself can be a great motivator to improved personal performance.

Unfortunately, management accounting information systems tend to be trapped in a fortress mentality within each company, preventing the efficient operation of benchmarking procedures. New initiatives are required to foster an attitude of co-operation with which to improve the competitiveness of all participants.

A number of barriers currently prevent the efficient cross-fertilization possible with benchmarking:

- Intercompany transfers are largely confined to the audit function, focused around tax and financial accounting. Financial comparisons with competitors are fraught with danger and unlikely to yield long-lasting benefits.
- A fear of revealing information which is of benefit to competitors (inside or outside the company) without receiving corresponding benefits, which acts to foster a defensive mentality.
- A fear that any benefits from co-operation will be one-sided – that the company will give but will not receive. A lack of preparation in this respect may result in closed-minded attitudes which ensure that no one reaps the full benefit of any collaboration.

All of these apparently insuperable obstacles can be easily overcome by shifting the focus away from contentious issues. This can be achieved by:

- collaborating not with competitors, but with companies engaged in similar fields, with like processes, but different markets;

- focusing on the process – what we do and how we do it – rather than on the numerical outcomes and key results; and
- tackling service-related areas or the adoption of new technologies, where collaborators are likely to be grappling with the same problems or experiencing like teething troubles.

CASE STUDY

Process Industry: A benchmarking field study

In this context, a benchmarking procedure was undertaken by a large Western Australian company with regard to the provision of its management accounting information services throughout that state. The company, the world's largest in its field, mines bauxite ore and refines alumina at three plants in Western Australia, exporting most of its product. It does have Australian competitors, but these were ignored for the purposes of the benchmarking operation.

Benchmarking was conducted in the context of a much wider total quality management (TQM) process. As part of the search for improvement opportunities, and the implementation of cost-effective solutions, three questions were posed:

1 What do we already do well?
2 What do we not do as well as we should?
3 What do we currently not attempt to do, but might?

Comparisons with other organizations were sought to provide answers to these questions and insights into the way other companies operated in the provision of similar services. Six large Western Australian process-based manufacturers, of comparable size, were selected for the purpose. All agreed to collaborate without hesitation. The two-way transfer of information and the mutual benefit of such transactions were emphasized throughout, so that both parties to the exchange were prepared to be as open as possible in all dealings. For each company the chief accountant and management accountant were asked to discuss key aspects of their roles within the following guidelines:

- *Accounting organization.* The number of accountants, their responsibilities, location and clerical support.
- *Systems.* Accounting systems and computer facilities; hardware and software compatibility and user-friendliness.
- *Reporting.* The timing, content and format of performance reports – their emphasis and target audience.
- *Planning.* The incidence, frequency and detail of short-term budgeting and forecasting, and long-term strategic planning.
- *Cost control.* The measurement and management of physical parameters and financial outcomes in key result areas.
- *Analysis.* The evaluation of business impact, performance analysis and commitment to TQM.

The findings of the survey demonstrated a great diversity of systems and procedures, representing the heights and depths of current practice. Interestingly, the survey indicated that the philosophy of TQM in the accounting area was not then well advanced. Indeed, considerable encouragement was gained from a recognition of the inadequacies of the systems operated by other manufacturers. This served to ameliorate somewhat the earlier depression of the accounting group with regard to the provision of their own services! More significantly, and of great concern, a number of common areas of deficiency were apparent, representing opportunities for all to make improvements of varying degrees.

The survey revealed a widespread absence of integrated, centralized database *systems*. Only one company integrated costs, budgeting, payroll, supply and accounts payable, as well as incorporating variance analysis. At the other extreme, three companies relied heavily on unlinked manual procedures, without any integrated on-line information system.

The inflexibility of systems frequently necessitated the downloading of information (manually) on to personal computers (PCs) in order to generate useful reports. The extent of this reliance on manual systems, particularly in the mine sites (where they were in the form of diaries, handwritten logs or card-based records) was surprising, and in sharp contrast to the refineries. The absence of PCs, and the consequent manual generation of reports, including hand-drawn graphs and diagrams, was remarkable given the relatively advanced information technology available even in the 1990s, but was attributed to the harsh physical conditions.

Many systems comprised a ramshackle assortment of hardware and software – including mainframes, networks, standalone PCs, home-grown software, and ready-made, purchased software – which were often not fully compatible and which necessitated an alarming degree of keying and rekeying of data. In far-flung outposts, 'HB' computer systems were common – entirely pencil-driven systems requiring extensive manual operation to pull together diverse items of information.

The timeliness of monthly *reporting* was not perceived to be a problem, even though only two companies generated routine reports within five working days. More apparent was the lack of focus for formal reporting. In particular, the survey revealed:

- a lack of any clear executive statement on corporate strategy which frequently made it impossible for management to pursue clear, coherent goals;
- a profusion of reports, prepared for nobody in particular, and with no apparent impact on the decision-making process;
- an absence of reporting downward through the organization, leaving supervisors in the dark regarding objectives, achievements and expectations;

CASE STUDY (cont.)

- a lack of user-friendly, managing-director-proof, executive-level information systems – most executives did not access accounting systems on-line, despite the observed need to do so, apparently because of the complexity of those systems;
- an emphasis on reporting upwards, matched by a pessimistic perception that such reports might be largely superfluous to requirements, merely providing historical documents containing information that was available in a more timely manner from other sources.

NFIs were in common use in the *measurement of process perform-ance*, but only two companies combined them with financial indicators in a single report. NFIs were much more of a problem in service areas where a diversity of approaches was apparent in both scope and definition. Alarmingly, only one enterprise conducted detailed post-project audits of capital expenditures to evaluate relative costs and benefits. Measures based on inter-site or interde-partmental comparisons were universally absent, even where the potential for such meaningful measurements was apparent. The overriding impression was one of management accountants as number-crunchers – too busy collecting and disseminating infor-mation to be able to spend the time to analyse and interpret its key features in a way which was meaningful to the user.

Overall, the benchmarking exercise was useful in a number of important ways, providing these responses to the questions posed earlier:

1 *What do we already do well?* The accounting group were encouraged that they were doing a good job. In most respects in-house systems were perceived to be superior to those of comparable companies.

2 *What do we not do as well as we should?* It was recognized that there were immediate opportunities for improvement available because current performance fell short of industry benchmarks. Most notably, the company could:
   (a) provide an executive-level interface allowing the on-line transmission of key results and corresponding trend data;
   (b) review the content and presentation of internal reports rela-tive to observed customer needs; and
   (c) abandon some traditional reporting practices, deemed to be either irrelevant or inappropriate.

3 *What do we currently not attempt to do, but might?* The company recognized a potential for further improving systems by:
   (a) questioning the extent of variance reporting;
   (b) implementing a systematic post-audit of capital expenditure projects;
   (c) devising and monitoring financial and non-financial meas-ures across plants to allow and encourage the comparison of performances; and

CASE STUDY (cont.)

(d) integrating non-financial and financial measures by developing software which aggregated the key features of the accounting and technical operating systems.

Changes implemented as a result of the study improved customer service and provided the basis for a more informed survey of customer requirements.

The success of this benchmarking exercise was greater than expected, encouraging its extension to other management accounting issues and other process manufacturers. Provided that the ground rules are established and observed, such initiatives have the potential to provide considerable benefit to all who participate.

Although this application was based within a large manufacturing organization, the benchmarking procedure was confined to service aspects of the organization. The principles adopted are equally applicable to small business and non-manufacturing organizations.

RESOURCE-BASED VIEW OF THE FIRM

The resource-based view (RBV) of the firm, based on the seminal works of Coase (1937), Selznick (1957) and Penrose (1959), views the firm as a bundle of resources and capabilities. The resources confer distinctive competences, so that the firm's performance is dependent on how it deploys them. The focus is very much internal, on factor market imperfections and the lack of transferability of corporate resources, and in many ways complements the external focus of the industry analysis view made popular by Porter (1980). The competitive advantage of the firm is then attributable to a set of specialized resources and capabilities that are scarce, difficult to imitate and difficult to trade (see, among others, Dierickx and Cool, 1990; Barney, 1991; Peteraf, 1993).

Theorists (e.g., Andrews, 1971; Wernerfelt, 1984; Grant, 1991; Stalk et al., 1992) recognize the importance of difference between firms and the way in which distinctive competencies and capabilities contribute to competitive advantage. Schmalensee (1985) and Rumelt (1991), among others, note the contribution that a resource-based view of the firm has made to our understanding of how profitability can be maintained over long periods independent of industry conditions. Indeed, Rumelt notes that firms often differ more from those in their own industry than they do from those in other industries. The rise in popularity of the RBV approach can largely be attributed to the Prahalad and Hamel (1990) paper on 'core competencies'. They defined these competencies, that core of skills and capabilities within the organization, as being the unique sources of value creation which held the organization together. The search for the development of corporate strategy based on core competencies led back to the RBV approach, and the recognition, first of those assets of a business which could be described as 'unique and valuable', and then of how these might be applied in new businesses or industries. RBV recognizes the unique and valuable role played by such as brand names and technologies, but highlights the need for continuous investment to maintain their critical role. Collis and Montgomery (1998: 162) highlight the manner in which Disney rebuilt its brand name in the 1990s and then sought to leverage the advantage provided by its cartoon resources (its 'Crown jewels') into new markets – by the transfer of the latest cartoon characters into all aspects of the business (theme parks, studios and consumer products).

Ambrosini (2002: 141) demonstrates how the RBV approach addresses the seven Cs of strategic management – context, competences, culture, competition, change, corporate strategy, and control – to illustrate how it is consistent with alternative approaches:

- *Context.* There is little attention to the external environment, so the RBV approach may complement the more traditional five-forces approach (Porter, 1980) in this regard. However, the absence of attention is deliberate – the external environment is viewed as common to all and not a generator of sustained competitive advantage.
- *Competences.* Since most tangible resources can be purchased, traded or replicated, intangible assets become the most important strategic resource of the firm. Hamel and Prahalad (1994) make it clear what are not included in the classification of 'core competences' – fixed assets, distribution channels, brand names, patents, etc. – in fact anything that might appear on the company's balance sheet!
- *Culture.* Organizational culture can encourage innovation, flexibility and the development of know-how. Barney (1991) suggests that because culture is complex and difficult to observe, it will yield competences which are difficult to imitate, and which may confer advantages. Tacit knowledge will usually be organization-specific, and depend on specific interpersonal relationships; it is likely that it will play a key part in the development of competitive advantage.
- *Competition.* Competition based on the use of internal resources means that firms must act to protect the advantages conferred by their current resources since these may be eroded, and eventually made obsolete, by environmental and technological changes. Firms must therefore act to improve their existing resource base and to build new resources.
- *Change.* The focus on intangible resources, and associated strategies, may cause great difficulty in practice. It may not be clear how they are creating competitive advantage, so that the absence of causal relationships make change strategies unpredictable. On the other hand, if managers cannot specify a cause, then neither can competitors, so they will find it impossible to imitate the source of competitive advantage.
- *Corporate strategy.* The resource-based approach supports diversification in order to transfer specific resources to new markets – as illustrated by the Disney strategies above. The exploitation of 'resource relatedness' may confer benefits in other business units, but the problem of 'resource specificity' may arise – the transfer may not be feasible, so that firms need to develop bespoke strategies.
- *Control.* If a firm is to control its rare and valuable resources, it first needs to establish what these competences are and who has them. But as we

saw above, not having a clear understanding of such relationships may be helpful, because it prevents imitation by competitors. This is a problem for management: inaction may make them vulnerable to a loss of key resources, but inappropriate actions designed to nurture resources may destroy them (e.g., restructuring to achieve cost savings or impose a more 'rational' organizational framework).

Amit and Schoemaker (1993) adopt a behavioural perspective to demonstrate how resource-based theory could drive the deployment of strategic assets. They use behavioural decision theory (see Zajac and Bazerman, 1991) to explain the existence and persistence of sub-optimal management choices. Amit and Schoemaker observe that firms will differ in their control of resources and capabilities both because of factor market imperfections (following RBV) and managerial discretion in decision-making (following behavioural decision theory). They attribute competitive advantage to what they term 'strategic assets', which include technological capability, brand management, distribution channels, customer relationships and reputation. They identify three issues – uncertainty, complexity and conflict – with significant implications for the management of 'strategic assets'.

- *Uncertainty.* Decision-making under conditions of uncertainty always provides the possibility of sub-optimal choices: psychological evidence (e.g., Kahneman and Tversky, 1979; Einhorn and Hogarth, 1986) suggests that managers may act in a biased and irrational manner with regard to their tolerance of both risk and ambiguity. Overconfidence, managerial arrogance and a blinkered search for 'confirmatory' findings make outcomes difficult to predict. While most individuals exhibit risk aversion, MacCrimmon and Wehrung (1986) identify risk-seeking behaviours in situations where either goals are unrealistic or ambitious targets, behaviours which parallel those in the well-publicized recent derivative trading episodes at Barings and at National Australia Bank. In uncertain conditions managers will tend to repeat past actions and pay too much attention to recent events (see Tversky and Kahneman, 1974). Indeed, past successes may create an illusion of control which biases future decision-making by precluding innovative solutions, challenges which might be overcome by recourse to organizational learning (see Senge, 1990). Both the measurement and management of risk are discussed in more depth in Chapter 9.
- *Complexity.* The simplification of data for decision-making purposes often involves the use of heuristic devices and rule-of-thumb guidelines which may result in the introduction of sub-optimal bias. Tversky and Kahneman (1974) identify hindsight bias and the adoption of unjustified assumptions regarding probability and causality as key drivers of sub-optimal choice. Mintzberg (1978) and Quinn (1980), among others, report on the adoption of arbitrary processes for strategy implementation which impact on the discretionary managerial choices relating to the deployment of strategic assets.
- *Conflict.* Conflicting demands from within the organization for the deployment of scarce resources may produce sub-optimal allocations. Where stakeholder groups have different levels of bargaining power we might anticipate that social and environmental conditions will add to the financial factors that must be considered in the decision-making process.

The RBV approach conflicts with Porter's (1980) framework by suggesting that positioning of itself is not enough, in that competitive advantages associated with cost leadership, niche marketing and branding would not be sustainable in the long term. Although a short-term competitive advantage may occasionally derive from imitable resources, a *sustained* competitive advantage is associated only with intangible resources classified as rare and not capable of purchase or imitation. As a strategic management tool the RBV approach is consistent with the SWOT approach (above) in that it emphasizes the strengths and weaknesses of the resource base; however, there are still relatively few case studies, and little empirical evidence to back up RBV theories. Porter (1996), reflecting on the absence of competitive strategy guidelines in the RBV approach, suggests that companies must identify those products and services which are the most distinctive and profitable and those customer relationships and activities which are the most effective, so that decisions can be made about the appropriateness of continuing past strategies.

PERFORMANCE MEASUREMENT ALTERNATIVES

The original balanced scorecard (Kaplan and Norton, 1992) adopts an unashamedly shareholder focus in establishing a performance framework which addresses other than financial measures (i.e., customer perspectives, business processes and long-term sustainability). The four dimensions have remained essentially the same (financial; customer; internal; and innovation and learning) though their constituents have varied with the changed emphases of subsequent iterations (Kaplan and Norton, 1993, 1996, 2004). The balanced scorecard in this original form has rightfully been criticized for its shareholder-only focus. Atkinson et al. (1997b) are particularly critical of its weakness in the area of employee and supplier contributions. Kaplan and Norton (1992) are also quiet on the selection of specific performance measures and on the role of performance targets.

Not surprisingly, then, the scorecard has frequently been adapted at the implementation stage to embrace other stakeholders, notably customers and suppliers. Thus Ax and Bjornenak (2000) report on the 'Scandinavian' version of the balanced scorecard. However, most of the established frameworks still fail to address the human resource dimension adequately, which as we saw in Chapter 2 has been identified by survey research as one of the biggest gaps between theory and practice in management accounting research. It is instructive to view alternative frameworks, both pre-dating and since the arrival of the balanced scorecard, to see how the embellishments have addressed the observed weaknesses.

The *tableau de bord* (see Epstein and Manzoni, 1997) was developed in the 1900s by French process engineers to establish the cause-and-effect relationships that would permit them to make production improvements. The controls were likened to those we might see on an automobile dashboard (and now in an aeroplane cockpit) to provide a simultaneous display of multiple measures. The tableau was subsequently adapted by managers in order for them to take an overview of a whole business or of a business unit. Within any business a number of tableaux might be developed to suit the individual requirements of particular units. The focus was mainly on financial measures, but controllable non-financial operational measures were also included. Monthly reporting was intended to induce the alignment of individual business unit objectives and performance with those of the organization as a whole. In practice, this myopic internal focus was dysfunctional, since what was required in the longer term was benchmarking against industry best performance.

The *five dimensions* framework (see Smith and Dikolli, 1991) revolves around five factors: goals, customers, employees, processes and information. Into each of these dimensions are mapped the management accounting tools which would provide the means of addressing issues of concern therein:

- The 'goal' dimension advocates the use SMA and NFIs for planning, the establishment of aims and objectives, and TQM to secure management commitment.
- The 'customers' dimension advocates the use of SWOT methods of industry analysis, SMA for a focus on competition, markets and the environment, and TQM to ensure ultimate customer focus.
- The 'employees' dimension embraces value-added management and total employee involvement to secure participation, team-building and creativity and TQM to change attitudes and behaviour.
- The 'processes' dimension addresses continuous improvement (through TQM), timely delivery (through just-in-time), waste elimination (through value-added management) as well as a number of process improvement facilitators, mainly confined to the manufacturing sector.
- The 'information' dimension focuses on the use of NFIs and feedback loops within an SMA environment aided by appropriate accounting and statistical systems.

Financial performance is the integrating factor for the framework, rather than a separate dimension, since each of the dimensions is seen as impacting on overall performance. The model is short on specific performance measures and has a short-term focus. Thus, while it does address customer, employee and supplier issues, it neglects organizational learning and innovation issues.

Beischel and Smith 1991 identified five *critical success factors*, thought to be universal for all manufacturing companies:

- *Quality* – defined for products (as meeting or exceeding customers' expected levels of satisfaction) and for processes (as reducing operational variances).
- *Customer service* – defined as external (for providing end-product satisfaction) and internal (for satisfying the requirements of other departments and colleagues).
- *Resource management* – concerned with producing optimal outputs from people, inventory and fixed capital.
- *Cost* – concerned with manageable reported levels of cost.
- *Flexibility* – defined in terms of the organization's ability to respond to changes in business circumstances (e.g., the environment, technology, markets, regulation).

The framework (which has clear similarities with the TQM approach for continuous improvement) recognized that a simultaneous approach was necessary if manufacturing performance was to be managed better. Beischel and Smith emphasized the importance of establishing causal relationships so that management's critical success factors could be linked to local performance measures (i.e., the link between 'top floor' and 'shop floor' that they envisaged). If the sets of measures did not align, or produced inconsistent directions, they should be abandoned. Once an appropriate set of manufacturing measures had been established, where demonstrable links to financial performance could be made, then they recommended the design of a number of 'scorecards'. These scorecards would provide a measurement system for each level of management and which reflected both the span of control for decision-making, and the frequency with which measures were reported. Scorecards, and measures, were only relevant if they preserved the link between local performance measures, manufacturing processes and critical success factors. Clearly this 'scorecard' framework has many similarities with its more famous brother, with both critically reliant on the establishment of causal relationships between measures used in different parts of the framework.

The *success dimensions framework* (see Shenhar and Dvir, 1996) suggests that the measurement of performance within only one time dimension might be misleading, and, as an alternative, identifies four time horizons (very short; short; long; very long) across which performance might be measured. This is combined with three organizational levels (project; business unit; company) to provide 12 cells of analysis. Despite the multitude of opportunities to do so, the framework does not suggest specific operational measures for each cell.

The *dynamic multidimensional performance model* (see Maltz et al., 2003) enables organizations to use different measures in each of five dimensions, viewed with varying degrees of importance, depending on industry and competitiveness of the environment. The authors argue that this model improves on existing models in the management literature, both by reflecting organizational performance in multiple time horizons, and through the inclusion of a 'people' dimension which recognizes the critical role of the human resource function in the success of an organization. The model consists of five dimensions in total: *financial*; *market/customer*; *process*; *people development*; and *future*. Within these five dimensions, 12 'baseline' performance measures are identified which might have general applicability to different organizations.

The model is not prescriptive in that it recognizes that one set of measures cannot 'fit' all organizations, but the authors suggest that it will allow an organization to map its performance measures into the five dimensions. However, the 'people' and 'future' measures in the model may, in practice, be too subjective for them to be operationalized consistently, posing potential problems of both generalizability and comparability.

The *performance prism* (see Neely, 2003) seeks to address the key flaw of the balanced scorecard by addressing stakeholder value, rather than purely shareholder value. The prism is a three-dimensional model based around strategies, processes and capabilities (being that combination of people, practices, technology and infrastructure necessary to sustain and improve on existing processes). Importantly, it addresses both 'stakeholder satisfaction' and 'stakeholder contribution', where 'stakeholders' would include not only investors but also customers, employees, suppliers and regulators.

Thus 'stakeholder satisfaction' identifies the important internal and external stakeholders in the organization, together with their requirements, while 'stakeholder contribution' identifies what is required from stakeholders if they are to maintain and develop the set of capabilities. A potential limitation of the performance prism is, however, that some the measures of 'stakeholder satisfaction' and 'stakeholder contribution' may be subjective in nature, and interestingly none of these developments have so far adequately addressed the human resources issue, so that further developments might be anticipated in this respect. Malina and Selto (2001) identify a potential barrier in that the implementation of knowledge-based strategies, necessarily with significant human resource implications, would not be encouraged by traditional financial performance measures should the associated resources continue to be treated as a current expense.

The balanced scorecard remains the most important of the performance measurement frameworks, and is discussed in greater depth in Chapter 8. Interestingly, Kaplan and Norton (2004) further blur the distinction between the four dimensions of performance. With their introduction of 'strategy maps', the 'internal processes' domain now embraces both customer management processes and innovation processes, while the 'learning and organization' quadrant provides the opportunity for the development of capabilities associated with intangible assets.

SUMMARY

The chapter provides an indication of the dynamic nature of performance measurement. Numerous alternative frameworks are examined, all with the potential to facilitate organizational improvement. In essence they provide guidelines, and must not be regarded as prescriptive: the one message that comes through loud and clear, and will be reiterated in Chapter 8, is that 'one size does not fit all' – the performance measurement framework must be modelled to fit the organization it is meant for or it will not produce the outcomes which are desired or expected. Alignment of corporate goals with performance measurement framework is essential. The frameworks in this chapter facilitate the conduct of comparative analysis and performance benchmarking, and establish the base for the analysis of implementation issues and alternative strategy approaches.

4   Strategy Alternatives

INTRODUCTION

Management decision-making is often constrained by inhibited thought processes and a blinkered approach. Frequently this will result in sub-optimal choices because too few feasible alternatives have been generated, making the selection procedure fatally flawed. Management accountants are often guilty in this respect because they have not been trained to think creatively and have not been equipped with management tools to aid innovative thinking. Creativity in accounting is not necessarily an impediment if it encourages a move towards non-traditional approaches to problem-solving.

One of the greatest potential benefits of the adoption of a new corporate culture – for example, a commitment to total quality management, value-added management, or theory of constraints – is a renewed emphasis on creativity in the workforce. Such benefits should accrue to the management accounting team where, as elsewhere, a creative approach is often constrained by the predominance of traditional reporting mechanisms.

When solving problems, making decisions and choosing between alternative courses of action, we need to determine the optimum solution, rather than falling back on the prevalent attitude that close enough is good enough. But our selection can only be as good as the alternatives from which our choice is made. More attention needs to be devoted to the generation of ideas and alternatives if the search for an optimum solution is not to be inescapably constrained.

Training will underlie any attempt at effecting a change in attitudes. Management accountants are too rarely taught to think, and too rarely equipped with the management tools which facilitate the process. Indeed, the word 'creativity' itself – most usually encountered in the context of 'creative accounting' – immediately conjures up images of fudging, of blurred edges, economy with the truth, and even fraud. Such negative perceptions must be overcome, or at least softened, if a less blinkered approach is to be encouraged. Psychologists have identified a number of thinking aids as tools to facilitate creativity. They include brainstorming, lateral thinking, synectics, affinity diagrams and force fields techniques whose application to the management environment is well established. As practising accountants we are prone to be too backward in embracing the ideas of other disciplines and incorporating them to advantage in our own processes, though such practices are well established and accepted in accounting research (see Smith, 2003: 1).

We should aim to avoid jumping to conclusions and offering quick-fix solutions without sufficient emphasis on the options and the consequences of our actions. Problems rarely exist in isolation, and the chain of dependent events must be examined in each case. Understanding the root problem, not merely its symptoms, is often the greatest challenge, requiring clarity of thought and the avoidance of obscurity. It is thus fruitless to identify a problem as 'communication difficulties' or 'low morale'; if a solution is to be discovered then it is essential to frame the problem much more specifically than this. We should approach each issue in well-defined, bite-sized chunks. A team approach is very much to be preferred in the generation and evaluation of ideas. A structured, group decision-making process for assigning priorities and reaching consensus provides an environment conducive to the development of creative solutions.

CREATIVE THINKING

Delbecq and Van de Ven's (1971) nominal group technique is one such systematic approach. The technique embraces a number of key stages:

- Team members' suggestions for improvements are collected without discussion, criticism or evaluation, in order to encourage contributions.
- Team ideas are aggregated prior to evaluation and the identification of trends and patterns.
- A group process is initiated for the ranking of ideas for importance and the selection of key opportunities for further analysis. This voting system helps to eliminate 'pet' ideas with scant group support and to alleviate the effects of status differences between team members.
- Selected ideas are assigned to teams for further investigation so that recommendations and preliminary action plans can be developed.

The success of the technique will usually depend on the combined strength of the team members, their commitment to the process and their training in the appropriate management tools. It may be a frustrating exercise initially, since many contributors will see the solution as 'obvious' from the outset. If they recognize the acceptability of alternatives as a result of the creative processes then this revelation will have made the process worthwhile.

Consider the familiar portrait of the wife and mother-in-law in Figure 4.1. This ambiguous picture was originally drawn by W.E. Hill and appeared in the 6 November 1915 issue of *Puck*. It was subsequently employed in psychological research by Boring (1930). The picture may be perceived differently by individuals because of the way they relate the figure to its background. Some observers see only the old woman, with hooked nose, jutting chin, slit mouth and headscarf. Others see only the profile of the young woman,

FIGURE 4.1

Female perception alternatives

with pert nose, mascaraed lashes and plumed headwear. Many observers still fail to see both figures even when they are aware that the portrait contains two likenesses. Their search for alternatives has ceased because they have found one acceptable interpretation of the figure – they fail to go on to consider the existence of alternative interpretations.

In a management accounting context, we wish to avoid focusing inappropriately on the obvious, so providing an opportunity for generating acceptable alternatives. This means searching for more, potentially better, strategies; we wish to create a management environment where we do not stop looking for better solutions because we have already found a satisfactory one.

Consider the problem in Figure 4.2 suggested by Edward de Bono (1970). Most people can generate three alternatives very easily, but tend to grind to a halt once they have reached the stage illustrated in Figure 4.3. Further progress requires a change in attitudes and a questioning of the fundamental assumptions we are working with. What is a continuous line? Does it have to be straight? Can it be stepped? Appropriate answers to this last question frequently generate the alternatives shown in Figure 4.4. This is the critical step. Once taken, it becomes apparent that there are many alternative kinds of lines which will provide acceptable solutions. Once the lines become curved, as in Figure 4.5, we realize that an infinite number of potential solutions might be generated through infinitesimal variations in the curvature.

The de Bono problem: use two continuous lines to cut this square into areas which are equal in size and shape

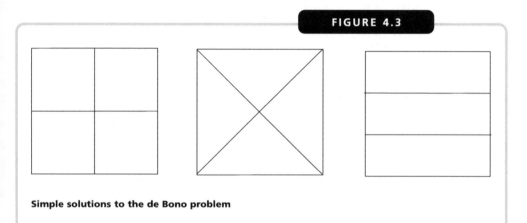

Simple solutions to the de Bono problem

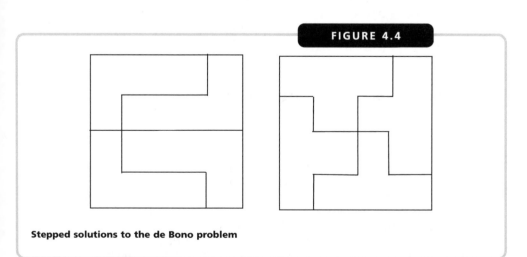

Stepped solutions to the de Bono problem

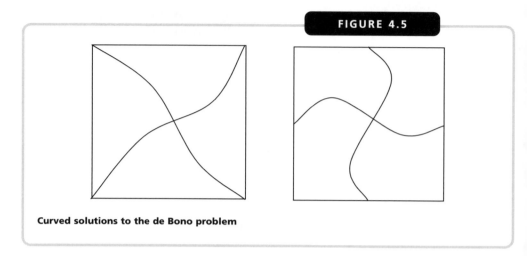

FIGURE 4.5

Curved solutions to the de Bono problem

The requirements for problem-solving in a management accounting environment are clear:

- a precise definition of the problem, with an awareness of inhibiting constraints;
- a willingness to accept the existence of alternatives; and
- the avoidance of a closed-minded attitude which focuses on a single, obvious solution.

Figure 4.6 provides an example of a flawed decision-making process. Adapted from an actual instance of management reporting in an Australian manufacturing company, it illustrates the consequences of responding inappropriately to a problem rather than examining the root causes of potential difficulties. By rushing into a quick-fix solution, time and money are needlessly expended in producing an outcome which offers no improvement on the original! More considered thought and wide-ranging problem analysis prior to implementation ensures that we are aware of the likely consequences of actions and the eventual outcomes that are desirable.

The messages of creativity, innovation and lateral thinking are thus not confined to problem-solving and decision-making, but can be extended to the management processes and the reporting environment.

DEVELOPING AN INNOVATION CULTURE

Long-term improvements in economic performance demand that firms develop an adaptive culture in which innovation features prominently. To nurture an innovative and flexible workforce which facilitates product and process changes, an environment must be created which eliminates cautious and protective attitudes and encourages risk-taking. The harnessing of the creativity of the workforce in order to promote innovation remains problematic in most companies. We know that innovation is good for us, but how do we achieve it? What systems and work environment need to be in place to encourage innovation? How do we change the culture of the

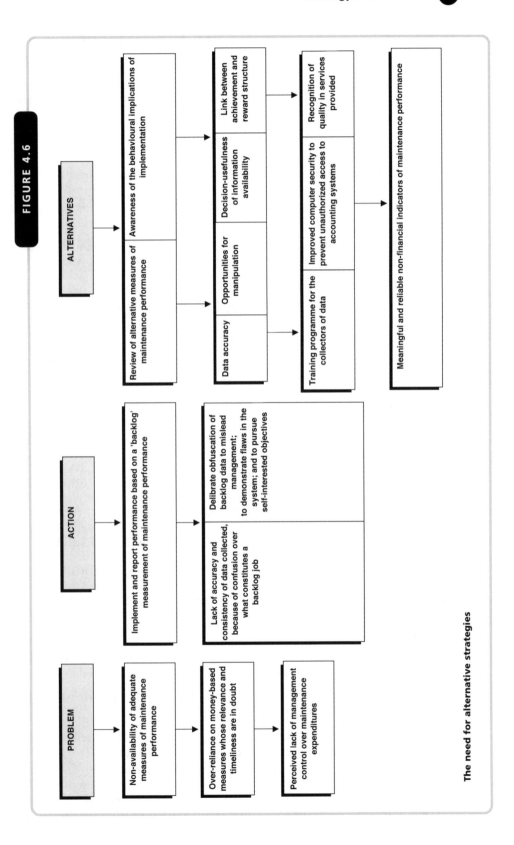

FIGURE 4.6

The need for alternative strategies

organization to make innovation a central part of it? All fundamental questions, to which the academic literature and the experience of practitioners can provide guidance, if not a complete solution.

For example, Collins and Porras (1994) observe that long-lived companies, with financial performance which has established them as industry leaders, often share a number of common qualities:

- core values, which dictate the behaviour and recruitment of employees;
- alternative goals to that of 'making money';
- a focus on continuous self-improvement, rather than just beating the competition;
- recognition of the importance of trial and error, and learning from failures.

A culture which embraces learning from mistakes, rather than inculcating a 'get-it-right-the-first-time' mentality, therefore provides a link with longevity, linking the latter with an innovation culture.

Kotter and Heskett (1992) detail a relationship between organizational culture and profitability, in which long-term financial success was associated with:

- visionary leadership, clearly articulating future directions;
- walking the talk, so that there is no conflict between words and action;
- attentiveness to the needs of all stakeholders;
- empowerment of employees, and
- dedication to continuous improvement.

Common characteristics emerge in commitment from the top, team working and the encouragement of creativity, which are all factors in the creation of an innovation culture.

Inventions will not just emerge; conditions must be established to encourage their emergence. For our particular organization we should be aware of where the ideas for innovations will come from so that they can be sourced properly. Ideas will usually be generated internally (from the workforce) or externally (from customers or suppliers) but inter-industry differences are inevitable.

There is some evidence to suggest that the 'type' of innovation will be important in determining its likely source. Thus we have the matrix of Figure 4.7 to dictate the likely source of 'product' or 'process' innovations.

We also have to decide how we intend to generate ideas:

- Are they to be problem-specific?
- Are they to be random? In which case we seek lots of good ideas in the knowledge that relatively few will actually be implemented.

The reactions of those generating the ideas are paramount in deciding which approach to adopt:

- If we encourage the generation of ideas, then sit on them without taking any action, we will not get ideas generated in the future.
- If we reject some ideas out of hand without providing an adequate justification, we will lose the goodwill and creativity of these individuals. De Bono (1992) presents an interesting alternative to the simple accept/reject decision, in which ideas are graded as directly usable, good

FIGURE 4.7

SOURCE / IDEA	Internal	Customer	Supplier
Product	✓	✓	
Process	✓		✓

(Column group header: **External** spanning Customer and Supplier)

Source of innovations

but not for us, good but not for now, needing more work, powerful but not usable, interesting but unusable, of weak value, or unworkable.

- If ideas are rejected publicly, trivially or jokingly, so that participants lose face as a result, we will alienate a whole segment of potential creativity.
- If ideas are converted into successfully implemented innovations without the innovator being adequately rewarded, then this too might stifle the future flow of ideas. We have to counter the 'why should I bother?' mentality. Precisely what form this reward should take causes a good deal of controversy. Much of the US literature suggests the use of plaques, blazers and ties rather than monetary rewards. Experience elsewhere suggests that it is dollars that counts – and big dollars for innovations that generate million-dollar savings.

Sourcing ideas outside the organization demands closer ties with external organizations:

- Suppliers might be interested in innovation-sharing, so that technological ingenuity is not confined to one company.
- Subsidiaries may prefer to pay royalties to the parent company to share in the benefits of innovations; though the implications may be that individuals feel that the 'pressure is off' and innovation is no longer part of their job.
- For the solution to specific technological problems, outside scientific agencies might be sourced to provide alternatives at a fraction of the cost charged by consultants.
- Close links with local universities might be developed to provide a 'think tank' atmosphere for creative solutions.
- Customer surveys and marketing research should be used to identify unsatisfied needs and potential innovative opportunities.

Many organizations have the perception that the customer often does not know what they want until they see a new development in the marketplace. There is plenty of anecdotal evidence to suggest that there is some truth in this, which makes it important for organizations to have effective screening systems in place to deal with the multiplicity of ideas under consideration. Figure 4.8 provides a representation of the innovation process, showing the importance of the 'sourcing' and 'screening' activities.

Market-based evidence suggests that as many as 40% of new products launched fail in the marketplace, and that 46% of the industry resources devoted to new products are spent on failed or cancelled projects. Management needs to be able to spot probable new product winners early, and to allocate development resources to these projects. This makes the 'screening' stage of the innovation process so vitally important. Most projects will be killed off at the 'screening' stage for new products, but two errors will be made:

- some 'losers' may creep through the process, and
- some viable projects which are just too innovative may be rejected by too rigid a screening mechanism.

We need to weigh the cost of lost opportunities against the cost of misallocated resources, and balance rejection and acceptance errors. However, the screening decision remains an investment appraisal under extreme uncertainty and with no accurate financials until the end of the product development or, indeed, commercialization. A further problem is illustrated by the dilemma of what precisely constitutes a 'good' innovation. If what has been judged as a 'good idea' is subsequently a commercial failure because of marketing and implementation errors, does that, in hindsight, make it a 'bad idea'? Similarly, if an idea viewed subjectively to be 'poor' is successful because it hangs onto the coat tails of a new market craze, does that suddenly make it a good idea? Some judges would make commercial success the only criterion for a 'good idea', but we have to have alternative judgement criteria in order to clear the previous hurdle, that is, to decide whether or not to bring the idea to market.

The most popular screening methods involve the rating of product attributes, and the subjective assessment of the project to give a numerical project score. It is usually assumed that the success of a project can be predicted from an examination of the product profile and that future successes/

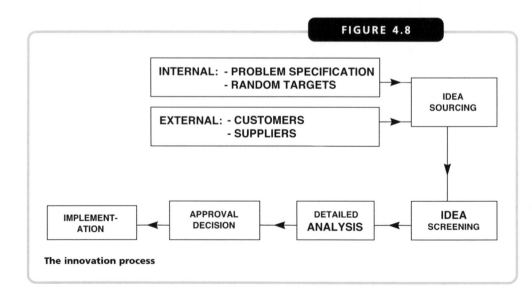

FIGURE 4.8

The innovation process

failures will have similar product profiles to previous successes/failures. This form of 'failure' modelling is therefore very similar to that for bankruptcy prediction (see Chapter 9) whereby appropriately weighted financial factors for current companies are compared with the corresponding financial profiles of known previous failures.

To identify successful future products, R.G. Cooper (1985) suggests that there are four key factors:

- market – size, growth and level of competition;
- product advantages – uniqueness and superiority;
- project–company fit – in terms of technology and distribution networks;
- size and complexity of the project – relative to the firm's readiness to innovate.

In each of these areas, Cooper identifies the characteristics sought in order to promote successful adoption and implementation of innovations. The *market* should be large, have high growth and exhibit high need, low competitive intensity with few competitors, few new products and little price competition. The *product* should be of higher quality, have greater reliability, encourage new customer behaviour, be highly innovative, and first to market. The *project–company fit* analysis will hopefully point to synergies in market research, managerial skills, sales and distribution, advertising and promotion, technology, and research and development. Finally, the *firm readiness analysis* may reveal disadvantages associated with diversification, particularly those associated with moving to a new product class with new types of user and new competitors, new processes and new technology. Cooper claims a high success rate for his commercial project, NewProd, which incorporates the above factors, appropriately measured, into a model to predict the success of product innovations.

What is apparent from the innovation process is that we need to recognize industry differences, and to have a system in place which is capable of both generating and screening ideas. Both require the development of an innovation culture within the organization. The firm's readiness and flexibility to innovate will be influenced by accounting factors relating to both strategic direction and management controls. Within a management accounting context, Askarany and Smith (2004) have shown that the work of Rogers (1995), in the management field, can be extended to demonstrate those important characteristics of accounting innovations which are associated with implementation and adoption.

A number of authors (notably Miles and Snow, 1978; Porter, 1980; Miller and Friesen, 1982; Covin, 1991) have developed alternative typologies to characterize the organizational strategies that are associated with success. These are helpful in clarifying the attributes we would expect to find in innovative companies. Miles and Snow suggest prospector/defender categories, Porter differentiator/cost leader categories, and Miller and Friesen (amplified by Covin) entrepreneurial/conservative categories. Each of these groupings represent extremes in their attitude towards innovation. Combining the three research works allows us to consider the characteristics of two distinct types:

- Prospector–differentiator–entrepreneur: emphasize innovative aspects of firm activity; minimize customer sensitivity to price; offer products unique in design and brand image.
- Defender–cost leader–conservative: emphasize stability; promote cost leadership through controls; focus on asset use and employee productivity;

seek maintenance of current market niche through quality, superior service and/or lower prices.

The first of these strategy types (prospector–differentiator–entrepreneur) is the one we seek to promote in the pursuit of innovation, and which generates congruent strategies:

- aim to be first to the market, rather than being content with being 'good at what we do now';
- change products and services frequently and implement active search processes;
- respond flexibly to market opportunities;
- promote a team-based empowered approach to new product development;
- reduce delays by delegating responsibilities; avoid hierarchical bureaucracies and the rigidity of long chains of command;
- emphasize new product and production technologies, rather than efficient mass production.

When considering the role of organizational control in innovation Waldersee and Sheather (1996) emphasize the incompatibility of an innovative and flexible workforce with the rules, procedures and top-down management which typify a conservative strategy. Where managers are forced to focus on efficiency and cost control the benefits of participation and consensus may be less apparent.

Prospectors–differentiators–entrepreneurs actively pursue innovation; control systems might be used to warn against excessive innovation, especially if its long-term objectives threaten the short-term survival of the enterprise. Defenders–cost leaders–conservative types are likely to have detailed control systems focusing on problem-solving and reducing uncertainty, but providing little assistance in new product development or the need for innovation.

Smith (1997) suggests that the traditional sources of competitive advantage (detailed by Porter, 1985) – efficiency, productivity and throughput as a result of technological leadership and low cost per unit – may no longer be appropriate in an environment pursuing competitive advantage through innovation.

With the adoption of advanced manufacturing philosophies, the implications for control systems at all levels need to be addressed. It is quite conceivable that the administrative controls introduced to facilitate administrative change (e.g., activity-based costing) may be incompatible with the pursuit of innovation.

Rogers (1995) suggests that innovation may be thought of as progressing through four stages;

- adoption – where the need for change is recognized, but where a high level of uncertainty exists;
- preparation – the process of training, consulting and data collection;
- implementation – introducing and evaluating its impact;
- routinization – where innovation becomes a normal part of everyone's job.

As management accountants we need to review the control systems, performance measures and reward systems that we have in place, to ensure that this four-stage process can proceed efficiently and is consistent with the strategies outlined above in pursuit of innovation.

EVALUATION

The positive and negative aspects of all alternative strategies which generate desirable outcomes must be considered with respect to corporate priorities and the likely results of different courses of action. Evaluation may reveal evidence of potential conflict between corporate strategy and performance measurement. For example, we might anticipate that this would appear in:

- *Different time-horizon reference points*. While senior management might be pursuing medium and long-term objectives, the focus at lower levels will more likely be short term, or even, in a manufacturing environment, exclusively shift-based.
- *Different emphases attached to the importance of costs*. Where senior management might focus on cost control and adherence to budget, at lower levels cost considerations may be secondary, cursory or even non-existent as 'getting the job done' assumes priority.

The latter point is potentially damaging because it may lead to a lack of goal congruence, where the pursuit of individual target indicators (such as production volumes, or labour and equipment productivities) may not be consistent with strategic corporate goals.

In manufacturing industry, nowhere is the measurement issue more fraught with danger than in the maintenance function. Studies by the author in both the UK and Australia highlight a laudable degree of experimentation in attempts to measure quality of workmanship and standards of performance in the provision of a maintenance service. This provides an excellent example of the problems which the management accountant faces in formulating measures which inspire confidence in management without provoking a matching scepticism at leading-hand level and below regarding the accuracy of data inputs.

Job cards completed by operators or contractors may be notoriously inaccurate if they necessitate the recording of:

- job numbers or area categories – often involving six-figure costing codes consistent with cost information systems;
- hours on the job or time of completion;
- allocation of overtime hours between alternative jobs; and
- allocation of equipment time to alternative activities.

As well as inaccuracies due to accident, design or complacency, there exist opportunities for self-interested manipulation as illustrated in Figure 4.6. Such opportunities are manifestly apparent in measures of the backlog, either in time or the number of jobs – popular in the literature, but often eliminated as unworkable in practice. Three critical questions arise:

- What is a backlog item? Can it be dropped from the schedules with ease to reappear as forward scheduling or breakdown maintenance?
- Can jobs be closed early to reduce backlog – only to reappear as new jobs or reworks?
- Is it in the interest of the maintenance team to reduce backlog? In practice, it will only be in their interest if their reward structure is linked to the performance measure. If, as a result of their increased efficiency,

some men are redeployed or the supply of available overtime dries up, then the motivation to seek further improvements will be curtailed.

The human factor – both in terms of data accuracy and in the manipulation of data – is central to the successful measurement of outcomes and, therefore, an appropriate evaluation of alternatives. Any comparison of outcomes with expectations must be viewed systematically. It is pointless focusing only on apparently underperforming projects because this biases the review – there may be opportunities for improvement in strategies which are already performing to expectation.

The post-implementation review provides the opportunity for uncovering errors and bias, deliberate or otherwise, in the original objective statement. The negative aspects of the evaluation arise in terms of the possible witch-hunt when projected results have not been achieved, generating finger-pointing and the need to find someone to blame. This makes it difficult to rely on the effective co-operation of those involved, and may prevent a complete evaluation taking place.

This is a great pity and a lost opportunity for learning where errors are likely to occur and where bias can most easily be introduced. An unbiased evaluation of alternatives – including those not implemented – has potentially great benefits for the organization, but is dependent on more enlightened views of the nature of the investigative procedure.

Any appraisal of the quality of investment decisions should address the way in which the decisions have been taken as well as their consequences. This would include the following stages:

- Project generation: which projects are put forward for examination?
- Cash flows: how and by whom are these estimated?
- Analysis: what methods and assumptions are employed?
- Selection: importance of financials/non-financials in project choice.
- Authorization: documentation of monitoring process for project implementation.
- Evaluation: do the project outcomes match/exceed expectations?

A post-audit investigation can potentially have a significant impact on the manner in which future appraisals are conducted. Problems with implementing post-audit schemes range across the whole gamut of which? where? how? and by whom? Big companies may be able to audit internally, others may need to employ consultants. Either way, the continued co-operation of those individuals involved in implementing the project is essential. Any breach of confidence will reduce the levels of active co-operation and, potentially, destroy the learning opportunities. The post-audit could extend over:

- all projects currently underperforming;
- all projects implemented (underperforming or not);
- all projects considered (implemented or not); and
- a sample of any of the above.

In practice, post-audit evaluations appear to be conducted rarely, except for the very largest of projects. The reasons for not doing so usually range from 'Not enough time: too busy with appraising new projects' to 'What's the point? the money has been spent'. We might speculate that the real reasons are more likely to do with the 'witch-hunt' that might arise if errors were to be found.

The following case is particularly rewarding because the post-audit was conducted by a group of master's degree students, three years after the investment had been implemented (to avoid sensitivity of individuals), who were granted access by the company to such papers that still existed relating to the project decisions.

CASE STUDY

Alumina PLC: Post-audit of capital investment expenditure

BACKGROUND

Alumina PLC has recently purchased a new platform and a crane to replace the old ones with the intention of improving work practices and reducing the need for equipment hire.

The old platform is too large to operate in confined areas and requires the erection of scaffolding for maintenance access. Scaffolding takes on average in excess of three days to erect and disassemble and disrupts production over the corresponding period. Sometimes a similar and smaller machine is hired to perform such duties. The crane does not have an operator's cab and would not normally be permitted by the appropriate safety and licensing authorities for crane and lifting operations. If the cab is to be installed, then this crane cannot be used in confined spaces, which would drastically limit the maintenance department's effectiveness. Both pieces of equipment are over 25 years old and have accumulated high maintenance costs over the last five years. The maintenance costs are set to rise as spare parts are no longer available, and have to be manufactured in most instances.

The replacement machines were jointly evaluated during the process, and a detailed cost justification was presented in the evaluation report. This exercise has resulted in the purchase, as recommended in the evaluation, of a Grove low-profile mobile crane at $140,000 and a Longreach mobile aerial platform at $60,000. This equipment replaces the existing Steelweld crane and mobile work platform.

A post-audit study was conducted on the capital expenditure evaluation process on which the purchase decision was based, with the objective of:

- identifying any deficiencies in the evaluation procedure adopted;
- identifying any key and related issues regarding the purchasing decision; and
- making recommendations to improve capital expenditure evaluation procedures in the future.

CASE STUDY (cont.)

Economic justification for purchase

Alumina PLC currently operates an aerial work platform with a 40 ft (12.2 m) high reach aerial work platform and a Steelweld crane in its major bauxite refinery operation. The work platform is used in various locations for maintenance access to valves, piping and structures, while the crane is used extensively by maintenance personnel, particularly shift maintenance, in buildings where access is tight and confined. Both units are essential for maintenance departments to carry out day-to-day activities that require aerial access or lifting capabilities in confined areas.

Mobile aerial work platform. The physical dimensions of the platform are too large for it to operate in confined areas. This then requires the erection of scaffolding to gain access to equipment such as valves, pumps and piping structures. Scaffolding takes on average in excess of three days to erect and dismantle when an appropriate aerial work platform would take less than a day. Sometimes a similar and smaller machine is hired to perform such duties. The slow travelling speed (0.5 km/hr) of the existing platform is a disadvantage and causes its non-return to the central cranes parking area. This then ties up personnel time in trying to locate the machine for use in other areas.

Steelweld crane. The existing Steelweld crane is considered to be an asset to maintenance users as it is the only crane on site that can be used in confined areas and in the rod mills, due to its low profile height and slewable jib. This crane does not have an operator's cab, and its use would not normally be allowed by the appropriate safety and licensing authorities for crane and lifting operations. If the cab were installed, then the effect on the crane's profile would mean that it could not be used in any of the confined areas for which it is currently uniquely suitable. This would drastically limit the maintenance department's effectiveness.

This crane is not easy to maintain as virtually all parts have to be manufactured and downtime can be considerable. This type of crane is obsolete and vendor technical expertise is virtually nonexistent. Maintenance costs for both pieces of equipment have become exorbitant, over the last five years $37,000 for the work platform and $17,000 for the crane; further overhaul is not recommended on either since the same parts difficulties would still be encountered. The proposed replacement equipment comprises the latest models available. They are more capable and can provide a service which reduces or removes costly work practices and reduces the need for equipment hire.

Proposal

It is recommended to replace both machines with the Grove low profile mobile crane at $140,000 and the Longreach mobile aerial work platform at $60,000. These replacement machines would enhance maintenance effectiveness by providing the same maintenance service plus additional duties not provided by the older machines. Grove cranes are already used extensively at sister refineries and have been very reliable, accumulating low maintenance costs. The load range and extendable boom would also allow the use of this crane in areas normally serviced by the existing Steelweld crane as well as reducing hire requirements.

Another advantage is the carry decks which will eliminate the use of a dogman to accompany the crane. It is proposed to install a forklift and work platform accessories to provide additional capabilities for maintenance.

The aerial lift mobile work platform will be utilized in confined areas of low height and width and can reach up and over obstructing pipework and structures. These capabilities will eliminate the need to build scaffolding to reach valves and piping to carry out maintenance work. It is estimated that the erection and dismantling of scaffolding could cause in excess of two to three days' downtime of precipitator tanks.

Benefits

The replacement of this equipment will generate the cost savings and profit improvements detailed in Tables 4.1 and 4.2 by reducing the need for scaffolding and increasing production opportunities due to the earlier return of out-of-circuit equipment to production.

Details of the project appraisal are shown in Table 4.3. The analysis is conducted over 20 half-year periods with a tax rate of 39%,

TABLE 4.1

Cost savings for crane and platform

Cost savings ($'000)	Year 1	Year 2	Year 3	Year 4	Year 5
Crane					
Labour savings	50	50	50	50	50
Scaffold inventory	–	–	–	–	–
Increased production	–	–	–	–	–
Maintenance reduction	4.2	5.6	8.4	11.2	12.6
Hire reduction	1.28	1.28	1.28	1.28	1.28
Total	55.48	56.88	59.68	62.48	63.88
Platform					
Labour savings	–	–	–	–	–
Scaffold inventory	10	10	10	10	10
Increased production	54	54	54	54	54
Maintenance reduction	1.8	2.4	3.6	4.8	5.4
Hire reduction	5.12	5.12	5.12	5.12	5.12
Total	70.92	71.52	72.72	73.92	74.52

CASE STUDY (cont.)

TABLE 4.2

Cost savings and increased profits ($)

Savings/profits	Year 1	Year 2	Year 3	Year 4	Year 5
Labour savings	50,000	50,000	50,000	50,000	50,000
Scaffold inventory	10,000	10,000	10,000	10,000	10,000
Increased production	54,000	54,000	54,000	54,000	54,000
Maintenance reduction	6,000	8,000	12,000	16,000	18,000
Hire reductions	6,400	6,400	6,400	6,400	6,400
Total	126,400	128,400	132,400	136,400	138,400

discount factor of 13% and depreciation rate of 18% compound. Depreciation is charged half-yearly on a reducing balance basis.

Evaluation of this project leads to the following conclusions: a net present value (NPV, at 13%) of $342,000, an internal rate of return (IRR) of 54.3%, and a payback period (discounted) of 1.8 years. A post-audit of this project needs to make recommendations for the improvement of the procedure adopted. Assumptions are necessary to deal with some of the uncertainties associated with the joint consideration of costs and revenues, so a detailed sensitivity analysis is necessary to allow the two components of the project to be appraised separately.

POST-AUDIT ANALYSIS

The crane and the platform are independent of each other in the sense that they operate independently and perform their own functions in the maintenance process. There is no apparent reason for these two machines to be appraised together. The joint evaluation reveals a payback period of 1.8 years, an NPV (at 13%) of $342,000 and an IRR of 54.3% for the combined project.

When separate analyses are performed for the crane and the platform, and a comparison with the 'combined' analysis is made, an interesting picture emerges. The combined cost savings figures are shown in Table 4.2, and the following assumptions are necessary to separate the cost savings for the crane from those for the platform:

- The labour savings are entirely attributed to the crane because the new crane will eliminate the use of a dogman.
- The scaffold inventory is attributed to the platform because the old platform could not be used in confined areas, and scaffolding is required instead for maintenance.
- The increased production is attributed to the platform because the need to build and dismantle scaffolds could cause in excess of 2–3 days' downtime and consequent loss of production.
- The maintenance reduction is apportioned to align with the historical maintenance costs of the crane and platform. Based on

TABLE 4.3

Alumina PLC project appraisal

	Base	Y1		Y2		Y3		Y4		Y5		Y6		Y7		Y8		Y9		Y10	
		Y1H1	Y1H2	Y2H1	Y2H2	Y3H1	Y3H2	Y4H1	Y4H2	Y5H1	Y5H2	Y6H1	Y6H2	Y7H1	Y7H2	Y8H1	Y8H2	Y9H1	Y9H2	Y10H1	Y10H2
Investment and depreciation																					
Investment	200.0																				
Depreciation		18.0	18.0	14.8	14.8	12.1	12.1	9.9	9.9	8.1	8.1	6.7	6.7	5.5	5.5	4.5	4.5	3.7	3.7	3.0	3.0
Depreciated value	200.0	182.0	164.0	149.2	134.5	122.4	110.3	100.3	90.4	82.3	74.1	67.5	60.8	55.3	49.9	45.4	40.9	37.2	33.5	30.5	27.5
Working capital	0.0																				
Salvage	200.0																				
Cash flow from operations																					
Cash from Operations		63.2	63.2	64.2	64.2	66.2	66.2	68.2	68.2	69.2	69.2	69.2	69.2	69.2	69.2	69.2	69.2	69.2	69.2	69.2	69.2
plus salvage	0.0	0.0	0.0	0.0	0.0	0.0	0.0	0.0	0.0	0.0	0.0	0.0	0.0	0.0	0.0	0.0	0.0	0.0	0.0	0.0	0.0
less depreciation	0.0	18.0	18.0	14.8	14.8	12.1	12.1	9.9	9.9	8.1	8.1	6.7	6.7	5.5	5.5	4.5	4.5	3.7	3.7	3.0	3.0
Taxable income	0.0	45.2	45.2	49.4	49.4	54.1	54.1	58.3	58.3	61.1	61.1	62.5	62.5	63.7	63.7	64.7	64.7	65.5	65.5	66.2	66.2
less tax paid				43.1		38.6		42.2		45.5		47.6		48.8		49.7		50.5		51.1	
After tax cash from operations	0.0	65.2	45.2	6.4	49.4	15.5	54.1	16.1	58.3	15.6	61.1	14.9	62.5	15.0	63.7	15.0	64.7	15.0	65.5	15.1	66.2
less working capital	0.0	0.0	0.0	0.0	0.0	0.0	0.0	0.0	0.0	0.0	0.0	0.0	0.0	0.0	0.0	0.0	0.0	0.0	0.0	0.0	0.0
less investment	200.0	0.0	0.0	0.0	0.0	0.0	0.0	0.0	0.0	0.0	0.0	0.0	0.0	0.0	0.0	0.0	0.0	0.0	0.0	0.0	0.0
plus depreciation		18.0	18.0	14.8	14.8	12.1	12.1	9.9	9.9	8.1	8.1	6.7	6.7	5.5	5.5	4.5	4.5	3.7	3.7	3.0	3.0
Net cash flow	–200.0	83.2	63.2	21.1	64.2	27.6	66.2	26.0	68.2	23.7	69.2	21.6	69.2	20.4	69.2	19.5	69.2	18.7	69.2	18.1	69.2
Accumulated Net cash flow	–200.0	–116.8	–53.6	–32.5	31.7	59.4	125.6	151.6	219.8	243.5	312.7	334.3	403.5	423.9	493.1	512.6	581.8	600.5	669.7	687.8	757.0

TABLE 4.3 (cont.)

	Base	Y1		Y2		Y3		Y4		Y5		Y6		Y7		Y8		Y9		Y10	
		Y1H1	Y1H2	Y2H1	Y2H2	Y3H1	Y3H2	Y4H1	Y4H2	Y5H1	Y5H2	Y6H1	Y6H2	Y7H1	Y7H2	Y8H1	Y8H2	Y9H1	Y9H2	Y10H1	Y10H2
Discounted Cash Flow																					
Discount factor %	13.0																				
Net present value	–200.0	–121.9	–66.2	–48.7	1.3	21.4	66.8	83.5	124.7	138.2	175.1	185.9	218.4	227.4	256.0	263.6	288.9	295.3	317.6	323.0	342.7
Benefit–cost ratio	0.0	0.4	0.7	0.8	1.0	1.1	1.3	1.4	1.6	1.7	1.9	1.9	2.1	2.1	2.3	2.3	2.4	2.5	2.6	2.6	2.7
IRR		0.0	0.0	0.0	13.6	22.2	35.3	38.7	44.8	46.2	49.3	50.0	51.6	52.0	52.9	53.1	53.6	53.7	54.0	54.1	54.3
Discount factor period		0	1	2	3	4	5	6	7	8	9	10	11	12	13	14	15	16	17	18	
NPV		757.0	710.3	666.9	626.4	588.7	553.5	520.7	490.0	461.3	434.5	409.3	385.7	363.5	342.7	323.1	304.6	287.2	270.8	255.4	

the calculation, a 70–30 split of this cost variable is derived for respectively the crane and the platform.

- The hire reductions are apportioned so that 80% is due to platform and 20% due to the crane. The new platform can access confined spaces while the new crane can handle extreme lifting requirements.

This yields the separate cost saving figures in Table 4.2 for subsequent analysis. These figures, together with nominal salvage values of $10,000 for each machine, allow the calculation of the return on investment in terms of NPV and IRR:

	Crane	Platform
NPV ($000)	94.8	244.9
IRR (%)	30.3	111.9

It is apparent that the NPV for the platform is consistently above the 'combined' NPV, whilst the NPV for the crane is below that for the combined project. This shows that the return on investment for the new platform *subsidizes* the investment for the new crane.

The payback period for the platform is less than 1 year, whilst the payback for the crane is about 4 years. It is clear that the 'combined' evaluation has obscured the true picture if the machines are appraised separately.

Based on the cost savings for the crane and the platform a sensitivity analysis can be conducted by varying the cost savings factors. A standard variation of ±30% is adopted for the pessimistic and optimistic cases. Table 4.4 shows the NPVs of each investment

TABLE 4.4

Sensitivity analysis for crane and platform

Cost Savings	Crane			Platform		
NPV ($'000)	Pessimistic	Expected	Optimistic	Pessimistic	Expected	Optimistic
Labour savings	39.9	94.8	149.6	244.9	244.9	244.9
Scaffold inventory	94.8	94.8	94.8	234.0	244.9	255.9
Increased production	94.8	94.8	94.8	185.7	244.9	304.1
Maintenance reduction	90.3	94.8	99.3	234.4	244.9	255.5
Hire reduction	93.4	94.8	96.2	239.3	244.9	250.5
IRR (%)						
Labour savings	20.5	30.3	39.7	111.9	111.9	111.9
Scaffold inventory	30.3	30.3	30.3	107.3	111.9	116.6
Increased production	30.3	30.3	30.3	87.3	111.9	137.2
Maintenance reduction	29.6	30.3	30.9	109.2	111.9	114.6
Hire reduction	30.0	30.3	30.5	109.6	111.9	114.3

with the separate variation of each of the cost saving factors. The outcomes highlight the importance of accurate estimates of labour savings and production improvements resulting from the investment. The scaffold inventory, maintenance and hire factors are all relatively robust in their impact. The worst scenario occurs where all cost saving factors are at −30% of their expected estimates, and the best scenario is defined where all cost saving factors are at +30% of their expected estimates.

The return on investment for the crane and the platform for best and worst scenarios is as follows:

	Crane		Platform	
	Best	Worst	Best	Worst
NPV ($000)	155.5	34.0	331.3	158.6
IRR (%)	40.6	19.5	146.9	77.6

Given the absence of any clear logic in the amalgamation of the two projects for evaluation, we might speculate that the manager put together the evaluation of these machines for the following purposes:

• to cover the embarrassingly high return on investment for the platform, which might have led the management to question why the purchase was not proposed much earlier;
• to cover the lower than expected return on investment for the crane, which might not be as appealing when it was evaluated independently (a better picture could be presented when combined with the high investment return of the platform);
• to ensure the purchase of the crane when it was neither economically viable, nor justifiable on health and safety grounds.

The report presented focuses on the financial justification of the replacement machines. The non-financial aspects of the investment are not explored. Issues such as the safety standard and after-sales services of the machines should be considered. Human factors of the investment should be considered, too. The proposed elimination of the dogman with the purchase of the new crane might result in union objections.

RECOMMENDATIONS

1 The immediate purchase of the platform would be a good investment decision, but the purchase of the crane could be delayed for a few years due to its less favourable return. The delay in purchase of the crane would give the management more time to explore alternatives.
2 Sensitivity analysis on the variables that impact on the cash-flow situation of the investment gives management a much better picture. The labour savings factor has the most impact on the

cash-flow situation for the purchase of the crane. Management should look more closely at financial and non-financial implications of variation of this factor. Increased production is the most significant factor in the purchase of the platform. Management should study possible variations in production and its effect on the cash-flow situation.

3 The findings of the post-audit should be well documented and incorporated into the company's knowledge base such that the experiences gained could benefit the whole company. When the findings of this evaluation were reported to the company they immediately outlawed the (then still current) practice of amalgamating unrelated investment projects for the purpose of evaluation.

SUMMARY

Although 'costs' might be perceived to be the major focus of this chapter, hopefully they can now be perceived from both a qualitative as well as quantitative perspective. While we adopted some relatively sophisticated methods of data analysis, our focus was drawn more to the 'beginning' and 'end' of the appraisal process. We were concerned with where the numbers came from: the assumptions and hidden agendas involved, and the creativity in their generation. We were also concerned with the sensitivity of our outcomes to alternative assumptions. But, most importantly, we were concerned with the non-financial factors which are potentially the overriding influence in the decision-making process, and some of the behavioural considerations which make them so.

5 Product and Customer Profitability

INTRODUCTION

In this chapter we reflect upon some of the failures of financial accounting systems and their implications for management decision-making. This leads us to consider alternative measurement systems in the evaluation of both product and customer profitability. The chapter concludes with a wider consideration of 'customer' issues, which embraces some of the most recent empirical research in the area. Again we conclude that traditional financial accounting measures are flawed, potentially resulting in a dysfunctional allocation of resources.

ACCOUNTING SYSTEM IMPLICATIONS

Strategic management accounting provides us with a decision-useful information base, and the foregoing SWOT analysis is essential to a fundamental reappraisal of a company's present and future position. Most of the recent developments in management accounting are best considered under the umbrella of strategic management accounting, as methods and philosophies which help us to improve the information base and develop strategies which are consistent with the overall thrust of management strategies. These tools include:

- *activity-based costing* – the recognition of activities and the identification of *drivers* which cause costs to be incurred;
- *target costing* – an activity aimed at reducing the life-cycle costs of new products;
- *total quality management* – a process of continuous improvement seeking to identify and rectify operational deficiencies;

- *value-added management* – a focus on zero defects in order to eliminate waste and non-value-adding processes from operations;
- *non-financial indicators* – an awareness of the importance of non-monetary outcomes and their integration with traditional financial data sets;
- *the balanced scorecard* – a combination of financial and non-financial measures to give a balanced impression of overall performance;
- *theory of constraints* – a focus on production bottlenecks which targets the single most binding constraint for remedial action.

These are important developments; each of the succeeding chapters will discuss in detail the benefits provided by each of these sub-tools of SMA. First, however, we will consider their direct impact on product and customer profitability.

PRODUCT PROFITABILITY

A number of surveys have repeatedly suggested that manufacturers are unaware of the relative profitability attributable to individual products because they have unreliable information relating to product costs. This lack of reliable information is largely attributable to two factors:

- the incorrect allocation of overhead costs to products; and
- an over-reliance on financial reporting measures for internal management decisions.

The result is an information base which makes cost control difficult and decisions on pricing and product mix unsound.

The dangers of using financial accounting measures for management decision-making have already been addressed, but the problems of managing overhead costs require further discussion. We need to avoid the worst-case scenario in which the application of rigid but foolish rules for the allocation of overhead costs to products result in profitable products being eliminated from the mix and unprofitable products remaining undercosted.

It is a relatively simple process to trace direct material and labour costs to jobs and processes, but manufacturing overheads are not so easily traced because they may bear no obvious relationship to individual units of product. However, some assignment of overheads to products must be made in order to have a complete picture of cost occurrence. The assignment is made via a volume-based activity base (or cost driver), ideally so that products which cause large amounts of overhead costs also require large amounts of the cost driver. Such an ideal ignores any strategic considerations and is based on a 'right' or 'fairest' way of doing things. Thus the allocation of maintenance costs might be made on equipment usage even though a strategic goal of the enterprise might be to encourage innovation and technological leadership. In practice, many different bases are possible, usually based on numbers, areas, volumes, value or hours.

Absorption costing attributes all production overheads to units of output, though most systems do not attempt to allocate administration, selling or distribution overheads. However, many activities are not directly related to production volume. Ordering, delivery, transportation, equipment set-up, machining and administration, for example, require non-volume-based cost drivers if costs are to be appropriately traced. Hence the development of activity-based costing (ABC) systems.

Survey evidence has consistently shown that the majority of manufacturing companies recover overhead costs on the basis of direct labour or machine hours, despite the declining significance of direct labour to many products and services. The continued allocation of costs on such a basis is wholly inadequate for product costing purposes and can only be justified if it meets strategic considerations.

If we are to believe everything we read in the management accounting literature, then ABC is either a revolutionary tool which will solve all of our problems if we are prepared to abandon our traditional and misguided ways; or it is nothing new, being a repackaged version of absorption costing. In practice, it is probably neither – but, by considering the insights provided by ABC alongside other innovations, we have a potentially powerful set of tools.

ABC came to prominence as an alternative tool at a time where there was widespread concern that traditional methods of allocating overhead costs might be providing misleading product cost information. The basic elements of traditional costing systems have been around for a very long time, as Table 2.1 indicates. The fear is that technological advances have rendered some aspects of these systems redundant, particularly the treatment of non-volume-related overhead costs. ABC recognizes that many significant overheads are related to activities which are independent of volume and seeks to identify those cost drivers which consume resources prior to the determination of process and product costs. The fundamentals of ABC are not complex and might be illustrated by the perennial restaurant problem – how to average the bill while still maintaining equity (see Table 5.1).

In this example, courses and covers equal activities and products. The use of averaging procedures demonstrates how some individuals or products are undercosted. It also highlights significant differences in the consumption of resources by different courses or activities. The message is simple; the use of averages smooths out the variations which we must recognize if we are to cost products properly.

TABLE 5.1

The Mediterranean restaurant example

	Starter (£)	Main course (£)	Dessert (£)	Drinks (£)	Total (£)
Alan	10	15	7	4	36
Brian	0	12	8	8	28
Carmen	15	12	0	14	41
Dallas	14	14	14	8	50
Edward	21	17	11	16	65
Total	60	70	40	50	220
Average	12	14	8	10	44

The pioneering work of Kaplan, Johnson and Cooper has generated much activity among management accountants with a common concern about how traditional internal accounting systems support advanced manufacturing strategies. The abandonment of traditional volume-related absorption costing bases for product costing leads to the inclusion of non-production overheads in activity-based analysis.

Following Kaplan, design, engineering, servicing, production, distribution, marketing and after-sales service are all considered relevant activities. Only excess capacity costs and research and development costs are excluded – respectively being treated as period costs and asset capitalization – on the grounds that they would introduce unnecessary distortion.

Many overheads typically classified as fixed costs under a traditional system are, in fact, variable in response to activity-based changes. Purchasing, scheduling and set-up costs are instances of these. The essential characteristic of an ABC system is thus the differentiation between volume-driven costs and non-volume (activity-driven) costs. Direct costs (labour and material) are not normally a problem in this respect, but overhead costs necessitate some assumptions before they can be allocated to individual products. This is especially true where no volume-based relationship can be established. The detailed benefits and limitations provided by ABC systems are considered in more detail in Chapter 6.

No single adaptation of our present accounting systems can hope to solve all of our problems. The improvement of existing systems is essential to allow better performance measurement and improved management reporting. ABC serves a purpose in this context in that, at the very least, it forces us to look at alternatives and to recognize deficiencies in the way in which we currently do things. By applying the wider philosophies implicit in ABC, rather than rigidly applying its techniques, we can reap some real benefits. However, survey evidence (e.g., Chenhall and Langfield-Smith, 1998) consistently shows a low take-up of new management accounting initiatives (including ABC), suggesting that potential users may consider that the costs of implementation (financial and non-financial) exceed the expected benefits.

CUSTOMER PROFITABILITY

The recent innovations in management accounting have emphasized the importance of a customer focus and of remaining competitive through satisfying customer needs. In so doing, they have largely overlooked the complementary requirement that customers satisfy the strategic needs of the supplier. Customer profitability analysis (CPA) is a useful tool for the evaluation of the portfolio of customer profiles.

There is a danger that the dual focus of customer satisfaction and product costing pursued by TQM and ABC may unnecessarily divert attention from strategic considerations. The resultant attention to customer requirements and product profitability may mean that we fail to question the strategic importance of the product, who buys it, and the manner in which customers satisfy the company's goals. In some circumstances customer profitability, rather than product profitability, may be a more appropriate focus.

Companies frequently fail to undertake the detailed analysis of customers and associated service–cost differences. Such an analysis may be justified if:

- the cost of obtaining and maintaining information is not excessive; and
- the information generated is useful in the making of strategic decisions.

Analysis of the revenue streams generated by customers, relative to their service costs, may lead to some customers being eliminated from the business or, at least, a change in the way in which resources are allocated between customers.

Kaplan (1992) discusses three types of potentially unprofitable customer that might be retained:

- new and growing customers, who promise profitable business in the future and who may provide a stepping-stone for penetrating lucrative new markets;
- customers providing qualitative rather than financial benefits – these would include customers at the leading edge in the development of new markets who provide valuable insights into likely trends in consumer demand;
- customers providing increased credibility because of their status as recognized leaders in their markets or fields of expertise.

Despite the potential strategic advantages of a continuing trading relationship with such customers, their lack of current profitability must be balanced against the likely future benefits and the inherent risks of failure, both quantifiable.

What we must avoid is any attempt to apportion total costs over all customer groups. The consequential effects of doing so, should we choose to drop a customer and subsequently respread the costs over the remaining customers, are potentially ludicrous. We might find ourselves in the position of continuing to drop customers and respread costs until no customers remain. We should only attempt to differentiate, say, senior management costs and ordering costs between customers if there are significant discrepancies between customers. This can be illustrated by a simplified example similar to that employed by Robin Cooper in his classic Camelback Communications case study on product profitability (R. Cooper, 1985).

Suppose we have four products (A, B, C and D) utilizing the same equipment and each costed on the basis of materials plus labour plus allocated overheads. Overheads are allocated on the basis of direct labour hours and prices are established through reference to industry standards. The company looks to price with a 40% mark-up, but if costs are too high to allow this it is prepared to tolerate a minimum 25% mark-up. Products which cannot yield a 25% mark-up are eliminated from the product mix.

If the product profile were:

Product	Mark-up (%)
A	15
B	120
C	30
D	70

then product A would be dropped and the overhead reallocated to the three remaining products. The consequences of the reallocation might well be:

Product	Mark-up (%)
B	90
C	20
D	60

Product C would now fail the mark-up yardstick and be dropped from the product mix. Overheads reallocated over the two remaining products would increase product costs so that:

Product	Mark-up (%)
B	70
D	15

Product D is now also dropped and then all the overheads allocated to product B. The product B mark-up then fails to meet the 25% requirement and it is dropped too! The company has now dropped all of its products! The case illustrates the lunacy of charging surplus capacity to products, even where changes in product mix have no bearing on the production economies of the particular product. When combined with a rigid rule to determine the optimum product combination this lunacy is further compounded, resulting in the nonsense of successive product elimination.

While the TQM philosophy promotes competition based on the provision of customer service, we have to be aware that a diverse customer base will consume resources. Current management accounting practice will usually be to classify customer-related costs as period expenses, and even ABC systems will not usually analyse cost drivers in these areas, despite the likelihood of their not being volume-dependent. Sophisticated ABC systems may manage more effectively, depending on their objectives and the nature of the product. Where their objective is to determine product profitability, then the cost drivers selected are likely to be quite different from those selected for a customer-related resource consumption analysis. Distribution costs, in a mass-manufacturing environment for example, might be assigned to customers based on distance travelled, but where product profitability is the ultimate objective we cannot expect there to be a direct linear relationship between profits and distance. Large custom-made orders and the associated delivery costs can be attributed directly to the customer, but, where the orders are mass-produced, activity-based analysis makes it much more difficult to assign costs to customers.

The elimination of non-value-adding, customer-related expenses is best approached by developing a matrix comparing customer types and expense types. Table 5.2 illustrates such a matrix. We wish to identify customer-specific expenses. In order to do so we must be aware of those which are necessarily linked to a particular market or a particular distribution channel, which we may not be able to avoid by eliminating a particular customer.

Customers might be positioned in the wholesale, retail or industrial markets, each with different expectations of the service to be provided by a supplier. Similarly, distribution channel differences may be associated with large discrepancies in sales; the market may demand a direct sales

TABLE 5.2

Customer expense matrix

	Resource dependency		
	Customer specific	Market specific	Distribution channel specific
Purchasing patterns			
Delivery policy			
Accounting procedures			
Inventory holding			

approach employing agents and representatives or, alternatively, telephone sales or mail order by catalogue.

Customer-driven activities and associated expenses can be conveniently examined in some detail under a number of expense categories. The first category, *purchasing patterns*, includes:

- the cost of volume discounts;
- the size of agents' commissions;
- the cost of field service to maintain products distributed by customers – Ward (1992) observes that it might be possible to differentiate between the cost of those sales calls devoted to the maintenance of existing customers and those used to generate new customers;
- the cost of sales support – this might vary from the extremes of one customer requiring no visits at all, to one who requires not only frequent calls but also assistance with administrative operations, in-store displays, the physical merchandising of goods and the regular monitoring of inventory levels.

The associated on-costs of employing sales staff and motor vehicles is an important consideration here. They would embrace all vehicle operating costs, as well as superannuation, fringe benefits and payroll tax, holiday and long-service leave entitlements, workers' compensation and insurance. In practice, several of these items may conveniently be omitted from a customer profitability analysis because of the complex analysis required to divide general ledger amounts between the activities of different salespersons. The second category, *delivery policy*, includes:

- distribution expenses;
- shipping frequencies; and
- freight fleet requirements.

Profitable customers would be located close by and employ standard packaging and barcode readings, while less profitable customers would require unique, capacity-consuming packaging and delivery. *Accounting procedures* include:

- sales credits;
- settlement discount costs;

- debtor collection support; and
- order processing – this might vary between one customer who maintains large, regular bulk orders and one who requires immediate crisis deliveries resulting from stock-outs, but whose order details are so complex and ambiguous that multiple queries result before the transaction can be completed. Finally, *Inventory holding* includes:

- inventory support;
- distribution support; and
- holding requirements, which may vary enormously depending on the product range and the extent to which just-in-time (JIT) scheduling procedures have been adopted.

While product profitability analysis emphasizes the identification of undercosted products, resulting from low volumes, high wastage and high levels of rework, customer profitability analysis aims to identify low-volume and low-margin customers the servicing of whose orders requires a disproportionate amount of time and expense. Recognizing the 80–20 rule is not enough; we need to quantify the extent to which 80% of costs are attributable to 20% of customers, identify the customers and eliminate or modify the service provided to the unprofitable ones. We must recognize that no two customers are the same, even when they are in receipt of an identical product. Profitability between customers varies greatly because of the service commitment, but conventional accounting methods rarely reveal such differences.

The incremental costs of customer service and price elasticities of demand must be examined in order to establish a customer loyalty profile. What will customers bear? How sensitive are they to prices or to the levels of service provided? How will our internal costs change in response to variations in the level of service provided? A fundamental analysis of customers, performed properly, will answer these questions and provide the information base to support strategic decisions relating to the customer base.

Activity drivers will assist in the assignment of activity costs to customers where arbitrary allocation methods would otherwise be employed. Thus, distribution costs might be assigned on a zone basis dependent on the delivery destination activity, rather than being spread across all customers in an arbitrary fashion.

Hart and Smith (1998), exploring customer profitability in the banking sector, note that traditional methods of costing banking products have failed to allocate individual resources to either products or accounts in a satisfactory manner; they suggest that the inherent variation in 'number of accounts' or 'number of transactions', when these are used as cost drivers, makes the calculation basis insufficiently accurate for customer profitability measurement.

The need for a strategic approach is paramount. We must not be tempted to pigeon-hole TQM, ABC or CPA and examine each in a blinkered fashion. They must be employed simultaneously so that all aspects of customer focus can be considered, with projected costs and revenues appropriately quantified.

The following case study highlights the differences in profitability possible when different customers are in receipt of essentially the same product. It provides the opportunity for developing a customer portfolio, along BCG matrix lines, as part of a customer profitability analysis.

CASE STUDY

Derrick's Ice-Cream: A customer profitability analysis

Derrick's Ice-Cream is located in modern premises and manufactures and distributes 30 different ice-cream product lines from its suburban base. The products are distributed by Derrick's own fleet of refrigerated trucks to six major wholesale distributors.

Annual sales are currently around the £10 million level, distributed among the wholesalers as indicated in Table 5.3. Derrick's controls about 35% of its metropolitan market, but this shrinks to less than 10% in outlying areas where there are many small competitors.

Derrick's will usually hold up to four weeks of stock in its central cold stores to meet the distribution requirements of its six major customers. The cold stores cost approximately £500,000 p.a. to run, but excess capacity can be hired out to other non-competing firms. This becomes especially important during the winter months when consumer demand is considerably reduced. Even during the summer months demand is highly sensitive to temperature; Derrick's, therefore, bases its sales on a deseasonalized forecast, related to increases in disposable real incomes, and hopes that stocks will be adequate to cope with sequences of extreme high temperatures.

The raw materials – vegetable oil, butter, milk and sugar – are relatively inexpensive. They arrive at Derrick's by tanker and are stored on site. Ice-cream is then manufactured in two major processes, mixing and forming, followed by packaging to meet the specific customer requirements.

The requirements of meeting the, sometimes uniquely specific, requirements of customers have been causing Derrick's management some serious headaches recently. They recognize the importance of a client-focused approach to marketing and distribution, but are beginning to feel that they are being exploited by some customers who are never satisfied with the level of service provided, however extensive it may be. The satisfaction of customer whims is beginning to cost big money, so Derrick's has determined to conduct a

TABLE 5.3

Market shares for six customers

Customer	% Sales
Ardron's Wafers	19
Butler Ices	12
Cahill's Cones	25
Donleavy Ices	9
England Wedges	14
Frankston Chocs	20
Others	1
	100

detailed analysis of the customers and their varying requirements. These have been abbreviated below:

- *Ardron's Wafers* employs standard packaging and bar-code reading systems. It insists on only low discounts for volume and maintains large regular orders. Consequently its delivery requests and inventory holding requirements are highly predictable.

- *Butler Ices* is located nearly 150 miles north of Derrick's base and requires packaging which is unique to itself. Despite its distant location, it insists on free deliveries and requires large discounts for volume orders. Its internal inventory control procedures are not well developed, resulting in not uncommon requests for 'crisis' deliveries to deal with stock-outs.

- *Cahill's Cones* has the reputation of always paying on time and requiring low discounts and commissions. Its inventory holding procedures are perhaps the best in the business and it has a JIT scheduling system which is entirely compatible with Derrick's own. Deliveries require no special packaging or fleet requirements for the refrigerated vehicles.

- *Donleavy Ices* always pays late but demands all available discounts, even when strictly they are not applicable. It insists on daily deliveries, with the requirement of additional deliveries should demand merit it. It has threatened to take its business elsewhere if all its inventory holding requirements are not met in full.

- *England Wedges* relies on bulk orders which are shipped on an infrequent basis. It requires minimal volume discounts, rare visits from Derrick's personnel, and is prepared to collate sales credits and make monthly claims.

- *Frankston Chocs* is not noted for the strength of its internal organization. It is closely located to Derrick's base, but requires frequent calls which extend to assistance with administrative operations and help with the merchandising of stock and in-store displays. It initiates separate sales credits for each item of product returned and inevitably generates complex orders whose detail is unclear, so that multiple queries follow almost every transaction.

We are required to use the above information as the basis for a customer profitability analysis using the suggested framework, or a suitable alternative, in terms of purchasing patterns, delivery policy, accounting procedures and inventory holding. The analysis will then allow us to develop alternative strategies for the manner in which Derrick's might act on the outcomes.

CASE ANALYSIS

There has been surprisingly little written in the accounting literature about customer profitability analysis. In the main this has comprised exhortations in the professional journals for practitioners to pay attention to factors other than product profitability (e.g., Anandarajan and Christopher, 1987; Shapiro et al., 1987; Bellis-Jones, 1989; Smith, 1993; Connolly and Ashworth, 1994; Foster

CASE STUDY (cont.)

et al., 1996). There have been case-based approaches (notably the celebrated Kanthal case in Cooper and Kaplan, 1991), but surprisingly few empirical studies. Frameworks are established for analysis in Howell and Soucy (1990), Foster et al. (1996) and Smith and Dikolli (1995), but reports of field studies are rare (e.g., Hart and Smith, 1998; Shanahan, 2002). Thus, over a fifteen-year period, we have fewer than one major paper per year devoted to CPA, suggesting that researchers perceive product profitability to be a difficult enough issue, and that the problems associated with CPA appear insuperable. A challenge indeed for future researchers!

Analysis of the profiles of the six firms which provide Derrick's customer base allows the classification of their requirements in terms of purchasing patterns, delivery policy, accounting procedures and inventory holding. This analysis, following Smith and Dikolli (1995), is detailed in Table 5.4. The Howell and Soucy (1990) framework is similar, but more detailed, and suggests the measurement of a number of expense categories not detailed in the case: cost of volume discounts; size of agents' commissions; cost of product maintenance; cost of sales support; distribution expenses; shipping frequencies; freight fleet requirements; sales credits; settlement discount costs; debtor collection support; order processing; inventory support; distribution support; and holding requirements.

The narrative descriptions provide a qualitative 'feel' for the relative costs of each of the customers. This 'feel' can be quantified by allocating a numerical indicator to each of the attributes; although this approach can only be approximate, and is limited by the availability of the case information, it does facilitate the ranking of the customers in terms of the costs of providing service. If we allocate a score of +5 where a customer has the best possible attributes, of 0 where the customer is neutral, or no information is available, and of –5 where the customer has the worst possible attributes, then by rating each customer on each attribute between these limits we can generate a composite cost index. A typical response is detailed in Table 5.5.

The fact that we have no information available in some categories is problematical, as is the judgement required in assigning a particular numerical score. We are in a decision-making under uncertainty scenario here which requires a trade-off between reliability and relevance: we know that our scores cannot be 'right' in an absolute sense, but if the approximations still allow us to make useful inferences then they will have been worthwhile.

Following Kotler (1994: 70) the relative profitability of each customer is measured in terms of its contribution to Derrick by way of sales. This is calculated as

$$\frac{\% \text{ Market share}}{\% \text{ Share of market leader}}$$

and is fractional for all customers, except the market leader, calculated as

$$\frac{\% \text{ Market share}}{\% \text{ Share of closest competitor}}.$$

TABLE 5.4

Derrick's Ice-Cream customer requirements

	Ardron's Wafers	Butler Ices	Cahill's Cones	Donleavy Ices	England Wedges	Frankston Chocs
Purchasing patterns	• require low discounts on volume orders	• require large discounts for volume orders	• require low discounts and commissions	• demand available discount, even if not applicable	• require rare visits from personnel	• require frequent calls extending to assistance: with admin., help in store
Delivery policy	• delivery requests predictable • standard packaging • maintain large regular order	• 150 miles away • unique packaging • insist on free delivery • 'crisis' deliveries	• no special fleet requirements for refrigerated vehicles • JIT scheduling • no special packaging	• insist on daily deliveries, additional deliveries if demanded	• infrequent shipping • minimal volume discounts	• close location to base • require frequent assistance
Accounting procedures	• no information available	• poorly developed internal control procedures	• reputation for paying on time • 'best in the business' accounting procedures	• demand all settlement discounts, even if not applicable • always pay late	• collate sales credits and make monthly claims	• initiates separate sales credits for each item returned • multiple queries before each transaction can be completed • require frequent assistance
Inventory holding	• predictable delivery requests	• 'crisis' deliveries • insist on free delivery to remote location	• compatible scheduling systems	• will take business elsewhere if requirements are unmet	• infrequent shipping of bulk orders	• weak internal organization

CASE STUDY (cont.)

The results are detailed in Table 5.6 after converting to the log format recommended by Kotler (1994).

These tables provide the data which form the basis of a BCG matrix, with relative market share on the horizontal and cost basis on the vertical, the former using a log natural transformation. The conventional axes of the BCG matrix are relative market share (as a proxy for cash inflow) and market growth (as a proxy for cash outflow); here cost is substituted for the market growth variable. The two axes are represented together in Figure 5.1, with grid lines positioned at $Y = 0$ (a neutral cost position) and $X = 1$ (i.e. $\ln X = 0$) to identify market leaders.

The use of market share relativities, relative to the performance of the industry leader, and a log scale on the horizontal causes some problems in practice. Only the industry leader will have a 'relative

TABLE 5.5

Customer requirements index

	Customer					
Criteria	Ardron's	Butler	Cahill's	Donleavy	England	Frankson
Purchasing patterns:						
• Discount required	4	−3	5	−5	4	0
• Quality of organization	5	−2	5	−1	5	−5
Delivery policy:						
• Delivery distance, etc.	0	−5	0	0	0	5
• Unique packaging required	5	−5	5	0	0	0
• Urgent order frequency	5	−3	4	−4	5	−3
Accounting procedures:						
• Payment record	0	0	5	−5	0	0
• Credit returns handling	0	0	0	0	5	−5
Inventory holding:						
• Volume of sales	4	2	5	1	3	4
• Order frequency	5	3	3	−5	5	−3
Total	+28	−13	+32	−19	+27	−7

TABLE 5.6

Log transformations of relative market share

Customer	Market share	Relative market share (M)	$\ln(M)$
Ardron's Wafers	19	0.76	−0.27
Butler Ices	12	0.48	−0.73
Cahill's Cones	25	1.25	0.22
Donleavy Ices	9	0.36	−1.02
England Wedges	14	0.56	−0.58
Frankston Chocs	20	0.80	−0.22

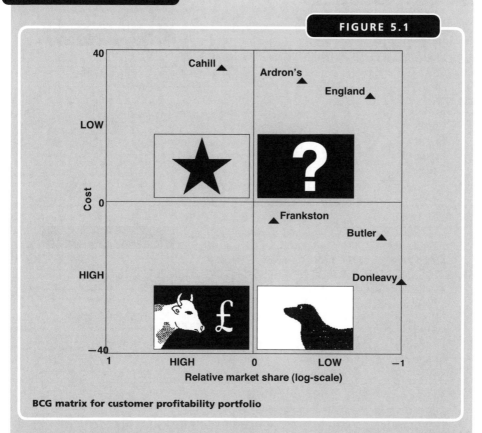

FIGURE 5.1

BCG matrix for customer profitability portfolio

market share (M)' greater than one, so all other competitors will have negative log scores on the horizontal axis. Consequently, only one company can appear to the left of the central vertical, meaning that we can have a 'star' company or a 'cash cow' company, depending on cost levels, but not both! Alternatives to this standard Kotler (1994) approach might, therefore, be explored in practice.

The approximations in the data-gathering make it difficult to argue a unique correspondence of company to BCG category, even though the relative positioning of the companies is in less doubt. However, it is possible to demonstrate the robustness of outcomes by questioning some of the assumptions and evaluating their sensitivity:

- 'Volume of sales' is represented above within a simple 1 to 5 ranking. We might argue that consistency demands a ranking over the full range of –5 to +5, which would produce different absolute scores. Thus if the complete eleven-point ranking were applied to sales over the range 0–25% we would produce the version A scores of Table 5.7; if the ranking were applied to the sales of the six major companies (i.e., 9–25%) we would produce the version B scores.

- The 'order frequency' category of 'inventory holding' also suggests alternatives. While the extremes ('infrequent shipping' for England, and 'daily deliveries' for Donleavy) are straightforward,

CASE STUDY (cont.)

TABLE 5.7

Alternative scores for 'volume of sales' category

	Version A	Version B
Ardron	2.6	1.25
Butler	–0.2	–3.125
Cahill	5	5
Donleavy	–1.4	–5
England	0.6	–1.875
Frankston	3	1.875

TABLE 5.8

Alternative scores for 'order frequency' category

	Version C	Version D
Ardron	5	4
Butler	–5	–3
Cahill	5	0
Donleavy	–5	–5
England	5	5
Frankston	–5	–5

it is not absolutely clear what the implications for delivery frequencies would be for 'predictable requests' (Ardron), 'crisis deliveries' (Butler) or 'JIT scheduling' (Cahill) – the latter could potentially be demanding despite its apparent compatibility with Derrick's systems. The alternatives of Table 5.8 are thus generated.

Combining the A–D alternatives of Tables 5.7 and 5.8 with the more certain elements of the Table 5.4 matrix of customer requirements generates four more sets of scores, presented in Table 5.9.

Table 5.10 compares the final scores for the original matrix and the four alternatives and highlights their close similarities. The split between positive scores (ACE) and negative scores (BDF) is common to all the alternatives. CAE is the consistent order for the 'best' performers, except where pessimistic assumptions are made regarding the impact of Cahill's JIT scheduling. FDB is the consistent order for the 'poor' performers except where optimistic assumptions are made regarding Butler's order frequency. Other interpretations are possible, but they are unlikely to produce a radical reordering of company performance.

In the light of the similarity of these alternative profiles, the more important issue becomes the recommendations we might make to improve Derrick's position.

The BCG matrix highlights the position of Butler Ices and Donleavy's Ices as 'dogs', who are very expensive to service but

Alternative customer requirements indices

TABLE 5.9

	Alternative 1						Alternative 2						Alternative 3						Alternative 4					
	A	B	C	D	E	F	A	B	C	D	E	F	A	B	C	D	E	F	A	B	C	D	E	F
Purchasing :	4	-4	4	-5	0	0	4	-4	4	-5	0	0	4	-4	4	-5	0	0	4	-4	4	-5	0	0
Discount	4	-4	4	-5	0	0	4	-4	4	-5	0	0	4	-4	4	-5	0	0	4	-4	4	-5	0	0
Organization quality	4	-5	5	-4	5	-5	4	-5	5	-4	5	-5	4	-5	5	-4	5	-5	4	-5	5	-4	5	-5
Delivery :																								
Distance	5	-5	0	0	0	0	5	-5	0	0	0	0	5	-5	0	0	0	0	5	-5	0	0	0	0
Packaging	5	-5	5	0	0	0	5	-5	5	0	0	0	5	-5	5	0	0	0	5	-5	5	0	0	0
Urgency	5	-5	5	-4	5	-5	5	-5	5	-4	5	-5	5	-5	5	-4	5	-5	5	-5	5	-4	5	-5
Accounting:																								
Records	0	0	5	-5	0	0	0	0	5	-5	0	0	0	0	5	-5	0	0	0	0	5	-5	0	0
Credit returns	0	0	0	0	5	-5	0	0	0	0	5	-5	0	0	0	0	5	-5	0	0	0	0	5	-5
Inventory :																								
Sales volume	2.6	-0.2	5	-1.4	0.6	3	1.25	-3.125	5	-5	-1.875	1.875	2.6	-0.2	55	-1.4	0.6	3	1.25	-3.125	5	-5	-1.875	1.875
Order frequency	5	-5	5	-5	5	-5	4	-3	0	-5	5	-5	4	0	0	-5	5	-5	4	-4	5	-5	5	-5
Total	30.6	-29.2	34	-24.4	20.6	-17	28.25	-30.12	29	-28	18.125	-18.125	29.6	-27.2	29	-24.4	20.6	-17	29.25	-32.125	34	-28	18.125	-18.125

TABLE 5.10

Comparative consumer requirements index scores

	Ardron's	Butler	Cahill's	Donleavy	England	Frankston	ORDER
Original	28	-13	32	-19	27	-7	(CAEFBD)
Alternative 1	30.6	-29.2	34	-24.4	20.6	-17	(CAEFDB)
Alternative 2	28.25	-30.125	29	-28	18.125	-18.125	(CAEFDB)
Alternative 3	29.6	-27.2	29	-24.4	20.6	-17	(ACEFDB)
Alternative 4	29.25	-32.125	34	-28	18.125	-18.125	(CAEFDB)

CASE STUDY (cont.)

who, nevertheless, are together responsible for over £2 million of annual sales. Change strategies must be introduced, but with a good deal of management sensitivity, especially in the short term. A sympathetic approach, and one which recognizes the mutual benefits of changes in internal systems, should be pursued. Priority actions revolve around making both of these customers less expensive while, if possible, maintaining their business. In the case of Butler Ices, strategies might include:

- imposing charges for its unique packaging requirements;
- restricting free deliveries to fewer visits – those on the regular runs;
- imposing punitive charges for crisis deliveries; and
- offering assistance to reorganize inventory control procedures – this offer might make the first three strategies more palatable to Butler.

For Donleavy's Ices, strategies could similarly include:

- strict adherence to the discount availability mechanism to discourage consistent late payment;
- restricting the availability of free deliveries;
- imposing punitive charges for crisis deliveries;
- tighter specification of mutual responsibilities, with the clear acknowledgement that Derrick's is prepared to sacrifice Donleavy's business in the absence of improved co-operation and better management controls.

Frankston Chocs is a more marginal 'dog' and offers significant improvement opportunities. It is too big a customer for Derrick's to risk its loss (annual sales of £2 million), but its accounting and merchandising procedures are expensive and need attention. Derrick's might explore closer links with Frankston in order to exploit its future potential. At the very least it might offer assistance to reorganize inventory control procedures, and ordering and credit procedures, with the ultimate aim of converting it to '?' status.

Cahill's Cones is the star performer in Derrick's customer portfolio. As well as being the largest, it makes the fewest demands on Derrick's organization. It is well organized and progressive, as reflected by its adoption of the latest management accounting techniques. It might also provide a suitable joint-venture partner in the development of new outlets in areas where Derrick's currently exerts minimal influence.

Ardron's Wafers and *England Wedges* similarly make few demands on Derrick's, being reliable and regular in their requirements. Although individually less important than Cahill, and accorded '?' status, together they account for one-third of Derrick's sales.

The BCG matrix gives a simple (sometimes simplistic) overview of the current relativities in Derrick's portfolio and limitations arise in its implementation when trying to devise strict dividing lines. As we have noted, the textbook analysis dictates that there will only be one market leader, that is, only one company assigned to the left-hand quadrants, and therefore only one company which is termed a 'star' or a 'cash cow' – with the requirements score determining its precise position. However, it forces us to take an overview of all customers and highlights individual contributions.

The case seeks to highlight that conventional accounting methods will fail to reveal differences in costs attributable to different customers: customer-related costs will usually be treated as period expenses, and even traditional ABC methods may have difficulty in analysing cost drivers in these areas, despite the likelihood of their being non-volume-related, because of measurement issues. Whereas product profitability emphasizes the impact of undercosted products resulting from low volumes, high wastage rates and high levels of rework, customer profitability seeks to pinpoint low-volume/low-margin customers who consume more than proportionate expense in servicing orders. The aim is to identify problem customers and eliminate or modify the service provided to unprofitable ones.

CUSTOMER RELATIONSHIP MANAGEMENT

The gap between theory and practice, and the empirical evidence, much of it conflicting, make customer relationships an important focus. Despite what financial accounting may tell us, customer value is important, and the customer should be viewed as an asset to the firm (e.g., Berger et al., 2002). Empirical studies have shown market-based assets (e.g., customer asset value, customer relationships and channel relationships) to be positively associated with the financial performance (notably shareholder value) of participant firms (e.g., Sheth and Sharma, 2001; Srivastava et al., 1998; Ward and Ryals, 2001; Hogan et al., 2002). Because customers play such an important role in the value of a firm, increasing the value of customers is consistent with a goal of maximizing shareholder wealth, but to do so we must be able to measure the value of customers in a reliable manner. CPA can be employed, but where contractual relationships with customers exist (e.g., in financial services or banking operations) customer lifetime value analysis is more likely to be used than CPA (e.g., Jain and Singh, 2002; Gurau and Ranchhod, 2002).

Customer relationship management (CRM) aims to align customer strategy and business processes in order to improve customer loyalty and, hopefully, profitability (Rigby et al., 2002). CRM impacts on both customer satisfaction and shareholder value by providing customers with consistent, high-quality experiences (Kale, 2003). It seeks to identify a company's most valuable customers and to increase customer loyalty by tailoring products and services to meet customer requirements. In doing so it tries to control the costs of servicing such customers to improve both retention and acquisition prospects. The focus of CRM is on data and measurement, and concerns the organization's ability to leverage customer data innovatively and efficiently to establish an effective relationship between customers and firms.

However, Rigby et al. (2002) also report on the failure of CRM profits, with the anticipated benefits not achieved: one in five executives had abandoned CRM altogether, saying that it drove away valuable customers. Some reasons (McKim, 2002; Kale, 2003) causing firms to abandon implementation include:

- lack of preparedness;
- failure to accurately specify business problems;
- lack of a common definition of CRM;
- absence of appropriate measurement; and
- breakdown of communication in customer relationships.

While most of these points are common to implementation failures and the abandonment of business initiatives in general (see Rogers, 1995), the measurement issue is one that arises less rarely elsewhere.

Customer satisfaction

Satisfaction is defined in terms of customer evaluation of a product or service as to whether that product or service has met customer needs and expectations (e.g., Bitner et al., 1997). Jones and Sasser (1995) highlight four main elements that affect customer satisfaction:

- the basic elements of the product or service that customers expect all providers to deliver;
- the existence of basic support services, such as customer assistance and order tracking;
- a process for dealing with complaints and providing satisfactory solutions to 'bad' customer experiences;
- memorable service that exceeds the customer's expectations.

Levels of satisfaction will vary according to the specific circumstances of the transaction, with customers liable to be influenced in their evaluation by relatively small events surrounding the delivery of the product or service. The measurement of satisfaction will also be influenced by variations in the scales used to collect the data, as well as the data collection methods (Wilson, 2002).

Customer loyalty

Customer loyalty is usually the focus of the development of retention strategies. Many firms believe benefits can be generated from long-life customers, such as lower service costs, an ability to charge high prices and the power of 'word of mouth' of loyal customers (Reichheld and Sasser, 1990). However, Reinartz and Kumar (2000) provide empirical evidence that casts doubt on all these assertions. They show that:

- long-life customers are not necessarily profitable in a non-contractual setting;
- the lower service cost rule is industry-specific;
- the relationship between loyalty and higher prices is not strong;
- the power of 'word of mouth' is difficult to measure without reference to both attitudinal and behavioural factors.

Customer equity

Customer equity is defined by Dorsch and Carlson (1996) as the value of the complete set of resources, tangible (e.g., money) and intangible (e.g., knowledge and commitment), that customers invest in a firm. Since Blattberg and Deighton (1996) coined the term 'customer equity', many authors have advocated growing customer equity as a means of growing shareholder value (Hogan et al., 2002; Fornell, 2000). Dorsch et al. (2001) refer to customer equity management (CEM) as the management of that portfolio of resources that customers invest in their firms, and provide for the calculation of customer equity in terms of the NPV of cash flow generated from present and potential customers. This information should help managers to determine the optimal balance between acquisition and retention strategies (see Blattberg and Deighton, 1996; Blattberg et al., 2001).

In studies of large US and UK companies, respectively, Fornell (2000) and Doyle (2000) suggest that the market value of these companies is predominantly made up of intangible assets, and that customer relationships are a major feature of these intangible assets. Hogan et al. (2002) suggest that customer equity is a means of growing shareholder value, but that conventional accounting has treated marketing expenditures as costs rather than an investment in intangible assets. He emphasizes the importance of increasing the lifetime value of individual customers in a way that maximizes customer equity. Srivastava et al. (1998) emphasize that the most appropriate customer-related strategies will lead to increased customer satisfaction and loyalty and then produce a positive impact on customer equity. As long as customer equity increases, then shareholder value should increase too.

Effective CEM requires a business to identify a target customer equity profile, and to compare it with the actual customer equity profile. Any incompatibility between observed and expected profile highlights a gap in the firm's CRM practices which may occasion investment inefficiencies for the firm. Firms will wish to allocate limited resources to the most appropriate customers and to implement the management practices necessary to generate an optimum customer equity profile. Bayon et al. (2002) highlight the increasing use of CEM practices as a management tool, to influence lifetime values of current and future customers, and eventually customer equity.

The influence of customer satisfaction and customer loyalty on the profitability of the firm continues to receive a good deal of attention in the literature, though few of these examples are currently drawn from the accounting literature. Increasingly customers are being treated as assets, which can be managed and measured, despite the associated financial accounting difficulties (Blattberg et al., 2001; Berger et al., 2002). Srivastava et al. (1998) suggest that the increasing focus on the enhancement of shareholder returns has led firms to recognize that the relationship between marketing and finance must be managed systematically. Therefore, firms are taking a more customer-focused approach to their strategy formulation, instead of the traditional product-focused approach (Jain and Singh, 2002). In particular, the three customer-related measures identified above (customer satisfaction, customer loyalty and customer equity) are each deserving of more attention in the literature, and might even be addressed simultaneously to determine their impact on financial performance.

A four-pronged strategy: customer satisfaction, customer loyalty, customer profitability and customer equity

According to the concept of the service–profit chain, once customer satisfaction increases, customer loyalty must increase accordingly and then profitability increases (Heskett et al., 1994). But the empirical evidence is less convincing; the relationships between satisfaction and loyalty (Jones and Sasser, 1995), satisfaction and profitability (Scharitzer and Kollarits, 2000; Anderson et al., 1994; Ittner and Larcker, 1998a; Soderlund and Vilgon, 1999), and loyalty and profitability (Reinartz and Kumar, 2002) have been the subject of empirical investigation, but have produced conflicting outcomes.

Anderson and Sullivan (1993) and Fornell (1992) suggest that there could be a positive or negative relationship between customer satisfaction and customer loyalty. A number of alternative explanations are possible: for example, industry conditions, the regulatory environment, provider switching costs, prevailing technology and loyalty programmes might all have an impact. Some of the empirical evidence even suggests that there is no significant relationship between customer satisfaction and profitability at all (Ittner and Larcker, 1998a; Soderlund and Vilgon, 1999; Scharitzer and Kollarits, 2000; Hellier et al., 2003). As a consequence it is conceivable that some firms will be investing their limited resources in totally inappropriate (potentially unprofitable) customers. Further empirical evidence casts doubt on the commonly held belief that loyalty programmes improve profitability; Reinartz and Kumar (2002) found that in some cases a negative relationship between loyalty and profitability existed, which they explained through the existence of customers groups termed as 'barnacles' (i.e., high loyalty but low profitability) and 'butterflies' (i.e., low loyalty but potentially high profitability). These counter-intuitive empirical findings in the literature are a cause for concern and provide further motivation for a study focusing on the measurement and modelling of customer-related variables.

CRM measurement issues

Shareholder value, as the NPV of future projected cash flows, is not new to the literature (e.g., Rappaport, 1986) but has gained prominence due to the economic value-added debate. Since the inclusion of cash flow as a major variable in marketing studies the influence of marketing activities and customer relationships on shareholder value has increased (Srivastava et al., 1998, 1999). A short-term focus on accounting profits will lead to under-investment in intangible assets, such as staff, brands, and customer and supplier relationships, making a shareholder value approach increasingly important for the firm in evaluating financial performance. Additionally, since market-based assets do not normally appear on the balance sheet (on the grounds that financial accountants do not believe that their value can be measured accurately enough), they will be treated as costs rather than investment, and not be depreciated, which may lead to insufficient spending on developing brands, retaining customers and creating channel partnerships (Doyle, 2000).

Since shareholder value analysis is not based on accounting conventions, but is derived on a cash basis, it becomes a more reliable measure of financial performance when evaluating the impact of marketing assets and customer-related strategies. Alternative indicators have been developed to evaluate shareholder value, of which undoubtedly the most popular is economic value added (Stern et al., 1996), a measure which emphasizes the residual wealth creation in a company after all costs and expenses have been charged, including the firm's cost of capital. However, empirical evidence casts doubt on the strength of the relationship between economic value added and shareholder value (e.g., Farslo et al., 2000; Abdeen and Haight, 2002; Sparling and Turvey, 2003).

Market-based assets, such as customers and distribution channels, are assets that must be cultivated over time to deliver shareholder value (e.g., Hunt and Morgan, 1995; Srivastava et al., 1998). Lusch and Harvey (1994) indicated that organizational performance is increasingly being tied to intangible assets such as corporate culture, customer relationships and brand equity, but such off-balance sheet items are difficult to measure and value. As a potential solution Srivastava et al. (1998) suggested a framework which links the contribution of market-based assets to market performance and hence financial performance. They suggest that shareholder value can be evaluated by:

- an acceleration of cash flows – since market-based assets accelerate cash flows by reducing the market penetration cycle time;
- an increase in the level of cash flows – since well-developed customer relationships will enhance cash flows by reducing working capital requirements;
- reduction in the risk associated with cash flows – since the volatility of cash flows will be reduced if the firm can retain a stable customer base, without incurring the costs of acquiring new customers, and
- the residual value of the business – since long-term customer loyalty might eventually result in a lower cost of capital and enhance the future values.

SUMMARY

This chapter has discussed some of the implications for accounting systems consequent upon technological and administrative changes within the organization. It notes that the pace of change in this regard is slow – a stark contrast from what we perceived with regard to performance measurement. Clearly the benefits from management accounting change do not match the costs, since the difficulties apparent with existing (financial accounting oriented) systems persist. The same cannot be said for performance measurement initiatives, since any improvement opportunities proffered in this regard appear to be grasped more readily. A 'product' and 'customer' focus is maintained in the chapter in readiness for the more detailed discussion of 'process' and 'people' aspects in the two succeeding chapters.

6   Know Your Processes

INTRODUCTION

A much simplified cybernetic process of the type in Figure 6.1 provides a suitable basis for the analysis and measurement of a series of activities. We should have a model in place which can predict the volume and quality of outputs, depending on the volume and quality of inputs. The degree of predictive success will depend upon the complexity of the process and the number and type of variables which may impact on the outcomes of the process. If the model does not work well we should aim to develop a new one which better reflects the involvement of key variables.

If activity-based systems do nothing more, they will at least force us to look at our cost structures again, to reappraise the systems in place and improve measurement patterns. Knowledge of process and cost behaviour is an essential feature of decision support. The database necessary to support activity-based systems requires a keener awareness of interrelationships between activities than is currently apparent in many organizations. Accordingly, these issues provide the focus for this chapter.

COST BEHAVIOUR: RANDOM VARIATION AND INTERDEPENDENT EVENTS

Fundamental to the development of predictive process models are three features:

- *Identification of the critical indicators*. We may not be completely aware of these if the process is complex and not clearly documented. It is likely

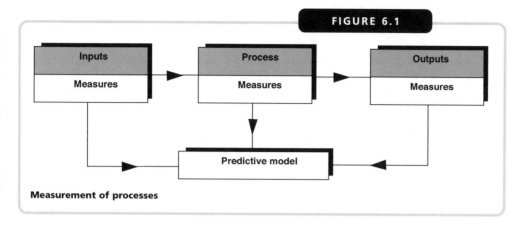

FIGURE 6.1

Measurement of processes

that we do not record data for many potentially useful variables; and, depending on the costs involved, we may be forced to collect data on new variables in case they feature strongly in the revised model of process.

- *Awareness of the mathematical relationship between variables*. This is achieved through a detailed analysis of cost behaviour. Gone are the days when management accountants can 'average' at whim and make straight-line assumptions when none are applicable. Statistical software facilitates the exploration of relationships and the development of knowledge relating to cost structures.
- *Weighting of the key factors*. We need to recognize the appropriate weighting to be given to the key factors in a parsimonious data set suitable for modelling and forecasting.

We can only reduce the variation in systems by understanding their cause and effect. By studying variation, rather than demanding unnecessary managerial explanations, we can implement changes appropriate to customer expectations. Variation is frequently attributable to random fluctuations, with its magnitude amplified by the effect of interdependence among functions. Such variation does not stop the process from being in control; by taking appropriate action in trying to compensate for the variation we will simply make things worse and fail to meet customer targets.

For example, familiar but inappropriate management practice would include:

- demanding explanations from managers for adverse variances and taking action to correct those variances when they merely comprise random fluctuations within a normal curve;
- adjusting budgets based on one month's results – usually the last one – although those results may neither be representative nor reflect performance trends;
- increasing sales targets in response to a shortfall in the previous week rather than projecting fluctuations in the series over time;
- overreacting to a single customer complaint, without appropriate analysis of its cause or justification;

- revising detailed plans and schedules based on the outcome of a single job – the previous one – which is assumed to be representative of all such outcomes; and
- changing key process variables (such as time, temperature or pressure) based on the quality of the output from the most recent production batch, when the outcome may be attributable to batch-specific input causes.

Such inappropriate actions result from common misconceptions regarding the nature of variation. All of these outcomes conform to systematic statistical distributions, with means and standard deviations. Variation within such distributions is inevitable and, in itself, should not be questioned. What we need to establish are answers to two questions:

1 Is the system in control? In other words, is the observed variation consistent with statistical expectations?
2 Is the system capable of satisfying customer requirements? That is, are the observed variations within specified, acceptable limits?

These two questions require different solutions; action taken on stable systems (in control), in an effort to compensate for variation, will only increase the variation and, inevitably, increase costs.

Figure 6.2 illustrates the nature of distributions and the extent to which they are both in control and capable. 'In control' basically means that a process is operating normally between statistical control boundaries, but not necessarily as the customer wants it. A process deemed to be 'in control' can still fail to meet customer specifications. The three cases shown in Figure 6.2 follow precise statistical distributions, but only case A fits tightly within the specified limits. Case B displays unacceptably large amounts of variation attributable to random fluctuations. Case C is wrongly targeted so that the specification limits are unrealistic and customer requirements go unsatisfied.

'Capable' refers to a process that is achieving the customers' requirements, operating between statistically defined limits. In Figure 6.2, only case A describes a system which is both 'in control' and 'capable'.

Variation in any system may be due to:

- common causes, inherent in stable and predictable systems, producing random fluctuations within specified limits; or

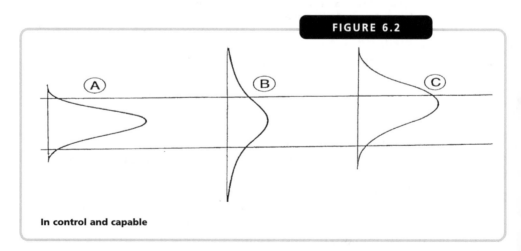

FIGURE 6.2

In control and capable

- special causes, events due to factors external to the system which result in instability and unpredictability.

Common causes contribute to output variability because they themselves vary, resulting in a random aggregate variability. If a process has only 'common causes' it is deemed to be in control and requires fundamental change if further improvement is to take place. Different actions, impacting upon external factors, are required to correct variations attributable to special causes. Problems arise where inappropriate actions are taken.

If the source of variation is common cause (random fluctuation), adjusting the system will result in errors – we should not tamper with a stable set-up. But if the source is a special cause (external to the system) things will get worse if we do nothing. We must identify and eradicate the effects of external factors impacting upon the system. It is, therefore, essential that we recognize the nature of the cause to which variation is attributable, because this determines the appropriate form of managerial action.

This situation is further exacerbated by the existence of a chain of interdependent events, each of which is subject to random fluctuation. Now the nature of the dependence and the extent of the individual fluctuations will determine the variation.

Consider the situation where service costs (C) are dependent upon the time taken to complete two tasks (X and Y). The tasks are normally distributed with a mean time to completion of 2 minutes and 3 minutes, and standard deviations of 1 minute and 2 minutes, respectively. The functional relationship is $C = f(X, Y)$, but the variation in costs attributable to common causes differs enormously depending on the nature of the relationship. If

$$C = 18X + 12Y,$$

(case 1) then the mean cost is $72 with a standard deviation of $24.70. But if

$$C = X^3Y^2,$$

(case 2) then, while the mean cost is still $72, the standard deviation blows out to $276. Figure 6.3 illustrates the impact on our 'in control and capable' programme. If we specify an upper control limit of two standard deviations, our definitions of 'in control' would be vastly different – under $121.40 for case 1, but under $624 for case 2! Clearly cost behaviour must be carefully examined.

A further complication arises if one event cannot take place until after the completion of another. Here the accumulation of fluctuations will act to increase inventory and reduce throughput. Despite the existence of a balanced system, random fluctuations of the two (or more) variables in the dependency will cause the variation of subsequent events to be determined by the maximum of preceding ones. Because of the dependency, departments get behind and work-in-process inventory builds up, the usual consequences being:

- overtime work;
- flexibility of operatives;
- management stress; and

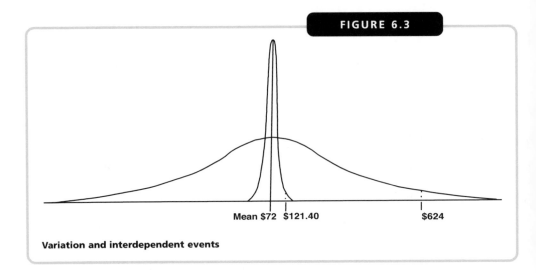

Mean $72 $121.40 $624

Variation and interdependent events

- pressure on employees to get the product out of the door and reduce inventory.

This process will then inevitably be repeated because of the interdependencies unless action is taken to reduce the level of variation applicable to individual events. The alternative – stopping the production line to allow some sections to catch up – is still frowned upon because of the idle time created, even though it might reduce the cost of work in process.

Where multiple events are concerned, the fluctuations may average out, but for interdependent ones they will just accumulate. If we do not know our process then there may be nasty surprises awaiting us. The fundamentals of statistics are essential if we are to comprehend the workings of the processes and the intricacies of cost behaviour.

ACTIVITY-BASED COSTING

The abandonment of traditional, volume-related, absorption costing bases for product costing leads to the inclusion of non-production overheads in activity-based analysis. Design, engineering, servicing, production, distribution, marketing and after-sales service are all usually considered to be relevant activities. Only excess capacity costs and research and development costs, respectively treated as period costs and asset capitalization, are normally excluded. Purchasing, scheduling and set-up costs, typically classified as fixed costs under a traditional system, respond to activity-based changes.

The essential characteristic of an activity-based costing (ABC) system is the differentiation between volume-driven costs and non-volume (activity-driven) costs. Direct costs (labour and material) are not a problem in this respect, but overhead costs necessitate the adoption of some assumptions before they can be allocated to individual products. This is especially true where no volume-based relationship can be established.

Rather than the traditional approach of allocating overhead costs to production departments and then to product lines via volume-based overhead rates, ABC introduces an intermediary: cost pools. The revised system is still a two-stage one, but ABC charges overhead costs to activity-based cost pools and on to product lines through rates based on cost drivers. Figure 6.4 illustrates the stages.

Three further fundamental elements of ABC are therefore:

- the choice of cost pools, based on the identification of the major activities which cause overhead costs, such as maintenance, purchasing, supply and processing;
- the allocation of overhead costs to the cost pools, which will require some indication of the significance of each major activity in incurring overhead costs; and
- the choice of cost drivers for each activity-based cost pool, which will require judgement regarding the homogeneity of the activity and the representativeness of the cost drivers.

ABC systems have been put forward as a possible solution to the fact that absorption cost systems do not normally embrace marketing expenses – this despite studies which suggest that marketing costs can comprise as much as 50% of the total costs of many product lines. Physical distribution costs may be a major factor in internal operations, impacting on performance measurement and possibly preventing the implementation of just-in-time systems. The application of ABC principles in tracking marketing costs to products suggests that we should adopt a number of possible cost drivers for each sphere of activity, as in Table 6.1.

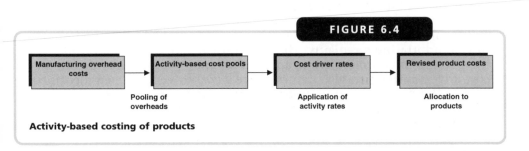

FIGURE 6.4

Manufacturing overhead costs → Activity-based cost pools → Cost driver rates → Revised product costs

Pooling of overheads   Application of activity rates   Allocation to products

Activity-based costing of products

TABLE 6.1

Allocation of cost drivers

Activity	Cost driver
Sales	Number of orders received
	Gross sales
	Number of sales calls
Distribution	Number of units
	Weight of units
Warehousing	Size of units
Accounting	Number of customer orders
	Number of invoice categories

Organizations may expect to benefit from the implementation of ABC in a number of areas of their operations. These include:

- in multi-product organizations, a completely different ranking of product costings, reflecting a correction of the benefits previously accruing to low-volume products;
- an improved awareness of the activities which are driving overhead costs and which may improve the control exercised over the incurring of such costs;
- the generation of an information base which facilitates the implementation of TQM by quantifying improvement opportunities;
- the use of non-financial indicators to measure cost drivers, providing measures of performance in addition to a means of costing production;
- the identification of non-value-adding activities;
- a new perspective on the examination of cost behaviour, and on planning and budgeting, through the analysis of cost drivers;
- costing information which is more credible and demonstrably more useful in the decision-making process, making ABC useful for inter-plant and inter-divisional comparisons.

However, despite its nuances and subtleties, an ABC system is still essentially a historic cost system. In certain circumstances the decision-usefulness of its conclusions is doubtful, especially where present and future cost considerations are of particular importance. As with all historic cost information, we should regard it as a starting point for future cost information rather than as a direct input into the decision-making process.

Far from eliminating arbitrary allocations of overhead costs, an ABC system may actually increase the number of such apportionments. The manner of the allocation may be more systematic but, nevertheless, a hint of arbitrariness remains. Thus we must determine decision rules for the pooling of common overheads into separate cost pools and common cost drivers into separate activities. Once a cost driver has been identified, there is the danger of trying to employ it alone to explain the cost behaviour of a whole cost pool, even though it may not be entirely representative. It is likely that a combination of cost drivers, appropriately integrated, will often provide a better means of explaining cost behaviour.

An alternative approach is to adopt a strategic approach to the choice of cost drivers. By choosing drivers which are consistent with strategic goals, rather than 'correct' in some sense, we may deliberately penalize certain parts of the production process whose operation is not congruent with corporate goals.

An often neglected problem of ABC systems is that of data collection. To justify the sophistication and potential complexity of ABC, the training of those inputting data into the system is essential. They must be able to measure the NFIs employed as cost drivers and must appreciate the importance of accuracy and reliability to the credibility of the whole system. Similar problems exist with financial indicators under traditional cost systems.

While ABC studies documented so far have predominantly been conducted in manufacturing environments, the extension of the ABC methodology to the service sector in more recent studies is a welcome extension, allowing more accurate measurement of indirect costs and more appropriate service costing. Reported cases include successful applications in banking (Mabberly, 1992; Hart and Smith, 1998) and in airlines, hotels, telecommunications, transport, marketing, wholesale and distribution, health and information services (Cooper and Kaplan, 1992; King et al., 1994; Banker et al., 2000).

The emergence of ABC has undoubtedly forced management accountants to reappraise their costing systems and to identify improvement opportunities. Clear advantages have been demonstrated in particular working environments, notably in multi-product organizations. However, equally clear doubts have been expressed about the costs of changing to an ABC system, especially when there have been few documented studies of successful implementations, to suggest, conclusively, that ABC generates bottom-line improvements in profitability. The findings of Kennedy and Affleck-Graves (2001) are important in this regard in that they show that for a matched sample of UK firms, those adopting ABC outperformed the non-adopters by 27% over a three-year period; they suggest that ABC adds value through cost control, asset usage and access to greater financial leverage. The take-up of management accounting innovations is slow worldwide, and ABC implementation provides a good example: Innes and Mitchell (1995) reported adoption rates in the UK of less than 14%, while in the USA Ness and Cucuzza (1995) report that fewer than 10% of ABC adopters continue to support the innovation. The evidence seems to suggest (e.g., Askarany and Smith, 2004) that the perceived benefits of implementation do not outweigh the costs, and that this perception is borne out among adopters too.

OPERATIONALIZING ACTIVITY-BASED COSTING

The motives for pursuing an ABC implementation, or at least for investigating its feasibility, must be established at the outset. Most commonly, these will be:

- to improve product costing where a belief exists that existing methods undercost some products and overcost others; or
- to identify non-value-adding activities in the production process which might be a suitable focus for attention or elimination.

In practice, the former is the most quoted goal, even though the latter may be more appropriate. This is especially so for firms which are highly labour-intensive and which do not have a great diversity of products in their range, and where allocation of overheads based on direct labour hours may already function efficiently.

Direct costs, like materials and direct labour, are easily assigned directly to products. Some indirect costs, particularly those selling costs which are product specific (e.g., advertising), may be directly assigned to the product too. The remaining indirect costs are those which are problematical and provide the focus for ABC, with resource costs indirectly assigned to the cost object via cost pools and activity drivers. A number of distinct practical stages in the ABC implementation exist:

- *Staff training.* The co-operation of the workforce is critical to the successful implementation of ABC. They are closest to the process and most aware of the problems. Staff training should be, as far as possible, jargon-free, and create an awareness of the purpose of ABC. It should be non-threatening in nature, stressing that increased efficiencies resulting from a successful implementation will mean rewards, *not* redundancies. The need for the co-operation of staff in a concerted team effort, for mutual benefit, must be emphasized throughout the training activity.

- *Process specification.* Informal, but structured, interviews with key members of personnel will identify the different stages of the production process, the commitment of resources to each, processing times and bottlenecks. The interviews will yield a list of transactions which may, or may not, be defined as 'activities' at a subsequent stage, but in any case provide a feel for the scope of the process in its entirety.

- *Activity definition.* The problem must be kept manageable at this stage, despite the possibility of information overload from new data, much of which is in need of codification. The listed transactions must be rationalized in order to aggregate those in similar categories and eliminate those deemed immaterial. The resultant cost pools will likely have a number of different events, or drivers, associated with their incurrence.

- *Activity driver selection.* A single driver covering all of the transactions grouped together in an 'activity' probably does not exist. Multiple driver models could be developed if the data were available, but cost–benefit analysis has rarely shown these to be desirable. The intercorrelation of potential activity drivers will be so strong as to suggest that it really does not matter which one is selected. This argument might be employed to avoid the costly collection of data items otherwise not monitored, nor easily accessible.

- *Costing.* A single representative activity driver can be used to assign costs from the activity pools to the cost objects. If, for example, the number of engineering set-ups has been identified as a driver of process costs and the total set-up cost is £40,000 for a company producing four products (A, B, C and D) then the number of set-ups per product can be used to assign these costs. If product A requires two set-ups, B four set-ups, C 24 and D 10, then the average cost per set-up of $40,000/40 = £1000$, a misleading figure taken at face value, which does not imply the different demands of the set-up resource made by the different products. However, total set-up costs can be distributed to product groups in proportion to use (A, £2000; B, £4000; C, £24,000; D, £10,000) and then assigned to individual units of product in proportion to the total level of output. Thus if 20,000 units of A were being produced each would attract £0.10 of costs attributable to set-ups. This procedure can then be repeated for all material activities, as in the following case study. The existing literature suggests that the likely outcome will be a demonstration of costing errors of varying degrees; these will most commonly be the undercosting of low-volume products and the overcosting of high-volume products.

The onerous nature of this recosting exercise should not be underestimated and may make it advisable to concentrate on the most important products in the range. Thus for a 100-product firm a focus, at least initially, on the most prominent 20 products, say, could yield the outcomes desired. The question of how to use the revised costings resulting from the ABC implementation is more problematical. It may show that some products are unprofitable at current price levels, so that a financial analysis suggests that they should be dropped from the product mix. Such a decision should not be made without reference to inter-product implications and to strategic and non-financial considerations concerning the overall impact of the product concerned.

We now present a case study which highlights the deficiencies of traditional methods of product costing, employing single-volume methods of overhead allocation. It provides the opportunity to apply ABC methods in order to demonstrate differences in cost and price outcomes.

CASE STUDY

RAVE Holdings: Activity-based costing for pricing decisions

This case study highlights the potential difficulties associated with traditional methods of product costing which employ single-volume methods of overhead cost allocation. It provides the opportunity to explore alternative costing methodologies and to apply activity-based costing methods, and demonstrates both the differences in cost and price outcomes associated with different methods, and the marketing implications of the new cost information for pricing practice.

Teddy Rodhouse was born to be a salesman. He traded football cards and postage stamps at school, before he was 10, and by his teens was selling car radios, stereos and aerials from a market stall. School soon came to have little meaning for him because he loved buying and selling, always at a profit, and always in cash. He bought himself a van (the lack of licence and insurance seemed only a minor obstacle) and traded daily on the circuit of street markets in central and south Sydney. His absence from school was noted, and his father responded by cutting his pocket money, but at 16 Teddy was already earning more in a week than his father did in a month!

Teddy's genius was in spotting unmet consumer demand early, and taking rapid steps to supply it, particularly in the areas of home entertainment and audio-visual systems. Thus was RAVE Holdings born (Rodhouse Audio Visual Entertainment), initially as a selling arm, but increasingly as a vehicle for externally sourced and designed products. By providing products in anticipation of the market, and bringing them in ahead of competitors, RAVE became more profitable. Teddy had always been reluctant to do his own manufacturing, but as the organization grew in size and reputation, he recognized the enormous profit opportunities from vertical integration which made use of low-cost sources off Australia's northern shores. Twenty years on, Teddy Rodhouse is now Chief Executive of a thriving business with an enviable reputation among the market leaders for hi-tech products. But now Teddy's lack of schooling may become his Achilles heel; costing and pricing have always been low on his priorities because new, well-marketed products have always been successful in the past.

The management at RAVE are now worried, and the shareholders restless. Table 6.2 indicates why: the company's bottom line displays a disconcerting downturn for the second successive year – the first time this has happened in the company's 20-year history. The reason for this relatively poor performance is largely attributable to lack of sales revenue stemming from an inexplicable failure to win orders.

CASE STUDY (cont.)

TABLE 6.2

RAVE Holdings financial performance

Year Ending	31/12/2000 ($000)	31/12/1999 ($000)	21/12/1998 ($000)
INCOME STATEMENT			
Sales Revenue	336,420	229,716	218,928
Profit before Tax	17,680	18,580	24,410
BALANCE SHEET			
Current Assets	292,848	174,754	148,012
Inventory	89,856	35,496	24,624
Current Liabilities	501,648	262,053	140,423
Total Assets	460,162	316,842	265,813
Total Liabilities	723,157	396,101	266,647

The Chief Executive feels that the pricing policies must be wrong and has called for a full investigation of current procedures in order to identify deficiencies.

RAVE has always prided itself on staying at the cutting-edge of new manufacturing technologies and has diversified to take advantage of new marketing opportunities. It reckons itself to be the most efficient producers worldwide of its two traditional products:

- Astra, an efficient and cost-effective portable compact disc system, originally designed for in-car use but successfully adapted as a portable single-disc system integrating radio and double tape-deck.
- Bueno, a streamlined and sturdy six-head video cassette recorder with G-code and a reputation for reliability.

Both the Astra and the Bueno are mature and proven products. They regularly receive minor upgrades, but this requires a minimal investment commitment.

The future of RAVE Holdings is heavily dependent on the success of its two recently launched products:

- Cisco, an attractively designed flat screen TV targeting the bottom end of a still emerging market, and which quickly achieved prominence just a short time after initial penetration, taking advantage of the demand for new technologies.
- Delta, a compact and lightweight DVD unit, targeting the top-end of the market and with advanced features relating to picture quality and theatre-style 'surround sound'.

The initial success of the two new products has surprised even the most optimistic of management. Although the new products have been successfully launched, it is the sales of the traditional products which are the greatest cause of concern. RAVE has lost out to competitors

CASE STUDY (cont.)

TABLE 6.3

Breakdown of average monthly sales revenues 1999/2000

	2000		1999	
	UNITS SOLD	REVENUE ($)	UNITS SOLD	REVENUE ($)
ASTRA: PORTABLE CD	20,000	7,200	23,000	8,280
BUENO: VCR SYSTEM	15,000	9,585	17,000	10,863
CISCO: FLAT SCREEN TV	8,000	4,680		
DELTA: DVD SYSTEM	10,000	6,570		
		28,035		19,143

that it views as inferior and less efficient. Inferior producers have been able to tender at more competitive prices, suggesting that there is something wrong with pricing procedures at RAVE.

An analysis of the breakdown of monthly sales revenue (in Table 6.3) confirms the decline in the sales of the two traditional product lines. Teddy Rodhouse's worst fears are confirmed when he checks out the current selling prices of comparable products in the Toshiba, Samsung, Panasonic and Sony ranges:

	Selling Price ($)	
	RAVE products	Competitors' products
Portable CD	360	323 (Panasonic)
Six-head VCR	639	529 (Sony)
Flat screen TV	585	899 (Samsung)
DVD system	657	775 (Toshiba)

Teddy orders an urgent investigation and re-evaluation of costing and pricing methodologies.

Each of the products proceeds through the same four-step production process, though the time spent and resources consumed at each step varies between products:

1 supply of raw material components;
2 set-up and run of production engineering;
3 vacuum packing of finished product;
4 distribution of product to wholesalers and retailers.

Table 6.4 shows the monthly cost information which is employed by RAVE in its current pricing procedures.

Prices are currently calculated with respect to unit costs computed on the basis of direct labour, direct material and a share of overhead costs. Overheads are allocated on a direct labour hour (DLH) basis, using an overhead rate of $10,800,000/90,000 = \$120$ per DLH. Table 6.5 illustrates the calculation of selling prices for each of the products.

CASE STUDY (cont.)

TABLE 6.4

Cost information for four products

	Astra	Bueno	Cisco	Delta	TOTAL
			TOTAL		
Units of Output	30,000	20,000	8,000	10,000	68,000
Resource Use per Unit:					
Raw Materials	4	5	10	15	450,000
Labour Hours	1	2	1.25	1	90,000
Machine Hours	1	1	2.5	1	80,000
Production Costs per Unit:					
Raw Materials ($)	72	90	180	270	$8,100,000
Direct Labour ($)	48	96	60	48	$4,320,000
Overheads:					
Machining ($ per hour)	$60	$60	$60	$60	$4,800,000
Engineering Set-ups	3	7	20	10	$240,000
Component Receipts	20	40	240	100	$2,400,000
Orders Packaged	10	2	20	18	$1,800,000
Distribution Deliveries	10	10	25	20	$1,560,000

TABLE 6.5

Product pricing

	PRODUCT			
	Astra	Bueno	Cisco	Delta
Direct Labour ($)	48	96	60	48
Direct Materials ($)	72	90	180	270
Allocated Overhead ($)	120	240	150	120
TOTAL COST ($)	240	426	390	438
Mark-Up (50%) ($)	120	213	195	219
SELLING PRICE ($)	360	639	585	657

We are required to examine the current method of establishing product costs and prices and make recommendations for an improved system. Our report should embrace a consideration of the impact on prices of alternative cost bases and of alternative methods of allocating overhead costs to products.

CASE ANALYSIS

The traditional products have not been performing well lately, as a result of which RAVE's profitability has been adversely affected.

CASE STUDY (cont.)

For the first time in its history, RAVE has experienced a downturn in profit for the second successive year. This relatively poor performance is mainly due to loss of orders.

Although the new products have exceeded management's expectation in sales performance, the sales of traditional products are apparently the greatest cause of concern.

A SWOT analysis is performed to identify the internal factors and external factors that have impact on RAVE. Detailed findings of the analysis are presented in Table 6.6. In general, the rapidly changing nature of the hi-tech electronic industry provides both opportunities and threats. RAVE excels in anticipating customer needs, but shows lack of emphasis on the revenue-generating functions of the business, with the result that, despite the superior quality of its traditional products and popularity of its new products, profits have still fallen.

However, analysis of RAVE's financial performance in Table 6.7 demonstrates the extent of the problem. The build-up of inventory because of the lost sales of Astra and Bueno products has seriously impacted on liquidity, with the quick assets ratio (QA/CL) down to a low of 0.40 from 0.88 just two years ago; the current ratio (CA/CL) shows a similar decline. The gearing ratio (TL/TA) has deteriorated over the period and has now become a matter of concern. The cash-flow issue must be addressed in order to reduce the growing liabilities. Attention to the profit ratios highlights a further cause for alarm: a decline from a relatively healthy position in 1998 which has been exacerbated by the launch of the two new

---

TABLE 6.6

SWOT analysis for RAVE Holdings

Strengths	Weaknesses
• Respected position among market leaders	• Little attention to costing/pricing strategies
• Ability to anticipate market needs	• Insensitive to market competition
• New manufacturing technologies	• Failure to win orders for the Astra and Bueno products
• Efficient producer	
• Ability to diversify product range	

Opportunities	Threats
• Constant market demands for new products	• Low barrier of entry to the industry
• Possible product upgrades	• Short Product Life Cycle (PLC)
• Diversification	• Astra and Bueno products at mature age of PLC
• Command instead of respond to market needs	• Fast competitor catch-up
• Promote product quality	• Huge R & D investments on new products
	• Price competition

CASE STUDY (cont.)

TABLE 6.7

Financial ratio trends (1998–2000)

Year Ending	31/12/2000	31/12/1999	31/12/1998
Profitability:			
PBT/S (%)	5.3	8.1	11.1
PBT/TA (%)	3.8	5.9	9.2
Liquidity:			
CA/CL	0.58	0.67	1.05
QA/CL	0.40	0.53	0.88
Gearing:			
TL/TA	1.57	1.25	1.00

products; while the Cisco and Delta have expanded sales revenue, profits have fallen. Clearly something has gone wrong here, and the pricing methodology and associated product costing require urgent attention.

RAVE currently employs an *absorption* or *full costing* method to derive unit costs for its products. The unit costs consist of variable cost components and fixed cost components. Overheads are allocated on a DLH basis at a rate of $120 per DLH, as explained above. A cost-plus approach has been adopted. The unit cost of each product is marked up 50% to cover selling and administration expenses and the profit.

The current costing method is *full-cost single-volume costing*, which includes sunk cost and could potentially lead to sub-optimum decision-making, especially where overheads are allocated on a DLH basis.

The Cisco and Delta products are relatively more complex and have used up more units of overheads than the mature Astra and Bueno products. However, they are not allocated higher overheads. This suggests the single-volume method using DLH as its basis is inappropriate.

The composition of total production costs for these four products, as indicated in Table 6.4, is: direct labour cost $4,320,000, direct materials $8,100,000, and overhead costs $10,800,000. An analysis of the composition of production costs shows that the direct labour cost component constitutes only 18.6% of RAVE's total production costs, whereas raw materials make up 34.9% and overheads 46.5%. DLH is therefore unlikely to be the most suitable basis for RAVE's overhead allocation as it does not reflect the total cost structure. As a consequence, the high-volume products are overcosted and the low volume products are undercosted.

RAVE adopts a convenient and simplistic approach in pricing its products. It imposes a 50% mark-up across the board, which does not provide any incentive for cost reduction. This pricing approach does not recognize the necessity of considering the individual characteristics and position of each product. It is not sensitive to

CASE STUDY (cont.)

the market and the actions of competitors. It would be preferable were pricing determined within a marketing framework with due consideration given to the marketing mix of individual products.

The apparent overcosting of the Astra and Bueno products must hamper their competitiveness in the market. A 50% mark-up on these already overcosted products results in a market price for the products which is just too high. As a result, these products lose their competitive edge in a hostile retail environment despite their superior product quality.

The Cisco and Delta products are more successful because they are new products with good market demand, and also because they are undercosted and subsequently underpriced. It is possible that, despite the apparent success of these two products, when compared with their actual full costs, RAVE is suffering a loss on each unit of these products sold. If the marked-up prices simply do not cover their actual production costs, then this will significantly contribute to the sudden decline in RAVE's financial position.

There are clear deficiencies in the current method of establishing product prices. We need to investigate alternative means of costing and pricing the four products under consideration to embrace single- and multiple-volume methods for the allocation of overhead costs to products.

Alternative costing methods

The original allocation of overhead costs to products based on labour hours (alternative 1) is potentially misleading, especially since much of the overhead is incurred on a non-volume-related basis. The arguments for using DLH are unconvincing and we might initially consider the use of alternative single-volume-based methods.

Alternative 2 might be to switch from DLH to machine hours in the allocation of overhead:

$$\frac{\text{Total overhead}}{\text{Total machine hours}} = \frac{\$10,800,000}{80,000} = \$135 \text{ per machine hour.}$$

Overhead allocated to each product would then be $135 instead of $120 for Astra, $135 instead of $240 for Bueno, $337.5 instead of $150 for Cisco, and $135 instead of $120 for Delta. Thus the total costs per unit would be $255, $321, $577.5 and $453 respectively, still not adequately reflecting the range of activities. Bueno benefits from its relative labour intensity, although Cisco is penalized for its use of technology.

Alternative 3 might be to switch from DLH to raw material utilization as the basis for allocation:

$$\frac{\text{Total overhead}}{\text{Raw material volume}} = \frac{\$10,800,000}{450,000}$$
$$= \$24 \text{ per raw material component.}$$

Overhead allocated to each product would then be $96 for Astra, $120 for Bueno, $240 for Cisco, and $360 for Delta, and total costs per unit would be $216, $306, $480 and $678 respectively. This method greatly benefits the old products (Astra and Bueno) but penalizes the new ones, especially Delta. We might argue that this single-volume base is more appropriate than either DLH or machine hours alone, because of the relative prominence of raw material costs to the total costs of the operation.

Alternative 4 might be to combine the three basic resources to form a multiple-volume-based allocation method comprising the extremes of the three separate measures. We thus split the total overhead of $10,800,000 as follows. The overhead directly attributable to machining is $4,800,000. If the remaining $6,000,000 of overhead is attributable to raw materials and labour, then an estimate of the split between the two can be made using the production costs applicable from Table 6.4: $8,100,000 for raw materials and $4,320,000 for labour. Simple proportions would then give a breakdown of the remaining $6,000,000 overhead as:

$$\frac{8.1}{12.42} \times 6,000,000 = 3,913,044$$

for raw materials and

$$\frac{4.32}{12.42} \times 6,000,000 = 2,086,956$$

for labour. Then the labour allocation rate would be

$$\frac{\$2,086,956}{90,000} = \$23.16 \text{ per DLH},$$

the machine time allocation rate

$$\frac{\$4,800,000}{80,000} = \$60 \text{ per machine hour}$$

and the raw materials allocation rate

$$\frac{\$3,913,044}{450,000} = \$8.70 \text{ per component.}$$

This combination would give allocated overheads as follows:

	Astra	Bueno	Cisco	Delta
Labour	23.16	46.38	28.98	23.16
Machinery	60.00	60.00	150.00	60.00
Raw Materials	34.80	43.50	87.00	130.50
Total	117.96	149.88	265.98	213.66

resulting in total costs per unit of $237.96 for Astra, $335.88 for Bueno, $505.98 for Cisco and $531.66 for Delta. The Astra costings are little altered from the original, but the Cisco costings are reduced and a considerable trade-off has taken place between Bueno and Delta, reflecting the 'raw material' penalty to which these products are subject.

The three new alternatives highlight the differences in product costs consequent upon the adoption of different bases. But none of them is obviously 'right'; we might argue, for example, that alternative 3 over-emphasizes machine costs and gives an insufficient allocation to raw material components. All of the methods considered thus far ignore non-volume-related alternatives.

Alternative 5 adopts a more radical activity-based approach, eliminating DLH as an allocation base altogether and directing attention to five overhead components.

We might allocate the whole of the overhead on the basis of a single allocation base (cost driver) – that is, for machinery, set-ups, receipts, packaging and distribution separately, as we did for the three resources above. But it is probably more appropriate to allocate each additional component of the overhead in accordance with the weighting attributed it:

$$\text{Cost per set-up} = \frac{\$240,000}{40} = \$6000,$$

$$\text{Cost per receipt} = \frac{\$2400,000}{400} = \$6000,$$

$$\text{Cost per package} = \frac{\$1,800,000}{50} = \$36,000,$$

$$\text{Cost per delivery} = \frac{\$1,560,000}{65} = \$24,000.$$

The resultant allocation by activity is shown in Table 6.8. Reallocating the activity costs to products on the basis of the cost (see the final row of Table 6.8) gives total costs of $204.60 for Astra,

TABLE 6.8

Cost allocation for four products

	Astra	Bueno	Cisco	Delta	Total
Machinery	1,800,000	1,200,000	1,200,000	600,000	4,800,000
Set-ups	18,000	42,000	120,000	60,000	240,000
Receipts	120,000	240,000	1,440,000	600,000	2,400,000
Packaging	360,000	72,000	720,000	648,000	1,800,000
Delivery	240,000	240,000	600,000	480,000	1,560,000
Total	2,538,000	1,794,000	4,080,000	2,388,000	10,800,000
No. of units of output	30,000	20,000	8,000	10,000	68,000
Costs per unit	84.60	89.70	510.00	238.80	

CASE STUDY (cont.)

TABLE 6.9

Effect of alternative overhead allocation bases on product costs

Overhead Allocation basis	Product costs ($)			
	Astra	Bueno	Cisco	Delta
Single-Volume:				
1 Direct labour hours	240	426	390	438
2 Machine hours	255	321	577.50	453
3 Raw materials	216	306	480	678
Multiple-Volume:				
4 Labour/Machinery/ Materials	237.96	335.8	505.98	531.66
Multiple Non-Volume:				
5 Machine time/Set-ups/ Receipts/Packaging/ Delivery	204.60	275.70	750.00	556.80

$275.70 for Bueno, $750.00 for Cisco and $556.80 for Delta, and selling prices, based on a 50% mark-up, of $306.90, $413.55, $1125.00 and $835.20 respectively.

The differences from our original costing/pricing combination apparent from Table 6.9 are startling. The variations in the non-volume-related costs favour the traditional products (Astra and Bueno) and penalize the new ones, suggesting that Cisco and Delta products are vastly undercosted (and underpriced) when DLH is the only consideration.

The returns on costs from the 'old' products, Astra and Bueno, are excellent at 76% and 132% per unit. But they are too high, because they disguise a selling price per unit which is hitting sales revenue hard because too few units are being sold. The markets for these products are extremely price-sensitive, so that price reductions (though perhaps not to the extent suggested by the analysis of alternative 5: $53 per unit and $225 per unit, respectively) will increase sales volume and probably sales revenue.

Table 6.10 demonstrates that the 'successful' launch of the two new products is indeed a myth: Cisco is not covering its product costs, and Delta is making only a modest contribution to profits. Such low prices may have been justified on market penetration arguments, but they are unsustainable in the long term. The analysis of alternative 5 suggests that price increases of $540 per unit and $178 per unit are required; clearly these are impossible to achieve in the short term. Of most concern, Cisco needs to generate an additional $165 per unit just to cover its production costs.

The logical extension of Table 6.10 highlights more problems for RAVE Holdings. Table 6.11 shows that Cisco is contributing an annual loss of approximately $15.8 million, but even so the four products

TABLE 6.10

Product profitability at RAVE Holdings

	Astra	Bueno	Cisco	Delta
Current Price per unit ($)	360	639	585	657
Product Cost per Unit suggested by activity analysis ($)	204.60	275.70	750	556.80
Contribution per unit ($)	155.40	363.30	(165)	100.20
Return on Costs (%)	76	132	(22)	18
Revised Selling Price (ALT.5)	307	414	1125	835

TABLE 6.11

Contributions to profitability in 2000

	Astra	Bueno	Cisco	Delta
Contribution per unit ($)	155.40	363.30	(165)	100.20
Units sold per month (2000)	20,000	15,000	8,000	10,000
Average Monthly Contribution to Profit ($000)	3,108	5,449	(1320)	1,002
Annual Contribution to Profit ($000)	37,296	65,394	(15,840)	12,024
Total Contribution ($000)	98,874			
Reported Profit before Tax ($000)	17,680			

together contribute nearly $99 million annually to corporate profits. Yet reported profit before tax is less than $18 million, suggesting that RAVE Holdings must urgently pay more attention to its selling and distribution expenses and the costs of product development.

Alternative pricing methods

Establishing the most appropriate costing method to be employed is only one of the priorities. The appropriate pricing method to be used has a direct impact on the profitability of individual products, and thus the overall bottom line of the company. RAVE's 50% across the board mark-up pricing method is too cost-oriented, inflexible and not sensitive to market and external factors. A more sensitive, 'outward-looking' method is required.

One alternative would be to base the pricing on the nature of individual products. For instance, the Astra and Bueno products are in the mature stage of their product life cycle, a stage characterized by keen price competition. Although the products are of superior quality and product differentiation is possible, there is little scope

CASE STUDY (cont.)

for non-price competition. The only way to excel in this market is to drive prices down in order to compete on a price basis. Reference to variable costs is essential in making strategic pricing decisions for these products. As long as the prices are sufficient to cover the variable cost, RAVE can maintain the low price policy in the market and win orders. By doing so, the profit derived could contribute to the recovery of fixed costs. Continued production of these products could utilize the investment in production line by reducing the slack in manufacturing capacity.

On the other hand, the Cisco and Delta products have been exceptionally successful since their launch in terms of number of units sold. This is largely attributable to their being undercosted and subsequently under-priced. For the Cisco even the existing 50% mark up on DLH cost does not cover actual manufacturing costs so that RAVE is suffering a loss on this product and a minimal profit on the Delta. These two products are at the growth stage of the product life cycle, and the company might have derived a better profit performance from them. For new products RAVE might have adopted a cost-plus approach, with a variable mark-up to a level that the market can bear. This approach is market-sensitive, and maximizes return on investment in new products.

In practice, several factors must be considered to derive effective market-driven pricing strategies. Among the internal factors are the following:

- Pricing policies should align with the company's corporate goals and marketing objectives. Different strategies could be formulated for different objectives, be they profit maximization, increased market share or product images.
- Pricing strategies should be formulated in conjunction with the market mix of the products. A market skimming strategy would suggest a high price, whereas a market penetration strategy might suggest a lower price.
- Cost is a significant factor in any pricing decision, with different costing approaches impacting on the market prices of products.
- Organizational factors should be considered in establishing product prices. For example, it would be difficult for RAVE to promote high-quality, high-price products if the company were known in the market as a cheap product provider.

The external factors are as follows:

- A detailed assessment should be made of market demand and product price elasticity in order to establish a realistic pricing approach for individual products.
- Market intelligence is an important aspect of market competition, and information gained from competitors should be used in setting product prices in order to maintain a competitive position in the market, and to be aware of likely competitor reaction.
- The condition of the economy should be considered in setting product prices. Consumers may be able to afford higher prices in

boom time, but they tend to be more careful of their spending during a recession.

- Government may impose restrictions in price setting in order to protect the industry as a whole. Such regulations should be examined carefully when setting product prices.

RECOMMENDATIONS

RAVE should assess its position in the market and establish long-term and short-term corporate goals. This is important for the company's long-term development and allows the formulation of congruent short-term and long-term strategies.

- For the traditional products, Astra and Bueno, a reduction of product prices should be implemented as soon as possible to contain the loss of market share. A target costing approach might be adopted to regain competitiveness. Competitive prices should be determined from market intelligence to facilitate successful tender bidding.
- In future, RAVE should consider adopting activity-based costing as the basis of new product costings. Where possible, RAVE should establish itself as price leader for its new products, setting a price close to what the market will bear.
- As for the two new products, prices below cost have already been established in the market. Therefore, it is necessary to increase the product prices in order to return to profit for these two products. However, the market is not able to absorb a sudden surge in prices, which could turn away potential customers or create an unfavourable image of the company. Sales volume is likely to drop as a result. Therefore, RAVE should offer and promote product enhancements as far as possible and take the opportunity to adjust the prices. A phased enhancement programme might be implemented and prices adjusted upwards on a gradual basis.

Thus, for Cisco, RAVE might promote enhancements in product reliability, picture and audio quality, while the further inclusion of a digital decoder might justify modest price increases. For Delta, enhanced picture quality functions, multiple-disc facilities and a 'karaoke' function might be added at a modest investment cost, to justify a price hike.

CONCLUSIONS

The case of RAVE illustrates the importance of costing and pricing policies to the revenue and thus the profitability of a company. Costing policies should best reflect the cost structure of products, and correspond with the corporate goals of the company. Allocation of overhead costs results in cross-subsidization among the products, and the basis of allocation should support the company's marketing strategies.

Apart from the costing and pricing issues, other issues should also be considered in view of the company's long-term development

> **CASE STUDY (cont.)**
>
> and growth. The costing system should be regarded as a component of the company's management information system. Internal costing information, production capacity and efficiency, together with external market and competitor information, should all be utilized for corporate decision-making.

TARGET COSTING

Target costing is a simple idea with potentially powerful cost-reduction capabilities. Its adoption has spread from Japanese companies (e.g., Sakurai, 1989; Tanaka, 1993) to manufacturing operations in Europe, the USA and Australia. The major objective of the tool is cost reduction, but the focus is moved from the production stage to the planning and design stages. The ultimate aim is to explain 100% of product costs at the initial planning stages and then to implement tools which reduce their incidence, particularly through the control of design specification. Target costing therefore moves away from standard costing and towards management and engineering.

It may be defined as:

> a comprehensive program to reduce costs, which begins even before there are any plans for new products. It is an activity which is aimed at reducing the life-cycle costs of new products, while ensuring quality, reliability and other consumer requirements, by examining all possible ideas for cost reduction at the product planning, research and development and prototyping phases of production. (Kato et al., 1995: 39)

This definition recognizes that most product costs are committed through decisions made at the planning and pre-production stages. Philosophies such as total quality control (TQC) and kaizen, which focus on continuous improvement, once production has already commenced, can only address a relatively small proportion of total costs (perhaps as low as 5%). Cost-cutting post-implementation therefore has a very restricted scope compared to the potential savings that might be made in the planning stages. Target costing shifts the focus to the determination of an acceptable level of costs, consistent with both corporate profit requirements and customer price expectations, so that:

$$\text{Target cost} = \text{Target price} - \text{Target profit}.$$

These costs are those necessary for surviving in a global market, since 'price' is essentially determined by the competition, and 'profit' set at a level determined by wider corporate requirements. Once price and profit targets have determined a target cost, management must act to 'fill the cost gap' by designing the product so that costs can be reduced appropriately.

The management accountant plays an important role in this process by providing cost estimates and by investigating cost behaviour relationships for the different activities involved. Activity analysis is an important aspect of this work too, in order to specify cycle time. The achievements of the target costing approach in practice have been impressive: cost reductions of the order of 30–50% without loss of quality, reliability or increasing time to market. These successes have been confined to mass manufacturing industry (most notably the motor industry) and as yet there is no evidence of the successful implementation of target costing in process industry.

Customer focus is paramount in the procedure, in that products must be of high quality and must satisfy customer needs, but beyond that target costs are set early on in the specification stage.

Targets are attained through:

• value-engineering customer-required functions;
• the use of standard costs at the production stage; and
• the search for continuous improvement throughout.

There is a downside to the implementation of target costing. A trade-off must be achieved between cost cutting and customer-oriented product development: costs may be reduced by reducing the number of product varieties, for example, while additional new products may attract customers without necessarily increasing profits. Supplier fatigue and dissatisfaction are inevitable, since if manufacturers have difficulty in identifying ineffi-ciencies they will put even greater pressure on suppliers to cut costs. Design engineers will face similar pressures in that a cost focus may reduce motivation because innovative flair is less rewarding. Internal organiza-tional conflict is inevitable too, as target costing seeks to change the corporate culture with a mindset that combines minimum cost with customer pref-erence; resistance and manipulation will be apparent much the same as is observed with TQM implementations. In the medium-term the effects of this can be overcome with training, documentation (in the form of target costing manuals) and the encouragement of employee creativity in diffusing target costing techniques down the organization.

Ramesh and Woods (1996) detail some of the design changes that the big motor manufacturers are making, to save millions of dollars by elimi-nating little-noticed non-essential items from their specifications.

• Ford reduced the range of its horn tones from 37 to 3 in number, and saves $0.40 per car by not painting the inside of the ashtray.
• Toyota no longer uses a white cigarette symbol on the lighters of some models.
• Mercedes dropped the spring-loading from the ashtrays on its E-class sedans, and replaced the oil pressure gauge with a warning light.
• Honda replaced the electric aerial on its Civic coupé with a manual one.
• Rover introduced generous employee incentives for those who can identify cost-cutting opportunities which do not perceptibly change the look of the car.

Although these changes to specifications reap cost savings for manufacturers, they also provide the opportunity for the introduction of innovations (e.g., airbags, air-conditioning) which target customer preferences through competitive diversifications.

ACTIVITY-BASED MANAGEMENT

The limitations of ABC discussed earlier mean that we must recognize that it is not a holy grail nor a universal panacea for management ills. We are *management* accountants, not just *cost* accountants; while ABC is a useful starting point, we must not be blinkered by the vested interests involved in its marketing. There are other, arguably more important, aspects which must be considered too.

All the evidence suggests that it will be impossible to eliminate arbitrary allocations of overhead totally, even under an ABC system, so perhaps we should be looking beyond product costing to a more appropriate emphasis on process management.

The key to the extension of ABC into activity-based management (ABM) is a wider appreciation of the concept of 'drivers'. We can no longer focus on cost drivers alone, but must investigate the manner in which resources are consumed in non-monetary areas. Current research suggests that customers have perceived needs in four areas, all of which must be satisfied simultaneously: lower costs, higher quality, faster response times and greater innovation. Management information systems must therefore embrace drivers across each of the areas shown in Table 6.12, focusing on all without giving undue emphasis to one. Let us consider the four elements of competition, in each case referencing appropriate activity drivers. Smith (1990), referred to in Chapter 8, surveys the range of NFIs in use in manufacturing and service industry. This approach can be adapted to give an indication of the type of non-financials that would be useful in each of our four areas.

Costs

The scope of ABC applications and implementations must be extended in both directions from traditional process activities to:

- a reappraisal of traditionally fixed costs, so that costs might be classified as product- or process-sustaining, allowing increased tracing of cost to product;
- a consideration of white-collar service areas traditionally consigned to the 'too-hard' basket; and
- the adoption of radical cost reduction strategies, such as business process re-engineering (BPR).

Table 6.13 lists a number of useful non-financial measures of costs.

TABLE 6.12

The drivers of ABM

Customer needs	Drivers
Cost	Cost behaviour and distribution
Quality	Factors inhibiting improved performance
Time	Bottlenecks and inertia
Innovation	New product and process inflexibility

TABLE 6.13

Non-financial measures of cost

Area	Measure
Quantity of raw material	Actual v. target number inputs
Equipment productivity	Actual v. standard units
Maintenance efforts	No. of production units lost through maintenance; no. of production units lost through failure; no. of failures prior to schedule
Overtime costs	Overtime hours/total hours
Product complexity	No. of component parts
Quantity of output	Actual v. target completion
Product obsolescence	Percentage shrinkage
Employees	Percentage staff turnover
Employee productivity	Direct labour hours per unit
Customer focus	Percentage calls; percentage claims

Business process re-engineering

Business process re-engineering is a radical technique designed to encourage radical organizational change – frequently by starting from scratch and attempting to rebuild the organization from the bottom up.

Hammer and Stanton (1995: 3) define re-engineering as 'the fundamental rethinking and radical redesign of business processes to bring about dramatic improvements in performance'. Unfortunately, the implementation of re-engineering has been clouded by the interpretation of the Hammer and Champy (1993) definition of the technique which focuses on short-term profit through a blinkered commitment to cost-reduction programmes where 'head-count' is the measure which features most appropriately. Radical redesign to create breakthrough performance means cost-cutting and rapid downsizing; employees may be retrenched, but the volume of work remains the same.

In practice this will be a short-term expedient; as Mumford and Hendricks (1996) point out, BPR results in companies becoming 'lean and lame' rather than 'lean and mean', with negative effects on both profitability and future vitality. Short-termism with respect to issues, contracts and management behaviour will produce an alienated workforce, working longer hours under greater stress, and no longer able to identify with the long-term goals of their employer.

Eisenberg (1997) details the negative impact that BPR will have on the competitiveness of the organization by discouraging both innovation and risk-taking. When downsizing is employed without reference to a clearly articulated vision of the future:

• teamwork will deteriorate, because more is expected of those that remain;
• delays will take place in decision-making for fear of making an error;
• support functions, always the most vulnerable to retrenchment, will be crippled;
• conditions of anger and anxiety will cause decreased creativity, and lost opportunities from lost incentives to contribute;
• caution and protective attitudes will predominate, to preserve the employment of those who remain.

Eisenberg despairs that companies continue to repeat the mistakes of the past, making major errors when dealing with rapid change because too little time is devoted to assessing critical success factors and learning from historical precedent. He highlights the damaging impact of BPR and rapid downsizing on organizational morale and performance, citing numerous examples of BPR failure, and makes a plea for enlightened decision-making in the pursuit of long-term economic performance fully utilizing the intellectual capital of the organization.

Adopting a more positive perspective, Booth (1995) looks upon BPR as a means of identifying and prioritizing the key processes within any organization so that they can be grouped into one of four categories:

- supply chain management – defining customer requirements from order to despatch and specifying delivery and scheduling operations, capacity management, supply procurement and inventory supervision;
- customer development – acquisition, maintenance and the management of customer profitability;
- business development – product planning, brand management and product/service development;
- business maintenance – attention to activities which may not be directly value-adding, but which must be undertaken for the organization to continue (e.g., human resource management, financial management, infrastructure maintenance).

Process mapping specifies the linkages between the major processes of a typical company and aids an understanding of the interrelationships; activity mapping can locate the activities within each of these processes and highlight errors and omissions. However, the decomposition of processes and activities may not identify conditional paths. Ideally process modelling should:

- help to eliminate duplicated or redundant activities;
- avoid unnecessary data collection;
- simplify the process by avoiding unnecessary decision points;
- offer opportunities for moving from a serial process to a parallel process (with consequent lead time reduction, better due date performance and the elimination of duplication);
- achieve economies of scale by combining currently separate operations; and
- help to avoid unnecessary product movement and data transfer.

Quality

The cost of quality is a potentially important component of management accounting systems which may facilitate the implementation of total quality management. The classification of quality costs is useful in order to allow a closer examination of the drivers of quality:

1 *Prevention costs.* These include the costs of plant, product and process planning, preventive maintenance, training and the implementation of statistical process control systems.
2 *Appraisal costs.* These include the costs of inspection and testing of both incoming and outgoing materials, and the cost of maintaining and

administering appraisal systems and equipment.
3 *Failure costs.* 'Failure' here embraces both the internal and external aspects of operations. Failure costs thus include:

    (a) at the internal level, the costs of scrap, rework, redesign and safety stocks necessary to provide a buffer against such failure; and
    (b) at the external level, the cost of repairs, customer returns, warranty claims, investigations and losses associated with customers, good will and reputation.

Measurement and analysis of the costs of external failure is increasingly becoming the focus of attention in this area, reflecting the renewed customer orientation of management accounting.

Table 6.14 lists a number of useful non-financial measures of quality.

Time

Surveys of manufacturing executives in large, successful companies in Europe, the USA and Japan consistently rank three time-based characteristics among their top five competitive priorities: dependable delivery, fast delivery, and rapid design changes. A time-based focus has a number of positive implications for the management accountant in designing improved management information systems which:

- ensure that our decision-making is linked to an appropriate time horizon by matching short-run and long-run costs with decisions which have corresponding time implications;
- reduce new product lead time by halving planning and engineering lead times for manufacturing operations – the amount of process time is often less than 10% of the total manufacturing lead time for many organizations, with the remaining 90% adding costs but not value;
- monitor customer feedback regarding the reliability of delivery and develop new indicators to measure delivery and distribution performance;

TABLE 6.14

Non-financial measures of quality

Area	Measure
Quality of purchased components	Zero defects
Equipment failure	Downtime/total time
Maintenance effort	Breakdown maintenance/total maintenance
Waste	Percentage defects; percentage scrap; pecentage rework
Quality of output	Percentage yield
Safety	Serious industrial injury rate
Reliability	Percentage warranty claims
Quality commitment	Percentage dependence on post inspection; percentage conformance to quality standards
Employee morale	Percentage absenteeism
Leadership impact	Percentage cancelled meetings
Customer awareness	Percentage repeat orders; number of complaints

- focus on product cycle time and use throughput time as a measure of performance; and
- focus on bottlenecks in the production or service processes with a more appropriate emphasis on activities which alleviate bottlenecks.

The focus on throughput time and bottlenecks highlights the question of capacity and constraints in the production or service process. Capacity, and the associated availability of services to meet demand, may require management science techniques such as queuing theory to determine acceptable delays and appropriate provisions. Constraints require the identification of bottlenecks, together with stringent efforts to increase their efficiency and, potentially, inventory build-ups to ensure that idle time at the bottlenecks is avoided. The issue of interdependent events suggests that the use of productivity and utilization performance measures among non-bottleneck activities is pointless. Further, we may have to tolerate, or even encourage, idle time for these activities in order to prevent the build-up of unnecessary inventory.

Table 6.15 lists a number of non-financial measures which might prove useful in the analysis of time-related factors. The 'time' dimension of ABM has become such an important feature that a separate section is devoted to its operational aspects later, and to the theory of constraints here.

Theory of constraints

Goldratt and Cox (1986) developed the theory of constraints (TOC) as a technique to increase sales, and reduce inventory, by focusing on production scheduling. TOC is a consequence of criticism of the negative consequences of a cost focus in management accounting, particularly:

- the neglect of sales and operating costs by focusing totally on overheads;
- the neglect of throughput and optimum profitability by focusing on lowest cost per unit; and
- overproduction and the build-up of unnecessary inventory resulting from a focus on equipment efficiency.

TOC focuses on bottlenecks, targeting the single most binding constraint in the production process for action. Improved efficiencies elsewhere in the production process are deemed a waste of time and money, since they serve merely to build up queues and inventory in front of the bottlenecks. The focus on throughput, and increasing profitability by

TABLE 6.15

Non-financial measures of time

Area	Measure
Equipment failure	Time between failures
Maintenance effort	Time spent on repeat work
Throughput	Processing time/total time per unit
Production flexibility	Set-up time
Availability	Percentage stockouts
Labour effectiveness	Standard hours achieved/total hours worked
Customer impact	No. of overdue deliveries; mean delivery delay

generating more sales revenue per period, necessitates an appreciation of the interdependence of process events and the random fluctuations evident in processing times. Although 'breaking' a bottleneck involves additional equipment expenditure, increasing cost per unit, more finished product passes through the production process per period, allowing more to be sold. The 'drum–buffer–rope' mechanism is central to the Goldratt and Cox methodology, where the 'drum' is the constraint which governs the pace of production, the 'buffer' protects that binding constraint from disruption from other causes, and the 'rope' signals the release of materials.

Blackstone (2001) argues for closer communication between production and marketing departments. Awareness of the differences in 'throughput dollars per constraint' between products should allow salesmen to shift the focus away from products with the highest selling prices, or highest contribution margins, since these factors may not determine the optimum short-term product mix in practice.

The focus of throughput implementations is normally on the reduction of manufacturing cycle times – that is recognition that improving efficiencies in non-critical activities will not impact on overall throughput. Its impact is, therefore, necessarily short-term in nature. However, a number of authors (e.g., Carter and Hendrick, 1997; Chen and Kleiner, 2001: Buzby et al., 2002) emphasize that this oversimplifies the situation. They suggest that manufacturing cycle times may account for a very small proportion of total job flow time, and that the time spent in processing the customer purchase order will frequently exceed the product manufacturing time. They highlight that the next area of focus must be on the services which support manufacturing and an analysis of the links between cycle time and financial performance.

Consider, for example, the following case study, adapted from Darlington et al. (1992) Garrett Automotive illustration.

CASE STUDY

Orion Signalling: A TOC case study

Orion operates a manufacturing process with three sequential processes: A,B,C. Units of product pass through each of the processes where they are engineered by machines A, B, and either C or D. The current (stage 1) production flow is illustrated in Figure 6.5. Each process operates with a target schedule adherence of 80%. The plant operates a 125-hour week at 90% utilization (i.e., 112.5 usable hours). Weekly output is 2025 units. The bottleneck in process B restricts the total throughput to only 18 units per hour, even though process A and process C have the capacity to deal with many more (30 units/hour and 80 units/hour, respectively). The management at Orion wants to break the bottleneck in process B and increase the throughput.

CASE ANALYSIS

At stage 2 Orion invests in a new piece of equipment (machine E) at a cost of £6000 to relieve the pressure in process B. As a result a

CASE STUDY (cont.)

FIGURE 6.5

	Process A	Process B	Process C	Throughput
Stage 1	Machine A	Machine B	Machine C Machine D	18
	30 units/hr	18 units/hr	80 unit/hr	
Stage 2	Machine A	Machine B Machine E	Machine C Machine D	21
	30 units/hr	21 units/hr	80 unit/hr	
Stage 3	Machine A	Machine B Machine E Machine D	Machine C	24
	30 units/hr	24 units/hr	26 unit/hr	

Throughput at Orion Signalling

throughput of 21 units per hour can be achieved. At stage 3 Orion adapts a piece of machinery currently in use in process C (a non-bottleneck activity) at a cost of £2000 to increase the throughput further, even though process C will operate less efficiently. As a result a throughput of 24 units per hour can be achieved, and although process B remains the production bottleneck, process C is now a constraint on further improvements.

The changes in the production system mean that 2362 units are processed at stage 2 and 2700 units at stage 3. The increased throughput will have an immediate impact on cash flows as long as it is sold and not consigned to finished goods inventory.

The marginal cost per unit will be higher than at stage 1:

- £6000 invested to secure an additional 337 units per week throughput;
- £8000 invested to secure an additional 675 units per week throughput in total.

The whole process at stage 3 may appear less efficient in cost per unit terms than it did at stage 1. But manufacturing efficiency is measured to include unwanted units, those produced for inventory; throughput focuses on making the most of capacity to produce immediate sales. The interdependence of the process makes schedule adherence paramount. Orion must produce:

- the right amount;
- the right mix of components;
- on time.

Even so, with 80% schedule adherence in each of three consecutive processes the customer may only expect 51.2% adherence (i.e., $0.8 \times 0.8 \times 0.8$). Unscheduled production, in either quantity or mix is, therefore, potentially very disruptive.

There will be problems in implementing a bottleneck-breaking scheme like Orion's, when it is used simultaneously with a policy of eliminating inventory (except for buffers in front of bottleneck process B):

- It may become more difficult to identify bottlenecks in the future, especially as processes become more complex.
- Inventory reductions will give a one-off profit reduction.
- Reduced inventories will highlight new problems, most seriously those associated with suppliers unable to meet delivery schedules.
- Corporate culture must change by learning to accept the existence of idle time at non-bottleneck activities.

Innovation

'Innovation' may include pure and applied research, developmental applications, new product development, operational and process development and cost reduction techniques. Innovation is essential to the long-term survival of an enterprise and to the maintenance of its market share and competitive advantage. The uncertainty associated with innovation may make traditional management accounting systems inappropriate for a variety of reasons. Such systems may:

- focus on short-term financial performance, so having an adverse effect on products or processes at the early stages of their life cycle;
- use measurement indicators which, while suitable for mature products and processes, emphasize cost minimization to an extent unsuitable for new methods; and
- judge management performance on the basis of a manager's success in implementing cost-reduction strategies, with deleterious consequences on creativity and innovation.

These problems suggest the need for non-financial indicators which reflect the special requirements of innovation, including the ability to introduce new products, the flexibility to accommodate change, and a reputation for leading-edge operations. The special requirements of innovation necessitate the development of a new range of NFIs (Table 6.16).

The overlapping of the requirements and corresponding measures of cost, quality, time and innovation is inevitable, as is shown by the development of new accounting measures to monitor the effectiveness of companies in bringing new products to the market promptly. We might speculate that new product strategies will focus on the cost of lead times in bringing new product concepts to the market, in conjunction with the time taken to recover research and development and marketing expenditures from the projected sales of a quality product.

Existing measures of throughput are weak (see Waldron and Galloway, 1988) and demand more attention. Horngren et al. (1994) detail the break-even time (BET) measure developed by Hewlett Packard to measure market lead times and industry leadership. BET, a variation of the discounted payback procedure, measures the time which elapses between the initiation of a project and the time when the implemented project breaks even for the first time, that is, when the cumulative present value of cash inflows equals the cumulative present value of total cash outflows.

Shorter break-even periods, and lower BET values promote earlier sales revenue consistent with reduced product-to-market times. This accelerated product development also acts as an innovation indicator contributing to the company's competitive advantage.

BET therefore provides a dual indicator of lead time and innovation, and a potentially powerful measure. Innovation measures are often difficult to cite, partly because of difficulties associated with definitions of innovation. In practice, real-world problems often involve simultaneous concerns about costs, throughput and innovation.

Common issues in the implementation of each of the cost, quality, time and innovation strands of ABM are:

- the considerable demands on the time of those involved, necessitating widespread co-operation and total organizational involvement;
- the need for a commitment to change which must come from the top, especially if an unreceptive corporate culture needs to be overcome – an

TABLE 6.16

Non-financial measures of innovation

Area	Measure
Ability to introduce new products	Percentage product obsolescence; no. of new products launched; no. of patents secured; time to launch new products
Flexibility to accommodate change	No. of new processes implemented; no. of new process modifications
Reputation for innovation	Media recognition for leadership; expert assessment of competence; demonstrable competitive advantage

awareness that improvements are possible in the way in which we operate is a good starting point;

- the need for appropriate kinds of documentation and data which will, most likely, not exist, so that key drivers and non-financial indicators need to be determined and measured; and
- the need to identify cause and effect carefully with an eye to potentially damaging organizational and behavioural consequences.

Doubts have been expressed about the costs of changing to ABC and ABM systems, especially since studies to suggest that they generate sufficiently large bottom-line improvements in profitability are rare. There have still been far too few documented instances of success which take into account both the problems of implementation and the wider implications of an ABM environment.

INNOVATION AND THE ACTIVITY-BASED MANAGEMENT TRADE-OFF

Given the perceived needs of customers in terms of cost, quality, time and innovation, management accounting information systems must address drivers in each of these areas (see Table 6.12). Cost, quality and time have received much attention in the management accounting literature, innovation very little. The balanced scorecard (Kaplan and Norton, 1992, 1993, 1996, 2004) has raised the profile of innovation, and the factors driving innovation, by emphasizing new goals (new products and processes, technological advantage, manufacturing learning) and new performance measures (time to market, time to develop innovations, process time to maturity).

The focus on cost, quality and time has generated a plethora of management changes with significant accounting implications: activity analysis, ABC and BPR, where the accent is on cost, continuous improvement and TQM, where the concern is with quality; and JIT, throughput and TOC, where time is of interest. But it may not be possible to pursue innovation as a key success factor while simultaneously tackling the other three areas with the above tools. There may need to be a significant trade-off because of the conflicting cultures involved. Let us consider each in turn.

Cost

Traditional performance indicators and costing methodologies developed for mature products and processes may be unsuitable for new developments. Activity-based costing could be the enemy of product diversification. By burdening low-volume new products with punitive levels of overhead, ABC threatens the opportunities for successful innovation.

Where management performance is judged on success in the implementation of cost-reduction strategies, the long-run consequences for innovation and creativity could be devastating. Cost-reduction programmes based on drastically cutting head count may have a deleterious long-term effect because of the loss of skills and morale.

Quality

Possible cost–quality trade-offs are readily apparent where cost reduction strategies (and the short term) are seen to have greater priority than quality (and the long term). Eskildson (1995) notes that successful turnarounds are rarely, if ever, accomplished through numerous incremental improvements, and that the fundamental reasons underlying downturns are not quality, but high costs, excess debt, strategic errors and inventory control problems. He notes the many companies and divisions in the USA which have received the prestigious Malcolm Baldrige National Quality Award and have subsequently:

- failed;
- scaled back operations;
- downsized in quality management departments, because programme costs outweighed benefits;
- replaced their chairman because of substantial and sustained corporate losses; or
- expressed disillusionment with TQM.

Harari (1997) suggests ten reasons why TQM methods have failed business:

- The focus is on internal processes and not external results, so that forward-looking, customer-oriented improvements are subjugated by attention to current procedures. He notes that 'before we invested in TQM we turned out poorly made products that customers didn't want; now, after TQM, things have changed; we turn out well-made products that customers don't want'.
- The focus is on minimum standards – but zero defects is no longer enough; there needs to be an 'excitement' factor which generates customer preference. Quality alone may be losing its role as a differentiator between the top companies, with innovation growing in importance to take its place.
- TQM is much too bureaucratic. Involvement in a TQM implementation employing Deming's (1986) 14-stage procedure (or similar) can be a very frustrating experience. The sequence of painful meetings designed to progress from stage 2 to stage 4, say, is often too much for the participants; they start to vote with their feet or arrange other meetings which 'accidentally' coincide with the TQM timetable. Continuous improvement has its appeal, but even the mention of the TQM acronym may be sufficient to raise the barriers and the hackles.
- Quality cannot be delegated. Where quality becomes the domain of a 'champion' and does not receive support from the chief executive sufficient to ensure commitment, ownership, identification and involvement from all, then it is doomed to failure. Quality must become a normal part of everyone's job, at all levels, if it is to stand a chance of success.
- Radical organizational reform is rarely addressed, and the focus throughout is on small incremental changes. TQM is 'orderly, sequential, linear and predictable, while real quality emerges from a chaotic, disruptive, emotional process that tears the organization apart and then rebuilds it from the bottom up'.

- TQM is divorced from issues of management compensation. In traditional TQM schemes there is no link between quality achievements and reward systems, merely an appeal to the self-motivation of the individual. More realistically firms implementing TQM have adopted ingenious schemes to reward and encourage participation. For example, the awarding of 'points' to the participants of TQM teams based on the impact of a successful implementation; at year's end these points are aggregated and team members can use their points to buy items from a catalogue as a quasi-financial reward in a manner similar to airline frequent flyer schemes.

- TQM ignores the value chain and relationships with outside partners. Symptomatic of the internal navel-gazing, the focus on small improvements and blinkered value-adding may be losing sight of the long-term big picture and the interdependencies of modern business.

- TQM appeals to quick fixes with the minimum of confrontation, because it is often associated with small, even trivial, instances of change. Though the bureaucracy of the scheme is designed to slow the decision-making process down, to eliminate quick fixes, it may also constrain the generation of innovative alternatives because of the desire for a satisfactory short-term solution.

- TQM drains entrepreneurship and innovation from the corporate culture. Obsession with internal processes, the standardization and routinizing of internal procedures so that there is a single, acceptable 'right way', may slow down the development of path-breaking innovations. The 'do it right first time' stricture may be a dangerous long-term policy if it impairs organizational entrepreneurship and innovation. The paradox is one of TQM pursuing continuous improvement and zero defects with what it already has, while the organization needs to encourage risks and tolerate errors to create something new.

- TQM lacks excitement. It has become unemotional, detached and mechanical and may potentially facilitate the development of a matching corporate culture. Where the new challenge is to create an innovation culture within an organization to sustain high value-added operations in a global economy, then successful players are unlikely to have a TQM orientation.

If the conflict between TQM and innovation in the quality arena is apparent, does BPR fare any better? Some authors suggest that TQM and BPR can co-exist happily within most organizations, with continuous improvements taking place between radical changes, with both emphasizing customer focus, teamwork and empowerment. An alternative view suggests that morale among the survivors of BPR is so terminally damaged that the incentive to involve themselves in TQM is destroyed.

This alternative view is more widely accepted. Siew and Boon (1996) warn that the abandonment of traditional management control functions, like segregation of duties, in a BPR environment, may mean that by ignoring critical risks such systems will fail. With compression of responsibilities, empowerment of the workforce, reliance on external partnerships and reductions in checks and controls there will be fewer opportunities to control individuals and more reliance on self-management. In such an environment the development of an innovation culture may be difficult, and serious doubts arise about the compatibility of TQM and BPR.

Time

Improvement techniques such as JIT attempt to squeeze all of the variation out of a process so that there are fewer surprises. A rigid system pursuing a single 'right way' is unlikely to reinforce risk-taking, innovation and entrepreneurship. Interdependence of events means that normal variations in time and quality for sequential operations will reduce the overall rate of throughput below that of the slowest operation. Simplifications, standardization, conformity and adherence, terms all commonly linked with JIT, are not the words one would normally associate with an innovation culture.

The throughput approach, with its emphasis on those completed products actually sold, is more cash- than profit-based; it seeks to focus on the rate at which a product contributes money in an undeniably short-term manner. By focusing on bottleneck constraints and ignoring other binding constraints until they become bottlenecks, a tightly targeted approach for investment is enforced. This may encourage innovation in the short term by facilitating the search for alternative solutions to the bottleneck creating problem; it would discourage the random generation of innovative ideas which might have allowed improvements to take place in non-priority areas.

Teamwork and wholehearted commitment from the top are essential ingredients of the successful implementation of improvement schemes like TQM, ABC, JIT and TOC. Properly implemented JIT can be used to improve lead times and due date performance, TQM to improve interpersonal relations, ABC to provide non-financial data and TOC to provide a focus for the whole improvement process. But competent implementation requires a shift of the corporate culture to accommodate and encourage change.

The changes in corporate culture required to encourage organizational innovation are not necessarily the same. Evidence from Gosselin (1997) suggests that the most entrepreneurial of organizations are *not* the ones that fully incorporate administrative procedures like TQM and ABC, but are the ones that flirt with activity analysis and continuous improvement. He suggests that specific aspects of the organizational structure drive the adoption of accounting initiatives. The implication is that these firms are taking on the useful and creative aspects of the new tools, those that will aid their innovative pursuits, but are not interested in the bureaucracy or data burden associated with full adoption.

Until we are less uncertain about the best way to develop an innovation culture in our organizations, we might have to conclude that systems which encourage and facilitate new products and processes are not necessarily consistent with accounting innovations.

OPERATIONALIZING ACTIVITY-BASED MANAGEMENT: THE TIME DIMENSION

One of the major benefits of the focus on activity-based relationships has, not surprisingly, been the development of new non-financial measures. These may have been employed as cost drivers in activity-based costing but have a potentially wider application when they also impact on the quality, time and innovation dimensions.

Focus on product cycle time, throughput time, bottlenecks and delivery reliability highlights the need for new measures of operating performance and better indicators to measure delivery performance and the degree of operations interdependence. The use of some measure of 'set-ups' provides a useful illustration. Set-up times as a cost driver will inevitably penalize small batches and encourage larger batches. While set-up cost can be reduced through shorter set-up times, it can be more easily lowered by fewer set-ups, larger batches and consequently higher inventory levels. Reducing set-up times to make more set-ups possible provides a flexibility facilitating the meeting of customer requirements. But more product lines and smaller batches mean more non-productive set-up time. The congruence of production objectives and measurement implications must be ensured. Set-up times tend to ignore the question of dependence, both in terms of the way jobs are sequenced and backlogs generated, and in the way that set-up is a variable subject to the impact of special causes (e.g., unpredictable external factors) and common causes (e.g., random fluctuations within otherwise stable systems).

Just as the focus on the efficiency of machines may not be particularly useful in a sequence of operations, so may be set-up times. Increasing the efficiency of non-bottleneck operations incurs expense but also creates spare capacity and unnecessary units of production. Similarly, the consequences of a set-up on a bottleneck operation, with the generation of idle time in a constraining activity, will far outweigh that on a non-bottleneck activity.

Recognition of the existence of a bottleneck where demand exceeds supply for a resource, and the focus on processing time, leads naturally to a consideration of throughput, and throughput accounting. Throughput accounting represents a movement away from ABC, since it is not concerned with overhead costs, and represents a movement towards ABM, the time taken to generate profits and the rate at which raw materials are turned into sales. It identifies selling price, sales volume and material cost as the three key variables determining profitability and focuses on product flow, by treating overheads and labour costs as fixed in the short term. As with the linear programming approach to the solution of product-mix problems, throughput focuses on scarce resources and the relative contribution per unit of such resources for each product. As a result, a single bottleneck activity will usually become the focus of attention. Other binding constraints will exist, but these will only become bottlenecks, in the future, as a result of successful investment in overcoming prior bottlenecks. A number of consequences of throughput focus quickly become apparent:

- It is pointless investing resources in order to increase the efficiency of non-bottleneck resources. This will not improve throughput until the bottleneck activity has first been attacked.
- Queues will develop in front of bottlenecks which increase production lead time. However, such inventory provides an essential buffer to eliminate the possibility of idle time in the bottlenecks.
- Throughput will reduce inventory and work in process, making efficient JIT procedures and reliable supplier relationships essential.
- Lower inventory will mean fewer overheads available for carrying forward under absorption costing and a likely negative impact on short-term profits.

CASE STUDY

Crustybake Pies: A throughput case study

Crustybake Pies is a small food manufacturer which produces two varieties of catering-size pie – meat (X) and vegetarian (Y). Each type of pie undergoes six separate operations in the production process, using the same equipment resources but requiring different amounts of time in each resource. Resource capacity, material costs, selling price and operating time are all detailed in Table 6.17. These figures allow the calculation of relative contribution per unit for each of the products.

A linear programming (LP) problem for the determination of optimum product mix of the two pies will maximize contribution (π) subject to the operating constraints. (There are many PC-based LP programs available commercially; even spreadsheet software, such as Excel's 'Solver' function, facilitates the solution to small problems like this one.)

The aim to maximize contribution yields an objective function, $\pi = 5X + 3.20Y$, which is to be as large as possible, subject to the time capacity constraints:

$$0.10X + 0.20Y < 6500 \quad \text{(for operation 1)}$$
$$0.30X + 0.15Y < 6000 \quad \text{(for operation 2)}$$
$$0.15X + 0.30Y < 9600 \quad \text{(for operation 3)}$$
$$0.20X + 0.25Y < 8000 \quad \text{(for operation 4)}$$
$$0.40X + 0.30Y < 9600 \quad \text{(for operation 5)}$$
$$0.10X + 0.20Y < 7000 \quad \text{(for operation 6)}.$$

TABLE 6.17

Resource capacity at Crustybake Pies

	Operations time (hours per unit)						
Products	1	2	3	4	5	6	Total (Hours)
X	0.10	0.30	0.15	0.20	0.40	0.10	1.25
Y	0.20	0.15	0.30	0.25	0.30	0.20	1.40
Capacity	6500	6000	9600	8000	9600	7000	

	Material Cost (£)	Labour Cost (£/Hr)	Selling Price (£)	Direct Costs (Material & labour)	Contribution (£/Unit)
Products					
X	5	12	25	20	5.00
Y	5	12	25	21.80	3.20

CASE STUDY (cont.)

Since we cannot produce *minus* quantities of product, we also have two non-negativity constraints, $X \leq 0$ and $Y \leq 0$. The above matrix yields only two binding constraints (operations 2 and 5) and three potential optimum combinations as corner points on the feasible region of available combinations:

- option A, where $X = 0$ and $Y = 32,000$;
- option B, where $X = 12,000$ and $Y = 16,000$;
- option C, where $X = 20,000$ and $Y = 0$.

Examination of the objective function reveals the total contribution from the three alternatives to be £102,400 from option A, £111,200 from option B and £100,000 from option C. So the LP solution suggests that the optimum product mix is $X = 12,000$ and $Y = 16,000$, a total production of 28,000 units per time period.

A closer inspection of the maximum possible throughput of product for the sequence of operation reveals:

Products	Operations time (hours per unit)					
	1	2	3	4	5	6
X	65,000	20,000	64,000	40,000	24,000	70,000
Y	32,000	40,000	32,000	32,000	32,000	35,000

CASE ANALYSIS

For each of the three options A, B and C above there are only two binding constraints. Only operations 2 and 5 are used to capacity, providing an effective constraint on production. Considerable excess capacity exists in each of the remaining operations. Operation 2 is the production bottleneck, restricting the throughput of product X to the marketplace to a maximum of 20,000 units per period.

Although product X has a superior profit contribution to that of product Y, and a combination of X and Y yields a greater contribution per batch than producing Y alone, it is possible to bring more of product Y to the marketplace (32,000 units) than of X and Y together. Sales revenue would be optimized by producing/selling 32,000 units of Y (yielding £800,000) rather than the optimum X, Y combination (revenue of £700,000). We can process twice as many units of Y (40,000) through the bottleneck operation 2 as of X (20,000). But the constraints in successive operations restrict the output per period to only 32,000. A throughput approach would justify a switch to product Y if the faster processing allowed more units to be marketed and sold, despite the lower contribution per unit. The approach is, therefore, more cash- than profit-based, seeking to focus on the rate at which the product contributes money, but might be justified were 'sales revenue maximization' the preferred strategic goal.

LP yields a static solution based on several inflexible assumptions. It ignores set-up times between operations, variation in the time taken to complete operations and the intricacies of job scheduling.

CASE STUDY (cont.)

Scheduling complexities may lead to substantial operating delays, especially where we have more than two products all relying on the same equipment resources and competing for processing time. Each batch – 32,000 of Y, or 16,000 of Y with 12,000 of X – will take a total of 9600 hours to process but delays will occur at operations 2 and 5, the effective constraints on production. The mixed product, within the batch, can be brought to the market quicker through an X followed by Y sequence (1.65 hours) compared to 1.7 hours for two of product Y, as illustrated by Figure 6.6. The mixed product (X, Y) system has material queuing in front of the binding constraints (operations 2 and 5) whereas the single product (Y, Y) system has idle time in the bottleneck resource (operation 2).

If we had treated the production of products X and Y as multiple events, instances of fluctuation in operating time might have averaged out. But where, as here, one event cannot take place until the

FIGURE 6.6

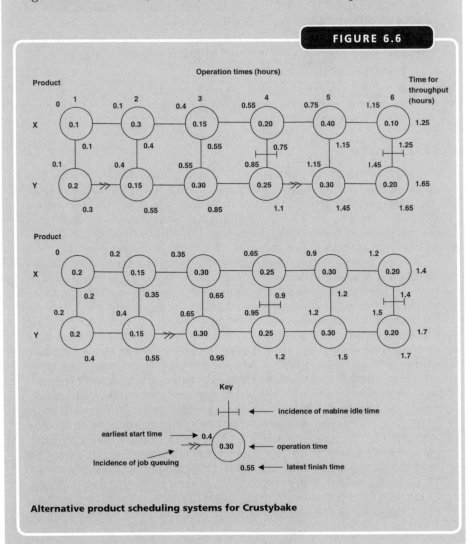

Alternative product scheduling systems for Crustybake

completion of another, the fluctuations will accumulate. With product queuing for machine availability, coupled with enforced machine idle time, inventory will increase and throughput will be reduced. Even with a balanced system, random fluctuations will cause the variation of operating time to be determined by the maximum variation of the preceding operations. Interdependence will continue to increase inventory levels and reduce throughput unless we reduce the level of variation applicable to particular operations, or create idle time by stopping that non-bottleneck part of the line in which the inventory build-up is occurring, to allow the bottleneck activities to catch up. Knowledge of the process and the statistical implications of operation dependencies are essential if bottlenecks are to be managed effectively.

Throughput time and project lead time are frequently the variables to which project outcomes are most sensitive. We need to estimate both the likelihood of delays (as part of a risk management strategy) and their financial impact (as part of an analysis of the sensitivity of returns). There may be some scope for varying the order in which the project is completed or the amount of resources each component consumes. Either way, we need to know the alternatives available and be aware of their costs and benefits, as part of our detailed analysis. Trend diagrams, Gantt charts, network and critical path analysis are all useful techniques to assist choices concerning timing and associated costs.

The most common form of individual scheduling problem, for both batch and process production flows, is job shop scheduling (JSS). This is characterized by the ordering and allocation of multiple jobs (n) to alternative machines (m). There are a very large number of alternative schedules even for a relatively small number of jobs to be processed (e.g., the scheduling of only five jobs on three machines produces $(5!)^3$ or 1.7 million alternatives).

In practice, technological restrictions and the existence of specified processing routes will reduce the number of alternatives. Jobs may be sequentially ordered (with all jobs subject to the same procedures in the same sequence), sequentially broken-ordered (so that certain jobs miss out certain stages) or randomly assigned (non-sequential and non-ordered). Even so, the feasible set of alternatives is still usually too large for complete enumeration and results in the adoption of heuristics to provide satisfactory solutions. These short-cut rules generate alternative schedules which may be judged on their achievement of particular targets, for example:

- minimum time to complete the entire current job schedule (makespan time);
- minimum number of jobs in progress;
- minimum waiting time for jobs in the queue; and
- minimum lateness of completion (i.e., delivery date minus due date).

Scheduling problems can be represented graphically or through networks, similar to those used in the Crustybake Pies example. Calculations of expected completion time are complicated both by the variability in job processing times and the interdependence of jobs and machines. Unless both jobs in process and machines are free simultaneously then a delay will result because one is waiting for the other. This is characterized by either machine idle time or job queuing. These complications are identical to those associated with earliest start/latest finish time for sequential projects. Although heuristic rules are rarely developed from scientific principles, they are generally better than intuition and may provide optimum solutions in specific circumstances. A number of commonly employed rules of thumb (heuristics) exist for the ordering of jobs:

- first come, first served (FCFS);
- shortest operating time (for entire job) first (SOT);
- shortest operating time (for first processing operation) first (SPT);
- longest operating time (for first operation) first (LOT)
- critical ratio method (work content ÷ time remaining available) lowest (C/T)

Simulation-based research has shown that adoption of the SOT rule will, on average, minimize the targets specified above. But it may have some socially unacceptable disadvantages, in that some jobs may remain in the queue for a very long time! A truncated SOT rule may, therefore be necessary in practice so that normal priorities can be overridden to bring a job to the front of the queue if it has been in the system longer than a specified time. This could be accomplished less arbitrarily by using C/T as a priority index in conjunction with the normal SOT rule. This would allow higher priority to attach to a job as its due date approaches, but complicates the single-rule method.

Consider another simple numerical example: a manufacturer, Ashby Furnishings, processing an order for three different styles of chair, designated jobs 1, 2 and 3 respectively. Each of the jobs passes through the same operations in the same order, but each makes different requirements of the resource. Job 1 requires 5 hours in cutting, 6 hours in machining and 3 hours in staining and polishing. Job 2 requires 4 hours in cutting, 3 hours in machining and 4 hours in staining and polishing. Job 3 requires 6 hours in cutting, 3 hours in machining and another 3 hours in staining and polishing. The minimum time to process each job separately, independent of the requirements of the others, is, therefore, 14 hours, 11 hours and 12 hours, respectively.

Ashby's target time for the completion of all three jobs is 16 hours, but they wish to minimize total throughput time while at the same time ensuring that machine idle time, job waiting time and job delivery times are as low as possible. They are investigating alternative job schedules.

The Gantt chart, detailed in Figure 6.7, shows how resources are consumed and jobs completed relative to the horizontal time scale. It provides a means of facilitating job scheduling, but one which might be improved upon with a matrix approach. The latter shows waiting time, resource slack and the completion times for each separate operation more clearly. Figure 6.8 shows the outcome of adopting the FCFS scheduling rule processing the jobs 1, 2 and 3 in that order. It shows all jobs to be completed within 21 hours using the FCFS (i.e., 1–2–3) rule, but with the incurrence of both machine idle time and job queuing time. Job 2 must wait for 2 hours for the availability of resource B (machining), and spare capacity of 1 hour exists in machining while it waits for job 3 to clear cutting. Both jobs 2 and 3 fail to meet the target time of 16 hours; job 2 is 2 hours late and job 3 is 5 hours late (i.e., 3.5 hours per late job on average).

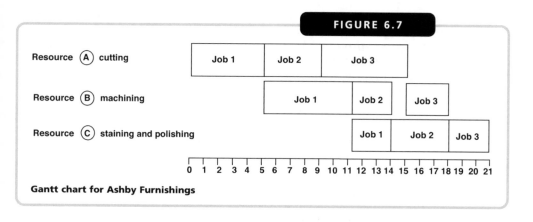

FIGURE 6.7

Gantt chart for Ashby Furnishings

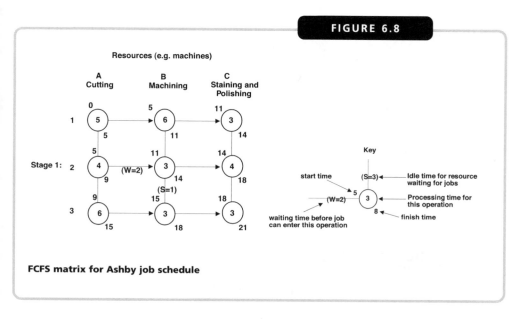

FIGURE 6.8

FCFS matrix for Ashby job schedule

Several more heuristics might be employed to schedule these jobs, with the following results. The SOT (2–3–1) rule results in:

- a total processing time of 24 hours;
- waiting time of 0 hours;
- idle time of 7 hours (5 in B and 2 in C); and
- only job 2 fails to meet the delivery target, but it is 8 hours late.

The SPT (2–1–3) rule processes the Jobs 2, 1, 3 and results in:

- a total processing time of 21 hours;
- waiting time of 0 hours;
- idle time of 6 hours (2 in B and 4 in C); and
- both job 1 and job 3 failing to meet delivery target, being 2 hours and 5 hours late, respectively.

None of the other alternatives, 1–3–2, 3–1–2 or 3–2–1, results in a total throughput time of less than 21 hours. In choosing between FCFS and the widely used SPT scheduling, Ashby must rank their requirements for minimizing job queuing time or machine utilization. Similar matrix-based approaches can be employed in the analysis of larger projects and capital expenditures. Thus, network techniques represent the jobs by nodes and designate the schedule sequence with arrows for an 'activity on node' approach, or vice versa for an 'activity on arrow' approach like critical path analysis or the programme evaluation review technique. Whichever method is employed, they all recognize the same basic features:

- the time taken to complete the operation;
- the earliest time at which the operation may start;
- the latest time at which the operation may finish; and
- the interdependence and sequencing of operations.

Realistic problems acknowledge that in practice all of these are variables because:

- time to complete will follow a distribution with a mean and standard deviation. The degree of acceptable variation will be critical to the progress of the project;
- time to complete an activity may be reduced by employing additional resources; and
- the degree of interdependence might be influenced by additional equipment and/or job flexibility to reduce bottlenecks.

We now consider a case which highlights the problems arising when a company lacks clear strategic goals or the management accounting control procedures to supply the information necessary to monitor or direct the progress of the business. It provides the opportunity to identify and correct serious bottleneck problems.

CASE STUDY

Lincoln Furniture: An ABM case study

Lincoln is a manufacturer of high-quality lounge suites run by its two directors, the husband-and-wife team of Eileen and Paul Hayton. The company produces leather and fabric output in its Norwich factory and operates exclusively on a factory-direct basis in East Anglia and through appointed agents and retailers in the South of England. They have no other outlets in East Anglia other than the factory showroom.

The company has been established for 10 years and recently moved to purpose-built accommodation adjacent to its original site to coincide with a rapid expansion into the South East and the markets of western Europe. While producing a range of standard lounge suites, its output is largely market-led, with the great majority of suites produced in response to orders. With the exception of minimal showroom requirements, no suites are specifically produced for stock and three product lines account for nearly 90% of total production. The goal of avoiding mass production techniques has allowed the company to stay small, employing only eight full-time staff: two in the frameshop; one in the cutting room; one in sewing;

CASE STUDY (cont.)

and four in upholstery. Each of the staff works a standard 40-hour week and each of the processes functions independently, apart from the matching up of orders at the sewing and upholstering stages.

Each suite, whether fabric or leather, undergoes four production stages. In the frameshop, the frame is constructed, assembled and polished; in the cutting department, fabric and/or leather is cut to size, ready to be sewn in the sewing shop; in upholstery the webbing is fixed to the frame, the foam cut to shape, the fabric and foam combined and the result stapled to the frame. The employee mix and inflexibility of functions effectively governs Lincoln's productive capacity. The maximum number of units of output for each process over a three-week cycle is:

Frame-making 60 (120 hours × 2 employees @ 4 hours per suite),
Cutting   15 (120 hours × 1 employee @ 8 hours per suite),
Sewing   15 (120 hours × 1 employee @ 8 hours per suite),
Upholstery   34 (120 hours × 4 employees @ 14 hours per suite).

The directors are keen to expand their presence in the South East further and can accommodate the additional four or five production staff that this would require without significant capital expenditure outlays. Currently they are only operating at 70% of maximum productive capacity.

Lincoln has no formal stock control records or procedures. Orders for leather and fabric are placed in response to orders, and availability of materials is generally good (about one week) with the exception of local materials (lead time greater than four weeks). No economic order levels are set for materials and consumables and just-in-time manufacturing procedures have never been considered appropriate. Therefore stock-outs, and consequent disruptions to the production process, have been known to occur because of minimal stocks of raw materials, and, despite this, work in progress, in the form of assembled frames and sewn materials, is very high and consistent with mass production manufacturing techniques. The standard suite produced comprises a two-seater settee and two armchairs. Production scheduling is on a three-week cycle with local sales requirements completed in week 1, those for the South East and western Europe in weeks 2 and 3. This schedule is consistent with the existing three-week period between deliveries to customers in the South East and overseas, but imposes constraints which are contributing to the company's existing cash-flow problems.

Full absorption costing is employed at present so that factory overhead (including an idle capacity allowance) and general overheads are incorporated. The hourly direct labour charge would thus be calculated as follows:

	£
Direct labour	12.00
Factory overhead @ 45%	5.40
General overhead @ 125%	15.00
	32.40

CASE STUDY (cont.)

Standard direct material costs, including a 10% wastage allowance, are added to these direct labour costs when the product is initiated, but no subsequent comparison is made with actual costs. The existing accounting system at Lincoln classifies all consumables and electricity as cost of goods sold. This, together with absence of recognition of the closing values of work in process and finished goods, contributes to reported losses in net profits.

The nature of the business, with a standard selling price in excess of £6000 per unit, dictates that the majority of sales are on credit. Bad debts are rare, but most debtors are converted into cash in a period ranging from 60 to 120 days. This long delay contributes to the cash-flow problems of the company; the debt ratio (calculated as total liabilities/total assets) has blown out to 100%, and retailers in the South East (responsible for 70% of sales) are seen to be the major culprits. But the directors are wary of pressurizing debtors for fear of losing business in a sensitive and competitive market. The directors acknowledge that the cash-flow problem did not exist prior to the South East and European marketing ventures.

The growth in sales is not being matched with corresponding profits, and the directors wish to examine the strategic alternatives available to Lincoln which make the management controls in place consistent with the goals of the company.

CASE ANALYSIS

The fundamental problem the company faces is an absence of accurate, reliable and relevant information upon which sound decisions can be made and the appropriate action taken. The specific problems that can be identified, detailed below, can be considered to be symptoms of this major deficiency.

Tracking systems

Under the existing system, there is no method of monitoring each order through the various stages of production. The business is unable to ascertain what stage a particular order is at, or the amount of resources used at any time during the production process. This creates difficulties in determining the actual costs of production, the timing and volumes of inventory required, and prevents the identification of factors that inhibit efficient production processes. The net effect is to reduce profitability and place unnecessary strain on cash flows.

Inventory and work in progress

Lincoln have no formal stock control records or procedures. The availability of materials is subject to fluctuations and leads to stockouts and disruptions in the production process. Bottlenecks in the production process add to the inventory problems. Differences in output capacity have resulted in inventory (work in progress) levels increasing at a disproportionate rate at each stage of the production process. The absence of any recording or monitoring system prevents management from recognizing this problem.

Staffing mix

The present design of the manufacturing process constitutes a poorly organized, uncoordinated and segmented mass production line. This is contrary to the directors' stated desire of seeking a quality handcrafted product. Failures to staff and monitor work-flow correctly have resulted in constantly increasing inventory levels.

The present staffing arrangements, detailed below, highlight two significant bottlenecks in the production process:

Process	Frameshop	Cutting	Sewing	Upholstery
Standard hours	4	8	8	14
Number of employees	2	1	1	4

Bottlenecks occur at the end of the frame-making and sewing processes. For each unit the upholstery section is able to complete, the sewing section completes 1.75 units and the frameshop 3.5 units. Because each unit operates independently of the capacity of the following unit the inventory accumulation and associated problems are inevitable.

Debtor management

Since expanding into the South East the company has experienced long delays in payments from these clients, and this has con-tributed to the cash-flow problems. While bad debts are rare, most debtors are converted into cash in a period ranging from 60 to 120 days; such a debt collection period is likely to be higher than the industry average. However, the directors are reluctant to pressure the debtors for earlier payment for fear of losing business in a sen-sitive and competitive market.

Gearing

The debt ratio of 100% implies that the company has a minimal equity component and is almost totally financed by borrowings. The directors' apparent reluctance to reinvest a portion of the annual profits back into the firm to reduce existing borrowings or build up working capital hampers the company's financial flexibility by making a further injection of capital a pressing need.

CASE STUDY (cont.)

Costing systems

The full absorption costing method used by the firm allocates costs on the basis of factory and general overheads, direct labour, and wastage and idle capacity allowances. This methodology does not provide the business with the capacity to identify the costs associated with each product line and each market. The absence of any effective order tracking mechanism also prevents the business from comparing actual production costs with forecast production costs, upon which the selling price is based.

By not being able to discriminate between costs, or make the comparison between projected and actual costs, management is unable to determine accurately the profitability of each product and each market. The ramifications impact directly on the long-term viability of the business.

Financial reporting

The current accounting system does not follow recognized accounting procedures. The absence of critical items in the financial analysis and a lack of consistency in recording other details (e.g., recognition of revenue and expense items) will provide a distorted view of the company's profitability.

Even after allowing for work in progress, the company's profit will still be understated due to an apparent inconsistency in recognizing revenue and expense items. Had revenue been recognized when the delivery contract was complete and not upon receipt of the actual funds, recorded profit for the period would be much higher. This recognition problem would have been accentuated with the move into the South East market where debtors are taking between 60 and 120 days to effect payment.

These deficiencies in the company's financial reporting systems prevent the business from being able to draw accurate conclusions from previous data, or forecast future trends with any degree of certainty. Distorted quarterly profit figures will result in incorrect decisions being made by internal and external users of the information.

Customer satisfaction

Long delivery times and unacceptable wastage rates may detract significantly from customer service perceptions. Expenditure on advertising is considerable and its effectiveness requires a detailed evaluation. There is no evidence of the business undertaking any market research or monitoring what they are selling, where, or to whom. There appears to be little monitoring of information at any level relevant to the effective functioning of the business.

RECOMMENDATIONS

The directors of Lincoln Furniture have a myopic perception of the overall company situation. This is highlighted by the failure to acknowledge and respond to the ever increasing levels of work in progress, evidenced by the quantity of furniture frames that has built up in the factory. The directors need to take an overall perspective of the company's position and determine:

- its objectives;
- the information and strategies necessary to support these objectives; and
- the systems necessary to provide the required information.

The following suggestions assist the directors in implementing recommended actions and also address each of the immediate concerns detailed above.

Tracking systems

The ability to track orders and monitor inventory levels through the production process is critical to managing issues such as quality, timeliness, costs and production problems. The current system is disjointed and has contributed to the current unsatisfactory situation. In particular, the existing system does not provide a comparison between actual and forecast costs incurred in the production of a lounge suite or highlight the inventory stockpiling problems.

The company should invest in a computerized monitoring system for orders and inventory levels, to provide meaningful information on which production and pricing decisions can be made.

Inventory and work in progress

It is inevitable that new financial and non-financial performance measures will be required in the provision of a modified management accounting information system.

One alternative to clear the inventory stockpiles and improve both profitability and cash flows in the immediate future is for the frameshop, the cutting section and the sewing section to stop producing until the upholstery section has been able to clear the backlog of frames and sewing output. If the staff involved in the frame-making, cutting and sewing sections have the necessary skills to assist in the upholstery section then they can be directed to this area. If they cannot be of assistance and cannot add value to the firm while waiting for the upholstery section to clear the backlog, then consideration can be given to clearing any accrued leave entitlements. Alternatively, they might participate in training that will enable them to assist in other aspects of the production process on future occasions.

Casual or temporary staff could be used in the upholstery section to correct the imbalance and increase the level of output above the other sections. This will overcome the need to stop production in the other sections and will lead to a reduction in inventories. The completion of a larger number of ordered lounge suites sooner than expected will assist in resolving the cash-flow and profitability concerns. Such an arrangement would require the redeployment of

CASE STUDY (cont.)

one frame maker to bring this section into line with the sewing and cutting sections.

Staffing mix

A longer-term and more permanent solution requires a restructuring of the staffing mix in the production process to remove bottlenecks. Such a restructuring could also include the company's plans to recruit more staff to lift output levels.

The current staffing mix might be restructured accordingly:

Process	Frameshop	Cutting	Sewing	Upholstery
Standard hours	8	8	8	8
Number of employees	1	1	1	7

This revised staffing mix requires one frame maker to be reassigned to the upholstery section, with training as appropriate, and an additional two upholsterers to be employed. Under this structure bottlenecks are removed and each section is completing a unit as it is required by the following section.

A commitment to multi-skilling employees, where possible, in each section will also assist in maintaining the production process during periods of absenteeism.

Debtor management

Apparently Lincoln does not want to pressurize retailers in the South East market for fear of losing business. However, it may undertake other measures to help improve debtor collections. Discounts may be offered for prompt payment. The debt collection period would be reduced if debtors were to take advantage of the discounts, and this would have a positive effect on cash flow.

Prior to offering discounts to all debtors a closer examination of individual debtors may isolate particular problem areas. These may then be addressed by offering selected discounts or applying other measures considered appropriate. The company could enter into an arrangement with a finance company or bank to provide loans to purchasers. This would alleviate the need for the company to carry the funding costs associated with the purchase of lounge suites, providing immediate cash flows plus a commission.

Gearing

The highly geared nature of the company supports a recommendation that the directors re-examine the company's funding mix. In particular, serious consideration should be given to using a portion of future profits to clear lending commitments which have an adverse effect on liquidity. Depending on the directors' resources, they may even consider an injection of equity or a directors' loan to improve liquidity.

Costing systems

The directors must re-evaluate the effectiveness of the existing costing systems and methodology. The basic need is for a system that divides costs into appropriate manageable components while providing sufficient detail, in an easily understood format, to enable quality decisions to be made.

In order to assess the relevance of any costing method the directors might consider these fundamental reasons for developing a costing system:

- valuation of inventory for financial and tax reporting;
- control of resources required and consumed;
- determining costs associated with each product and each market; and
- to understand how costs are incurred in the business in order to plan the introduction and design of new products or variations to current products.

Financial reporting

The directors should adopt a financial accounting system that conforms to standard accounting practices and procedures. This would include a consistent approach to the timing of recognition of revenues and expenses and incorporate all relevant details, such as work in progress, in the profit and loss statement.

Customer satisfaction

Many of the problems in this area arise from the physical location of the business and the rapid international expansion. With 70% of company sales occurring in the South East and further expansion planned in these markets and those overseas, a relocation strategy might be considered. The analysis would need to consider quantitative effects such as profitability and also qualitative issues. These qualitative issues would require an analysis of the firm's goals, the attitudes of the directors and their families to relocation and the likely loss of experienced staff who know the company and its products.

The key requirement for any recommended system change is to consider the individual requirements of Lincoln Furniture and the skills and abilities of the directors and staff. Any new systems must be accepted by the people involved and provide useful information that can be easily interpreted. The principal objective is to generate relevant, reliable and accurate information to enable decisions to be made that are in the best interests of the company.

VALUE-ADDED MANAGEMENT

Value-added management (VAM) is concerned with the identification and elimination of all non-value-adding, and thus wasteful, activity in the manufacturing process. As such it focuses principally on the following:

- *Overproduction*. This leads to wasteful stock build-ups, often deliberate or attributable to production planning errors.
- *Waiting*. Job queues and excessive work in progress.
- *Transportation*. Time spent transporting materials or product.
- *Inventory*. The level of stockholding, including safety stocks and often attributable to excessive batch sizes.
- *Motion*. Non-value-adding movement of materials or products.
- *Defects*. The production of sub-standard items and their reworking.
- *Unused creativity*. Ignoring feedback from the shop floor.

VAM is concerned with maximizing the processing time spent adding value to the product and minimizing the effects of each of the above. It aims to remove, or at least reduce, the wasted effort associated with delays (i.e., inventory), excess (scrap) and unevenness (overtime). The identification and elimination of the causes of such waste require the co-operation of everyone in the organization. The whole VAM system can be thought of as comprising three sub-systems:

- *Just-in-time*. The reduction of wasteful lead time.
- *Total employee involvement (TEI)*. The co-operation and creative involvement of the workforce.
- *Quality control (QC)*. The attempt to achieve a zero-defect objective.

The systems are not mutually exclusive, but might be considered as overlapping features of the purchasing and production aspects of operations.

McIlhattan (1987) suggests that senior management efforts are disproportionately devoted to direct labour costs, even though they usually account for less than 10% of total manufacturing costs, with an inappropriately small amount of time devoted to the control of material and overhead costs. Williams et al. (1995) suggest that this might be an overstatement, in that manufacturing remains labour-intensive, typically accounting for 30% of costs and 70% of value added, with figures of 10% for labour costs attributable to standard costing methods hiding indirect labour on the one hand, and the labour costs included within materials on the other hand. Both agree that the great majority of the lead time associated with a product adds *cost* but *no value* to the product, with the great majority of the time spent in queuing and waiting (through activities such as handling, moving, picking, inspecting, counting and monitoring). Williams et al. (1995) highlight the manner in which management accounting in the manufacturing environment has become out of touch with engineering practice. They welcome the initiatives due to the likes of Cooper and Kaplan, but criticize their focus, on the grounds that we need to devote more attention to the real problems than to more arbitrary allocations. They note that while materials typically account for 50% of manufacturing costs, these can be controlled through improved attention to design issues and supplier relations.

Neely et al. (2003) observe that as companies outsource more and more of their non-core activities, so suppliers become increasingly important stakeholders, making performance measures to monitor supplier relationships vital. Their absence from the normal balanced scorecard framework is not tolerable, though its absence from the original 1992 framework may be excusable on the grounds of 'changing business circumstances' over the last 20 years.

VAM is concerned with attacking this non-value-added waste and reducing total lead time. The great benefit of a line of attack directed at non-value-adding activities is that it is usually a low-cost option. The disadvantage is that it requires a change of attitude away from the traditional 'us and them' employee–management confrontation.

Traditionally, accounting procedures measure organizational performance on the basis of the three Es of evaluation:

- *Efficiency*. The utilization of equipment and the efficiency of the workforce.
- *Economy*. The optimum use of material.
- *Effectiveness*. The achievement of target outcomes.

Such measures are more concerned with the productivity of the business than with throughput. There is no normal measure of the flow of materials (hence the perseverance of the use of progress chasers). Little emphasis is placed on the reduction of lead times and the time spent to transform material into product.

The use of traditional daily monitoring measures may be inappropriate and misleading, with the benefits of changed processes only apparent at year end. Apparently 'inefficient' operations (where less time is spent in production, with more product change-overs) may in practice be the most appropriate. The management accountant has a duty to act positively with respect to five key issues:

1 Existing performance indicators are inadequate, placing too much emphasis on short-term profitability to the exclusion of non-financial aspects. Traditional budget variances should no longer be the focus of attention; more emphasis needs to be devoted to non-financial measures, including such factors as elapsed time, distance moved, space occupied, number of different part numbers and variances concerned with quality, cycle time and product complexity. (See Chapter 8 for a detailed consideration of non-financial indicators.)
2 The response of accountants in providing feedback to manufacturers is too slow. Too often decisions are based on incomplete or misleading information, so that product costings, product mix and pricing are all inappropriate. The allocation of overhead costs to products in other than an arbitrary manner remains an unsolved problem. Clearly, direct labour and direct materials are no longer appropriate bases under a JIT production system. Non-volume-related overhead allocation bases (as discussed in Chapter 6) may be the answer, but more work needs to be done in this area, especially in small businesses and the service sector.
3 Performance measurement should not be relative to industry averages, since this increases the acceptability of non-optimum levels of achievement. The aim should always be 100% perfection. Similarly, the focus on standard cost comparisons and variance reporting should be rejected as

lacking decision-usefulness. Indeed, if we adopt a 'get it right first time' philosophy we might be able to eliminate variance analysis totally.

4 Wherever possible, actual costs should be substituted for standard costs. Less concern should be shown for labour and equipment utilization, and more should be shown for maximizing the value added aspects of production.

5 The accounting system must provide an appropriate, decision-useful information back-up to the manufacturing process which does not rely excessively on externally reported financial information. That is, there must be a timely, relevant and reliable management information system.

Unfortunately, there is some credence to the view that existing accounting measures actually work contrary to VAM by encouraging waste. Thus:

- standard costs institutionalize waste and idle time within expectations;
- cost centres direct attention away from improvement opportunities and cost reductions;
- absorption costing encourages excess inventory by allowing production for stock to contribute to income;
- labour efficiency variances encourage more output, and potentially over-production, in the cause of the productivity of the workforce;
- price variances encourage bulk-buying and unnecessarily increase inventory;
- machine utilization rates encourage the pursuit of equipment productivity, with consequential overproduction and overstocking; and
- scrap cost rates encourage costly reworks in order to avoid measured scrap outcomes.

The three VAM components – JIT, TEI and QC – form a single overlapping system, rather than three completely separate areas. We consider TEI in Chapter 7, within our 'people' focus, so we now turn to a more detailed discussion of the other two components and their mutual interaction.

Just-in-time

The advent of JIT manufacturing systems has created an attitude among many management accountants which places undue emphasis on stock control methods. JIT should be considered as part of the wider VAM process of value-added management, in which attitudinal changes are central to the development of more efficient management processes and generate the adoption of more decision-useful management accounting measures.

JIT is a production technique aimed at manufacturing and delivering components in a production line immediately they are needed by processes further down the line. JIT is dedicated to the notion of zero defects and reduced buffer stocks through the search for continuous improvement in operational control. Ultimately, under JIT, customer orders might be expected to initiate a demand pull, rather than demand-pushing the manufacture of goods.

JIT is, therefore, much more than a vendor–supplier relationship, though this is important. Reduction of inventory by insisting that suppliers hold on to materials until required simply transfers the problem to the supplier and may, in the longer term, induce financial distress, and possibly failure, in trading partners.

Overall, JIT is concerned with the generation of increased profit, increased cash flow, and better-quality goods through a reduction in material costs. Lower inventory can be achieved only through co-operation with suppliers, not by attempts to exploit their apparent dependency.

There are two important aspects of JIT: inventory and supplier relationships.

Inventory

The use of buffer stocks provides a production safety net – but at a cost. The stock provides a breathing space for the unexpected and for management incompetence but consumes valuable work-space and incurs additional and unnecessary interest payments. Work in progress should be reduced, but slowly, so that the consequent problems which arise can be identified and solved. The gradual reduction of inventory allows the solution of the core problems for which the inventory was originally being stocked.

The adoption of traditional economic order quantity principles dictates large batches in order to attract discounts, so that change-over times between products are relatively large and tooling-up problems are extensive. The suggestion is that the advantages of large runs may be outweighed by the rigidity of an unwieldy stocking system. The consequence is inflexibility and non-value-added waste.

The reduction in batch sizes and the elimination of unnecessary inventory may act as a catalyst, generating improved quality and a reduced level of defective output. Increased flexibility goes hand in hand with product and process simplification.

Supplier relationships

The aim is one of reliability in raw material supplies in order to satisfy a zero-defect policy. This means that gaining the lowest price is no longer necessarily the most appropriate priority. An underlying need exists to work with the supplier to the mutual benefit of both parties. A close working relationship with suppliers can lead to:

- single sourcing;
- long-term contracts;
- short lead times;
- rational and achievable design specifications;
- the use of local sources, wherever feasible; and
- guarantees of quality assurance by suppliers.

Each of these factors can have extensive mutual benefits, but each requires a re-evaluation of traditional producer–supplier working attitudes.

The abandonment of lowest-price tenders focuses attention on quality and availability, even where these come at higher prices. The implication for management accounting is a reduced emphasis on purchase-price variances. Favourable purchase-price variances may be attributable to quantity discounts or the acceptance of lower-quality supplies. These contribute, respectively, to increased inventory and more wastage and reworking.

Adverse production variances may result, but the VAM system is much more concerned with *overall* performance trends than with individual variances.

Quality control

Quality control is concerned with converting a quality problem into a productivity increase, at low cost, through more attention to product detail. The alternative is to overproduce in order to ensure the production of a serviceable set of units of acceptable quality, with the consequent buffer stock problem discussed earlier.

The JIT philosophy means that management prefers an idle workforce if the alternative is that the workers are producing for inventory. This has serious consequences for management accounting methods. A focus on labour utilization and overhead absorption as measures of the efficiency and productivity of the manufacturing process encourages overproduction and the generation of excessive inventory and has no relevance in an integrated VAM system.

The key aspect of QC is an attitude change – one of attention to and respect for quality on the part of the workforce, rather than one which aims only to ensure that a product 'passes' the monitoring inspector. The objectives are:

- The production of perfect parts every time (i.e., zero defects). High quality is viewed as being totally consistent with low costs, rather than the reverse.
- The transfer of production responsibility to the operators, so that they have the ability to monitor and improve production processes where continuing serious faults are apparent.
- An attitude of mutual respect between colleagues in the workforce to ensure the transfer of acceptable-quality product between them (with workers regarding the next person in the assembly line as their customer). The emphasis on teamwork and co-operation between employees means that the focus of attention must be diverted from the individual worker. Piecework payment plans must be eliminated, and an emphasis on labour variances within production units is no longer appropriate.
- Generation and analysis of relevant data, so that production quality decisions are based on a reliable management information system. This includes, for example, information about average set-up times, days of production in inventory and the average distance travelled by products during production.
- The identification of the fundamental causes of problems to ensure that the disease responsible for poor quality production is cured, rather than the symptoms treated.

Ideally, QC should be approached at the *prevention* stage through the co-operation of the workforce, rather than by facilitating opportunistic behaviour aimed at defeating the system. Such an approach dictates a new role for standard costing. Traditionally, measurement of performance relative to standard emphasizes output, not quality of output. Rather than using standards to which costs can be compared *after* they have been incurred, costing standards should provide a more decision-useful guide to prevent costs being incurred *before* they arise.

Operationalizing value-added management

Reference back to Figure 3.1 highlights the importance of discriminating between value-adding and non-value-adding activities in the measurement of process performance. Recognition of corporate goals and specification of cost drivers and critical indicators are all steps in the pursuit of VAM goals.

The application of VAM principles aims:

- to reduce costs by reducing lead times, change-over time, inventory, cycle time, floor space, raw material stock, wastage, work in progress, reworking, and interest payments;
- to increase quality by increasing flexibility, employee involvement and productivity.

The adoption of these principles has demonstrable and significant benefits for manufacturing industry and revolutionary consequences for management accounting. The principles underpinning VAM can be applied equally well in non-manufacturing environments with similar benefits.

For the VAM system to operate effectively, management accountants must be able to provide decision-useful information. This must allow managers to make the decisions necessary to generate long-term profitability, rather than merely monitoring current operations or providing data for the financial reporting function.

To quantify and integrate the potential benefits of value-added management, more non-financial and qualitative information is needed to complement traditional sources. Such data collection is potentially expensive and time-consuming, especially if we are unsure which non-financial indicators are the most appropriate. The following chapter considers this issue in more detail, while the following case study considers some of the issues and attitudes which prevent the successful implementation of VAM.

CASE STUDY

Chester Ltd: A VAM case study

Chester Ltd provides an example of a suitable case for treatment. Its characteristics are typical of organizations requiring a re-evaluation of their business strategies to allow the alignment of customer focus and employee involvement. You may even recognize your own organization in the CHESTER acronym!

- Conflict levels are high and increasing. Interpersonal conflict among colleagues is common, making for an unpleasant work environment dominated by rumour, back-biting, innuendo and gossip.
- Heavy-handed control is perceived to be necessary in order to preserve the *status quo* of 'them and us'. There is little delegated responsibility and trivial cost-cutting exercises assume the proportion of major issues. We might expect the stationery cupboard to resemble Fort Knox and up to three signatures to be required before a fax can be dispatched.
- Energy is high, but frequently misdirected. Middle managers work long hours and always take work home with them. The training of junior ranks is apparently too arduous and consequently there is no delegation of decision-making.

CASE STUDY (cont.)

- Stress levels are also high, with frequent short absences and doctors' appointments. The preponderance of red eyes and grey faces does not augur well for future stability.
- Turnover among staff is high, either because of movement elsewhere or because staff members actively seek internal demotion to less stressful occupations. Worse, staff turnover is tacitly accepted as a part of normal operations.
- Entrenched views and work practices persist: 'We have always done things like this and why should we change tried and tested procedures?'
- Rationalization after the event takes place on a regular basis in order to attribute blame elsewhere. High levels of inconsistency are perceived to exist in the environment, so that external factors can always be located in order to explain failure.

The solutions to Chester's problems are not easy. They require fundamental changes throughout the organization so that new attitudes allow all to give the best of themselves:

1 Variations in systems and procedure are inevitable. They are not a cause for panic and recriminations, but a database for the investigation of our processes. Similarly, there are no 'failures' as such – mistakes provide us with feedback, allowing the re-evaluation of subsequent strategies. We must constantly look for improvement opportunities, means of doing the job better and evidence to substantiate improved job practices.
2 The aim is to increase customer satisfaction with the service provided by the company. Management must establish this vision with their employees. What we do should promote customer happiness, so we must be aware of those current practices which positively reduce customer satisfaction. The identification of key problem areas will allow the implementation of solutions which vastly improve the quality of customer service, in a manner which is not transaction-specific. But that alone is insufficient. Employee attitudes must change so that employees view constant improvement as part of their job and can act in a manner which implements individual improvements.
3 Empowerment is a key factor. Devolved decision-making is essential to allow individuals the power to implement customer-focused solutions. In the short term, such actions may reduce profitability, but the goal is long-term, and as long as customer satisfaction is increased, along with the long-term value of the assets, short-term hiccups have to be tolerated.
4 Barriers and enablers to successful implementation must be evaluated. The major barriers will most likely be in two areas:
   (a) *Attitudes to change.* Top management commitment must be wholehearted and must permeate down through all management levels. Adherence to the vision must eventually become part of everyone's work practices. Deliberate obstruction and agitation must be countered with, first, the

opportunity to conform, then with damage limitation via transfer or resignation.

(b) *Institutionalized procedures.* Entrenched work practices, relics of previous corporate goals, must be made more flexible or eliminated in order to give full rein to individual creativity. The consequent reduction in formal controls is balanced by the encouragement of self-auditing to ensure that new work practices are consistent with the vision.

5 The major enablers will be:

(a) Management encouragement of individuality and risk-taking. The devolution of decision-making should develop responsibility and self-importance through an 'it's up to me' approach. A careful balance must be maintained here between job descriptions and managerial roles to prevent buck-passing and the elimination of *any* control by not asking subordinates to make decisions in areas outside their areas of competence.

(b) The provision of documentation detailing procedures and working methods deemed to be industry best practice. Individual creativity should therefore not be required at the level of fundamentals but can be devoted to original situations.

(c) A training programme which emphasizes creativity, assertiveness and teamwork to facilitate the smooth devolution of customer-focused decision-making.

SUMMARY

This chapter offers a wide-ranging discussion of cost measurement and management, and the opportunities offered by new methods. The chapter progresses from a predominantly 'cost' focus (with ABC and target costing) to a more 'managerial' focus, concerned more with implementation issues and waste reduction. In doing so, it highlights the variations in current practice and the improvement opportunities available.

7 Know Your People

INTRODUCTION

Recent studies, such as those referred to in Chapter 2 (see Jazayeri and Cuthbert, 2004), have highlighted the gap which exists in the management accounting literature with respect to papers devoted to human resources issues. Chief executives consistently attach great importance to human resources topics, and they are popular in the practitioner journals, but they remain relatively neglected in the pages of refereed academic journals. This chapter attempts to partly close this gap by devoting more attention to 'people' issues.

TOTAL QUALITY MANAGEMENT

As recently as the late 1950s, Japanese products were denigrated in the West for their shoddiness and unreliability. The transformation in the reputation of Japanese goods by the 1990s – led by the electronics and motor sectors – has much to do with their readiness to accept and apply the latest management principles. Their flexibility to do so lies substantially in the restructuring of unions and institutions following the Second World War, allowing the changes necessary to incorporate just-in-time, value-added management and total quality management to take place. Interestingly, activity-based costing has never received widespread approval, or been widely adopted, in Japan. The initial forays into South-East

Asia during the 1950s of W. Edwards Deming, the celebrated US guru of quality management, meant that his ideas were incorporated at a time when the inflexibility of attitudes and union resistance to change prevented them from being adopted in his home country. The considerable competitive advantage that Japanese companies were able to establish in quality and timeliness, compared to their US and European counterparts, is more than a little attributable to their readiness to recognize these American advances. Subsequently, Easton and Jarrell (1998) found a positive association between the implementation of TQM and long-term financial performance, measured using both accounting and market-based measures.

TQM is too often viewed as a technique whose potential usefulness is confined to manufacturing processes. This section argues that TQM assumes greater importance as a tool for addressing human resources issues to produce improved efficiency in service areas. By focusing on the management accounting function, we will devise a process through which quality improvement methods might be used to highlight problem areas and facilitate their solution. An initial understanding of the difference between the three major 'quality' terms – quality control (QC), quality assurance (QA) and quality management (QM) – is essential to the short-, medium- and long-term focus of business:

- QC is concerned with the *past*, and deals with data obtained from previous production which allow action to be taken to stop defects being produced.
- QA deals with the *present*, and concerns the putting into place of systems to prevent defects from occurring.
- QM is concerned with the *future*, and manages people in a process of continuous improvement targeted at the products and services offered by the organization.

Thus while QA is responsible for systems which prevent departures from budgeted costs and corrective mechanisms to prevent future departures from budgeted costs, QM uses the skills and participation of the workforce to reduce the costs of production of goods and services. It becomes TQM when it embraces the whole organization.

In this section we will consider an in-depth study of the implementation of the TQM process in the management accounting function. A systematic process is adopted to identify and implement solutions to prioritized opportunities for improvement. The TQM approach highlights the need for a customer-oriented approach to management reporting, eliminating some of our more traditional reporting practices.

TQM seeks to increase customer satisfaction by finding the factors that limit current performance. The practice of TQM in a manufacturing environment has produced tangible improvements in efficiency and profitability as a result of many small improvements. The generation of similar results in the areas of overhead costs and, particularly, indirect labour productivity is long overdue. Performance measurement and quality improvement are not the sole domain of manufacturing industry, but they dominate the literature. This chapter focuses on an implementation in the professional service environment and details the opportunities for improvement available in a management accounting environment.

On the shop floor, quality concepts have been based around the involvement of employees and an approach according to which each worker sees the next person on the assembly line as their customer. The application of quality concepts to service areas, like the accounting function, requires a similar approach, necessitating a focus on customer requirements. The 'customers' are the receivers of a 'product' – in this case periodic management accounting reports – and their 'satisfaction' is determined by the usefulness of this product in the decision-making process.

There is a danger of viewing TQM in terms of statistical processes and control charts. It is much more than this. Quality is not some vague utopian ideal associated with 'goodness'; it can be seen as requiring that we conform to very specific performance requirements. Close enough is not good enough in this respect. The cost of quality is the monetary impact of a failure to conform, a measurable characteristic which can be reduced through a system of prevention in much the same way as safety standards are implemented.

In a manufacturing environment the cost of quality might be viewed as the sum of the costs associated with scrap, reworks, warranty claims and inspection expenses. The same costs are those associated with management accounting procedures which produce inaccurate, error-prone or untimely services for their 'customers'. Errors in the wages function, for example, are perceived as intolerable, so it is inappropriate that they be any more acceptable elsewhere.

The following example is concerned with operationalizing TQM and with the commitment of a large Australian manufacturer to a TQM process seeking greater organizational attainment through constant improvements and the co-ordination of individual efforts. The focus is on the accounting function within Australian operations with the objective of implementing a process which will lead to the adoption of new strategies, the solving of problems and the elimination of identifiable deficiencies. The section describes the process adopted together with details of internal deliberations, giving valuable insights into the problems and benefits associated with TQM implementations.

OPERATIONALIZING TOTAL QUALITY MANAGEMENT

Figure 7.1 outlines a systematic process for the examination of a number of fundamental questions. The first four stages of this procedure are conducted internally within the management accounting team. They comprise a situation audit of current practice embracing corporate culture, product and customers.

A team approach was adopted to generate priorities in the identification of customers (stage 1) and critical issues in the provision of decision-support information. This provided a structured, group decision-making process for reaching consensus through the assignment of ranked priorities, together with an environment conducive to the development of creative suggestions. The nominal group technique discussed earlier was employed.

A multi-voting technique was employed to prioritize the list of customers and provide a focus of services. The ranking of perceived customer

FIGURE 7.1

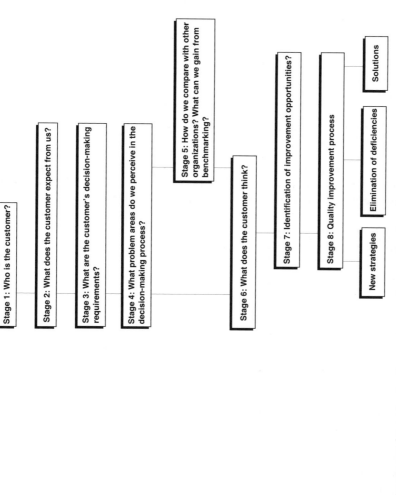

Stage 1: Who is the customer?

Stage 2: What does the customer expect from us?

Stage 3: What are the customer's decision-making requirements?

Stage 4: What problem areas do we perceive in the decision-making process?

Stage 5: How do we compare with other organizations? What can we gain from benchmarking?

Stage 6: What does the customer think?

Stage 7: Identification of improvement opportunities?

Stage 8: Quality improvement process

New strategies

Elimination of deficiencies

Solutions

The process for reviewing the management accounting function

importance reveals the priority customers for management accounting services as:

1 managers;
2 engineers; and
3 leading hands.

Managers having been identified as the priority group in receipt of accounting output, a second brainstorming session was used to generate a comprehensive list of their perceived expectations of the accounting function (stage 2). Multi-voting was again used to identify the relative importance of these expectations, providing a ranking of 12 accounting functions:

1 compliance with procedures;
2 focus on problems;
3 performance reviews;
4 provision of budget information;
5 assessment of proposals;
6 payment of salaries;
7 tax advice;
8 management processes advice;
9 information forecasting;
10 commercial training;
11 information-processing skills; and
12 professional advice.

Turning now to the customer's decision-making requirements (stage 3), brainstorming revealed a list of 18 processes perceived to be major elements of the service provided by management accountants:

1 pay people (wages and salaries);
2 pay accounts (vendors and contractors);
3 keep the books of account;
4 budget;
5 forecast;
6 audit;
7 conduct business-impact analyses;
8 manage authorization procedures;
9 issue guidelines;
10 maintain a library of procedures;
11 analyse performance;
12 manage licences;
13 contribute to meetings;
14 manage property;
15 carry out strategic planning;
16 train others;
17 evaluate insurance requirements; and
18 produce *ad hoc* reports.

Combining management perceptions of customer expectations and the importance of the various functions, we find four processes clearly ranked as the key areas of importance to managers:

1 performance analysis;
2 *ad hoc* reporting;
3 strategic planning; and
4 contribution to meetings.

This series of steps, therefore, establishes managers as the priority customers for management accounting reporting and procedures, while performance analysis is the priority consideration in their use of management accounting information.

Typically, management accountants focus on the analysis of total performance in cost centres, using cost-per-unit comparisons and calculations of variance to generate plans. Where the focus is on quality improvement, the overriding need is to stay close to the customers and follow their suggestions. In this way, a decision-support system can be developed, incorporating both financial and non-financial information, which provides a flexible reporting system meeting user requirements. In order to do this properly, we need to know:

• the nature of the decisions being made;
• the nature of the decision-making process; and
• the degree to which information requirements are being met.

A survey of users is required to provide this information, but critical issues can be identified and prioritized in advance, in order to refine the necessary survey questions.

The process next considers the problem areas perceived to be in the decision-making process (stage 4). Once again using brainstorming and multi-voting, the team ranked the characteristics of an accounting information system thought most desirable from a decision-making point of view, as follows:

1 *Relevance*. A targeted decision-making process.
2 *Congruence*. Consistency with the long-term strategy of the business.
3 *Comprehensibility*. Systems should be readily understandable, and therefore readily usable, by customers.
4 *Linkage to non-financial indicators*. Systems need to reflect the monetary impact of physical parameters.
5 *Timeliness*. Systems should be on time and on-line.

These characteristics were perceived as being areas of weakness where the greatest impact could be achieved through the implementation of improvements. It is instructive to consider some of the actual situations that might be associated with improvements in these areas.

• *Lack of relevance*. If line managers ignore most of the data reported to them by traditional cost accounting systems and treat head office cost analysts with disdain, they may prefer to perform their own specific cost investigations to determine the cause of deviations from plan, seeing management accounting reports as irrelevant and technically unrealistic. These informal systems may incorporate superior information which would be of benefit to all and which would be better incorporated within a global management information system. The solution: develop formal and informal reporting mechanisms targeted to the needs of the user.

- *Lack of congruence.* Where the management accounting system focuses entirely on the measurement of costs, then it is not surprising that employees adopt a similar focus. Where the plant-level emphasis is on production and productivity, a detailed analysis of process performance evaluation may reveal that the pursuit of efficiency measures is not necessarily consistent with the stated strategic goals of the organization as a whole. For example, a reputation for industry leadership and innovation might be aided by a strategy of rapid asset replacement. Where divisional performance – and management rewards – are based on return on investment (ROI) type indicators, a short-term perspective might be adopted, inconsistent with corporate strategy. But the revaluation of old assets, no longer depreciable, through inflation indices might promote their replacement with new, more efficient assets. The solution: develop a robust process to ensure that the accounting department's performance analysis is linked to strategic direction.

- *Lack of comprehensibility.* If management accountants believe that they prepare detailed financial reports for their managers to enable them to report to the managing director at the monthly board meeting, and the managing director declares that he or she is already aware of all the relevant reported material from informal sources, well in advance of the meeting, then clearly the customer for existing management accounting reports is not the managing director. Where such reports do not embrace the full extent of information generators, and fail to target a designated customer, there is room for a distinct improvement in the service offered. This may derive from more timely reporting, the provision of NFIs, new performance measures, or a complete reformatting of the reporting process. The solution: generate accounting information systems of a format and content suitable to meet user requirements.

- *Absence of a link to non-financial indicators.* The focus of management accounting must move beyond summary, financial measures of manufacturing operations if it is to maintain its central evaluation and control role. If a corporate goal of rapid internal growth is being pursued through a strategy of introducing automated production processes requiring less direct labour, then products using automated machinery intensely will be undercosted if direct labour hours are used to allocate manufacturing overhead costs to products. A more flexible allocation procedure should be adopted incorporating NFIs, such as inspection and set-up times, in order to provide a 'fairer' distribution. In the absence of a 'right' answer, corporate strategy might serve to provide more guidance. Perseverance with an allocation on the basis of direct labour penalizes those products reliant on manual operations and provides an incentive to automate, consistent with the corporate strategy. The solution: generate a concise group of NFIs which reflect the overall performance of the company.

- *Lack of timeliness.* Suppose that the management accounting team prides itself on producing its monthly operating report on the eighth working day of the following month. An unexpected equipment failure means that it is unable to meet its accustomed deadline until the fifteenth working day. The team receives no complaints or enquiries during the interim on timeliness. The following month it produces, but does not distribute, the report. There is no response from the customer. The team continues this practice for the next three months until an internal memo indicates that the customer no longer wishes to receive the report – it is now surplus to requirements. In this case, the relevance of the whole reporting process is questionable and a close look at the distribution list of any given report, if not the existence of the report itself, is advisable. The solution: generate reports in a form and time envelope which meet the needs of the target customer.

Detailed and systematic internal deliberations allow the accounting team to develop a clear idea of their own strengths and weaknesses and of the areas of most significant deficiency. The benchmarking exercise at stage 5 of the TQM review process allows us to see how other similar companies are coping with similar problems and opportunities. (The details of the benchmarking process itself were considered in Chapter 3.)

Stages 1–5 provide an information base developed without reference to the key player – the customer. This is rectified at stage 6 with a survey of representative customers which embraces their views on perceived problem areas. Respondents to the survey were encouraged to talk freely about their attitudes towards accounting information services, within a semi-structured outline covering:

1　the nature of decisions made;
2　the use made of existing formal reports;
3　the preferred format (graphical, tabular or narrative) for formal reporting;
4　other information sources employed;
5　information, currently unavailable, which would aid decision-making; and
6　NFIs used in performance appraisal.

Attitudes to the management reporting process were particularly illuminating, and directly applicable to other organizations. Monthly variance reports as a means of control were viewed as pointless by senior management, conscious of inevitable process fluctuations during the year, and by junior management, who viewed budgets as unrealistic and no major constraint on their spending.

Formal reports were generally perceived as having four positive features:

- highlighting and reinforcing the existence of large variances, especially when close to the budget setting period;
- reporting unanticipated items associated with unexpected and late accruals, end-of-month 'adjustments', and misallocations to inappropriate accounts;
- providing information which might change priorities; and
- communicating a degree of analysis not available through on-line systems.

However, a number of criticisms of content were widespread. The reports were considered to:

- place too much emphasis on the reporting of unfavourable variances constituting insignificantly small monetary amounts rather than focusing on an explanation of large expenditures actually incurred;

- expend too much energy chasing inconsequential items representing minor out-of-budget fluctuations, rather than focusing on wrongly trended items (even where in budget);
- show an unrealistic concern with comparisons of actual versus budgeted outcomes where unfavourable variances were in fact inevitable and symptomatic of inflexible budgeting and time shifts; and
- report too many items for their own sake rather than to satisfy particular objectives or meet the requirements of particular individuals.

Unsatisfied needs embraced three major areas:

- Ease of access to labour information to facilitate: the quantification and explanation of severe downturns in maintenance productivity; the distinction between normal and overtime hours on maintenance jobs, replacing inadequate composite hourly rates; and accounting for non-productive hours per worker resulting from the adoption of a more participatory style of management.
- Predictive models concerning: early warning of massive deteriorations; forecasts of monthly maintenance expenditures; relationships between breakdown and scheduled maintenance expenditures; the impact on performance of safety training; probability-based analysis of risk to facilitate the management of maintenance expenditures.
- Trend information, ideally weekly and on-line, covering: downtime and cost of breakdowns; operating supplies; maintenance materials; purchased services; and statistical process control.

The outcomes of the customer survey, benchmarking, and internal analysis, provide the raw material for stages 7 and 8 of the review process: the identification of improvement opportunities and the implementation of a formal improvement process. Table 7.1 depicts the framework for the six-step analysis, identified by the acronym 'PRAISE'. The successful adoption of this sequence of steps demands discipline and commitment. The goal of quality improvement is paramount and guides the actions of the change team throughout. Difficulties will be experienced at each step:

1 The symptoms or observed effects of a problem may be readily apparent, but it may be more difficult to identify a measurable improvement opportunity. Attempts to identify problems broadly as 'communication', 'organization', 'morale' or 'productivity' should be resisted – much more specific target areas are required to allow a focus on precisely what is wrong.
2 It may not be possible to achieve consensus because of the pet projects of a minority of the team members. Multi-voting may therefore be necessary to provide a focus in a democratic manner.
3 Lateral thinking may be helpful to encourage a wide-ranging discussion and to avoid a blinkered approach to the nature of the problem. The required objective is the identification of the root cause, and this is unlikely to be one that promotes a quick-fix solution.
4 'Innovation' and 'creativity' are the key words to encourage a multitude of suggested solutions. These may then be evaluated in terms of the

TABLE 7.1

The PRAISE six-step quality improvement process

Step	Activity	Elements
1	Problem identification	Areas of customer dissatisfaction Absence of competitive advantage Complacency regarding present arrangements
2	Ranking	Prioritize problems and opportunities by: • perceived importance; and • ease of measurement and solution
3	Analysis	Ask 'why?' to identify possible causes Keep asking 'why?' to move beyond the symptoms and to avoid jumping to premature conclusions Ask 'what?' to consider potential implications Ask 'how much?' to quantify cause and effect
4	Innovation	Use creative thinking to generate potential solutions. Operationalize these solutions by identifying: • barriers to implementation; • available enablers; and • people whose co-operation must be sought
5	Solution	Implement the preferred solution Take appropriate action to bring about the required changes Reinforce with training and documentation back-up
6	Evaluation	Monitor the effectiveness of actions Establish and interpret performance indicators to track progress towards objectives Identify the potential for further improvements – and return to step 1

extent to which they may be converted into operating plans which achieve the required objectives. A systematic evaluation of positive and negative aspects of each strategy is essential – but remember, no matter how sophisticated the analysis, the final solution is only as good as the original list from which it is chosen.

5 The implementation of the solution may require a great deal of diplomacy, especially in divisions or departments resistant to change. Possible side-effects must be identified and the whole process smoothed through with the co-operation of the workforce at all levels, efficient internal communi-cation, training programmes where appropriate, and feedback throughout.

6 The evaluation at this step may indicate the trouble-free implementation of a strategy which has solved 100% of the problem. More likely it will not! As part of the drive for continuous improvement in quality, several other areas capable of improvement will emerge. As such, this step is not the last stage in the process but the first stage in a renewed process. The

new problems emerging here provide fresh improvement opportunities ready for restatement at step 1 and prioritization at step 2.

Central to the whole PRAISE system are both quality control – the search for continuous improvements in quality – and total employee involvement – the co-operation and commitment of employees. This dual approach provides a single focus – the customer – whose increased satisfaction remains the primary goal of the procedure.

A number of essential requirements emerge, therefore, for successful implementation, which may be described as the six Cs of TQM:

- *Commitment.* If a TQM culture is to be developed, so that quality improvement becomes a normal part of everyone's job, a clear commitment from the top must be provided. Without this all else fails. It is not sufficient to delegate 'quality' issues to a single person since this will not provide an environment for changing attitudes and breaking down the barriers to quality improvement. Such expectations must be made clear, together with the support and training necessary to their achievement.
- *Culture.* Training lies at the heart of effecting a change in culture and attitudes. Management accountants too often associate 'creativity' with 'creative accounting' and related negative perceptions. This must be changed to encourage individual contributions and to make 'quality' a normal part of everyone's job.
- *Continuous improvement.* Recognition that TQM is a 'process' not a 'programme' necessitates that we are committed in the long term to the never ending search for ways to do the job better. There will always be room for improvement, however small.
- *Co-operation.* The application of TEI principles is paramount. The on-the-job experience of all employees must be fully utilized and their involvement and co-operation sought in the development of improvement strategies and associated performance measures.
- *Customer focus.* The needs of the customer are the major driving thrust – not just the external customer (in receipt of the final product or service) but the internal customer (colleagues who receive and supply goods, services or information). Perfect service with zero defects is all that is acceptable at either internal or external levels. Too frequently, in practice, TQM implementations focus entirely on the external customer to the exclusion of internal relationships; they will not survive the short term unless they foster the mutual respect necessary to preserve morale and employee participation.
- *Control.* Documentation, procedures and awareness of current best practice are essential if TQM implementations are to function appropriately. The need for control mechanisms is frequently overlooked, in practice, in the euphoria of customer service and employee empowerment. Unless procedures are in place, improvements cannot be monitored and measured nor deficiencies corrected.

Difficulties will undoubtedly be experienced in the implementation of quality improvement and it is worthwhile detailing procedures that might be adopted to minimize them. To these, then, we now turn.

OVERCOMING TOTAL QUALITY PARALYSIS

Little attention has so far been paid to the practical problems of overcoming the inertia of organizations and the reluctance of some individuals to embrace management accounting change. This section argues for a systematic approach to overcome the apparent paralysis besetting many companies in implementing a quality policy.

A quality improvement process like the PRAISE system restricts the adoption of sub-optimal quick-fix solutions and increases the participants' awareness of the barriers to change. However, it does not overcome completely some of the behavioural difficulties associated with individual motivation and group dynamics. The problem is not one of an awareness of the usefulness of TQM but rather the ability to do something about it: the inertia associated with total quality paralysis. Some fundamental requirements in getting started are:

1 A clear commitment, from the top, to TQM ideals. Without this, all else fails. It is not sufficient to delegate 'quality' issues to a single person, since this will not provide an appropriate environment for changing attitudes and behaviour and breaking down the barriers to quality improvement. The aim is to develop a TQM culture so that quality improvement becomes a normal part of everyone's job. This expectation must be made clear, and whatever support and training are necessary to its achievement must be provided.
2 Managers must be provided with the skills, tools and techniques to pursue systematic improvement. Training should be practical, avoiding unnecessary abstractions and keeping management jargon to a minimum. It may even be necessary to avoid the acronym 'TQM' itself, because of the barriers associated with buzzwords, reverting to reference instead to the phrase 'quality improvement process'.
3 The general awareness of improvement opportunities must be improved through the creation of a database documenting the *status quo* and covering those things that the organization currently does well, as well as its deficiencies. Such a database should contains answers to questions like these:
   (a) Where do we make errors?
   (b) Where do we create waste?
   (c) What should we do that we currently make no attempt to do?

Ideally, the quality improvement process should be a vehicle for positive and constructive movement within an organization. We must, however, be aware of the destructive potential of the process. Failure to observe the fundamental principles associated with the 'four Ps' of quality improvement may so severely damage motivation that the organization is unable to recover fully. Those four Ps are:

• *People*. It will quickly become apparent that some individuals are not ideally suited to the participatory process. Lack of enthusiasm will be apparent from a generally negative approach and a tendency to have prearranged meetings which coincide with the meetings of TQM teams! Where these individuals are charged with the responsibility for driving group success, progress will be slow or negligible. Quality improvement teams may have to be abandoned largely for associated reasons before they are allowed to grind to a halt.

- *Process.* The rhetoric and inflexibility of a strict Deming approach will often have a demotivating effect on group activity. It is essential to approach problem-solving practically and to regard the formal process as a system designed to prevent participants from jumping to conclusions. As such it will provide a means to facilitate the generation of alternatives while ensuring that important discussion stages are not omitted.
- *Problem.* Experience suggests that the least successful groups are those approaching problems that are deemed to be too large to provide meaningful solutions within a finite time period. Problems need to be approached in bite-sized chunks, with teams tackling solvable problems with a direct economic impact, allowing for immediate feedback together with a recognition of the contribution made by individual participants. For example, while 'communications' and 'morale' are frequently cited as key problem areas, they are too broad to provide successful quality improvement targets. Smaller aspects of these issues must be identified.
- *Preparation.* A training in the workings of Deming-like processes is an inadequate preparation for the efficient implementation of a quality improvement process. Additional courses on creative thinking and statistical processes are needed in order to give participants a greater appreciation of the diversity of the process. This training must quickly be extended beyond the immediate accounting circle to include employees at supervisory levels and below who are involved at the data input stage.

A three-point action plan for the choice of projects and the implementation of the process is as follows:

1 *Bite-sized chunks.* It is tempting to seek a large cherry to pluck, but big improvement opportunities are inevitably complex and require extensive interdepartmental co-operation. The choice of a relatively small problem in the first instance provides a greater chance of success.
2 *A solvable problem.* The problem selected should not be trivial, but it should be one with a potential impact and a clear improvement opportunity. Measurable progress towards implementation should be accomplished within three or four months (or less if possible) in order to maintain the motivation of participants and advertise the success of the improvement process itself.
3 *Recognition of participants.* The successful projects and team members should receive appropriate recognition throughout the enterprise, at the very least being 'mentioned in despatches' via company newsletters. Prominent individuals should be rewarded for their efforts both as personal recognition and as an encouragement to others. The precise nature of the reward may be the recognition itself, although in some situations material, but usually non-monetary, prizes may also be appropriate.

The implementation of TQM processes can provide long-lasting benefits as long as the achievement of quality goals is not in conflict with other objectives. This might be the case, where, for instance:

- bonuses are based on the volume of output alone; or
- retrenchments result from the increased efficiency associated with the quality improvement process.

By overcoming the initial obstacles, a TQM process can provide us with an additional tool to improve competitiveness and ensure long-term survival.

CONTROL: THE MISSING LINK OF TOTAL QUALITY MANAGEMENT

The fundamental principles of TQM focus on a process of continuous improvement which enhances the satisfaction of customer requirements by changing the attitude of the workforce. The reduction of waste is made implicit in each worker's task. This suggests the elimination of all non-value-adding processes, processes which include all control functions – monitoring, inspecting, progress chasing, even auditing – which would now be replaced by self-auditing as part of the change in corporate culture. Such extreme expectations are unrealistic. A control function, properly defined, is essential and can contribute to the achievement of TQM objectives.

The development of TQM provides a vehicle for the accounting function to achieve control, continuous improvement and maximum efficiency by ensuring that all of the processes carried out by that function are both in control and capable. Such movements will have a dramatic effect on the accounting function and may well redefine the audit function.

The basic requirement of accounting control is that a process is capable of meeting customer requirements, whether they are those of the directors, the shareholders, or the law. Techniques which have historically been used to achieve this control include procedures and audit, but these have major flaws. If we are not appropriately focused, it is possible that the process is *never* going to be capable of meeting customer requirements, no matter how complex the levels of audit or procedure adopted. Further, there will be no focus for the documentation of flaws and their subsequent reversal.

Qualitative and non-financial data, though vital for control, may not be subject to the same strict standards of measurement as financial and technical data. Their role in the quality programme may, therefore, be underestimated.

Documentation of the *activities* to be performed in the accounting function is an essential first step in identifying the dimensions of processes and the interrelationships between tasks. Table 7.2 details eight basic processes which may be identified in the accounting function, each covering multiple activities and crossing task boundaries.

A narrow control function is apparent in each process, but this is effectively just the checking or audit component of controllership. The controllership function interacts with the TQM process to impact upon the other six dimensions to provide timely and relevant information to

TABLE 7.2

Dimensions of the accounting function

Process	Activity
1 Planning	Strategic planning
	Operations planning
	Forecasts
2 Book-keeping	Costing
	Inventory accounting
	Project accounting
	Fixed capital
	Maintenance system
3 Discharging liabilities	Payroll
	Accounts receivable
	Accounts payable
	Cashier
	Contracts administration
4 Reporting	Corporate reporting
	Statutory reporting
	Management reporting
5 Business support	Project or opportunity evaluation
	Cost improvement
	Tax advice or guidance
	Operating centres
6 Corporate services	Tax
	Insurance
	Legal
7 Functional administration	Technology management
	Human resource management
	Non-accounting procedures
	TQM
	Agreements
8 Controllership	Accounting guidelines
	Accounting procedures
	Accounting policy and standards
	Internal audits
	External audits

decision-makers and to monitor compliance with corporate expectations where policies, procedures, ethical behaviour and professional conduct are concerned.

The quality manual is usually the major document controlling the implementation of the quality process. It defines the basic philosophy of the organization, the structure and responsibilities of managers and departments, and the relationship between them. It also contains the methods to be used to ensure quality, including the composition of teams, and the audit procedures to be adopted.

The definition of the process, inputs and outputs gives a framework for the writing of procedures and standard methods while also providing a focus for improvement opportunities. Underpinning both is a control and audit process, defining the way that the system is to be checked.

For every process within the accounting organization, a policy and procedures are established in accordance with industry best practice and communicated throughout the organization. The objective of these is to satisfy customer requirements and to identify improvement opportunities which allow the continuous extension of the customer service provided.

The writing of procedures and standard methods is a fundamental step in pursuing excellence of process. Procedures are concerned with the properties of the system that we are trying to influence (controlled parameters). Standard working methods are concerned with the process variables that are being manipulated in order to influence the system (control points). Thus, if we want to control the water level in a bath, the level is the controlled parameter, and the tap and plug are the control points.

By providing a sound control environment, which supports business decisions with appropriate measurement and analysis, the controllership function pursues complete customer satisfaction. The aim is to achieve acknowledged industry leadership for excellence of process, personnel and service. Underpinning this aim is an audit process that ensures that all of the above are in place and operating. The audit process is partly external, but largely internal, consisting of a control check system that monitors the critical processes of the system. Depending on the breakdown consequences and risk of failure, additional control points can be introduced into the process chain. Thus, the system allows for not only control but also continuous improvement. The monitoring of the data around a process will allow modifications which make it in control and capable. As changes or improvements are made they are documented and the system updated so that everyone uses the current best method.

The clear definition and documentation of procedures facilitates job flexibility, making control easier and increasing the level of productivity in the accounting department. Thus, a good control system facilitates continuous improvement by focusing on customer needs, identifying priorities, and relating processes to one another. Variation and inaccuracy are caused by poor control and incompatible systems. A quality system is therefore essential to reduce these problems.

The application of the PRAISE quality improvement process to the timeliness problem provides an excellent example of service improvement, one which observes the fundamental quality principles of waste elimination and doing things right first time. Documentation of key data on processes is the first, and arguably the most important, step in the procedure. By charting processes for each activity, establishing time barriers, constraints, priorities, degrees of difficulty and expected improvement times, a critical database is established. Small, dedicated problem-solving teams can be charged with developing solutions for task improvements, with the success of the process demonstrated by widespread internal reporting.

Significant further improvements are also likely to follow:

• the elimination of double handling and manual data delays in day-to-day operations;

- the acceptance of the quality process for problem-solving; and
- the highlighting of opportunities for interdisciplinary teamwork.

The reasons for the success of the improvement process in the area of timeliness are firmly grounded in the principles of TQM, embracing TEI and process measurement. These principles include:

- the clear exposition of the benefits of a project;
- the involvement of *all* customers and contributors;
- the elimination of non-relevant data;
- an understanding of the needs of the *whole* process;
- the use of graphical and pictorial techniques to achieve understanding;
- the establishment of performance specifications and targets;
- the use of errors to prompt continuous improvement; and
- the use of statistics to tell people how well they are doing.

The basic need for controllership is a practical reality and provides a springboard for the provision of accurate, timely data to manage and enhance a business. Control features are, therefore, essential constituents of the TQM process, facilitating the successful implementation of customer-focused improvements.

TOTAL EMPLOYEE INVOLVEMENT

The pursuit of TQM has increased awareness of the need for customer focus in the service sector. Changes in attitude and corporate culture necessary for the successful implementation of TQM strategies require total employee involvement and the empowerment of individuals, so that decision-making about issues affecting the quality of service becomes a normal part of the everyday workload.

TEI involves the maximum utilization of employee talents. Using a team-oriented approach to enhance co-operation, employees participate actively in the improvement of process efficiency and product quality. Accordingly, greater responsibility for operating decisions is assigned to employees, together with the development of a multi-skilled workforce to increase production flexibility and minimize idle time.

TEI aims to facilitate the creative involvement of the workforce by making best use of those closest to the sharp end of the production process. Like many management initiatives, it leans heavily on the development of an attitude of responsibility. An increased perception of customer service is a part of business strategy, essential to survival and long-term profitability. Research has demonstrated the strategic benefits of quality in contributing to market share and ROI as well as lowering manufacturing costs and improving productivity. TQM processes provide welcome relief from the short-term myopia of financial reports, in that they suggest we have to begin treating both customers and employees as assets, although neither appears formally in the balance sheet.

In achieving excellence and ensuring the long-term survival of the enterprise, five critical dimensions of service quality can be identified:

- *Tangibles*. Physical facilities and the appearance of personnel.
- *Reliability*. Accurate performance of promised service.
- *Responsiveness*. Prompt and willing help provided to customers.
- *Assurance*. Confidence resulting from employee knowledge.
- *Empathy*. Caring, individualized attention.

Customer perceptions of the quality of the service they are receiving may be a weighted combination of these five factors.

To provide customers with friendly service which minimizes the need for control and bureaucracy, a fundamental change in employee attitudes is required, embracing a number of important issues.

- **Leadership**. The leadership function involves setting directions in order to challenge the status quo and create a vision of the future. This vision must then be communicated from the top in order to encourage the alignment of subordinates with the new culture. A further, fundamental aspect of leadership is the motivation of sub-managers, supervisors and plant-level employees about the importance of group values and their importance as individuals in fulfilling the vision. Commitment from the top is critical, enforced by the visibility and accessibility of active leadership.
- **Goal congruence**. Strong leadership is essential if goal congruence from all participants is to be achieved. Attitudes must be changed, and entrenched views sometimes reversed, if the alignment of *all* employees is eventually to be achieved. Everybody must see how the vision affects them and how their support is vital for its achievement. TEI is, therefore, central to this aspect of team performance.
- **Training**. The enforcement of motivation through training in fundamental skills and competencies is essential to the success of the process. Benchmarking should establish industry best practice for working methods and procedures, and initiative and creativity should be encouraged in decision-making beyond these areas. Training in lateral thinking, brainstorming and similar management methods will facilitate successful implementation.

The aim is to provide a level of service which facilitates repeat orders and results in happy, satisfied customers. In this respect, customer service and price discounting are very different.

The participation of the workforce allows the encouragement of attitude changes which facilitate both quality control improvements and supplier relationships. TEI will allow the evolution of common goals and a work environment which is at least more pleasurable, at best fun. The delegation of day-to-day decision-making reduces the stress levels imposed on senior management and allows them to spend more time on strategic planning. Customers will benefit from a reduction in bureaucracy and from contact with representatives of the business who are fully empowered to deal with any issue which raises customer satisfaction.

A problematic small business scenario highlights improvement opportunities involving the employment of TQM and TEI methodologies.

Mercian Dry Cleaners: A TQM case study

Jack Taft has spent 10 years building a successful chain of eight dry-cleaning outlets in Birmingham, each situated in one of the shopping centres dotted around the West Midlands metropolitan area. He feels that the new millennium has brought a time for consolidation, and he has now abandoned ideas of expanding the chain to concentrate on improving the profitability of each of his existing outlets.

Each of the shops has a full-time manager and three part-time employees. Even the word 'manager' is something of a misnomer – supervisor being more appropriate – since Jack effectively manages the whole operation, with very little delegated decision-making. There is very little communication between the shops, virtually all information and direction being provided by Jack in his daily shuttle between the shops.

Jack monitors the competition carefully. He regularly takes pieces of his dry-cleaning to his rivals for service – one first thing in the morning and another last thing in the evening. The difference in the numbered dockets allows him to estimate weekly revenue and to make comparisons with his own takings. His survey findings show Mercian to be the second ranked outlet in each of the locations, with no single competitor consistently occupying the top position. The chain is doing well, with each of the outlets separately profitable, but Jack is anxious to occupy the top slot in at least half of his eight locations.

A number of alternative ideas have been tried out in his 'Blue Riband' shops, located in the Solihull and Sutton Coldfield centres, with a view to implementation across the whole chain if successful:

- close control on raw material usage in order to reduce the use of solvents while maintaining cleaning quality;
- implementation of a computer system to track items and costs and to give immediate feedback on daily progress;
- staff training to target 'lost' customers by encouraging knock-on sales; and
- repackaging of the existing product to provide a deluxe service, at an increased margin, to existing customers.

Staff reaction to the trials has not been favourable. They feel they are not trusted because of the close monitoring imposed – a perception recently magnified by Jack insisting on conducting the cleaning operations himself for both expensive items and 'celebrity' customers. The implementation of a new computer system without consultation or training has further advanced their perception of being watched constantly. The introduction of formal staff training sessions is associated with a feeling that they are not doing their jobs properly and need to be reinstructed, apparently in the basics of providing customer service.

CASE STUDY (cont.)

Jack is disillusioned by the lack of success of his attempts to implement improvements. He needs help in making recommendations for actions which will improve the performance of the Mercian chain.

CASE ANALYSIS

The SWOT analysis in Table 7.3 is an ideal starting point for the analysis of Mercian Dry Cleaners. It is apparent that Jack Taft has clear aims and has established a strategic direction for his business. Unfortunately, he has failed to match the duties and responsibilities of employees with either their skills or designated position, with the result that there is no goal congruence among owner, managers and employees and a potentially damaging atmosphere exists.

A number of major improvement opportunities are apparent, of which those below are, arguably, the four that need immediate attention:

- *The need for active leadership from Jack Taft*, whose highly autocratic leadership style restricts information flow between the operating units, with the result that neither job satisfaction nor business performance is at an optimum.

TABLE 7.3

SWOT analysis for Mercian Dry Cleaners

Strengths	Weaknesses
• Successful chain	• Owner's autocratic managerial style
• Well spread throughout metro area	• Lack of delegation to shop managers
• Staff structure appears to be 'lean'	• Little inter-shop communication
• Flat organizational structure	• Owner is conduit for all business communication
• Each shop profitable	• Shops have feeling that they are being watched
• Owner has a clear 'mission' for business	• No delegation
	• Jack's method of monitoring competition
	• Method of computer implementation

Opportunities	Threats
• Improvement through TQM	• Owner not getting optimism or enthusiasm out of staff
• Possibilities of a TEI approach	• Lack of goal congruence of employee and organizational objectives
• Computer as a tool to assist with TQM	• Computer implementation could result in a 'Luddite' attitude by employees
• Let his managers 'manage'	
• Inter-shop communication	
• Possibility of chain being more strategic	

- *The need for improved communications between Jack Taft and his staff,* apparent from the introduction of new systems without consultation and the absence of inter-store contact.
- *The need to encourage the involvement of the staff* in the day-to-day running of the business, apparent from the lack of empowerment of managers, the prominence of part-time staffing and the missed learning opportunities arising from employee feedback.
- *The absence of meaningful performance indicators* for either staff or business, which might be used to address staff morale, service quality, customer satisfaction and cost efficiency.

The identification of key improvement opportunities yields a number of strategies that might be adopted to correct existing deficiencies.

Strategies for improving morale and job satisfaction

- Leadership style must be addressed. Training for Jack Taft to facilitate the delegation of authority to managers – allowing them to increase their commitment, motivation and self-work. He must actively seek their feedback, encourage information flows and empower decision-making within organizational goals. Jack must himself be committed to the process of change and recognize the required impact on his autonomy and organizational structure.
- Encourage teamwork in pursuit of a top position within each location; establish teams to address improvement opportunities and provide a 'think-tank' to support Jack Taft.
- Provision of incentives to motivate improved performance. This might embrace changes in the reward structure, particularly if associated with team-earned bonuses.
- Training of managers and staff is essential to increase their awareness of: goals and strategies; quality and TQM processes; and their role in ensuring customer satisfaction.

Communications through a TQM process

Jack needs to establish open lines of communication between himself and the staff, and between staff at different outlets. The encouragement of teamwork and modified attitudes to change can provide a focus for improvement opportunities which are recognized and communicated across the whole business. This might be illustrated by the adoption of the PRAISE system (see Table 7.1) of quality improvement in order to trial new services.

1 *Problem identification*
   - Customer satisfaction may be improved by the introduction of the deluxe service and better service to customers in general.
   - Reduction in raw materials (solvents) may provide the same quality garment at reduced cost.

CASE STUDY (cont.)

- Computer systems improve costings on a daily basis and improve inventory control.

2 *Ranking of opportunities*
- Take an incremental approach to implementing improvement opportunities.
- Select the most important opportunity with the greatest significance, in this case customer satisfaction.

3 *Analysis*
- Autocratic leadership and staff mistrust have led to resistance to changes that would enable quality improvement. This limits the potential of any TQM approach to improving customer satisfaction.

4 *Innovative alternative*
- Delegation of authority from Jack Taft.
- Undertake staff training in TQM, team building and customer satisfaction.
- Provide incentives for improved performance linked to group effort and customer satisfaction.

5 *Solutions implemented*
- Begin with staff training to overcome distrust and lack of support.
- Improve communication with weekly meetings to review objectives and progress.
- Ensure that Jack Taft also has training in delegation and that leaders provide top management support.
- Implement change in smooth and efficient process. Ensure appropriate training, documentation and resources are committed to the process to ensure its success.
- Continuous evaluation and feedback both from and to employees to ensure understanding of change and its effective implementation.
- Identify any problems which were originally overlooked and address them.

6 *Evaluation of outcomes*
- Continually evaluate the effectiveness of the changes to ensure their continued success.
- Identify signals which suggest that the process needs further attention to maintain the gains achieved.

Implement a TEI process

This would embrace:

- active pursuit of customer feedback;
- communication between stores;

CASE STUDY (cont.)

- formal 'benchmarking' with competitor stores;
- empowerment of managers and delegation to lower ranks;
- a reward system linked to store performance; and
- involvement of employees in the strategic plan, to induce a commitment to goals and the strategies for their achievement.

Establish a systematic set of performance measures

These would embrace both financial and non-financial indicators and might be expected to include: measures of quality, such as customer perception of service (cleanliness, timeliness, accuracy, reliability), number of lost items, number of customer complaints, conformance to competitors' standards, durability of creases, speed and courtesy of service, knowledgability of operatives, staff turnover levels and absenteeism levels; and measures of cost, such as overhead variances, solvent usage, inventory build-up, returns per square metre on labour costs, and relative cost/profitability of service provision.

The case highlights the importance of 'commitment from the top' and a willingness to change the culture of the group in the successful implementation of a TQM process.

STRATEGIC INTERNAL CONTROL

Internal control has always been a strategic process which goes far beyond policy manuals and internal audit to embrace corporate goals and the people, at all levels of the organization, who are employed to achieve them.

Casual observation of management accounting control systems (MACS) within large, complex organizations suggests that they are all the same – a combination of short- and long-term planning, budgets, variance analysis and project reporting. Closer examination reveals that the manner in which the MACS are applied varies greatly and reflects the preferences of senior management. Where, for example, management signals its perception of the importance of NFIs in interactive control systems, we might anticipate that in consequence subordinates will focus on the monitoring of these activities and the development of new measures.

The goals of MACS address four key strategic areas:

- planning – the setting of goals and an overall vision;
- control – the monitoring of external events and the measurement of internal activities to ensure a direction congruent with these goals;
- motivation – concerned with getting the best out of employees and linked to participation, empowerment and reward systems;
- performance – evaluation of individual and group performance for consistency with objectives and ethical considerations.

Following the seminal work of Anthony (1965) the planning and control areas have provided the traditional link between MACS and strategy. The SPAMSOAP mnemonic, so familiar to students of examinations in the management control area, designates the eight elements of the traditional system of internal control:

- Segregation of duties
- Physical safeguards
- Authorization and approval
- Management review
- Supervision and audit
- Organizational structures
- Accounting and information systems
- Personnel arrangements.

Planning and control activities rely heavily on financial and non-financial performance measures, but the internal control process goes far beyond policy manuals and audit, because it is determined by people at every level of the organization. It is geared to the achievement of corporate goals, not just financial reporting, making it a strategic process.

As Hiromoto (1988: 22) points out, 'Japanese companies must value inventory for tax purposes and financial statements … but don't let these accounting procedures determine how they measure and control organizational activities.' He emphasizes instead a direct link between management accounting practices and corporate goals whereby MACS are used to support and reinforce manufacturing strategies aimed at process and product innovation. Although recognizing that such practices do not represent *all* Japanese companies, his study provides early evidence of the importance of NFIs in motivating employees towards innovative practices and improved performance.

Information systems and control procedures (embracing authorization, verification, reconciliation, review and reports against budget) are necessary but insufficient features of a successful control environment. The Institute of Chartered Accountants in England and Wales (ICAEW, 1993) identified additional features which contribute to our 'motivation' and 'performance' goals; features which have remained substantially unaltered through subsequent reports (e.g., ICAEW, 2002):

- commitment to truth and fair dealing;
- commitment to quality and competence;
- leadership in control by example;
- communication of ethical values.

Corporate integrity, culture and code of ethics are thus central to successful internal control and lead us to consider alternative managerial approaches to motivation as a means of overcoming non-goal-congruent behaviour and the exploitation of MACS gaps. The seminal work in this area is F.W. Taylor's treatise of 1911 on *scientific management* in which he assumes that unskilled workers can be motivated to work only by money and close supervision (see Taylor, 1947). The resulting control system is one based on standard costing, budgeting and variance analysis. The natural consequences of the tight identification and planning of resource inputs, costs and variances are:

- work study, to analyse jobs and processes and find the 'best' way that unskilled labour can perform the task;
- scientific selection of personnel for the task at hand;
- minute division of labour to short specialized tasks;
- incentive schemes and targets;
- deskilling and potentially dehumanizing the workforce;
- ensuring that management, and not craftsmen, controls production and the speed of the production line.

Taylor's principles were widely adopted in the 1920s, most notably by Henry Ford in the mass production auto industry. Subsequent theorists have suggested alternative roles for management and supervisors in the organization. The *human resources movement* of the late 1930s recognized that financial reward was only one aspect of what working people wanted from their employment. The importance of mutual respect, discretion and recognition of contribution to the organization became more apparent. The implications for MACS were a focus on interpersonal relations and the monitoring and measurement of morale and job satisfaction. Since the 1950s the *human resources model* has extended the focus on individual needs to embrace working conditions and the nature of supervision. The implications for MACS have been greater employee participation in decision-making, TEI and employee empowerment. Recognition that subordinates often 'know the job' better than their managers, and associated research, suggest that participation in decision-making and employee empowerment will lead to greater motivation, greater job satisfaction, improved morale and greater commitment to the organization. The human resources model blends the 'motivation' and 'performance' goals of MACS by suggesting that goal congruence will be achieved by:

- strong organizational leadership;
- satisfying work and appropriate rewards;
- opportunities for advancement; and a
- supportive work environment.

The simplistic Taylorist assumption that financial reward is the only motivator to improved performance causes distinct problems for reward systems under *scientific management*:

- a short-term focus;
- high costs associated with servicing the system (particularly with share option schemes);
- manipulation opportunities (particularly with bonus plan schemes);
- doubts about whether the actual rewards target the most appropriate employees and whether they increase shareholder value.

The *human relations movement* and *human resources model* promote team-working and reward systems associated with the contributions of individuals to the team effort. Rewards may take the form of non-cash payments (e.g., gifts, or points schemes leading to gifts). TQM is one philosophy which aims to encourage teamwork and rewards participants for their co-operation in instituting organizational improvements.

Cullen et al. (1994) suggest that internal control failures will result from one of five eventualities:

1 *Lack of integrity of top management.* This may be apparent from dishonest, fraudulent or unethical behaviour. The resulting ethical dilemmas will emerge in the form of conflicts between individuals and organizational values, and between an organization's stated and practised values.
2 *A weak control environment.* This may be associated with corporate culture (e.g., a culture of excessive and unrealistic risk-taking). Shields and Young (1989) suggest that it will be very difficult to change organizational culture, especially in those organizations with weak leadership and no clear direction, or where internal conflict is high because of autocratic rule. They suggest that change will be resisted because of fear of the new, the cost of change in terms of both time and money, and the resulting changes in the balance of power in the organization.
3 *Inconsistent or unrealistic objectives.* For example, it would be inconsistent to pursue a corporate goal of industry leadership through technological innovation while still allocating overheads to product costs in a manner which penalizes the use of high-tech machinery.
4 *Communication breakdown* resulting in the pursuit of conflicting objectives. For example, innovation in entrepreneurial firms may be constrained by the implementation of unsuitable control systems focusing on costs to the detriment of the innovation goal.
5 *Inability or inflexibility to react appropriately.* This may mean that corporate inertia prevents the organization from taking advantage of technological opportunities or responding to threats from the external economy. For example, Williams and Ashford (1994) highlight four of the changes in control systems and product costing systems that may be necessitated by new manufacturing technologies:

  (i) competitive pressures necessitating shorter product life cycles and the faster introduction of new products and services. MACS must respond with flexible management structures, project teams and new performance measures.
 (ii) emphasis on activity analysis and the supply chain. MACS must respond with much closer attention to long-term supplier alliances and investigate activity-based management systems and customer profitability analysis.
(iii) adoption of TQM. MACS must respond with an increased emphasis on NFIs, to observe internal and external failure costs, to monitor prevention costs and to measure the costs of quality.
(iv) adoption of JIT management. MACS must respond by making wholesale modifications to traditional systems based on labour productivities, machine efficiencies, rejection and wastage rates, and inventory holdings. These will no longer be appropriate and new NFIs must place the emphasis on service to customers and speed of delivery.

Roslender (1992), Puxty (1993), Atkinson, et al. (1995) and Otley (2001) all provide excellent summaries of the accounting literature relating to management control, but no generally accepted view of the adequacy of existing theories in explaining organizational behaviour emerges. Researchers (e.g., Porter, 1980) agree that an 'overall cost leadership' strategy requires sophisticated cost controls, but otherwise such studies have been of little help in the design of MACS. Porter's cost leadership strategy in pursuit of sustainable competitive advantage provides a grounding for much of the subsequent research in the areas of value-chain analysis and strategic management accounting. It has popularized strategic cost analysis, with its identification of a value chain between raw materials and end-user, and the specification of cost drivers and cost reduction opportunities for each activity of the chain to effect appropriate internal management. The value-chain perspective is explored in detail by Shank and Govindarajan (1992).

Companies with different management control systems compete in different ways. Goold and Campbell (1987) identify three different strategic control styles where the degree of control from the centre is dependent on the balance between the competitive and financial goals of the enterprise. Leadership and the manner in which controls are implemented emerge as key distinguishing features between companies. Future research must focus on the relationship between MACS and corporate strategy to provide empirical support for those systems and non-financial measures which promote the short- and long-term goals of organizations.

Anthony's (1965) initial definition of management control has spawned a number of variations to facilitate understanding. Thus we have administrative and social controls (Hopwood, 1976), output and behavioural controls (Ouchi, 1977), market, bureaucracy and clan controls (Ouchi, 1979), results, action and personnel controls (Merchant, 1981), and, formal and informal controls (Anthony et al., 2003). The latter emphasize the importance of 'informal' control approaches while acknowledging that they are notoriously difficult to measure, or even quantify.

Studies founded within a 'contingency' framework have made a significant contribution to the management planning and control literatures by identifying contextual factors with the potential to influence the operation of the organization's 'package' – rather than system (Otley, 2001) – of accounting and non-accounting information mechanisms, for planning and control (Ittner and Larcker, 2001). The most prominent contingent factors include the external environment, technology, organizational structure, size, culture, competitive situation, and industry characteristics. (e.g., Chenhall, 2003).

Otley (1999) argues that accounting controls have historically been viewed as the principal means by which management control is effected, but that this orientation is no longer sufficiently broad to capture contemporary approaches. He argues for more 'management' in management accounting (Otley, 2001). These views are shared by Merchant and Van der Stede (2003), who observe that accounting controls form only part of broader control systems. Chenhall (2003) is especially concerned about the spurious research findings that might result (and have resulted) from failing to study specific accounting controls, and other organizational controls with which they are inextricably linked, at the same time.

The way in which particular combinations of controls can be aligned with strategic imperatives in particular circumstances, for optimum impact, remains a key concern in management accounting research. Malina and Selto (2001) suggest that an effective management control device should have both 'strategic alignment' and 'positive motivation' if it is to generate the desired outcomes. For strategic alignment they identify, respectively, the following critical attributes:

- measures of critical performance variables, linked to strategy;
- measures of critical performance demonstrably linked to desired outcomes;
- effective performance measures for communication purposes.

Correspondingly, for positive motivation, they identify:

- controllable performance measures;
- challenging but attainable performance targets;
- performance measures linked to the reward system in a meaningful manner.

These attributes have found considerable support in the empirical research literature, and provide a sound framework for further investigations.

The importance of sound internal controls is illustrated by the following case study which details the need to operate in a strategic manner to deal with significant external pressures.

CASE STUDY

Bradford Funerals: Performance and internal controls

This case concerns a company, operating within a highly sensitive industry, which needs to adopt new planning and control procedures and performance measures in order to ensure its long-term survival. The case explores the characteristics of the UK funeral industry and the impact of the incursion of large overseas companies on the operation of small family businesses.

Porter's (1980) *competitive strategy* framework provides the opportunity for the analysis of generic strategies to secure competitive advantage, when cost leadership is not a practical possibility. Product diversification and niche marketing are explored instead, together with a renewed focus on the internal controls in place.

Bradford Funerals is the largest funeral director in West Yorkshire, and one of the larger family-owned businesses in England. Even so, with an annual turnover of £1.6m and a full-time staff of only 15 it must still be categorized as a 'small' business.

The nature of the UK funeral business has changed rapidly during the past five years. Competition is becoming increasingly intense

CASE STUDY (cont.)

with the entry of overseas competitors; traditionally bereaved families had a tendency to choose a funeral director close to their home to be near their loved one, and the Co-operative Society has thus carried out about half of all UK funerals. But now Service Corporation International (SCI) has secured a significant share of the market by taking over the only public limited companies devoted to funeral operation. SCI is now the largest provider of death-care services in the world, operating over 3000 funeral service locations, 400 cemeteries and 200 crematoria in 20 countries. Growth by acquisition has been phenomenal; during 1994 SCI expanded into the UK by acquiring 154 funeral homes, two cemeteries and 13 crematoria owned by Great Southern Group plc, and 380 funeral homes held by Plantsbrook Group plc. In so doing SCI instantly gained approximately 15% of the UK market and became the country's largest privately-owned death-care operator. SCI's success has been driven by lowering costs through a 'clustering' strategy: clusters of geographical groups of funeral homes and cemeteries share common resources (e.g., personnel, accounting, sales, vehicles). However, such rapid growth in an acquisition company has come at a cost, as illustrated by the trends of Table 7.4. Despite record revenues in 1999 of £3.32 billion, up from only £1.65 billion in 1995, SCI's debt levels, having peaked in 1998, had forced a reorientation to reduce overhead and increase cash flow, including the disposal of non-core assets in the financial services areas.

The maintenance of market share is a key goal for Bradford Funerals across each of the three sectors of the business: burials (relative importance 20%), cremations (70%) and repatriation (10%).

TABLE 7.4

Financial trends for Service Corporation International
(Source: http://www.moneynet.com)

Year ended	31/12/99	31/12/98	31/12/97
INCOME STATEMENT (£000)			
Revenues	3,321,813	2,875,090	2,535,865
Total expenses	3,153,067	2,223,159	1,915,034
Pre-tax income	(37,690)	518,527	579,973
Post-tax income	(34,297)	342,142	374,552
BALANCE SHEET (£000)			
Current assets	996,151	1,209,080	811,408
Total assets	14,601,601	13,266,158	10,514,930
Current liabilities	1,057,865	630,325	535,442
Long-term debt	3,636,067	3,764,590	2,634,699
Total liabilities*	11,106,328	10,112,056	7,788,296

*Total liabilities include 'deferred pre-arranged funeral contract revenues' and 'deferred pre-need cemetery contract revenues' which together account for almost the whole of the difference between total liabilities, on the one hand, and current liabilities plus long-term debt, on the other.

CASE STUDY (cont.)

Repatriation is a significant component for Bradford Funerals because of its location close to a large Muslim population; although some Muslims bury their relatives in the UK as many as 80% are flown back to Pakistan for burial. The operations of SCI mean that it is impossible for Bradford to compete on a cost-efficiency basis. They must be cost-conscious, but rely on alternative strategies to stay competitive. In terms of Porter's (1980) generic strategies, this suggests that Bradford Funerals must look at product diversification and niche marketing.

THE NATURE OF THE SERVICE

Funeral direction is primarily a 'service' organization, responsible for supplying coffin, hearse, limousines and appropriate personnel and ensuring a smooth, dignified operation. However, the public perception of a 'product'-based business is still widespread.

Most funeral providers are professionals who try to satisfy the client's best interests, but the wide variety of customer choice means that the cost of a funeral can vary greatly. Table 7.5 details the scope of the service that might be provided by the funeral director. The cost of a coffin can vary from as little as £50, for cardboard or lightly veneered chipboard, to over £700 for a mahogany vessel with top-of-the-range handles, lining and fittings. Even so, a basic funeral – with no embalming, and just a hearse with no following limousine – is likely to cost at least £1280:

Professional services, hearse, oak veneer coffin	745
Crematorium fees	225
Minister's fees	150
Doctor's fees	85
Obituary and acknowledgements	75
	1280

The addition of the costs of embalming and dressing the body, visiting fees for the chapel of rest, an oak coffin, flowers, limousines for mourners, etc. means that this figure will quickly exceed £2000.

Most crematoria are run by local authorities and fees have historically been modest, though increasing to meet the cost of addressing European Union anti-pollution requirements. By 2000 SCI owned 21 out of 242 UK crematoria (8.7%), despite the potential undesirability of a firm that sells funerals in an area also controlling its crematoria. Most UK crematoria allow only 30 minutes for a service, some 45 minutes, but only very exceptionally longer; extra time for grieving may be purchased.

MARKET SHARE

When a call comes in from the customer about a bereavement, funeral arrangements commence immediately, with the actual

CASE STUDY (cont.)

TABLE 7.5

Services provided by funeral directors (Source: http://www.yorkshireco-op.com.uk)

Funeral directors' charges may include:
• a personal interview to receive instructions
• arranging for the removal of the deceased at anytime of the night or day
• use of private chapel of rest facilities
• liaison and confirmation with clergy, church, cemetery or crematorium
• completing and forwarding legal documentation to the appropriate authority
• supply and fitting of the coffin or casket
• supply of the necessary bearers
• provision of the hearse and limousines as required (alternatively, horse-drawn hearse and carriages)
• liaison with the police and coroner
• arranging the dispersal or interment of cremated remains
• providing transport to the registrar (if required)
• professional attendance and supervision throughout the funeral
• retaining detailed records of each funeral for future reference by the family if required
• repatriation both to and from abroad

Supplies attracting value-added tax at the current rate:
• insertion of press announcements
• assistance in ordering and the receipt and care of floral tributes
• arranging for the production of service sheets, etc.
• arranging for catering either at home or elsewhere
• provisions of designs and estimates for memorials

Disbursements on behalf of the client may include:
• arranging for the completion and payment of medical certificates for cremation
• arranging for the removal of the memorial (if applicable)
• arranging for the purchase and preparation of the grave
• payment of minister's fees/church fees
• payment of cremation fees
• payment of honoraria and gratuities

funeral taking place within four or five working days. Muslim funerals, on the other hand, will often take place on the same day as the death, including weekends and public holidays. Although the speed of events frequently causes logistical difficulties, it also has the advantage of facilitating regular monitoring of demand and the impact of competition. The great majority of funerals are published in the local newspaper, and in 80% of cases a named funeral director is associated with a particular funeral. This is not surprising because it represents a cheap form of advertising for the funeral director, appropriately located in the newspaper, and at the

CASE STUDY (cont.)

customer's expense. Thus market share can be calculated very precisely for 80% of funerals, but further research is necessary to fill the gap posed by the unidentified 20%. Back-up information is available relating to every death in the area from death registrations at the local registrar's office; this information is published monthly by the Office of Population Census and Surveys, and broken down weekly by locality. This gives a more accurate indication of market share and how busy the competition has been over the corresponding time period. However, while the above indicate who has died within the locality, this does not necessarily correspond with the number having their funerals in the area; local deaths and registrations may result in repatriation or persons being transported to their home town for burial. The same sort of problem in a reverse direction causes data inaccuracies arising from transportation into the area for burial; this is occurring increasingly with hospital deaths in specialized units (e.g. cardiac, spinal, transplants) outside the locality. Market share is perhaps best measured as the percentage of those people who died in the area who also had a funeral within the area, but this is less easy to specify with confidence because local cemeteries and crematoria regard this information as confidential. However, for cremations it is quite easy to ascertain the share of the market: when clients request the return of their relative's cremated remains, within 24 hours of the funeral the local crematorium returns them to the funeral director, individually packed in a functional plastic ash casket, which bears the name of the deceased and cremation number. These numbers are sequential, and each crematorium operates the same system, so that it is easy to calculate the proportion of total cremations conducted by Bradford Funerals.

LOGISTICS

Bradford Funerals conducts about 1000 funerals a year, but the unpredictability of the funeral business means that there is great potential variation in the demand for staff and vehicles. It is almost impossible to forecast when a funeral will be needed or how often the Bradford service will be required during a given week. The only certainty is that the demand will be greater during the winter months (November to February) than during summer.

A core of full-time staff is required with the skills to conduct embalming, chauffeuring and funeral directing. Added to these are a pool of relatively unskilled chauffeurs/bearers who may be called upon at short notice, in order to provide the required degree of flexibility during periods of high demand.

Until recently Bradford used a single estate car to transport bodies from hospital/mortuary to their chapel of rest. This car could only hold two cadavers at a time, meaning a lot of wasted transportation time, particularly when the vehicles were travelling backwards and forwards to the same hospital. This situation has been considerably eased with the purchase of a converted private ambulance which

CASE STUDY (cont.)

allows the movement of up to five cadavers simultaneously from one or more place of death, before returning to the chapel.

Funerals can only be arranged with the cooperation of other interested parties, notably a religious minister to conduct the service, the crematorium or cemetery and the family, friends and relatives. Most funerals take place between 11.00 a.m. and 2.00 p.m., although the local crematoria are available from 9.00 a.m. until 3.30 p.m. at half-hour intervals. However, early morning funerals are very unpopular because of the difficulties of relatives travelling long distances to be there, and late funerals are unpopular because of the extra emotional burden it places on waiting family. Consequently the demands on the limousine fleet are very high over a relatively short period of time. Bradford has two hearses and three limousines, so that with careful timing it can conduct two funerals at the same time, starting one whilst the other is finishing. During exceptionally busy periods it has been known to conduct three funerals more or less simultaneously with the same core fleet, perhaps supplemented by a hired limousine. The hiring of additional hearses and limousines becomes essential due to exceptional circumstances:

- punctures or breakdowns to vehicles;
- last-minute requirements for additional limousines by clients wishing to transport additional family members; and
- families spending an excessive amount of time around the grave, talking, after the funeral.

These circumstances make mutual respect between competitors essential in the industry. All will be subject to the same difficulties, and all will be prepared to lend limousines to even their staunchest rivals at very short notice. There are no inter-company charges or transfers associated with this arrangement.

During such busy times job queues and excessive work in progress can arise. Sometimes in the winter months as many as 15 funerals need to be arranged for the same day, with the consequence that coffins are readied and cadavers moved to the chapel and placed in a queue awaiting embalming and then gowning once they have been placed in the coffin. The Bradford mortuary can only cope with two cases at a time, so that delays are inevitable during busy periods. The mortuary bottleneck is only relieved by staff working very long hours – often until very late in the evening – to ensure that preparations are complete for funerals taking place on the following day.

INVENTORY CONTROL

High build-ups in stocks of coffins, handles, gowns and shrouds are a feature of the business, associated with the irregularity of the service provided. An additional and not insignificant issue is the inventory associated with Muslim funerals. Bradford Funerals has an enviable reputation in this regard, which it has sought to

CASE STUDY (cont.)

encourage in order to expand market share. But Muslim funerals usually require repatriation to Pakistan for burial, and – because of the very tight time constraints imposed – Bradford must keep an inventory of hermetically sealed zinc-lined coffins in stock. These are a requirement of overseas carriage by air, and their inventory cost is right at the top of the range described earlier. These items frequently remain in stock at a cost of £6000 each for some months before they are required. Bradford's reputation with its competitors as the market leader for the provision of Muslim burials means that it is frequently called upon to supply zinc-interior coffins when their competitors have repatriation requirements. While the low level of demand experienced by competitors makes this a cost-effective strategy for them, for Bradford it imposes further inventory management problems as they seek to source coffins for all Muslim burials in the area, not just their own.

However, it is possible that some of the excess inventory may be attributable to bad planning and poor forecasting. The product range is extremely wide, catering for people of all shapes and sizes – from less than 20 cm in length for babies and small children up to a maximum length of about 220 cm and maximum width of 80 cm. The need for more than one style and type of coffin in the range means that an inventory in excess of 120 coffins will be held in a typical month. Even in relatively quiet times inventory holdings are high to provide a buffer against unanticipated increases in the workload. Given the 10% of high-value zinc-lined coffins required, this means that monthly inventory holdings will typically be £39,600. The average size coffin selection ranges from 150 cm to 190 cm in length and Bradford has coffin sizes at 5 cm intervals within this range. Consequently, size differences alone contribute to a substantial inventory, which arguably might be lower, since the occupant is unlikely to complain (nor the customers to notice) if the coffin is slightly too large. Bradford estimate that a halving in the number of coffin sizes they offer could cut inventory levels by as much as 15%, and reduce the value of inventory holdings by nearly £6000.

COSTING AND PRICING

A standardized costing and pricing system is the norm in the funeral industry, even though there may be significant cost differences between individual cases. Customers, especially those who lose a loved one out of normal working hours, expect a great deal in terms of attention, compassion, service and reverence from their funeral director, while at the same time wanting very little in the way of direct contact. The distress associated with ascertaining the precise requirements of the family necessitate the adoption of a standardized approach to both product and service. For example, a coffin 150 cm in length is much cheaper for the funeral director to supply than one which is 200 cm long, typically £300 rather than £350, but in providing an estimate of funeral costs an average figure is given to the

CASE STUDY (cont.)

customer rather than subjecting the bereaved to distressing questions relating to the height and weight of their recently deceased loved one.

Similarly, charges for the removal of the deceased back to the Bradford chapel for the funeral are standardized; the charge for a death occurring at 2.00 a.m. is the same as one at 9.00 a.m., both requiring immediate removal. The former is, in practice, a much more expensive service to provide, requiring overtime payments for attendance out of normal working hours as well as additional communications costs associated with keeping a team on call 24 hours a day, 365 days a year.

FINANCIAL INDICATORS

Bradford records creditors, debtors and bank statement balance on a month-by-month basis to allow comparisons against both budget and last year's performance. However, the budget is set on the basis of the actual performance in the previous year and involves no forecasting or projections. Capital expenditures in one year are entirely dependent on the profits earned in the previous year.

Cash flow is also monitored monthly, and debtors tracked from a period of three months, and thereafter every month. Bad debt averages only £8000, modest given that many customers have no savings or insurance cover, and may not be able to claim funding from the state (the Department of Social Security in the UK).

The financial accounts thus provide a 'broad brush' approach to the performance of the business, but they are regarded as reasonably accurate and perfectly adequate to meet the needs of day-to-day decision-making. The current annual position (at the end of 2000) is as detailed in Table 7.6.

TABLE 7.6

Bradford Funerals financial position as at 31/12/2000

Profit and Loss Account (£000)		Balance Sheet (£000)	
Revenue	1,600	Non-Current Assets	560
Cost of Sales	920	Current Assets: Cash	20
	680	Debtors	300
Wages & Salaries	370	Inventory	90
Rent, utilities etc.	60		410
Fleet maintenance	6	Current Liabilities:	10
Other expenses		Overdraft	
(including	12	Creditors	90
depreciation)	448		100
Net Profit	232	Long-Term Liabilities: loans	100
Taxation	72	Pre-sold funerals	70
Profit after Tax	160		170
		Share capital and Reserves	700

CASE STUDY (cont.)

We are required to make recommendations to Bradford Funerals about improvement opportunities that exist in the areas specified, together with a discussion of their implications for the strategies and control mechanisms that might be adopted to stay competitive.

CASE ANALYSIS

Bradford Funerals is a large family business, though still small when compared with the quoted service sector. Its goals appear to be survival as an independent company, while at least maintaining its market share.

The SWOT analysis of Table 7.7 highlights the internal weaknesses of the company and external threats to its survival. But it also offers some encouragement in the improvement opportunities that exist.

In examining Porter's three generic strategies for competitive advantage, cost leadership does not appear to be an option; Bradford cannot compete with the likes of SCI on cost or efficiency of operations. While it remains a family business it can ensure its independence, and with appropriate action to correct internal deficiencies be efficient enough to remain profitable. Such a focus should mean that Bradford can avoid the financial difficulties impacting on SCI, so apparent in Table 7.8. The ratio trends clearly demonstrate the need for the management actions currently being undertaken by SCI. Although debt levels are high, the gearing ratios have remained stable over the period, but both earnings and liquidity

TABLE 7.7

SWOT analysis for Bradford Funerals

STRENGTHS	OPPORTUNITIES
Largest funeral director in West Yorkshire	Increase market share
Amongst larger family-owned businesses in England	Improved forecasting
	More realistic costing methods
Family reputation	More personal service
Cooperation with rival funeral directors	

WEAKNESSES	THREATS
Small business (turnover £1.6m)	Intense competition from overseas
Logistical difficulties	Cost-cutting from larger operations
Staff inflexibility	
Average pricing policy	
Process bottlenecks	
High inventory levels	
Large product range	
Need for 24-hour cover all year round	

CASE STUDY (cont.)

TABLE 7.8

Financial ratio trends for SCI

Year ended	31/12/99	31/12/98	31/12/97
Profit Margin(%) – PBT/S	(1.13)	18.0	22.9
Return on Assets (%) – PBT/TA	(0.26)	3.9	5.5
Liquidity – CA/CL	0.94	1.92	1.52
Gearing – TL/TA	0.76	0.76	0.74

have declined, necessitating a renewed focus on improving cash flows and reducing overheads.

The financial accounts for Bradford demonstrate the relative strength of the balance sheet – very low levels of debt and high levels of liquidity (current ratio 4:1, quick assets ratio 3:2). But the profit and loss accounts reveal problems: the profit margin at 14.5% is good, but the net profit of only £160,000 may leave little room for future capital expenditure outlays. Both 'cost of sales' and 'wages and salaries' are too high and inconsistent with these revenue levels. The company needs to seek more profitable markets, balance its throughput better to avoid extensive 'out-of-hours' payments, and reduce the costs of its service provision.

Bradford can compete on service, and here its reputation as a sound local business is invaluable. It may also try to carve out a niche for itself as a specialist in particular funerals, for example for Muslims or small children, as well as in grievance counselling for the bereaved to break down the barriers of intrusive contact. Bradford Funerals is clearly already regarded by its competitors as the expert in Muslim burials, but this recognition has apparently not yet permeated to the whole of the market. The company needs to look at its markets more closely to determine why it is currently the funeral director of choice, and in what circumstances it might change the purchasing habits of potential customers.

Forecasting and inventory control

Levels of uncertainty in the funeral directing business are very low when compared with other industries (e.g., computer software). Even so, demand varies to such an extent as to make the use of resources (and idle time) very uneven. Bradford can significantly improve on the current situation by better forecasting of demand peaks and troughs, and making better use of existing resources.

Some form of simple time series analysis would assist in providing guidance of the expected highs/lows in demand and would reflect the seasonal patterns associated with high but variable demand due to climatic conditions. For any given month of the year their historical records will allow them to link climatic conditions

CASE STUDY (cont.)

with the range of likely demand. This analysis would allow Bradford to control resource use and allow inventory holdings to be kept in check, but would need to be monitored closely to avoid stock-outs. Given the contribution of the holdings of zinc-lined coffins to the value of inventory holdings, time series modelling of the incidence of repatriations could be very helpful in reducing inventory costs.

The data from the case suggests that the Bradford revenue of £1.6m is derived from approximately 1000 funerals, priced between £1300 and £2000, implying a mean cost of sales of £920 per funeral. The number of funerals peaks at 15, at the height of the winter, so that realistically the company will be conducting approximately 50 funerals per week during the winter months. Allowing for holiday periods, well over half of the annual number of funerals will be conducted between November and February, allowing an annual schedule similar to that below to be developed:

Month	Jan.	Feb.	Mar.	Apr.	May	Jun.	Jul.	Aug.	Sept.	Oct.	Nov.	Dec.
Funerals	120	200	100	30	30	20	20	30	30	100	200	120

Inventory holdings should match this anticipated pattern of demand, and modelling will allow the gap between actual demand and holdings to be minimized, especially during the relatively light April to September period. The case suggests a 'typical' monthly holding of 120 coffins (at a cost of around £39,600, based on 10% at £600 and 90% at £300), whereas a schedule of the kind developed would suggest that this is unnecessarily large for all but the peak months.

Activity analysis would allow the development of standards for time and quality for each of the sequential processes. It will also facilitate job scheduling to overcome some of the extremes of bottlenecks and excess capacity which exist at demand extremes. However, a stock turnover period of about $(90/1600) \propto 365 = 36$ days suggests that stock control is not the most serious problem facing Bradford Funerals.

Costing and pricing

Cost control is essential if Bradford Funerals is to survive in the long term, and the absence of an adequate costing system is perhaps their most pressing problem. Inventory should also be reduced, at least by the 15% envisaged, and probably more. This can be accomplished by radically reducing the size range of coffins held in stock, and their number. The forecasting methods referred to above should help in this regard too.

At present, price averaging means cross-subsidization across all the activities of the funeral director. There is no 'user pays' philosophy because activities in unsocial hours (e.g., early morning retrieval of corpses) and at peak periods (e.g., funerals between 11.00 a.m. and 2.00 p.m.) are currently all charged at a standard

CASE STUDY (cont.)

rate, in order to be able to quote a single price at the outset which causes the bereaved the least distress. However, funerals requiring more limousines (for example) will already be priced higher, so it should not be difficult to impose penalty charges for 11.00–2.00 funerals which encourage the use of facilities in non-peak periods. This would also help to smooth out resource use and make better use of capacity.

Bradford Funerals might consider the adoption of a total quality management approach to prioritize problems/issues and implement appropriate solutions with strategies consistent with the corporate goals.

Financial indicators

The 'broad brush' approach adopted by the company in the monitoring of performance means that they are focusing on a very restricted set of financial accounting numbers. There appears to be relatively little focus on profit performance, causal factors or on the three E's of management accounting: economy, efficiency and effectiveness. A better appreciation of the cost of provision of each part of the service would undoubtedly yield cost efficiencies and waste reduction. A renewed focus on budget setting might also highlight further improvement opportunities.

EMPLOYEE EMPOWERMENT

In the earlier section on strategic internal control we observed the trend away from the 'rational goals model' approach, so closely associated with the 'command and control' type regime of F.W. Taylor (1947). Instead we saw the development of human relations models, emphasizing participation, collaboration and teamwork, of which the TQM philosophy is so typical. Employee empowerment is an extension of this trend, with managerial control being sought through mechanisms which seek to encourage self-discipline and the assumption of responsibility.

The quality improvement process should be a vehicle for positive and constructive movement within an organization, but we must also be aware of the destructive potential of the process. Failure to observe the fundamental principles of quality improvement may destroy motivation irrecoverably. Some authors, notably Carlzon (1987), Albrecht (1988) and Albrecht and Zemke (1985), have criticized the direction that TQM implementations have tended to take in practice, in particular:

- the focus on documentation of process and ill-measurable outcomes;
- the emphasis on quality assurance rather than improvement; and
- an internal focus which is at odds with the alleged customer orientation.

Carlzon has revived customer focus with an emphasis on total employee involvement culminating in the empowerment of the 'front line' of customer service troops. The main features of his empowerment thrust have been:

- loyalty to the vision of the company through the pursuit of tough, visible goals;
- recognition of satisfied customers and motivated employees as the true assets of a company;
- delegation of decision-making to the point of responsibility by eliminating hierarchical tiers of authority to allow direct and speedy response to customer needs; and
- decentralization of management to make best use of the creative energy of the workforce.

Albrecht suggests that TQM may not be appropriate for service-based industries, because the standards-based approach of 'industry best practice' ignores the culture of organizations. He recommends a move towards total quality service (TQS), which is more customer-oriented and creates an environment to promote enthusiasm and commitment. Albrecht suggests that poor service is associated with sloppy procedures, errors, inaccuracies and oversights, and poor co-ordination, all of which represent improvement opportunities which can be achieved through tighter controls.

Not all managers adopt such collaborative and participative perspectives, so that differences persist in the choice between 'rational goals' or 'human relations' approaches in generating appropriate behaviours in particular circumstances. The following two case studies adopt alternative stances, but both illustrate the opportunities for dysfunctional behaviour. Thus the Harvey-Harris case pursues the employee empowerment route, with disastrous consequences, while the Borthwick Construction case follows the more traditional approach of bonuses awarded for reaching specified performance targets – again with undesirable outcomes.

CASE STUDY

Harvey-Harris Stores: Empowerment from the top floor to the shop floor

This case study focuses on the application of employee empowerment principles to a large retail group. It provides the opportunity to analyse the manner of the strategy implementation and the consequent impact on both individuals and the organization.

The case establishes significant financial underperformance in one part of a retail group and investigates the use of 'employee empowerment' techniques – following Carlzon (1987) – to provide a solution. The case illustrates the dysfunctional activity associated with implementing empowerment without either appropriate management control or staff training, together with the dire financial implications. The case analysis discusses alternative approaches that might have been adopted.

CASE STUDY (cont.)

Harvey-Harris operate 150 department stores across England and Wales, through two separate divisions which together offer a product range to cover all income groups. Thus, the 80 W.J. Harvey stores are targeted towards upper- and middle-income families and the 70 R.S. Harris stores target lower- and middle-income families. The Harvey stores are larger (often with two or three floors) while the Harris stores all operate on a single level. The stores are distributed as follows:

	Wales and the South West	East	Midlands	North East	North West	Anglia	Cumbria	Total
Harvey	15	38	10	4	8	3	2	80
Harris	26	18	10	6	8	1	1	70
	41	56	20	10	16	4	3	

The financial results for the current year (1999) are as follows:

	Group	W.J. Harvey	R.S. Harris
No. of stores	150	80	70
Sales revenue (£m)	4,846	3,718	1,128
Profit before tax (£m)	192	98	94
Selling area (sq m)	1,362,773	992,442	370,331
No. of employees	46,211	33,257	12,954

One of the factors which explains the poor performance of W.J. Harvey relative to R.S. Harris is that the latter is not involved in food retailing – which is traditionally low-margin and requires more selling space. Another is the expense associated with the provision of a superior decor in the Harvey stores.

Of more concern to the Group is the trend in sales and profitability. Harvey sales are static, Harris sales show only a modest increase over the last two years; both divisions are losing market share to competitors who are perceived to be more 'customer-friendly'. Table 7.9 details the trend, together with comparative industry benchmarks.

Clayton Watts, the Group Managing Director, commissions a customer survey across the W.J. Harvey division to determine what service customers really want. Table 7.10 details the outcome.

Clayton Watts prides himself on being well versed in the latest management techniques and is determined to apply them to correct the current weaknesses of the group. His intention is to redirect the group's objectives by introducing a new 'mission' together with employee empowerment to the 'front-line troops' of customer service personnel. He is looking for a system to push responsibility down to lower levels in order to free up senior management for strategic purposes. He has been impressed by the work

Relative performance at Harvey-Harris stores

	1999	1998	1997	1996	1995
W J Harvey					
No of Stores	80	77	75	74	74
Sales Revenue (£m) Food	364	359	360	356	350
(Total)	3718	3627	3563	3537	3552
Non-Food	3354	3268	3203	3181	3202
Profit before Tax (£m) Food	8	9	10	10	10
(Total)	98	102	103	106	107
Non-Food	90	93	93	96	97
Total Assets (£m)	1090	1019	1007	980	981
Finished Goods Inventory (£m) Food	62	58	56	54	50
(Total)	580	586	570	520	465
Non-Food	518	528	514	466	415
Selling Area (sq m)	992,442	954,220	930,435	917,030	917,030
No of Employees	33,257	32,032	31,256	30,780	30,796
R S Harris					
No of Stores	70	66	60	57	55
Sales Revenue (£m)	1128	1042	928.6	838.0	768.2
Profit before Tax (£m)	94	85	78	70	60
Total Assets (£m)	326	309	295	298	296
Finished Goods Inventory (£m)	280	275	260	258	240
Selling Area (sq m)	370,331	346,169	317,474	302,630	291,956
No of Employees	12,954	12,220	11,100	10,530	10,180
Retail Industry Benchmarks					
Food: PBT/S (%)	6.0	6.0	6.0	6.0	6.0
Sales/sq.m. (£000)	8.0	8.0	8.0	8.0	8.0
PBT/Inventory	10.0	10.0	10.0	10.0	10.0
Sales per Employee (£000)	150	150	145	145	140
Non-Food: PBT/S	10.0	10.0	10.0	10.0	10.0
Sales/sq.m. (£000)	4.0	4.0	4.0	4.0	4.0
PBT/Inventory	30.0	30.0	30.0	30.0	30.0
Sales per Employee (£000)	100	100	100	100	100

TABLE 7.9

CASE STUDY (cont.)

TABLE 7.10

Results of customer survey

Customer requirements

Pricing:
- all items clearly ticketed
- competitive pricing
- facilities for easy use of credit cards

Product range:
- departments easy to locate
- product available in the size and colour required
- good selection/variation of fashion items
- value for money

Speed of transaction:
- speedy, accurate purchases
- no long queues
- only one signature of authorization required

Staff availability:
- adequate staffing at peak trading times
- clearly visible staff to provide help
- staff with a pride in their appearance and sales performance
- no huddles of staff, talking or on the telephone

Staff service:
- complaints handled seriously and followed through to a satisfactory conclusion
- staff knowledgeable about products and alternatives
- genuine interest and attention to customer needs
- patience and courtesy shown at all times, especially when under pressure
- staff able to locate products and provide in-store directions
- staff provide careful and detailed advice
- acknowledge regular customers as special people
- respect customers as normal individuals

of Jan Carlzon (1987) in initiating the idea of employee empowerment to emphasize the role of employees in achieving customer focus, and sees empowerment as a means of facilitating commitment to corporate goals and recognition of the importance of both satisfied customers and motivated employees. To implement the strategy he intends to follow Carlzon by delegating decision-making to the point of responsibility by eliminating hierarchical tiers of authority, and allowing direct and speedy response to customer needs, and decentralizing management to make the best use of the creative energy of the workforce.

Since the W.J. Harvey division is apparently in need of the more urgent action the new approach will be implemented there first, and if successful then used in the R.S. Harris division too. First, he changes the mission statement of the group to reflect a shift in focus away from profitability and towards a customer focus. 'Customer satisfaction' is to be the new buzz-phrase, supported by a new responsive, friendly attitude to customers which is both helpful and genuinely respectful. Success will be measured by customer satisfaction and the degree to which customers return to make repeat purchases. To make the new initiative work the staff on the shop floor will be 'empowered' so that they have the authority to make immediate decisions without recourse to middle management. A new slogan, 'It's up to you', will be introduced to motivate sales staff to take the initiative in sales transactions. They will then be able to be 'responsive' to customer requirements and to ensure that they leave W.J. Harvey happy with their shopping experience.

The initiative was implemented in January 2000, with an immediate impact on the financial results as indicated below in the six months' figures to June 2000:

	Actual	Target
Sales revenue (£m)	1,950.0	2,000.0
Profit before tax (£m)	35.0	60.0
Profit margin (%)	1.8	3.0

Sales are almost on target, up 7.5% on the previous half-year, but profits have collapsed and the profit margin has slumped to a disastrous 1.8%. Clayton Watts orders an immediate investigation of the causes underlying this poor performance, with the focus on the way the 'It's up to you' policy has operated at sales floor level. The outcome is a devastating insight into the way employee empowerment has been implemented at W.J. Harvey:

- When staff on the sales floor have been reluctant to make a decision, and have appealed to middle management, the latter have retorted 'It's up to you' and failed to provide the necessary guidance.
- Sales staff have frequently become involved in bartering, allowing customers to negotiate generous discounts on the ticketed price of an item, in the belief that this is consistent with the 'customer satisfaction' objective.
- Staff have operated a generous refund policy on goods returned as apparently soiled or damaged. Even where there has been doubt about the cause of the damage, and the goods have been in the possession of the customer for up to three years, a full cash refund has been provided.
- Staff have operated a generous exchange policy too, for goods that customers believe not to have worn well, or to which they take a dislike. The abuse of the exchange policy has been most

CASE STUDY (cont.)

apparent in fashion departments where shoes have been replaced as they wear out, and dresses have been replaced after one or two wears. The sales staff perceive that they have been led to believe that such action is consistent with the new 'customer-friendly' policy.

- Sales staff are in the habit of complying with the requests of customers, however outrageous, once such customers start making a fuss or attract the attention of other shoppers with a raised voice.
- Generous policies have provided virtually a 'shoplifters' charter'. Thieves remove items from the shelves, abuse them (e.g., dirtying or pulling threads on fashion items) and take them for immediate refunds without even removing the goods from the store.

Clayton Watts knows that he must act quickly, if he is to save his own job and if he is to produce a satisfactory set of year-end figures for 2000. Employee empowerment has clearly been a complete failure which must be abandoned, and a new policy adopted in its place. Not being one for compromise, Clayton decides to change the whole complexion of the business. A new 'mission' statement will be drafted in which references to 'customer satisfaction' will be absent. Instead the focus will revert to short-term profitability in terms of the 'achievement of world best practice which creates shareholder value'.

To ensure the achievement of the new objective he implements two new strategies:

- Swingeing staff cuts. He eliminates a whole level of middle management, amalgamates the management and administrative functions of branches located in the same town, closes some small stores and cuts the sales staff by 20% across the board. Any undermanning on the sales floor will be covered by management at all levels; all must be prepared to be visible and facilitate sales.
- A strict policy of standard operating procedures for sales staff. Gone are the days of discretionary decision-making; in their place are rigid guidelines to control both exchanges and refunds (e.g., receipts must be produced) and the way in which sales staff react with customers. Rigid service standards are implemented which involve staff being scripted as to the form of words they can employ and the actions they can take.
- Both strategies are unpopular on the sales floor, and staff morale sinks to an all-time low. Skilled sales staff in the fashion areas are particularly aggrieved; they are commission-driven and are able to handle sales to up to six different customers simultaneously through their own personal approach. But Clayton Watts points to the bottom line; his actions have saved his skin and returned W.J. Harvey to respectability:

	2000 (1st half-year)	2000 (2nd half-year)	2000
Sales revenue (£m)	1,950.0	1,570.0	3,520.0
Profit before tax (£m)	35.0	60.0	95.0
Profit margin (%)	1.8	3.8	2.7
Selling area (sq. m.)	992,442	864,212	
No. of employees	33,257	23,744	

The results of the previous year have put all thoughts of extending the employee empowerment experiment to R.S. Harris out of his mind. But he does have some lingering doubts that had he done things differently the new initiative might have been successful. It is possible that he could make R.S. Harris even more successful than it already is.

We are required to identify the weaknesses in Clayton Watts' approach to the implementation of employee empowerment, and suggest what he might do differently were he to extend the initiative to R.S. Harris.

CASE ANALYSIS

The financial numbers for 1999 highlight the need for action at Harvey-Harris and pinpoint the W.J. Harvey stores as the major problem area. Table 7.11 details performance trends for the two sides of the business over the last five years. Sales per store are in decline for W.J. Harvey, where most alarmingly profit margin is only 2.6% and profit per square metre £82 (both figures a third of that achieved by R.S. Harris). Profit per employee, at £2947, lags way behind the Harris equivalent too. Neither store is performing outstandingly relative to retail industry benchmarks.

The adoption of employee empowerment may or may not be the best way to correct the imbalance; what is not in doubt is that the manner of its implementation has not given empowerment the chance to work. If Clayton Watts had given more thought and carried out research into the joint introduction of standard operating procedures and employee empowerment, then the dual management techniques could have provided excellent financial results while also uniting management and the sales force. There has been no consideration, for example, of whether the empowerment programme should be implemented differently in departments of the store responsible for 'food' and 'fashions'. Nor have the management controls been thought through, together with the associated implications for the management accounting and internal audit functions.

The fundamental weakness of the approach adopted is that the sales force have been empowered (i.e., given their freedom) without any corresponding establishment of ground rules for the implementation of this empowerment. If standard operating procedures had been documented in the first place then everyone would have

CASE STUDY (cont.)

TABLE 7.11

Harvey-Harris performance ratios

	1999	1998	1997	1996	1995
W.J. HARVEY					
Sales per store (£m.)	46.5	47.1	47.5	47.8	48.0
Sales per sq.m. (£000)	3.7	3.8	3.8	3.9	3.9
Sales per employee (£000)	111.8	113.2	114.0	114.9	115.3
Profit margin (%) (Overall)	2.6	2.8	2.9	3.0	3.0
Profit margin (%) Food	2.2	2.5	2.8	2.8	2.9
Profit margin (%) Non-Food	2.7	2.8	2.9	3.0	3.0
Return on inventory (%) Food	12.9	15.5	17.9	18.5	20.0
Return on inventory (%) Non-Food	17.4	17.6	18.1	20.6	23.4
Return on assets (%)	9.0	10.0	10.2	10.8	10.9
Profit per store (£m.)	1.2	1.3	1.4	1.4	1.4
Profit per sq. m (£)	82.2	106.9	110.7	115.6	116.7
Profit per employee (£)	2946.7	3184.3	3295.4	3443.8	3474.5
R.S. HARRIS					
Sales per store (£m.)	16.1	15.8	15.5	14.7	14.0
Sales per sq. m. (£000)	3.0	3.0	2.9	2.8	2.6
Sales per employee (£000)	87.1	85.3	83.7	79.6	75.5
Profit margin (%)	8.3	8.2	8.4	8.3	7.8
Return on inventory (%)	33.6	30.9	30.0	27.1	25.0
Return on assets (%)	28.8	27.5	26.4	23.5	20.3
Profit per store (£m.)	1.3	1.3	1.3	1.2	1.1
Profit per sq. m (£)	253.8	245.5	245.7	231.3	205.5
Profit per employee (£)	7256.4	6955.8	7027.0	6647.7	5893.9

understood the real objectives of the operation – 'to make a profit by satisfying customer needs'.

As it is, Clayton Watts' initiative is perceived to be a radical one by the sales force and they have responded likewise – by making radical business decisions. An apparently extreme business philosophy is matched by extreme business practice. Had the standard operating procedures been in place prior to the adoption of empowerment, then sales staff would have been able to improve service levels without giving away profits. Such a policy would have avoided the necessity of the draconian steps taken to reverse the chaos, notably the 'scripting' of staff for all transactions.

Should the new techniques be extended to R.S. Harris, then a number of pre-implementation steps are essential, if employee empowerment is to be given the chance to work:

1 Introduce a mission statement with the emphasis on 'profit through service'.

2 Introduce standard operating procedures, which would embrace at least service standards, an exchange and refunds policy, and merchandise selection and presentation. These would be modelled on the information gathered through customer surveys and detailed in Table 7.10.
3 Ensure that everyone knows their goals and limitations before empowering.

Follow-up work after implementation should include monitoring by further customer surveys and confidential staff surveys at two-month intervals. Deficiencies can then be corrected before the consequences are too serious, and Clayton can gauge levels of customer satisfaction and staff commitment.

If the strategy is successful R.S. Harris will benefit from improved financials and an upward shift of staff morale.

Borthwick Construction : A case study of dysfunctional bonus schemes

Borthwick Construction is a UK company based in Wolverhampton which is providing construction and building materials within the industrial West Midlands. It has a divisional structure, with each of the five divisions making a significant contribution to group profits, as follows:

	Builders' Materials	Corrugated Board	Plastics	Roofing	Glass
Contribution to group profits	15%	20%	35%	17%	13%
Bonus-related profit target	10%	15%	20%	12%	10%

The performance of each division is measured by reference to the profits it generates relative to its asset base. The bonus element of the divisional managers' compensation packages is highly geared to the achievement of a target profits/net assets performance ratio. Senior managers within each division receive bonuses which are a fixed percentage of that awarded to the divisional manager. For bonus calculation purposes, profit is defined as the annual trading profit, excluding any extraordinary items, and net assets are defined as the net book value of assets at the year end after netting off both cash and overdraft:

Net assets = [Fixed assets + (Current assets *less* Cash)]
                     −[Long-term liabilities + (Current liabilities − Overdraft)].

Cedric Black is head of the Plastics Division; his division consistently provides the lion's share of group profitability but

CASE STUDY (cont.)

the nature of the business requires investment in expensive high-technology equipment, increasing the value of the asset base. He feels that he is being doubly penalized by being asked to achieve a target profit ratio significantly larger than any other division in order to earn his annual bonus.

The Divisional Management Accountant (Antonia Bracken) has alerted Cedric to the likelihood of the 2004 target not being achievable. Bracken forecasts that at 30 June 2004 trading profit will be £350,000 while net assets employed at the year end will be £1.8m, resulting in a profit ratio of 19.4%, marginally below the 20% target for earning performance-related bonuses.

Cedric calls on his function managers – Bob Forrest (sales and marketing), Peter Dobson (production), and Dorothy Marsden (personnel) – together with Bracken, to come up with proposals which might avert a personal financial reversal.

Antonia Bracken highlights the reason for the shortfall: investment in new equipment essential for the division to remain competitive, at a cost of £250,000. This equipment will allow the Division to produce a range of products recently released by its competitors, and is expected to result in additional sales of £150,000 per year over each of the next 10 years. Variable manufacturing costs are approximately 40% of sales, and it will cost the Division an additional £5000 to install the machinery. The equipment will be depreciated on a straight-line basis, and it is estimated to have a salvage value of £10,000 at the end of its useful life. Borthwick's weighted average cost of capital is 10% and the company tax rate 30%. Bracken suggests that the simple solution to achieve the required 20% profit target would be to defer the £255,000 expenditure to the next financial year.

Dorothy Marsden is unwilling to endanger the long-term competitiveness of the Division and suggests a safer alternative, as long as the Division is prepared to bite the bullet by retrenching a few workers. She proposes to close down the small, but profitable, Biddulph plant with a loss of 25 jobs. This move would incur a disengagement payout approaching £50,000 and would reduce divisional profits by £10,000 per year. On the other hand, the sale of the plant would immediately raise £250,000 while reducing the book value of assets by £200,000.

Bob Forrest is amazed that such draconian measures are even being contemplated. He suggests that a simple manipulation of creditors would provide an appropriate solution. Plastics Division owes £100,000 to Jones Brothers, a small independent manufacturer and long-standing supplier. There are plenty of alternative suppliers and Jones cannot afford to lose Plastics' business. They are vulnerable to exploitation and Forrest suggests that payment of the debt be deferred from 14 June to 2 July. A £5000 late-payment penalty would result and Jones would likely have problems meeting their own creditors. But that was not Plastics' problem!

CASE STUDY (cont.)

Peter Dobson is unhappy with the unnecessary £5000 late-payment pay-out and suggests a time-shift in the opposite direction, by bringing forward customer receipts. He suggests that by introducing an extra shift, additional overtime working and cutting a few corners, he can complete the Vertex project four weeks ahead of schedule (20 June instead of 18 July). Quality might suffer a little as a result, but the customer could then be invoiced in June, increasing profits by £20,000, at a cost of only £2500 resulting from penalty production rates.

Cedric is encouraged by the ingenuity and creativity of his executive team, but requires guidance in choosing the most appropriate of the alternatives. After all, there is no point in implementing all of the policies. He is rewarded for beating target, not for beating target by 10%, and he does not wish to alert the group executive to the flexibility of his accounting procedures. Any one of the suggested alternatives will satisfy his immediate requirements, but each has different implications.

We are required to consider the relative merits of each of the proposals and to discuss any ethical issues that might be apparent. It is possible that we may be able to recommend to Cedric one alternative that is superior to the others, given the financial and behavioural implications. From an organization-wide perspective it is also clear that Borthwick Construction is in need of a new bonus scheme, and we need to explore the possibilities for an improved scheme.

CASE ANALYSIS

This case addresses the ethical issues that are raised when performance bonuses are awarded on the basis of accounting numbers. In the absence of self-control, or executive controls, bonus recipients are placed in a position where their decision-making is capable of distorting the intentions of the scheme for their own advantage.

The case provides the opportunity to discuss the potentially dysfunctional impact of such decisions on shareholders, employees and the community, when financial benefit to bonus recipients is apparently the only consideration. Corporate malpractice, ethical and unprofessional behaviour, provide a background in which alternative bonus schemes, of potentially long-term benefit to the organization and its stakeholders, might be explored.

Evaluation of the current situation reveals the extent of the problem as Cedric Black views it. The profitability ratio must exceed 20% in order for bonuses to be earned, but current projections from Antonia Bracken, Divisional Management Accountant, show

$$\text{Profitability} = \frac{\text{Trading profit}}{\text{Net assets employed}} = \frac{£350,000}{£1.8m} = 19.4\%.$$

CASE STUDY (cont.)

For the 20% barrier to be exceeded the profitability ratio must be 'modified' – either by increasing the numerator, or reducing the denominator, or both. Black's colleagues have come up with schemes which accomplish this, with the desired outcome, but with different emphases.

Antonia Bracken suggests a deferral of the proposed £255,000 investment in order to reduce the size of net assets employed:

$$\text{Profitability} = \frac{\text{Forecast trading profit}}{\text{Net assets} - \text{Deferred capital expenditure}}$$

$$= \frac{£350,000}{£1.8m - £255,000} = \frac{£350,000}{£1,545,000} = 22.65\%.$$

This measure satisfies the bonus conditions, but at what cost to the company?

The new investment yields a positive cash flow of £150,000 ∞ (1 – 0.4) ∞ (1 – 0.3) = £63,000 each year. With a projected life of 10 years and a cost of capital of 10% p.a., the present value (PV) of the proposed investment (including an allowance for salvage value) is

$$PV = (63,000 \times 6.1445) + (10,000 \times 0.386) = £390,964.$$

This figure is well in excess of the initial outlay, giving an NPV which is clearly positive and of long-term benefit to Borthwick Construction. The investment is essential to remain competitive, as Borthwick's competitors have released new product lines to the market. A delay in purchasing the new equipment (and consequent delay in offering competitive products) will enable these competitors to strengthen their market position. Such a delay may result in the proposed economic return of £135,964 (i.e., £390,964 less £255,000) becoming an opportunity cost greater than £135,964 through loss of market share. This investment may be even more profitable than stated, since interest and depreciation expense should be reduced if the equipment is not purchased, but such adjustments are assumed to be minimal.

Dorothy Marsden's suggested closure of the Biddulph plant would reduce the book value of the assets by £200,000 and divisional profits by £10,000 per year. The impact on the following year is:

$$\text{Profitability} = \frac{\text{Forecast trading profit}}{\text{Net assets} - \text{Book value of disposed assets}}$$

$$= \frac{£350,000 - £10,000}{£1.8m - £200,000} = \frac{£340,000}{£1.6m} = 21.25\%.$$

This figure would be even greater were the sale of the assets (£250,000) and retrenchment costs (£50,000) to be included in trading profit (i.e., profitability = £540,000/£1.6m = 33.75%). But it

CASE STUDY (cont.)

is likely that both of these items would be treated as extraordinary and not included in the profitability calculations for performance bonus purposes. However, the Biddulph plant is profitable (the PV of accumulated losses is £100,000 at 10% p.a. cost of capital) and its closure would be harmful to the company, its customers and employees. The adjustment nevertheless satisfies the bonus requirement, and might be justified on economic grounds, since the return on assets from the Biddulph plant (only 5%, based on annual returns of £10,000 from an asset base of £200,000) are well below the 20% target expected of the Division.

Bob Forrest's 18-day deferment of payment to a trade creditor will reduce net assets by £100,000 but cause the company to incur of a £5000 late-payment penalty.

$$\text{Profitability} = \frac{\text{Forecast trading profit} - \text{Late payment penalty}}{\text{Net assets} - \text{Increase in cash} - \text{Increase in accounts payable (due to penalty)}}$$

$$= \frac{£350,000 - £5000}{£1.8m - £100,000 - £5000} = \frac{£345,000}{£1,695,000} = 20.29\%.$$

The deferment is of no long-term benefit to the company and might even jeopardize a long-standing trading relationship if Jones' existence is threatened by the action. The company could earn interest on the deferred amount of £100,000 for an 18-day period, but at realistic rates the interest accrued would be nowhere near £5000.

Peter Dobson's solution is simpler, involving the expedition of the Vertex project. Early completion will increase profits by £20,000 and incur penalty production rates of only £2500.

$$\text{Profitability} = \frac{\text{Forecast profit} + \text{Increase in profit} - \text{Penalty charges}}{\text{Net assets} + \text{Increase in accounts receivable} - \text{Penalty charge}}$$

$$= \frac{£350,000 + £20,000 - £2500}{£1.8m + £20,000 - £2500} = \frac{£367,500}{£1,817,500} = 20.22\%.$$

The bonus requirement is again satisfied, but with an unnecessary reduction in profit margins resulting from the additional overtime working. Of even greater consequence is the potential long-term impact on customer perceptions and repeat orders resulting from reduced product quality and 'cut corners'. Vertex may appreciate the prompt delivery but have reservations later on if the order is unfit for purpose because of the number of defective items that are subsequently rejected.

Each of the four alternative forms of action is consistent with Cedric Black's guidelines. They correspond with our expectations of management manipulation practices, from the income smoothing literature, that is, where a lower bound for the award of bonuses exists we would anticipate upward manipulation, where feasible, to ensure that the bonus measure just crosses the line. In the

CASE STUDY (cont.)

Borthwick case crossing the line is all that is required – even a 21% return might be considered excessive! If a different bonus scheme was in operation, with rewards proportional to returns once the lower bound was exceeded, we might anticipate bonus-motivated management manipulation on an even greater scale. The danger of this course of action would be an increased likelihood of detection by group internal auditors.

Changes in the bonus scheme are an essential requirement in order to generate a 'profit ratio' whose achievement is more consistent with the goals of the company, and less easily manipulated by the Plastics Division. However, the attitude of the co-conspirators to this action (Bracken, Forrest, Dobson, and Black himself) is of much greater concern and must be addressed immediately. None of the four proposals is in any way justified if their purpose is solely to satisfy the requirements of the bonus recipients; the actions are unethical, and, in the case of Bracken, the management accountant, unprofessional too, since she will be breaching the accounting bodies' ethical codes. However, the actions might be justified, for other than bonus-earning reasons, if they were seen to be of benefit to the organization rather than individuals: for example, Dobson's proposal (the advance shipment of product) will increase short-term profit, and is the only proposal to do so; if it could be argued that this increase was of benefit to shareholders, through an increased share price, then it might be justified, despite its likely detrimental impact on long-term quality. Similarly, Marsden's proposal to close the Biddulph plant could be supported on purely financial grounds; the return on investment at Biddulph is a miserable 5%, and closure and reinvestment to yield 25% (i.e., £40,000 p.a.) would be of benefit to shareholders. However, no such arguments for financial benefit can be attributed to Bracken's and Forrest's proposals.

It is possible that Black's motivation to manipulate is partly driven by his view that the Plastics Division is disadvantaged relative to the other divisions. Plastics contributes 35% of group profits – more than double the contribution of all the other divisions, apart from Corrugated Board – and its profit target is correspondingly higher at 20%. Group action is necessary, in consultation with divisional managers, to determine a target structure which is deemed to be equitable. Modifications at this level, which benefit the Plastics Division, may reduce the need for accounting manipulation in the future.

Alternative bonus schemes

Bonus plans which are based on accounting numbers are open to manipulation by management who seek to maximize the possibility of achieving a bonus. The plan operated by Borthwick Construction appears to be particularly vulnerable for a number of reasons:

- It seems inequitable. The trading profit is divided by net assets to take account of the size of the division and the return on the investment. If net assets are an appropriate measure of size of the division the target ratio for each division should be the same, but this is not the case. The Plastics Division has the highest ratio of all the divisions, and the feeling that this is unfair may provide an incentive to manipulate the plan. This difference in ratios should be investigated to see if there is some valid reason for the different levels and whether this needs to be explained to the various divisions.

In addition, there may be a problem with using net assets as a guide to the size of division as some divisions may be asset-intensive. If Black is correct when he says that the Plastics Division is asset-intensive then it would appear that Plastics is being doubly penalized by having to achieve a higher target ratio as well as requiring larger values of net assets. The target ratio may, therefore, be unrealistically high and in need of investigation to determine whether it is appropriate.

- It is not progressive. As a result managers have no incentive to earn anything above the target level.
- Decision-making power is highly concentrated in those persons who are able to earn the bonus. It would be advisable to implement a system whereby an independent arbiter, such as Borthwick Construction's group accountant, is involved with each division of the organization to oversee the decision-making and achievement of the target ratio.
- There appears to be no consideration of non-financial factors in the bonus scheme. These might be equally important to the long-term survival of the company. These factors might be more difficult to measure, but their inclusion in the bonus scheme might make exploitation of the system more difficult, though on the down side they could encourage dysfunctional behaviour of a different manner!

A number of alternative bonus schemes are worth considering, which would eliminate some of the manipulation opportunities, correct some of the inequities of the present scheme and help in the pursuit of long-term objectives:

Alternative 1: Better use of the accounting numbers. Change the basis for profit distribution to one paid on the attainment of a specified sterling amount of profit for each division; this amount to be determined based on previous years' profit and general economic conditions. Provisions should be added to the scheme so that profits made above the specified levels are further rewarded. This will alleviate the possible inequities in the current bonus system because the allocation will no longer be dependent on the net assets employed by the division. In addition, increasing the bonus for attaining higher profits than necessary provides an incentive for

CASE STUDY (cont.)

the managers to maximize their profits. A switch from return on investment to residual income might be another approach, but there may still be problems with these alternatives because there is no change to the existing focus on short-term profit. The managers are still in a position to manipulate the accounting information and their objective will be to maximize their own rewards.

Alternative 2: A longer-term focus. Reward the divisional managers with shares, or stock options, in the company, instead of cash; the more profit made, the greater the number of shares. This could also be implemented so that the attainment of long-term profit targets is rewarded in a similar manner. Rewarding the managers with shares will encourage them to look at the long-term effects of their decisions on the profitability of the company. They will also want to make as much profit as possible, in order to obtain a larger number of shares. There is still the problem of perceived inequities if the basis for the bonus allocation stays the same. Attention to the terms of issue of the stock options must ensure that a long-term focus is preserved, otherwise the temptation to influence short-term profits remains: an increasing share value will facilitate disposals if the terms of issue so permit. Also, the managers may choose to sell the shares, in which case they will be focusing on short-term profits in order to maximize the price they can sell the shares for.

Alternative 3: A company-wide focus. Reward all divisional managers based on the price of the shares in the company; bonuses to be paid for increases in the value of the shares. Managers can be given the option to buy shares at a bargain price; the more the share is worth, the more valuable is this option. This alternative means that all divisional managers will be rewarded the same amount. If the price of shares increases, the bonus is paid; if the price stays the same or goes down, the bonus is not paid. This encourages the divisions to work together to achieve a common goal. The bonus can be made dependent on continued improvement in the price of the shares over a number of years. For example, performance over a five-year period might be rewarded to provide a focus on long-term profitability.

Alternative 4: A non-financial approach. A similar alternative would provide 'salary packaging' for the divisional managers in that they would be rewarded for increases in the value of the shares, but be able to select the way in which they are to be rewarded from a list of possible benefits (e.g., savings and superannuation plans, life insurance, travel expenses, extended or flexible holiday options or a company car). This allows the managers to choose the way in which they are to be compensated and the managers may be more motivated to increase the value of the shares because the reward is something that is highly valued by them. This option may increase morale and loyalty towards the company because it allows the divisional managers a considerable amount of autonomy over their own salary packages.

The challenge to Borthwick in rewarding executive performance is achieving an appropriate balance of short- and long-term incentives. Managers need some sort of ownership if their interests are to be aligned with those of shareholders, and stock options may help to provide such a motivation. If 'short-termism' is to be avoided, then stock options may help in this regard too. To reduce the incidence of dysfunctional activities the corporate culture must change; higher levels of monitoring and increased training in professional ethics may both be required in the short term.

SUMMARY

This chapter focuses on 'people' aspects – and in particular the 'internal' and 'external' customers of organizations. We begin by looking at TQM implementation as a group-based means of inspiring a customer-based philosophy throughout the company, and then progress to look at the control measures we might employ to ensure that our 'internal' customers are not performing in a dysfunctional manner. The chapter concludes with reference to reward structures, and the opportunities for manipulation when accounting numbers are involved.

8 Management Information Systems

INTRODUCTION

The message from the preceding chapters is clear: the focus of management accounting must move beyond the provision of summary, financial measures if it is to maintain its central role of evaluation and control. A fully integrated information system embracing both financial and non-financial indicators is required if the needs of all stakeholders are to be satisfied.

In manufacturing operations, for example, process parameters provide the means of exercising minute-to-minute control, performance measurement, forecasting and budget-setting, usually through on-line monitoring systems. The absence of comparable systems to monitor cost information will be a serious deficiency, leading to the generation of alternative work-effectiveness performance measures in service and non-process areas in order to gauge the likely impact of variations in procedure and practice.

The original purpose of management accounting was to provide a decision-making tool for management with any data considered relevant. But the requirements of financial accounting and external reporting have effected a retrograde change of emphasis, a change that must be addressed through the provision of relevant and timely information in an appropriate package.

NON-FINANCIAL INDICATORS

The declining relevance of traditional management accounting systems is attributed by Johnson and Kaplan (1987) to three types of failure:

- *Use-type.* A failure to adopt flexible budgets, to evaluate discretionary expenditures or to adopt appropriate measures to control fixed costs.
- *Relevance-type.* A failure to develop quality control and factor productivity measures or to highlight opportunity costs.

- *Control-type.* A failure to consider non-financial factors, through undue emphasis on short-term financial performance indicators and financial accounting considerations in most calculations.

Each of the three types can be overcome by the use of NFIs as measures which improve the decision-usefulness of management accounting information and facilitate evaluation and control. The accounting system should capture indicators which are good predictors of long-term success, measured in terms of consistency with the overall objectives of the enterprise. This may necessitate a preference for non-financial measures over traditional, standard costing and analysis of variance. Whitt and Whitt (1988) suggest a framework for NFIs extending over four aspects of a firm's performance – product, market, employee and customer – equally applicable to both manufacturing and service environments:

- product innovation, leadership and quality;
- market share and growth;
- employee skill, morale and productivity; and
- customer service, loyalty and delivery times.

An alternative framework based on the measurement of total performance in terms of the three Es (efficiency, economy and effectiveness), and devised by Gosling (1988), focuses on the use of resources and the success in achieving the intended results:

1 *Efficiency.* Work performance measures, covering:
   (a) process – efficiency, productivity, overtime and waste;
   (b) constraints – safety and environmental impact; and
   (c) temporal efficiency – milestone dates and elapsed time.

2 *·Economy.* Resource measures, dealing with issues such as input levels and 'budgeted versus actual' performance.

3 *Effectiveness.* Product measures concerning:
   (a) quantity – units and percentage completion;
   (b) quality – reliability, availability, obsolescence and safety; and
   (c) temporal effectiveness – delivery.

This classification amplifies the earlier, product-based classification. A combination of the two frameworks allow the development of a more comprehensive matrix, facilitating the calculation of NFIs which provide for more effective control over total performance.

Table 8.1 gives such a matrix, detailing 60 NFIs drawn from the relevant literature and from personal observation of accounting practice in manufacturing industry (Smith, 1990). The spread of performance measures is wide-ranging, embracing production, marketing and customer-orientation aspects. This is unsurprising, since the precise combination of performance measures appropriate in each case is industry- and strategy-specific.

Where output quality is seen as a key objective, it can be measured in a variety of ways. Thus, for instance, in a hospital, it might be measured by the number of on-ward accidents or the percentage of corrective surgery (patient reworks); while in an alumina refinery a key indicator of product quality might be found in the percentage of impurities, in an index of acceptability to smelter customers, or the community response towards rehabilitation of the environment. However, the potential exists for both inappropriate choices of NFIs and inaccurate and unreliable measurement – or worse, both! Weaknesses must be considered and behavioural implications evaluated prior to effective implementation. We must identify the key result areas in the provision of a particular product or service and ensure that those indicators selected for monitoring reflect the degree to which strategic objectives are being met.

Where direct labour hours measure costs, and the emphasis is on throughput, new measures such as managed hours per unit might be introduced, so that non-productive activities like maintenance and repair can be incorporated and appropriate actions taken to reduce this measure to an optimum level. Attention to equipment and machine efficiencies is aided by a focus on preventive and corrective maintenance measures in an effort to reduce the likelihood of their appearance in the breakdown maintenance statistics. By tracking machine performance and equipment histories, routine maintenance is facilitated and throughput time reduced.

Many authors argue that current methods of accounting for labour consume a cost out of all proportion to its significance in total product costs, and traditional utilization and efficiency measures do not provide good indicators of performance in just-in-time and world-class manufacturing environments.

It is important to avoid a myopic focus on equipment and labour productivities to the exclusion of all else. Where productivities are pursued as goals in their own right, rather than being seen as tools in the achievement of higher goals, throughput can be reduced and production costs increased. Where the emphasis is on keeping both men and machines busy at all times, work in progress will increase beyond economic levels, especially where insufficient attention is devoted to the random fluctuations and process dependencies inevitable within a manufacturing system.

Table 8.1 provides a useful framework for directing attention to the common measurement areas: product, market, employee and customer. It may be that as few as half a dozen NFI measures may be sufficient to give management the 'feel' that it requires for a status report on its current position with respect to its mission or with which to construct a model of performance. Their identification provides an opportunity to communicate and compare like measures throughout the organization, and motivate employers towards their achievement.

The choice of an optimum set of NFIs is inextricably linked to the goals of the organization. A given set of NFIs must provide measures consistent with the achievement of corporate goals. Where the goals change, the optimum set of NFIs will change too, and a system should be in place which is sufficiently robust to reflect these changes over time.

Said et al. (2003) provide empirical evidence to suggest that the adoption of non-financial measures of performance impacts positively on current and future stock market performance; however, they find only partial support for an associated improvement in accounting performance. A number of studies (e.g., Banker et al., 2000; Ghosh and Lusch, 2000; Hughes, 2000; Foster and Gupta, 1999; Behin and Riley, 1999; Perera et al., 1997; Amir and Lev, 1996; Barth and McNicholls, 1994) have shown that non-financial measures are useful leading indicators of financial performance. In particular, Banker et al. (2000) demonstrated a positive relationship between non-financial performance measures and future accounting performance for a hotel chain, while both Foster and Gupta (1999) and Ittner and Larcker (1998a) demonstrated an association between customer

TABLE 8.1

Matrix of NFIs

	Focus of measurement	NFI
Input	• Quality of purchased components	1 Zero defects
	• Quantity of raw material inputs	2 Actual versus target units
	• Equipment productivity	3 Actual versus standard units
	• Equipment failure	4 Downtime/total time
	• Maintenance effort	5 Time between failures
		6 Time between overhauls
		7 Time spent on repeat work
		8 Mean time to effect repairs
		9 Total time in backlog jobs
		10 Number of production units lost through maintenance
		11 Number of repeat jobs
		12 Number of backlog jobs
		13 Number of failures in planned jobs prior to schedule
		14 Percentage of failures: planned/unplanned jobs
		15 Preventive maintenance/ total maintenance
		16 Corrective maintenance/ total maintenance
		17 Breakdown maintenance/ total maintenance
Work performance	• Overtime	18 Overtime hours/total hours
	• Waste	19 Percentage of deficit items
		20 Percentage of scrap
		21 Percentage of rework
	• Throughput	22 $\dfrac{\text{Return per factory hour}}{\text{Cost per factory hour}} = \dfrac{\text{Return}}{\text{Total cost}} \times \dfrac{\text{Time available}}{\text{Time on key resource}}$
	• Production flexibility	23 Set-up time
	• Product complexity	24 Number of components
Product	• Quantity of output	25 Actual units
		26 Percentage completion: actual versus target
	• Quality of output	27 Percentage yield
		28 Index of key product characteristics
	• Safety	29 Serious industrial injury rate
	• Reliability	30 Warranty claims/costs
	• Availability	31 Percentage of stock-outs
	• Obsolescence	32 Percentage of shrinkage
	• Commitment to quality	33 Percentage dependence on post-inspection
		34 Percentage conformity to quality standards

TABLE 8.1 (cont.)

	Focus of measurement	NFI
Market	• Market share	35 Local, domestic or world volume
	• Market leadership	36 Percentage research and development expenditure
		37 Percentage of new product innovation
	• Growth	38 Percentage increase in market share
		39 New clients/total clients
	• Strengths	40 Index of competitive value
	• Competition	41 Index of vulnerability
Employees	• Employee skills	42 Index of educational attainment
		43 Percentage training costs
		44 Percentage of staff turnover lost to competitors
		45 Age or experience profiles
	• Employee morale	46 Percentage absenteeism
		47 Cost of employee downtime
		48 Leadership impact (e.g., percentage cancelled meetings)
		49 New staff/total staff
		50 New support staff/total staff
	• Employee productivity	51 Direct labour hours per unit
		52 Managed labour hours per unit
		53 Labour effectiveness

$$= \frac{\text{Standard hours achieved}}{\text{Direct} + \text{indirect hours worked}}$$

54 Output efficiency $= \dfrac{\text{Output}}{\text{Payroll cost}}$

	Focus of measurement	NFI
Customers	• Customer awareness	55 Percentage approval rating
		56 Percentage service calls/claims
		57 Number of complaints
		58 Percentage of repeat orders
	• Timeliness	59 Number of overdue deliveries
		60 Mean delivery delay

satisfaction and future profitability. The human relations literature (e.g., Becker and Huselid, 1998; Huselid, 1995) suggests that it is 'systems of NFIs', rather than individual measures, which are the more reliable indicators of firm performance.

We now present a case study concerned with the provision of a management information system (MIS), built around a series of NFIs. The focus here is on the provision of a system where currently very little of the available 'data' is collected and analysed by management in order to be turned into useful 'information'. We then turn to the use of NFIs within a balanced scorecard environment.

CASE STUDY

Whitlew Transport: NFIs for a management information system

This case concerns a company whose sales and client base have grown encouragingly, but whose MISs have not grown accordingly. It now faces external pressures from customers and the competition to improve its operations.

Whitlew Transport was founded in north Warwickshire in the late 1970s by Robert Whitmore and his brother-in-law, Richard Lewis. They started from humble beginnings, with two lorries that they drove and maintained themselves and in which they transported coal from open-cast workings to the nearby electricity generating stations at Rugeley and Hams Hall. Now there are more than 300 vehicles in the fleet, annual turnover is nearly £40 million and they have long since ceased to drive themselves.

The company's key activities are transport and warehousing. It provides a service to clients by storing goods, which arrive in bulk from overseas, and then delivering these direct to the customer in the agreed shipment sizes. The major costs incurred by Whitlew are, therefore:

- wages (for drivers and warehousemen);
- diesel fuel for the vehicles;
- maintenance costs for vehicles; and
- overheads necessary to operate the warehouse function.

Whitlew Transport has achieved a prominent position in the marketplace through delivering a satisfactory service whilst maintaining a low price. The pricing has been achieved through providing a service based on combining different clients' delivery and storage requirements, rather than dedicating vehicles and warehouse space to particular clients. As a result the storage peaks and troughs of individual clients can be smoothed, and on delivery several small orders for particular delivery points can be combined on one vehicle, yielding economies of scale, up to the size of a trailer.

The clients demand service of the highest quality which embraces:

- accurate receipt and checking in of their product. This information is then swiftly supplied to them so that they can process supplier payments.
- due care to maintain the quality of the product while warehoused, including the accurate rotation of date-sensitive food items. Any damage to stock through careless handling, or failure to rotate sell-by dates effectively, can lead to claims on Whitlew to the value of the inventory concerned.
- accurate picking and delivery of orders to their customers. Failures in this regard involve Whitlew in the costs of bringing the wrong products back to the warehouse – with even more opportunity for damage due to excessive handling – and of organizing emergency deliveries to correct mistakes.
- delivery of product to the customer, as ordered, and in a manner which meets the customer's satisfaction (and hence the client's

satisfaction). Since most retailers operate tight stock control procedures (and many JIT procedures in some sense) failure to deliver on time results in lost sales. Major retailers impose penalty charges on their suppliers for delivery failures and, where this is the fault of Whitlew, the charge is passed on. Even if there is no penalty charge, then the costs of making an emergency delivery to correct the situation will be incurred.

- accurate return of information clearly advising product delivered, for invoicing purposes. Any failure to record accurately, or communicate clearly, will result in discrepancies between the physical stockholding and the client records. Any shortfall is the responsibility of Whitlew as the warehouse keeper.

Any failure to meet the client's requirements means that additional short-term costs are incurred, and may mean long-term costs associated with loss of business.

Up to now Whitlew has been more concerned with the long-term costs associated with loss of reputation than with the short-term costs associated with slack operating procedures. Robert Whitmore believes that this attitude is no longer acceptable, indeed that a lax way of doing business is both losing the company money and damaging client relationships. He has therefore instituted a company-wide investigation targeting cost savings, inventory control, error elimination and improved customer service and focusing on the introduction of suitable controls in the twin areas of concern, those of transport and warehousing.

TRANSPORT

There are two major areas of potential waste in transport: vehicles making deliveries with less than a full payload; and vehicles moving empty, following delivery, to collect the next payload. In the long term computerized planning software will alleviate this waste, but its implementation is at an early stage, and is being faced by widespread dislike among the transport operatives. However, the information required to run such a system is already available and is already collected from drivers' time sheets for payroll purposes. It would be a relatively simple task to use this same information for different purposes.

The costs currently associated with this waste are suspected to be high, from direct fuel costs, wear and tear on vehicles, and tax and depreciation overheads. The savings from introducing new working methods are potentially great, but it is difficult to gauge precisely how well Whitlew is performing or whether it is improving over time. Without adequate measurement and monitoring of vehicle utilization it is possible that transport costs could quickly become out of control.

WAREHOUSING

Any spare capacity in warehousing cannot be charged to clients and is, therefore, not generating revenue. In order to utilize as much space as possible the warehouses are designed to offer total accessibility together with computer-controlled random location storage. But there are still two major factors which cause lower than acceptable utilization:

- low periods of demand (particularly in January and February). Additional business could be sought to fill the gap, but Whitlew would then run the risk of having insufficient capacity to cope with the demands of existing clients during their busy period (particularly in the run-up to Christmas).
- the mix of contracts across the country mean that it is easy to fill the premium central sites, but less easy for the outlying northern locations. Another leaseholder for the latter would allow smaller premises to be sought which could offer a transit delivery service to the less populous parts of the country.

A computerized stock control system, recording all activity through the warehouses, provides the basis for client feedback, and an information system against which Whitlew's performance can be judged. It is important that the information system provides Whitlew with the data necessary to protect itself too, against claims for stock loss, as far as is possible. In the past the inventory control system has been managed in a casual manner, with liaison with clients allowing the resolution of minor issues without any loss to Whitlew resulting. However, current market pressures and the squeeze on clients to achieve increasingly tighter margins mean that now virtually no stock loss whatsoever is considered acceptable. Whereas in the past minor pilferage at the point of delivery, and 0.5% stock losses relative to turnover, due to minor damage, were accepted, now all minor losses must be accounted for. Far greater detail is therefore required in the recording of stock discrepancies, a level of detail which the Whitlew information systems have difficulty in accommodating.

In the past Whitlew has kept clients in the dark about details of inventory control procedures, relying on its reputation and a sensitive handling of customers. In this way a vague approach has helped hide failures in service and facilitated the presence of inaccuracy in the control system. Now clients are much more aware of inventory issues and related problems; they demand attention to detail, making vagueness unacceptable. Losses to Whitlew are resulting as follows:

- Approximately 1% of goods despatched from the warehouses are refused at the point of delivery for one of a variety of reasons (usually damage in transit, goods not ordered, or the wrong goods having been sent). In the past, it has been assumed that these goods have been returned to the originating warehouse, returned to stock and made available for redelivery. These assumptions are no longer valid. However, it is not the goods that *are* received back in prime condition that are the problem; it is the goods which return in unsaleable condition, or never return at all, which must be traced. This involves much more time and effort spent on checking and recording the returns than has previously been the norm, and there is increasing client

CASE STUDY (cont.)

pressure for tighter controls on the product which they have consigned to Whitlew for safe-keeping.

- Where damage occurs within the warehouse there is no reliable procedure for its accurate recording. Warehousemen are concerned that they will be blamed for the damage, but the company connives in a policy of concealment, since clear reporting of the damage to the client will quickly attract an invoice! In so doing, Whitlew loses a learning opportunity, both of getting a clear appreciation of stock losses in this area and of motivating employees to reduce the costs associated with such damage. There is very little cost awareness within the warehouse. Pallets of goods typically vary in value between £400 and £20,000, but there is no recognition of the differing value of individual items, nor in the potential loss to Whitlew.

- Inaccurate picking of orders puts stock at risk; when a customer is short-delivered against an invoice they will quickly make a claim – but they are unlikely to provide comparable information for over-deliveries. When too much product is issued from stock, there is no customer feedback and that stock is lost.

- Client pressure on details of activity is being felt across the organization. In the transport department clients demand increasing levels of detail on delivery performance against agreed criteria and explanations for failure of on-time delivery.

Robert Whitmore recognizes that stock control procedures must be improved and new performance measures put into place. He agrees with the adage that 'what is measured is what is important' as a means of promoting improvement in key areas of the business, but also accepts that responsibility for Whitlew's present difficulties is ultimately his. The way in which the corporate culture has developed and the way that jobs get done both reflect the lax attitude that pervades the organization.

Historically there has been a lack of attention to detail unless the client specifically demands it. This lax attitude pervades the whole organization but can most easily be pinpointed in stock control. Any matter is not an issue until it becomes a problem; it only becomes a problem on receipt of an invoice, and a loss to Whitlew. It has suited Whitlew to maintain a slack attitude to systems because discrepancies can always be attributed to the paperwork rather than the delivery itself. Clients no longer accept such a rationalization, but the culture of 'vagueness' still pervades reporting procedures. Accuracy of operation is still not a vital issue to Whitlew, and too often inaccuracies in paperwork are regarded as merely a job for the pen-pushers to sort out.

The mission of the organization has become both diffused and confused since its inception. In its entrepreneurial phase profit maximization was paramount, to guarantee survival and to provide capital for growth. But the growth of the business from a 'no frills' haulage contractor to a provider of warehousing and distribution services has created confusing signals so that it is unclear whether 'low cost' or 'high-quality service' is now the top priority.

CASE STUDY (cont.)

The company remains internally focused, despite its role as a service provider whose reputation is judged relative to that of similar providers. Most of the Whitlew employees have been with the company for many years – some for the whole of their working lives and since Whitlew began. Their external experience is very limited and their interests often do not extend beyond those of the immediate client portfolio. There is little recognition of the marketplace or the actions of competitors; there is certainly no benchmarking against the performance of other companies, inside or outside the logistics industry. Warehousing is aware of the costs of lost stock; transport is aware of the costs in excess delivery charges; customer services are aware of the complaints from clients for failure to meet their requirements. However, the real costs of these failures are not collated, and many remain hidden completely within operating costs, without even being recorded. If the real cost is made clear to senior management, then the appropriate action will follow.

We are required to devise a strategy which will lead to the establishment of a management information system which will meet the current and likely future requirements of Whitlew Transport.

CASE ANALYSIS

Changes in customer expectations as to levels of service, and competition in the marketplace, have placed great pressure on Whitlew to provide 'quality' at a low price. The company's internal control systems have not grown to match turnover, so that the consequences are now being felt. The growth from being a 'no frills' provider to one offering a complete warehousing and distribution service, with associated infrastructure investment, has meant that the strategic direction of the company has become confused. There is currently no clear overarching company strategy, no means of measuring performance against standards, nor any opportunity to view the business as a whole, rather than the sum of its component parts. An MIS will provide Whitlew with a holistic view of the company, and provide a co-ordinated and systematic approach to information access and analysis of operational activities, which will allow more effective decision-making to take place. Critical to the successful development of any information system is commitment from senior management and the active involvement of all staff. This implies the existence of clear strategic goals to provide a focus for the setting and monitoring of performance standards.

Three key actions need to be taken in the establishment of the MIS:

- Establishment of a clear company strategy. Whitlew's days as a low-cost, no-frills transport company are long gone. The new strategic direction should make it clear, both to customers and employees, that Whitlew's new challenge is to provide a 'high-quality service'.
- Identification of core areas of concern. Whitlew needs to focus on five key areas to achieve its company objectives:

transport; warehousing; benchmarking; customer expectations; and corporate culture.

- Identification of specific performance indicators to measure, monitor, and control outcomes and behaviours in these areas.

The outcomes of these three actions should provide solutions to current problems, and address any pockets of resistance which might provide barriers to the establishment of the MIS and its further development. These are addressed in more detail below.

Transport

An effective transport policy requires low operating costs, high-quality customer service, and efficient scheduling to reduce the inventory holding costs associated with goods in transit. There are currently two major areas for concern: vehicles operating with less than full payloads on delivery runs; and vehicles moving empty, following delivery, to collect the next payload. Throughout the business there is a general lack of awareness of costs and resistance to the accurate recording of data relating to time and costs. This makes Whitlew vulnerable in the short term to 'surprise' movements (e.g., an oil price hike) which will impact significantly on their operations. These surprises might embrace: fuel costs, vehicle maintenance and depreciation of vehicles. Systems for recording and managing these costs better will help to reduce this vulnerability. While Whitlew has made some investment in new technology, there are further improvement opportunities. In the transport area, a GPS-type vehicle surveillance system could precisely locate vehicles and potentially facilitate return loading and alleviate the problem of empty vehicles.

Warehousing

There are two significant areas of concern for the warehousing operation: poor inventory control, resulting in damaged and lost stock, and inaccurate record-keeping; and large variations associated with occupation, related to the high and low periods of demand, and geographical differences. The warehousing operation could benefit from information systems to address specific issues:

- Fluctuating demand for warehouse space (with excess capacity in January and February). Offers of long-term storage discount rates might help to minimize the peaks and troughs in demand for warehousing.
- Difficulties in filling space in the outlying northern locations. The premium central warehouse sites can always be filled, but the northern excess capacity might be addressed by subletting the space allocation outside of peak periods
- Stock losses which are no longer being tolerated by customers.
- Information systems which are creaking, and incapable of dealing with complex customer stock requirements and reporting requests.

CASE STUDY (cont.)

- Errors in the despatching of goods to clients which are then returned, at no cost to the customer.
- Damage to stock whilst in storage.

In the warehousing area better stock control technology would reduce double-handling and improve the administration of the large amounts of goods in storage. Improvements in staff training are essential here too, so that such systems are correctly implemented. Then the maintenance of accurate stock data would avoid the current problems experienced with attribution of 'blame' for damaged and misplaced goods.

Benchmarking

Whitlew needs to look at external factors to get a better appreciation of the market. If possible the company should seek to benchmark its performance against that of other similar companies. Such data will help in the establishment of a competitive pricing structure, and as as a motivating tool both to recognize existing performance levels and to highlight improvement opportunities. Many of Whitlew's employees have worked for the company for the whole of their working lives, so that their external experience is very limited. Consequently, they have a limited appreciation of how their actions affect other areas of company or its competitiveness.

Customer expectations

Customers' expectations have changed greatly since the company's inception, and now customers are demanding higher levels of service and information regarding deliveries and inventories. Stock losses are no longer tolerated, and customers expect timely reporting about the condition and nature of their inventory. Attention to detail has become critical – the standards required are higher than the current information systems are capable of achieving.

Better data should enable Whitlew to develop an improved appreciation of customer profitability, so that they are able to vary the allocation of their own limited resources to fit customer variations. An adequate customer database might allow customers to be classified as 'high cost' or 'low cost', depending on their service-level requirements. A review of pricing structures may also be due, one that involves the specification of a standard service level. It is likely, for example, that the current pricing structure does not reflect some of the activities that customers have come to expect (such as the rotation of perishables and the provision of urgent and partial deliveries). A premium might be charged for such 'extraordinary' service, while discounts are offered to encourage full payload delivery quantities.

The implementation of new systems, to better satisfy customers' expectations and provide them with more timely and accurate information, might also be used as a justification for changes in price.

CASE STUDY (cont.)

Corporate culture

Employee support and input is crucial to making sure the whole MIS functions appropriately. Attitudes are currently very relaxed and there is little cost awareness, or understanding of the needs of those involved in other parts of the business. This culture has developed over a number of years, and will not be easily changed, but it is essential that changes are made here if Whitlew is to preserve its long-term competitiveness. Of critical importance is the resistance to change, when implementing the MIS, that must be addressed by senior management. Such resistance is inevitable, and may be widespread, driven by lack of understanding of the motives for change, fear of redundancy, fears of additional workload, and, for customers, fear of increased prices. Communication and participation will be necessary if this 'fear of the unknown' is to be overcome among the stakeholders to the business. When staff have an appreciation of the benefits of a MIS they should recognize that it will facilitate their doing a better job.

Specific performance indicators

Whitlew is already collecting a large amount of data from various areas of the business. However, the 'silo' mentality means that it is not successfully sharing this information within the business. The successful integration of this information is vital for the successful establishment of an MIS. Thus, Whitlew first needs to review how it can make better use of the data it already possesses. For example, raw data already exist in the form of consignment notes, delivery dockets, and drivers' timesheets, but they are used in isolation and no collective data analysis takes place to generate information for use in performance, productivity and efficiency monitoring.

These areas of concern allow the specification of particular performance measures to help monitor and control Whitlew's operations. These are detailed in Table 8.2.

Review and evaluation

The final stage in the MIS implementation process is the monitoring and review of the system. Improvements will need to be made which facilitate its adoption, and routinization, across the company. Such a review will ensure that the MIS:

- produces outcomes consistent with company objectives;
- employs performance measures which are aligned with corporate strategy;
- is based on accurate, reliable and timely data, collected in a cost-effective manner;
- appropriately incorporates feedback from employees and customers in the further development of the system.

TABLE 8.2

Performance indicators at Whitlew Transport

Focus	Measure	Data source

Transportation	% of full payloads
	Number of late deliveries
	% jobs completed on time
	Fuel economy (mpg)
	Maintenance time per vehicle
	Jobs lost though maintenance
	Preventive and corrective
	  maintenance compared with
	  general maintenance
		Driver
		  timesheets
		Client feedback
		Consignment
		  notes
		Manifests

Warehousing	Number of incorrect deliveries
	Number of stock discrepancies
	% of space used by month and
	  by warehouse
	Time spent on fixing errors
	Time spent on managing stock
	  per customer
	Claims for lost stock
	Claims for damaged stock
		Client feedback
		Staff timesheets
		Claims
		  paperwork

Market	% of state and national market
	  share
	% increase in market share
	Index of competitor services
	  offered
		Industry statistics
		Sales data from
		  accounts

Competitors	Index of competitor pricing
	List of major contracts held by
	  competitors
		Company
		  websites
		Competitor
		  marketing
		  material
		Word of mouth

Productivity	Direct labour hours per
	  completed job
	Ineffective labour hours
	  (relating to errors made)
	Completed jobs compared to
	  payroll costs
		Staff timesheets

Morale	Staff satisfaction Awareness of company goals % of absenteeism Staff turnover	Internal surveys Employee feedback Word of mouth

Customers	Amount of reports and
	  information requested
	Amount of time spent
	  generating reports for clients
	No. of complaints
	Customer satisfaction
	On-time payments by client
	% of total business by client
		Customer
		  surveys
		Invoice
		  payments
		Customer
		  database

THE BALANCED SCORECARD

A number of authors have argued over the last 30 years that management accounting information systems cannot rely on financial measures alone. They have suggested a combination of financial and non-financial indicators to give a more balanced impression of the overall performance of the enterprise. In Chapter 2 we discussed a number of alternative frameworks, from the original 'tableau du bord' to the more recent 'performance prism'; here we focus on the balanced scorecard. Kaplan and Norton (1992, 1993, 1996, 2004) give prominence to a 'balanced scorecard' originally developed from observing performance measurement in 12 large US companies. They emphasize the following points:

- Traditional accounting measures like return on investment and earning per share can give misleading signals when we are seeking continuous improvement or innovations.
- It is unrealistic to expect managers to focus on operational measures, such as cycle times and defect rates, when they are being appraised on the financials.
- A balance is required between the financials (results of actions already taken) and operational measures of innovation, internal processes and improvement activities.
- Managers need to be able to view performance across several dimensions simultaneously, dictating a multivariate approach.

The balanced scorecard therefore looks at performance from four perspectives:

- financial – how do we look to shareholders?
- customers – how are we viewed?
- internal – what must we excel at?
- innovation and learning – how do we continue to improve and create value? It then generates four groups of goals and a corresponding set of performance measures. A parsimonious set of measures is required and the example in Table 8.3 yields 15 key measures.

Although much of this information is available internally, the remainder has to be gleaned from elsewhere through customer surveys, benchmarking and inter-company comparisons. Different market situations, product strategies and competitive environments will require different scorecards – all will potentially suffer from the deficiencies common among traditional systems: lack of relevance and timeliness, unfriendliness and lack of communication throughout the organization.

Performance measurement of the kind advanced in the balanced scorecard has been suggested as a means of overcoming 'short-termism' – the tendency for companies and managers to pursue short-term profit and short-term stock price increases because they are of the greatest benefit to the individual (manager or shareholder).

Anthony et al. (1992) reiterate eight measures originally suggested by GEC:

- profitability (measured by residual income);
- market position (measured by market share);
- productivity (of capital and labour, compared to that of competitors);

TABLE 8.3

Typical goals and performance measures for a balanced scorecard

	Goal	Measures
Financial	Survival	Cash flow
	Success	Sales growth
	Prosperity	Market share
Customer	New products	% sales from new products
	Responsiveness	On-time delivery
	Customer partnership	Number of co-operative efforts
Internal	Technological edge	Competitive comparison
	Manufacturing	Cycle time
	excellence	Unit cost
		Yield
	Design productivity	Engineering efficiency
Innovation and learning	Technological edge	Time to develop innovations
	Manufacturing learning	Process time to maturity
	Product focus	% products = 80% of sales
	New product innovation	Time to market compared to the competition

- product leadership (measured by existing and new product development);
- personnel development (linking recruitment and training to future needs);
- employee attitudes (motivation);
- public responsibility (measured by ethics, environmental and community awareness);
- balance of long-range and short-range goals and strategies.

They highlight the dangers of adopting a short-term approach which focuses on financial measures alone, and advance a more realistic approach, where a longer-term perspective is adopted and the importance of non-financial measures appreciated.

Lewy and du Mee (1998) note that 70% of scorecard implementations fail and put forward their 'ten commandments' for success based on balanced scorecard implementations in the Netherlands. Their basic principles are consistent with those from other sources, when viewing the likely success, or eventual abandonment, of management accounting innovations:

1 Use the scorecard as the basis for implementing strategic goals, since its visibility makes it the ideal vehicle for doing so.

2 Ensure that a strategy is in place prior to the development of the scorecard, since *ad hoc* development will reinforce the wrong behaviours.

3 Ensure that there is sponsorship of the implementation from among the senior management of the company, and that senior managers are committed to its success, since it is important that the initiative is not seen just as the responsibility of accountants.

4 Implement a pilot stage to learn valuable lessons.

5 Introduce the scorecard gradually to each business unit after ensuring that the version of the scorecard being used will indeed serve their needs.

6 Do *not* use the scorecard as an extra level of top-down control, because there will be opposition to its implementation, rather than the collaboration and participation desired.

7 Do *not* adopt a standardized product; the scorecard must be adapted to the organization's needs and aligned with corporate strategy.

8 Do *not* underestimate the need for training and communication; the ideas may seem simple, but some people will need a lot of convincing.

9 Do *not* overcomplicate the scorecard by striving for perfection; it will never be 100% right, so do not delay its implementation by constant searches for 'better' indicators.

10 Do *not* underestimate the additional costs associated with recording, administrating and reporting the scorecard.

Commandments 3, 8 and 10 in particular will be familiar concerns addressed elsewhere in this volume in connection with both ABC and TQM implementations.

Though the balanced scorecard is a widely adopted managerial tool for performance measurement and strategic control, it remains a controversial one. Although it provides an overview of organizational performance through a range of financial and operational measures of customer satisfaction and internal processes, doubts still exist about the validity of the supposed cause-and-effect relationships within the scorecard, as suggested by Kaplan and Norton (1992). According to Norreklit (2000), there is no absolute causal relationships among the specified measures, only a logical connection, for example, between customer satisfaction and financial performance. The relationship has still to be demonstrated empirically in a convincing manner, and indeed Ittner et al. (2003b) suggest that while users exhibit higher degrees of satisfaction with a balanced scorecard system, there is almost no association with improved economic performance. Empirical findings on the relationship between customer-related measures and the financial performance of the firm suggest that there is no clear relationship between customer satisfaction on the one hand and customer loyalty and financial performance on the other (Reinartz and Kumar, 2002; Garland, 2002; Scharitzer and Kollarits, 2000; Ittner and Larcker, 1998a; Soderlund and Vilgon, 1999).

The following case study provides the opportunity to devise a balanced scorecard and plan for its implementation in a small business environment.

CASE STUDY

Bolehall Manor Motors: A balanced scorecard case study

Bolehall Manor Motors began life in the late 1970s when the three Lawrence brothers, Frank, George and Harold, joined as partners in a petrol station. Then they worked three shifts to provide a 24-hour service – still something of a novelty in those days. Then, as now, margins on petroleum sales were thin and the business would not support three full-time incomes without diversification. The brothers went to the local college of further education to attend courses in auto-mechanics, welding and metalwork, so that they could add service, maintenance and smash repairs to the facilities offered to motorists. The returns from service and repairs quickly outstripped those from petrol sales, although the revenue from the latter was still

CASE STUDY (cont.)

justified on the grounds of the number of people it brought into the garage. Smash repairs grew into a sophisticated bodyshop, which justified the buying-in of damaged vehicles for rework and resale. The profits from rebuilt second-hand cars promoted another strand to the business with the purchase of vehicles, usually at auction, for resale. The business has grown to a turnover in excess of £4 million so that it now supports the three brothers and 14 other full-time staff. The four aspects of the business might currently be described as follows:

	Turnover (£m)	Profit (£m)
Petrol sales	0.6	0.018
Service and repairs	1.2	0.240
Bodyshop	1.0	0.150
Motor sales	1.6	0.080
	4.4	0.488

Each of the brothers is responsible for one of the chief profit-earning parts of the business – Harold (motor sales), George (bodyshop), Frank (service and repairs) – while Harold's wife, Joan, oversees the petrol sales side of the business and the general administration. Together they take the decisions which establish the future direction of the business.

Further expansion of the business on its current site is not possible, so growth will have to come from more efficient operations. The bodyshop could accommodate one more fitter, but this would be at the expense of operating efficiency; the service and repair department has four bays, sharing two hydraulic lifts, and could only accommodate more vehicles by digging pits. The success of the business in the past has been based on customer care and attention to detail. This has resulted in the employment of perhaps more unproductive staff than is wise, and in the provision of free services to customers (e.g., car loan and chauffeuring) which might have to stop. Overstaffing has become part of the family image, and all of the brothers are reluctant to retrench anyone in the cause of efficiency and cost-cutting.

George spends most of his time supervising and quoting on bodyshop work. His department contributes significantly to bottom-line profits and customer goodwill. He has a great deal of pride in the product of his part of the organization, but accepts that his focus on the bodyshop has probably been at the expense of his influence on the control and direction of the organization as a whole.

Analysis of the bodyshop operations reveals margins close to the industry average, and delivery time targets which are almost always met. Stock issues are not significant because suppliers deliver only as necessary. However, the performance of the three fitters is not measured against quoted delivery times because George fears that this intervention would compromise their morale. He has considered promoting one of them to foreman, to promote teamworking, but has yet to evaluate the cost impact.

Frank Lawrence is responsible for the service and repair centre and is concerned that the 'customer care' mentality is becoming counter-productive. Problems in the centre are causing disquiet among customers because too frequently neither their cars nor their invoices are ready on time. There are early signs, although nothing substantiated, that customers may be going elsewhere because of the delays. The service and repair department is the major profit centre of the business, and one of its most successful components. However, a number of areas for improvement have been identified associated with non-value-adding activities:

- poor work scheduling;
- rework;
- constant movement of cars to create space;
- waiting for foreman availability, for stock to be delivered, and for a hydraulic lift to become free.

The service foreman's time is at a premium. He sorts out problems on the spot and provides on-the-job training for the mechanics when unfamiliar engines are being serviced. Some of his time, and that of the mechanics, is spent on fetching and carrying customers once their vehicles have been dropped off for service, but it is doubtful whether the labour charge-out rate fully reflects such activity. He frequently feels that he is doing Frank Lawrence's job as well as his own!

The service department provides a pre-delivery inspection on all vehicles that are sold, to ensure that they are fit for purpose. Delays here have an impact on car sales, a factor of great concern to Harold Lawrence.

Frank is being pressured by his brothers to become more innovative and so increase the throughput of the service centre. George wants him to allocate mechanics to customers (rather than cars) to encourage them to take more pride in their work and to take pressure off the foreman. George believes that if the mechanics are serving a final customer – rather than the foreman – there will be more urgency and a greater effort to 'get it right first time'. He believes the bodyshop does this already. Frank has set up a computerized database detailing a history of all the cars that they service, including all transactions, repairs and replacements. He cannot get anyone to show any enthusiasm for it, despite the likelihood that its adoption would take some pressure off Joan and her multiple responsibilities.

Harold Lawrence spends over 60% of his time at auctions, buying cars for subsequent resale. He is, therefore, rarely on site to help out with the actual sales function. The margins on motor vehicle sales are lower than they should be because many cars are sold at a loss, which casts serious doubts on Harold's ability to appraise trade-in vehicles and his understanding of the costs of converting bought-in cars into sales. This side of the business is much more competitive now than it has ever been. Harold blames the absence of Sunday opening, too few salesmen, pre-delivery inspection delays and the lack of space for his department's relatively poor performance. He can only display a maximum of six cars for sale at a time.

Although nominally the 'storeman', Reg Howarth has little stock to play with and no stock control systems. Most of his time is spent on other duties. The majority of parts are bought on demand by whoever is available – often the receptionist – resulting in upwards of eight deliveries per day. In emergencies Reg Howarth takes the van to pick up spare parts as required. The result is that stockholding costs are minimal, but delivery costs and the knock-on consequences create waste and incur costs:

- of management spending time sorting out problems;
- of customers not being attended to promptly;
- of uncertainty as to whether all purchases have been charged out properly; and
- of uncertainty as to how much time is wasted by the mechanics while they stand idle waiting for car spares to arrive.

Although, from the outside, administration looks to be the classic non-value-adding function, its support role for the three major profit centres cannot be underestimated. Joan Lawrence ensures that the antiquated computer system runs efficiently and her assistant, Diane Clegg, consistently meets her targets in updating their contents. However, they are only as good as the information with which they are supplied and the brothers (especially Frank and George) lack the vigilance to ensure the accuracy of the job-cards and other manual systems. Consequently, purchase invoices are not always passed on to administration, the credit note system has deteriorated, debt collection has fallen behind and the job-card invoice sequence system has some big gaps. Both Joan and Diane could spend more time clearing up these inefficiencies, but they seem to spend hours on the telephone chasing up jobs and complaints and trying to locate other personnel in the garage.

The management accounting system now in place provides detailed evidence of past performance broken up quite minutely, and is distributed to the management team (i.e., the brothers). It incorporates a number of indicators within each department, including:

- total on-cost of every car sold;
- total number of enquiries and conversion rates;
- lost time indicators in the bodyshop and service departments (per day per person);
- job-card and paperwork controls;
- daily turnover figures;
- debtor and stock analysis and trends;
- average charge-out rates.

The impact of this information has so far been limited. The lost time indicators in the service department did not highlight the reasons for last month's poor results. They should have highlighted reduced intake of work, repeat and poor workmanship, and poor management, but instead they impacted on the productive time figures and as a result the charge-out rate per productive hour dropped from £60 to £50.

It is apparent that the mechanics chose not to show the 'real' position. Did they realize by their action that they could have been seen as less inefficient? Do they care? Were they subconsciously matching workload to effort? In a similar period two months earlier they had achieved 33% more throughput, so the factors are consistent with their spreading the work to fit the available time.

The real problem, though, is why neither the foreman nor the manager (Frank Lawrence), who were responsible for recording the data, picked this up. The reason may have been lack of time, lack of interest, or lack of understanding of the purpose of the information system.

Performance indicators can only work if managed and if their purpose is known and properly communicated. This communication reinforces the intention. If used as a punishment, then data manipulation is likely to occur and so its purpose will be wasted. If not used at all (as in this case), only those mechanics who have any pride in their work will bother to make the effort to take it seriously. However, if used as intended, as a method to create a team spirit through regular meetings whereby opportunities can be identified, then perhaps the system may work, but it would be necessary to show that no interference to the mechanic's performance was underlying the implementation. Rewarding good performances may not be the answer either, since this may lead to manipulation of the incentive scheme.

None of the brothers is as young as he was. Harold is very set in his ways and sees no point in changing. He is the eldest of the three and will probably retire within the next five years. They realize that they have to streamline the business to make it more efficient, but are reluctant to bring in consultants to suggest solutions or solve problems. 'It's our business and we have to solve our own problems,' says Harold. The others nod in agreement. They meet informally throughout the day, most days, but rarely have formal meetings. Today they have done so to highlight weaknesses in current operations and improvement possibilities. They see the major weaknesses as:

- poor planning;
- poor paperwork controls;
- failure to monitor systems and indicators;
- failure to use the database;
- poor stock control;
- too much manual preparation of invoices;
- non-existent marketing systems, so that poor decisions result from lack of information;
- lack of space;
- independent operation of each of the departments.

CASE STUDY (cont.)

CASE ANALYSIS

For Bolehall Manor Motors to survive and grow over the next few years, it needs to recognize that changes are necessary. Firstly, a more appropriate structure needs to be implemented. Secondly, a strategic management plan needs to be developed, based on the balanced scorecard. For the plan to be effective, there needs to be significant employee input.

Problems

The first problem faced by this business is that its structure is too informal. Decision-making is conducted on an *ad hoc* basis, and regular and timely reporting does not occur. A properly executed company structure is required. Shares would be issued to the Lawrence brothers as directors, with provision for employee shares to be issued as part of an incentive scheme.

Regular board meetings with a structured agenda should be held at least monthly. The formalizing of reporting functions will enable continual monitoring of the business. The implementation of a company structure would help to solve the succession problem associated with Harold's contemplated departure five years hence.

Secondly, there is no strategic management plan with goals, strategies, relevant performance measurements and evaluation procedures. The business is small, therefore everyone should be encouraged to participate in the planning and decision-making processes. The balanced scorecard is an appropriate format on which to base the strategic management plan. Total employee involvement is fundamental to the success of this approach. Employees must be given the right to make suggestions and decisions, to assist in the establishment of monitoring procedures and to take responsibility for their decision-making. Workforce participation can facilitate an enhanced work environment, lead to goal congruence and improved profitability.

Thirdly, a detailed management accounting system exists, but it has not provided reasons for the business' downturn. The performance measurements used are either not easily understood or do not provide meaningful information. A more sophisticated computer system is required. Presently the management information system provides only financial measures, based on historical data, to monitor performance. With one of the organization's main objectives being to provide customer care and service, measuring and analysing customer complaints provides a good tool to establish the nature of the complaints and why they are actually arising. A database recording these details should be incorporated into the MIS. Another deficiency is the lost time indicator; again a financial measure was produced with little benefit in regard to measuring real performance. The foreman for each of these departments should be able to better analyse the operational reasons for the delays – machine down-time, rework, poor work scheduling. This type of non-financial information should be recorded as these directly relate to the cause of the delays and ultimately the quality of service.

CASE STUDY (cont.)

Finally, each department operates independently, to the detriment of the whole business. It is apparent that managers across the organization do not communicate effectively with each other or their staff. Effective leadership has a key role to play in both establishing a performance-enhancing culture and organizing people in ways that meet and anticipate customers needs. In implementing the above improvements, management (Frank, George, Harold and Joan) should be able to spend more time in establishing and reviewing the strategic objectives of the business. Managers should be consulting with their staff to enable these strategic objectives to be translated into operational objectives to which employees can relate. This consultation process will help to motivate employees, which is a key ingredient to effective performance. Having a layered objectives/goals approach will ensure all employees are focused on the strategic goals of the business. With the implementation of a new MIS, managers should be able to receive timely performance measures at a departmental and individual level. Incentive schemes may work more effectively under this new system. It is also essential to have a review and feedback system in place to ensure strategies are still working towards business goals, especially in today's competitive environment. Regular management meetings and staff meetings are essential to ensure effective communication in the organization.

The Bolehall Manor Motors balanced scorecard

The balanced scorecard approach looks at the performance of the firm from four perspectives: financial, customers, internal, innovation and learning. This approach moves away from the traditional approach of measuring performance based solely on financial criteria, which tends to reinforce short-run thinking. Financial measures produce untimely information and overlook factors such as customer satisfaction, quality and employee motivation. A scorecard focuses on the long-run strategic objectives by looking to the future and translates the mission statement into actionable terms that have meaning for the employees.

Under this approach we must identify performance measures for each strategic area and for the managers at each level in the business. The SWOT analysis in Table 8.4 can help here. The 'strengths' of the business can be the starting point on which to build the mission statement. The 'opportunities' can be the goals in the scorecard, whilst the 'threats' can serve as a reminder of the implications of not implementing a measure such as the balanced scorecard.

There are three steps involved in producing a scorecard. A combination of these three steps will produce a scorecard similar to Table 8.3. When applied to the Bolehall Manor Motors scenario we generate Figure 8.1.

In step 1 we *identify key missions* – that is, develop a mission statement to reflect the philosophy of the business. A mission statement should express the philosophy of the business and provide a long-term outlook. For example: 'To be a customer-oriented

CASE STUDY (cont.)

TABLE 8.4

SWOT analysis for Bolehall Manor Motors

Strengths	Weaknesses	Opportunities	Threats
• Turnover in excess of £4 million	• Lack of goal congruence	• More efficient operations	• Losing market share
• Customer care focus	• No room to expand at the current location	• Increase the customer base	• Decreased staff morale leading to decrease in productivity
• Diverse business	• Employees not consulted on decisions	• Increased repeat customers – can build loyalty	• Decreased profits
	• Presence of non-value-added activities, e.g., multiple orders in one day, moving cars, waiting time for foreman, parts to be delivered	• Implement total employee involvement (TEI), e.g., let the mechanics quote work times as they are closer to the operations	• With TEI, threat of building in 'slack time'
	• Outdated management accounting system in operation	• Increased profit	
	• No employee incentives		

company that cares about the customer and pays attention to detail'.

In step 2 we *identify the critical success factors* – those factors essential to the businesses continuing success. For example,

- customer satisfaction/responsiveness;
- quality of work;
- reliability;
- flexibility;
- acceptable use of finances.

In step 3 we *identify a set of performance measures* for each critical success factor and create the scorecard. The scorecard for the firm as a whole gives an overall perspective to the business philosophy. The main operational problems with the four areas of the business are:

- *Bodyshop*. The fitters need more direction; with no target to aim for they will not be encouraged to work at any set level.

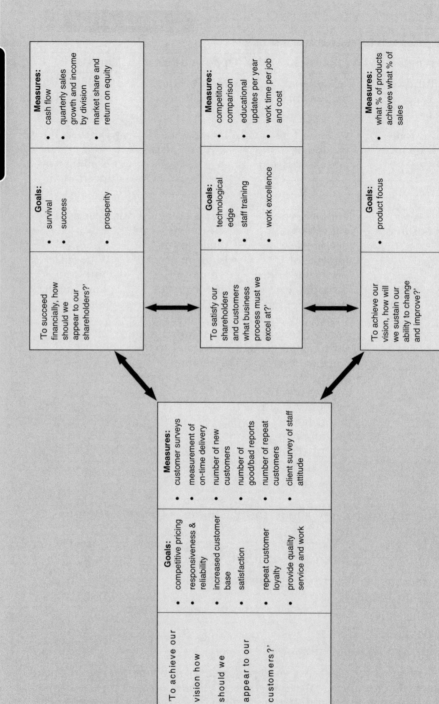

FIGURE 8.1

To achieve our vision how should we appear to our customers?'

Goals:
- competitive pricing
- responsiveness & reliability
- increased customer base
- satisfaction
- repeat customer loyalty
- provide quality service and work

Measures:
- customer surveys
- measurement of on-time delivery
- number of new customers
- number of good/bad reports
- number of repeat customers
- client survey of staff attitude

To succeed financially, how should we appear to our shareholders?'

Goals:
- survival
- success
- prosperity

Measures:
- cash flow
- quarterly sales growth and income by division
- market share and return on equity

To satisfy our shareholders and customers what business process must we excel at?'

Goals:
- technological edge
- staff training
- work excellence

Measures:
- competitor comparison
- educational updates per year
- work time per job and cost

To achieve our vision, how will we sustain our ability to change and improve?'

Goals:
- product focus

Measures:
- what % of products achieves what % of sales

Bolehall Manor Motors balanced scorecard

CASE STUDY (cont.)

TABLE 8.5

Balanced scorecard for each of the four areas

	Goals	Measures
Service and repairs	• efficient cash collection procedures • appraise mechanic performance • customer satisfaction	• number of debtors in one week • questionnaire of each customer • follow-up call
Bodyshop	• increase throughput of cars • flexibility during busy periods	• number of cars per week • attaining quoted times for repairs
Motor sales	• more efficient marketing plan • increase the sale of cars	• survey on effectiveness • number of cars sold per month
Administration	• increase the efficiency of administration work	• time spent on administration compared to time spent on non-value-added activities such as chasing staff

- *Service and repair.* Too often neither car nor invoice is ready on time.
- *Motor sales.* Many cars sold at a loss.
- *Administration.* Most stock is bought on demand which can result in deliveries up to eight times per day.

These problems are dealt with specifically and goals and measures are in force to give the employees strong direction of how to achieve their targets.

Table 8.5 develops the balanced scorecard for Bolehall Manor Motors. The scorecard is still incomplete; targets must be developed for each goal and measure, as well as incentives for achieving target. This can best be done by consultation with employees, by benchmarking, and by looking at the company's past performance.

The balanced scorecard links the mission statement and the goals and objectives of the company and reports on the company's performance in both the short and long term by using financial and non-financial performance measurements. The information necessary to evaluate the company's performance is contained in one report. The review process will easily identify which strategies are succeeding and recognize those which require change. It provides a learning mechanism that encourages ongoing modification for enhanced performance.

MEASUREMENT CHALLENGES FOR THE NOT-FOR-PROFIT SECTOR

Researchers have offered a variety of approaches for examining performance measurement and benchmarking across different organizations. The effectiveness of performance is traditionally measured in terms of the organization's ability to meet and exceed its objectives in each of a number of specified areas. However, this simple approach poses a number of problems:

- How do we accommodate inter-divisional comparisons where common objectives may not apply?
- How do we measure qualitative or intangible success factors? For example, corporate image, technological competence, learning, corporate culture, and employee morale.
- How do we express effectiveness in a relative manner in order to facilitate benchmarking, or a ranking of a company relative to its competitors?

Measurement in service industries is particularly problematical because many of the outputs are intangible and traditional success measures may be deemed inappropriate; service quality, for example, is notoriously difficult to measure. Dissatisfaction with the measurement difficulties associated with goal achievement modelling has led academics to investigate a number of alternatives, which include:

- contingency models (Burrell and Morgan, 1979);
- population ecology models (Aldrich, 1979);
- social justice models (Keeley, 1978);
- power models (Pfeffer and Salancik, 1978);
- political economy models (Nord, 1983);
- systems models (Weick and Daft, 1983);
- competing values models (Handa and Adas, 1996);
- analytic hierarchy models (Chan and Lynn, 1993).

However, the traditional 'goal achievement' model is the one that retains the most support. As long as we are aware of the difficulties associated with its implementation then it is still possible to make significant progress in the development of an acceptable measure of organizational effectiveness.

The management accounting and strategic planning literatures recognize the inherent relationship between formulating strategic goals and the identification of the key success factors for any organization. However, the critical factors for organizational success may be dependent on many variables, some of which are neither easily measured nor quantifiable. Where an overall integrated measure is difficult to achieve the focus of attention is frequently shifted on to a few quantitative measures, simply because the alternative is just too complex to be considered seriously. Innovation, for example, may be ignored for these reasons. In the area of financial performance, a simple earnings measure of effectiveness, like return on investment has been widely used. But is it good enough? Problems associated with life cycles and accounting methods will make comparisons difficult even within the same industry using such a measure. A large body of literature has suggested that measures which focus on returns to shareholders alone are inappropriate, and that some consideration of the needs of 'stakeholders' is also necessary.

If we venture away from purely financial measures to include a non-financial influence, we might focus on the popular '3 Es' framework of efficiency, economy and effectiveness considered in Chapter 7. This classification is particularly helpful in facilitating the generation of a host of suitable NFIs. However, in doing so it demonstrates flaws in a number of aspects:

- It does not help in the measurement of qualitative non-financials.
- It provides no indication of the variable weighting which would allow an integrated overall measure to be formulated.
- Its focus is undeniably internal, in circumstances where we require a measure which also reflects competitiveness and external conditions.

Reference to the particular problems of the service sector (e.g., Kraft et al., 1996) highlights some of the most pressing measurement problems, while providing indications of how they might be solved. A number of authors (e.g., Carlzon, 1987; Albrecht, 1988) have argued that performance measurement must more closely reflect a customer orientation, in order to encourage motivation and commitment among the workforce. In consequence they see 'satisfied customers' and 'motivated employees' as the true assets of the company. The latter is typical of the sort of measurement problem that arises here, and which is usually overcome through the use of proxy variables (in this instance the use of 'employee turnover' or 'level of absenteeism' would be common, if not entirely satisfactory, substitutes for 'employee motivation') and the adoption of rating scales, through which expert managers might provide subjective measurement of difficult variables.

Parasuraman et al. (1988) identify five dimensions of service quality:

- tangibles – physical appearance of facilities and personnel;
- reliability – ability to provide the promised service;
- responsiveness – willingness to provide a prompt service;
- assurance – ability of employees to inspire trust and confidence;
- empathy – caring and individual attention.

They develop a 22-item scale, called SERVQUAL, to measure the difference between consumer expectations and perceptions of the actual service received, so that 'service quality' increases when perceptions exceed expectations.

However, the problems of measurement already observed are suddenly magnified when we address the 'not-for-profit' sector. Such organizations include governmental departments, offices or instrumentalities that provide services and regulation, as well as private not-for-profit organizations. These private organizations are normally legally constrained from distributing residual earnings to those individuals who control the organization, but are not prohibited from earning profits or paying reasonable compensation to employees, though they must devote any surplus to the continuing operation of the organization. Wheelen and Hunger (2004) note that these conditions will generally exempt private not-for-profit organizations from the obligation to pay income tax under the jurisdictions within which they operate.

The importance of the not-for-profit sector should not be underestimated. In a recent study of not-for-profit organizations, Salamon and Wojciech (2001) found that this sector accounts for approximately one in every 20 jobs worldwide; in nine specified countries they noted that not-for-profit sector employment grew, on average, by 23% compared to only 6.2% for the rest of the economy over the period 1990–95. In Australia alone, for example, the Australian Bureau of Statistics (2002) noted the existence of almost 700,000 private not-for-profit organizations, and this excluded those based solely on volunteer activity. The sector embraced, among others, activities in the social services (26%); education and research (24%); culture and recreation (21%); health (15%); and business associations, professional associations and trade unions (2.5%). However, this level of importance has not been reflected in the management accounting literature, which is still dominated by studies devoted to the for-profit sector; indeed, it is interesting to note the rapid increase in published studies devoted to once public services consequent upon their privatization.

Parker (2001) notes the scant attention in the accounting and management literatures to the not-for-profit sector and suggests the need for more research in the area. Chenhall (2003) notes the particular challenges associated with research in this sector. A number of authors have also emphasized the major social and economic impact of the not-for-profit sector in society (e.g., Holder, 1987; Parker, 2001; Wooten et al., 2003).

The pivotal role played by measurement systems in the development of strategic plans, control systems and performance evaluation is well documented in the literature (e.g., Ittner and Larcker 1998b; Merchant and Van der Stede, 2003). Not-for-profit organizations offer particular challenges in the measurement of organizational performance. We have noted elsewhere in this volume the levels of dissatisfaction with traditional financial performance measures (e.g., return on investment, earnings per share) and the movement towards non-financial performance measures, often within a framework such as that provided by the balanced scorecard. With not-for-profit organizations we have no equivalent financials to start with and need to look at alternatives.

Forbes (1998: 184), among others, observes that while performance measurement in not-for-profit organizations is frequently addressed, the outcomes are largely inconclusive because such organizations have difficulty in developing appropriate quantitative measures because their goals are unclear and the services offered are difficult to isolate.

The performance measurement literature appears to suggest that the not-for-profits will continue to follow the for-profit sector in seeking to develop scorecard-type frameworks for management and control. However, as with the for-profit sector, guidance on the measures to be employed may be of limited help, other than to suggest that a 'one size fits all' scorecard will not work, and that organization-specific frameworks need to be developed. Otley (1999), for example, suggests that there is simply not enough evidence available yet to justify the widespread establishment of a comprehensive framework of quantitative measures of performance; he warns that, at the very least, this will not be an optimum position, and that in many circumstances such an approach may be counter-productive. Ittner et al. (2003a) provide supporting empirical evidence (though from the for-profit sector) in their example of a retail bank which found the degree of subjectivity in its balanced scorecard framework to be so great as to cause its abandonment, and a return to short-term financials as the predominant measures of performance.

There is a consensus in the literature, however (e.g., Cameron and Whetten, 1983; Smith, 1998; Sawhill and Williamson, 2001), that given the diversity among not-for-profit organizations, no single set of measures will work for all of them.

CHALLENGES OF TECHNOLOGICAL INNOVATION

A comprehensive electronic commerce strategy will embrace e-mail, electronic data interchange, barcodes and electronic funds transfer to remove non-value-adding activities from all operations across the purchase cycle. Given that as much as 90% of any organization's information base currently exists in an unstructured form (usually in narrative documents rather than database records), electronic document management remains a key issue. With the advent of the internet, organizations must change the way they conduct their operations, and their management of electronic documents will feature prominently in this process.

The internet has provided a wonderful opportunity for electronic trading. It is user-friendly and a low-cost delivery channel for a multitude of business applications. Despite the set-up costs, and inertia in some small businesses, the internet will ensure that electronic commerce will substantially replace traditional means of conducting business. For this transformation to be complete, there remain a number of challenges for management accounting control systems to overcome. Blanchard (1997) identifies three:

- authentication problems – a system of on-line authentication is required to facilitate the provision and verification of electronic signatures which goes beyond traditional 'password' mechanisms;
- confidentiality issues – encryption technology needs to be advanced to provide a cheap and simple means of scrambling the contents of messages, documents and records whose confidentiality is paramount;
- integration issues – compatibility of alternative applications is essential if electronic transactions are to be integrated with alternative media formats without the necessity for error-strewn scanning or repunching of data.

O'Donoghue (1997) likens the advent of the internet, and the resultant growth in communications capabilities, as 'back to the future' for accounting software; many organizations are now offering outsourcing services in a throwback to the accounting bureaux of the 1970s prior to the take-up of PC-based accounting packages. The next stage is the provision of accounting application services by professionally managed information technology (IT) organizations to a large sector of small and medium-sized enterprises.

The growing importance of the internet in business, and the increasingly important role of internet and intranet technologies for information delivery, makes it essential for web access capabilities to be explored in data warehouse projects. Data warehousing has become a key part of IT strategy in many organizations as they look for technology to yield a competitive advantage. As well as improving the accuracy of the information used in the decision-making process, and facilitating access to useful information stored across the business, data warehousing offers the opportunity for significant cost savings. Gibson (1998) identifies four compelling reasons for organizations to embrace data warehousing technology:

- improved market knowledge – for managing customers and new product development;
- data to support business process re-engineering initiatives;
- data for trend analysis and more accurate business forecasting;
- an infrastructure for goal-focused, strategic and tactical decision-making.

There has been a wide adoption of electronic commerce by big business – on-line transactions in the banking, insurance, travel and entertainment sectors are particularly common. But small business internet sites are often still little more than on-line catalogues which require access to traditional communication media in order to place orders, thus losing the opportunity for instant transactions. Small businesses must discard their old management accounting systems to conduct business on-line, saving processing costs, increasing productivity and building customer loyalty through an improved service consistent with the new technology.

As telecommunications technologies and electronic commerce pave the way for the 'virtual corporation', the traditional concept of capacity may fade. Strategic capacity management will still matter in such an environment, even though the measurement of outcomes becomes increasingly difficult.

SUMMARY

The chapter has focused on providing useful information to aid decision-making among all stakeholders of an organization. Whereas previous chapters have concentrated on costs and other financials, this time the initial focus is on the non-financial indicator and the part it plays in building a practical management information system. The two approaches (financial and non-financial) are then integrated in a formal balanced scorecard, again with illustrations of how it might be implemented. The chapter concludes by addressing current developments in the electronic sourcing of information and the particular challenges that this presents.

9 Financial Modelling

INTRODUCTION

Recognition of an optimum combination of financial and non-financial indicators which best measures current performance, or is capable of explaining or predicting future levels of performance, remains an area of current concern. The balanced scorecard provides the basis for a partial solution, through alternative measures and assumed relationships. But few of these internal relationships have been shown to exist empirically, making the prediction of outcomes from implemented strategies difficult to achieve. We need to be able to appraise our own performance, and that of our customers, suppliers and competitors, and we need to be able to make predictions about future performance, at least in the short term. The methods discussed in earlier chapters have identified techniques for tactical decision-making, and to support the analysis of product and customer profitability and of project viability. To date we have ignored the financial modelling and forecasting methods which are fundamental to budgeting and investment appraisal. This chapter looks at modelling methods to see how we can match methods with data availability, in order to explain and predict returns as well as evaluating risk.

FORECASTING METHODS

These methods might be classified according to the nature of the data available:

- quantitative – i.e., numerical (financial or non-financial), continuous or categorical;
- qualitative – i.e., non-numerical, descriptive, or narrative. Scales may sometimes be introduced to quantify what would otherwise be qualitative variables.

For both data types different forecasting methods might be employed, depending on whether the data are:

- time series data, where trend data are available for several variables across a number of successive time periods;
- cross-section data, where data are collected at a single point of time for several variables across a number of different cases.

With time series data we attempt to forecast values for future time periods, by making projections based on the components of the data. With cross-section data we attempt to forecast values for new cases outside the sample under consideration, based on what we have learned from the existing sample. We may also be able to 'explain' changes in forecasts in a way that makes it possible for us to instigate strategies which cause the forecast target to move in the desired direction. The primary methods available for different purposes might be categorized as follows, with methods of increasing sophistication corresponding with the quantitative data available:

- Delphi methods – popular in market research and often involving focus groups to gauge opinion and specify rankings or preferences;
- heuristic methods – essentially loose guidelines or rules of thumb used for decision-making in instances of uncertainty;
- probabilistic simulation – the specification of a range of 'possible' outcomes, together with associated probabilities, so that the alternatives may be modelled to simulate alternative scenarios.

All three of these methods start with very little in the way of hard data, though quantification might be introduced by attaching numbers to the alternatives and conducting detailed sensitivity analyses to test the robustness of the assumptions. The Derrick's Ice Cream (Chapter 5) and Casual Fashions (this chapter) case studies provide examples of the development of analysis, forecasting and strategies based on 'soft' data of this nature. The remaining methods require good quality numerical data, often a lot of it:

- time series methods (e.g., moving averages, exponential smoothing, Box–Jenkins) to identify systematic patterns in historical data and extrapolate forwards;
- causal methods (e.g., regression analysis for continuous data; discriminant analysis or logistic regression, where the dependent variables are categorical) to specify explanatory relationships and predict the effect of changes in the component variables.

DELPHI METHODS

Delphi assessment is a group process involving a panel of 'experts' who attempt to forecast future outcomes in situations where there is no direct knowledge, or at least a great deal of uncertainty. It is an intuitive procedure which relies on the subjective probabilities that participants attach to the likelihood of future events; it is also iterative in nature, so that individual opinion can be modified by the influence of other group members. The Delphi method attempts to generate collective expert opinion by making two substitutions: expert judgement for direct knowledge, and group for individual. Linstone and Turoff (2002: 223) note a significant convergence of responses for almost all forecast statements within three rounds of the process, and considerable stability of opinion thereafter.

However, Linstone (2002: 561) highlights the potential problems arising in the selection of 'expert group' participants:

- The differences in planning horizons for such a group may be wildly different from that for a more representative group; we expect loss of forecast accuracy when the time horizon expands for any group, but such variation needs to be controlled.
- The preferences expressed in an artificial planning session may differ from those in a real-life scenario, so that different approaches to risk taking, for example, are exhibited.
- The subjective probability basis of the technique makes it susceptible to the problems associated with heuristic devices, detailed in the next section.
- Poor selection of participants may lead to poor interaction and misleading outcomes; this is especially so with like-minded individuals not subject to differing opinions at either end of the spectrum.
- Groups are commonly over-pessimistic when making long-term forecasts, and over-optimistic when making short-term forecasts. This is complicated by individual traits of optimism/pessimism, though fortunately there is a great deal of consistency in individual behaviour in this regard.
- The process can be subject to deliberate deception if an assertive and articulate individual is able to disrupt the final outcomes through misleading and unrepresentative feedback.

However, despite these drawbacks, in some situations we may have no realistic alternative for generating any reasonable indication of likely future outcomes.

HEURISTIC METHODS

In practice, such heuristics may resemble trial and error, but are often 'rules of thumb' or standard operating procedures based on a wealth of knowledge and experience. For example, Thorngate (1980) provides examples of optimum decisions using decision-making heuristics, and Ashton (1976) demonstrates the robust nature of simple linear models used to approximate complex multivariate situations. The use of heuristic models has already been referred to with respect to both the resource-based view of the firm (Chapter 2) and the job scheduling problems of Chapter 6.

However, there is the danger that biased decision outcomes may result because inefficient information strategies have been adopted and/or the heuristics employed to overcome information overload are statistically inaccurate. Five particular areas of concern may be identified where heuristics can potentially cause bias:

- Availability – undue emphasis is given to recent or imaginable cases, for example recent instances of equipment failure may be accorded inappropriate seriousness because equipment histories and the probability distribution of breakdowns have not been examined.
- Representativeness – decisions are made on flimsy evidence which ignores prior probabilities. In practice hard numerical data giving the likely distribution of outcomes may be ignored, especially if 'softer' qualitative or narrative information is supplied simultaneously. Kahnemann and Tversky (1972) suggest that such narratives may be accorded a greatly inflated level of importance compared to their information content, a suggestion borne out by empirical evidence.
- Integration – inconsistent simplification methods might be adopted to combine information from different sources. For accounting information, this may coincide with the choice of inappropriate cues, inappropriate cue weightings, inappropriate mathematical relationships in the formation of multivariate models, or the erroneous amalgamation of time series and cross-section estimates.
- Concreteness – decisions are made using only explicitly stated information, ignoring that which may be assumed or derived indirectly. Inadequate investigations may, therefore, yield biased outcomes.
- Anchoring and adjustment – overconfidence in these initial estimates exists, which provides an 'anchor' to further adjustments made when additional information becomes available. Irrelevant information may form the basis of the initial 'anchor' so that subsequent adjustments result in hopelessly biased estimates.

The implication is that a heuristic approach, especially where conflicting messages are being conveyed by the available information sources, may result in biased outcomes.

PROBABILISTIC SIMULATION

Rather than limiting simplifying procedures to instances of 'information overload', some form of decision model may have to be introduced because of a lack of available data. Simulation or 'Monte Carlo' methods make it possible to 'create' hypothetical observations where no actual observations exist. In project planning and in predicting outcomes there may be no real observations, only estimates of values and relationships. This information is far from perfect, but is certainly better than nothing. It may be very representative of future outcomes and can be used to generate realistic future scenarios based on many fictitious observations where each of the outcomes satisfies known or assumed relationships between the variables, and each of the outcomes is representative for the variables.

The simulation approach necessitates the use of a computer model and multiple iterations (at least 100) to cope with the quantity of data, but the approach is essentially a simple one. Alternative approaches are possible depending on the assumptions made. This technique is best illustrated through reference to a numerical example, but since this will simultaneously address both 'risk' and 'return' issues, this illustration is delayed until our discussion of risk measurement later in this chapter.

The remaining sections of this chapter focus on analytic approaches to problem-solving using mathematical models for forecasting.

TIME SERIES ANALYSIS

Classical time series decomposition analysis assumes a relationship $Y = f(T, C, S, R)$ such that the variable to be forecast (Y) is subject to the influence of:

- a time trend (T), the directional trend of the series for Y over time, which may be upwards, downwards or static. The trend line may be linear or curved, either of which may be modelled with regression-type methods.
- the trade cycle (C), imposing short-term periods of boom and slump on the long-term trend. A curved pattern is likely, possibly extending over a period of many years. In practical terms it may be very difficult to isolate the 'cycle' and we may have to be satisfied with estimating a composite of 'trend and cycle' together, despite the errors so introduced.
- seasonal factors (S). Seasonal fluctuations do not necessarily correspond with seasons of the year; they are concerned with any systematic variation occurring within the time period under consideration. They would include quarterly variations within the year, monthly variations within the quarter, weekly variations within the month, daily variations within the week and hourly variations within the day. All are seasons as long as they are associated with a systematic variation within the time period, *whatever the time period*. The italicized phrase provides the clue to the elimination, and then isolation, of seasonal factors. If identical variation is attributable to Monday in any week, then Monday in week 1 is equated with Monday in week 2 for averaging purposes. Seasonal variation will cancel out completely when the week is totalled, and a moving average over successive time periods can be calculated.
- random fluctuations (R). Random fluctuations are by definition unpredictable. Over time we must expect positive and negative variations to cancel out. Summation of a series (provided that it is long enough) will eliminate random variation totally.

The irregular nature of the observed data usually means that a forecast of future values of Y cannot be made simply by eye. Instead we attempt to break up the series into its components so that each can be projected separately and the separate forecasts combined to give an integrated prediction. We therefore need to specify carefully the different components.

The simplest of assumptions allow basic arithmetic processes to be used to model the time series:

- Summation of the series eliminates R.
- Moving averages eliminate S. Subtraction of the remainder from the original series allows S to be isolated for each time period.
- Fitting a straight-line trend allows T to be identified, so that the C pattern can also be isolated.

However, before we proceed to fit the model and make predictions, we must expand the simple functional relationship $Y = f(T, C, S, R)$ into something more specific. Most commonly this would be either the simple additive model,

$$Y = T + C + S + R,$$

or the simple multiplicative model,

$$Y = T \times C \times S \times R.$$

The former is the easiest to fit and works well as long as the trend, T, is not too pronounced. When T is moving steeply (up or down) it will tend to blanket out all other fluctuations, so that a multiplicative model measuring the other factors relative to trend is to be preferred.

In practice there are infinite numbers of possible models, with various weightings and combinations. More sophisticated models can be introduced which weight the data items (e.g., giving greater emphasis to more recent time periods) as well as the components.

The additive and multiplicative models so far considered treat all items of data as of equal value, however outdated they might be, and weight all the forecasting variables equally. A number of alternative time series forecasting methods exist which attempt to relax one or both of these constraints. Their added complexity makes computer-based analysis essential.

Exponential smoothing uses a 'smoothing constant' at the moving average stage to place more emphasis on the most recent data items. Each smoothed data point is equal to the previous smoothed data point, plus a fraction of the difference between that and the actual data point. The calculations of successive values are linked so that they form an exponential series. Thus,

$$D_t = D_{t-1} + a(Y_t - D_{t-1}),$$

where Y_t is the actual data point, for time period t and D_t, D_{t-1} are smoothed data points. So, for $a = 0.2$,

$$D_t = D_{t-1} + 0.2(Y_t - D_{t-1})$$
$$= 0.2Y_t + 0.8D_{t-1},$$

a relationship which will smooth out 80% of the random errors in the data points Y_t. The value of a is chosen arbitrarily in the first place and modified in the light of the outcomes.

Similar smoothing methods can be used for trend and seasonal factors, each employing separate arbitrary smoothing constants, in order to build up a composite forecasting model. Thus a trend (T_t) is calculated from

$$T_t = (1 - \beta)T_{t-1} + \beta(D_t - D_{t-1}),$$

where β is the trend smoothing constant. A seasonal factor (S_t) is calculated from

$$S_t = (1 - g)S_{t-p} + g,$$

where g is the seasonal smoothing constant and p the length of the season in time periods. Forecasts are again based on trend (T) and seasonal (S)

components, but have the advantage of not requiring large quantities of historical data. But they are sensitive to the choice of arbitrary smoothing constant and may require fine tuning.

Fortunately a detailed knowledge of these algorithms is not usually necessary since most statistical software (e.g., SPSS-X) accommodates them within sophisticated time series forecasting models. For example, the Box–Jenkins procedure (Box and Jenkins, 1976) provides the opportunity for data transformation in the fitting and forecasting of time series using an iterative procedure requiring multiple computer runs in which the sensitivity of smoothing constants can easily be monitored.

REGRESSION ANALYSIS

Whereas time series analysis can provide us with trend projections for a key variable, in practice this may not be enough. If we wish to influence future values through appropriate management action, we need to know which variables impact on the values assumed by the key variable. In essence, we wish to establish

- degrees of association between variables (correlation) and
- causal relationships between variables (regression), in order to develop
- an explanatory relationship which allows us to show why a key variable is changing, not just how.

If we consider the simple two-variable situation (for a dependent variable Y and an explanatory variable X), then a scatter diagram with Y on the vertical axis and X on the horizontal would reveal the strength of any relationship between the two variables. Depending on the outcome, we might be able to speculate on the existence of a linear relationship of the form $Y = a + bX$.

The ordinary least-squares (OLS) method measures the deviation of points away from a fitted line, either vertically or horizontally, and ensures that the optimum fit is such that the sum of the squares of these distances, over all the points, is as small as possible.

The strength of the fit of the relationship may allow us to be confident about predicting values of Y for new values of X, but we must still be wary of making predictions outside the original range of X values. OLS regression methods attempt to estimate the actual relationship $Y_i = a + bX_i + m_i$ with an estimated relationship based on a finite sample size of n observations. The error term, m_i, in the relationship is estimated by the residual of the equation e_i.

OLS fits make a number of assumptions, the violation of which can result in unreliable equations. The most serious of these are autocorrelation in time series data (interrelated time periods) and multicollinearity for cross-section data, indicating that two or more explanatory variables are too closely related (i.e., essentially different measures of the same thing!).

For time series data we would therefore ensure that the Durbin–Watson statistic (d) is within acceptable bounds; and for cross-section data that correlation coefficients between potential explanatory variables are acceptable. Thus for an equation like $Y = a + bX_1 + cX_2 + dX_3$, we would need to check all combinations of correlations between the three X values to ensure that each was less than 0.8. Where the inter-correlations between the explanatory variables are all high and statistically significant we have a potential problem. The simplest solution is to avoid bringing one of the 'offending' variables into the equation.

In practice it is easy to miss evidence of multicollinearity, because changes of a large magnitude may not occur. The strength of the interrelationship may be destructive but may not, for example, cause sign changes in the regression equation. It is therefore vitally important that we monitor the inclusion of new variables into an equation on a step-by-step basis. We want to improve on the explanatory power of the equation, through the addition of new variables, while at the same time ensuring:

- coefficients remain statistically significant;
- coefficients and standard errors remain relatively stable;
- signs of coefficients remain intuitively correct.

In the regression process the construction of the correlation coefficient matrix is, arguably, the single most useful piece of preliminary information, because it serves three vital functions:

- It establishes the direction of any relationship, which should be intuitively correct and which would normally correspond with the sign of this variable in any regression equation.
- It suggests those variables likely to be useful explanatory variables, because they are highly correlated with the dependent variable.
- It highlights potential multicollinearity problems by specifying the inter-correlation between competing explanatory variables.

As with most of our analyses, it is just not enough to 'provide the numbers'. There must also be some indication of how these numbers might aid decision-making, and facilitate the implementation of new strategies. Sometimes regression analysis fails to satisfy these conditions because the key variables identified are beyond our control. Thus although the final regression equation may be a statistical optimum, it may be impossible to implement its recommendations (e.g., increase the value of those variables having a positive impact on the dependent variable), or a cost–benefit analysis may reveal that it is not financially viable to contemplate the changes envisaged. The treatment of regression analysis presented here is necessarily simplified, for mathematical expediency, but it attempts to demonstrate the potential strengths and pitfalls associated with the use of the technique.

DISCRIMINANT ANALYSIS: FAILURE PREDICTION AND CORPORATE TURNAROUND

The use of OLS regression methods, as in the previous section, requires a dependent variable which can be measured continuously. However, there will be occasions where the variable which we want to explain and predict is not of a continuous nature. It may be categorical – of the form high/medium/low, good/bad, or success/failure. These can be quantified by assigning dummy variables of the (1, 2, 3) or (0, 1) variety to reflect the alternative states, but in each case these are the only values that the dependent variable can take. Changes in the value of the explanatory variable cannot change the continuous value, only its classification into one or other of the categories. In such circumstances we cannot use simple regression methods, but seek an alternative. Linear discriminant analysis (LDA) can be used when:

- the groups being identified are clearly separate;
- the explanatory variables are close to being normally distributed, or can be transformed to be so – this ensures 'univariate normality' where the stricter requirement of 'multivariate normality' is more difficult to test for in practice;
- there is no multicollinearity between the explanatory variables.

We seek to construct an equation of the form:

$$Z = a + bX_1 + cX_2 + dX_3 + \cdots,$$

such that the resulting value of Z allows the categorization of cases. Effectively we are generating the equation of a line (or lines) which can be positioned to divide the cases into the required groups. If we return to our failure prediction model of Chapter 3, then the construction of a three-variable discriminant model based on financial ratios might be visualized relative to the space in a rectangular room where axes are constructed in the corner of the room: the profit ratio (P) stretches vertically towards the ceiling, and liquidity (Q) and debt (R) axes at right angles along the skirting boards. The company cases under consideration appear as points in space, representing three-ratio combinations, and discriminant analysis would try to position a plane in this space such that all the failed companies were on one side of this plane and all the healthy ones on the other. The equation of the optimum plane, even if it were impossible to classify all company cases correctly on either side, would be a discriminant equation of the form:

$$Z = a + bP + cQ - dR$$

where b, c and d are the weightings attached to each of the three ratios, P, Q, and R; a is a constant term whose value determines the cut-off between failed and non-failed groups; and Z is the value of the composite function, such that $Z > 0$ corresponds with a state of financial health and $Z < 0$ corresponds with a state of financial distress, in that the company has a financial profile similar to that of a previously failed company.

Discriminant analysis minimizes the number of misclassifications and determines the corresponding optimum variable weightings. Whereas various alternative multivariate techniques have been used to develop failure prediction models, including quadratic discriminant analysis (Altman et al., 1977), logit and probit (Ohlson, 1980; Zavgren, 1985), non-parametric methods (Frydman et al., 1985) and neural nets (Altman et al., 1994), there is no evidence of significantly superior performance associated with such approaches compared with traditional linear discriminant analysis (e.g., Hamer, 1983; Lo, 1986). Hair et al. (1998: 276) and McLeay and Omar (2000) argue that logistic regression is more robust than linear discriminant analysis when the univariate normality and homogeneity of variance–covariance assumptions are not met, and Collins and Green (1982) and Lennox (1999) suggest that a logistic regression model could identify failing companies more accurately than discriminant analysis, provided that specification problems are overcome. The univariate normality and homogeneity of variance–covariance assumptions are rarely satisfied in practice, but this does not appear to impact on the classificatory ability of discriminatory models, attributable by Bayne et al. (1983) to its robust nature and non-ambiguous group cut-off scores. For these reasons linear discriminant analysis continues to be the preferred method of analysis in many studies.

Failure prediction

Scope of models

There are considerable differences between the discriminant models constructed in different countries, both in terms of the financial ratio variables included and the weighting accorded them. Similarly, there are considerable differences between the models constructed for separate industry groupings. Pacey and Pham (1990) provide an excellent example of the dangers of over-aggregation and ignoring industry differentiation. Their model, embracing Australian companies across the whole of the industrial sector over a 20-year period (in order to generate a reasonable sample size) is, not surprisingly, an extremely poor predictor of impending failure.

An excellent instance of the need for different models in different industries lies in the application of the working capital ratio, given by

$$\frac{\text{Current assets } - \text{current liabilities}}{\text{Net capital employed}}.$$

Successful manufacturing companies will usually give a positive value for this ratio, indicating a positive net current assets balance. Successful large food retailers, however, will often exhibit negative values for this ratio because of the fast-moving, cash-based nature of their business and the power they can exert over their suppliers. Clearly, a single model for manufacturers and retailers could not normally accommodate such a ratio – necessitating the construction of separate models.

Nevertheless, a succession of authors have attempted to apply the US model developed by Altman (1968) to UK companies for which it was not intended, and, even more erroneously, to apply manufacturing models to non-manufacturing companies or to unlisted companies. The strict industry requirements of a particular model limit its application to a narrow sector of companies for which it was derived. Often a separate model will be necessary for each industry in each country, and we must recognize that there may be significant differences even between regions.

Ratio variables

Differences between countries and industries mean that no single optimum combination of financial ratios will exist, although we might expect that particular ratios are widely applicable.

Several studies have found a dividend-based ratio to be a useful discriminator, but it is absent from most UK models. Similarly, liquidity ratios have been found to be of only limited usefulness in models constructed outside the UK. Interestingly, Taffler's (1982, 1983) UK profitability ratio (profit before tax over average current liabilities) has been found to be a very useful discriminator for a number of industrial sectors of overseas models.

Whatever ratio combinations are employed in the construction of the model, it is essential that identical variables, variable weightings and cut-off points are used in their application. If such details are not publicly available then no attempt should be made to apply models 'approximately'. The errors which flow from this are unnecessary and have potentially dire consequences.

Models constructed on old data are not necessarily useless. The Altman (1968) and Taffler (1982) models, in the USA and UK respectively, are seen by some as remaining relatively robust and still of considerable use almost 40 years on, with reliable, long-term evidence of their discriminatory ability.

The definition of failure
There are numerous definitions of business or corporate failure, from the strict legal sense of liquidation to a more liberal definition of inability to repay monies as due. At least five common definitions of failure or distress, varying with their degree of stringency, might be employed: receivership; voluntary liquidation; compulsory liquidation; provisional liquidation; and stock exchange suspension or investigation. Models might be developed based on different definitions to suit user requirements; for example, Houghton and Smith (1991) included 'stock exchange investigation' as a failure measure, while Smith et al. (2004) included a PN4 designation by the Kuala Lumpur Stock Exchange in Malaysia within their failure definition. Almost all existing models suffer from the problem that they are based on artificially derived samples of companies and businesses, and therefore have an unreal probability of failure and non-failure. This problem is difficult to overcome without employing the whole population of listed companies so that the probability of failure is the same as the real-world incidence of failure.

The timing of failure
Most discriminant models will identify those companies exhibiting financial distress. Within this set they can highlight those most at risk – the worst companies, those most likely to fail within the following year. However, the precise timing of failure is determined by the bankers through their decision to appoint receivers or withdraw financial support. Financial profiles alone are therefore unable to specify the precise timing of failure, which is largely determined by the whim of the principal bankers. Clearly, the shorter the time between the prediction and the likely event the easier the prediction task is, but the less useful it would be in formulating an optimum investment strategy.

Predictive ability
Existing models are only predictive in the sense that they identify those companies which are currently trading but have financial profiles similar to previous failures. All models will highlight a 'distressed' set which overpredicts failure, in that it will also contain some companies who recover and some who will be taken over before they are allowed to fail. Recent studies argue that the cost of a type 1 error (missing a failed company) is much greater than a type 2 error (overpredicting failure). They suggest the relative importance of the type 1 error to the decision-making context is of the order of 40 : 1. Such factors should be incorporated into models and reflected in the cut-off point for predictions. Any reference to the overall classificatory ability of such models is fatuous if the type of error being made is not identified. Most researchers claim to demonstrate predictive ability while only demonstrating classificatory ability. All new models demonstrate only the

latter, and their usefulness as predictive tools can only be demonstrated with time and with the application of the models to new data.

Model development: *From univariate to multivariate models*

Whereas traditional univariate balance sheet ratios like those for liquidity may give an adequate indication of vulnerability to current and short-term fluctuations, longer-term predictions require a better indication of cash flows. In the absence of publicly available information relating to internal cash budgets, this must come via projections of cash-generating abilities from the published accounts.

The Altman (1968) study for listed US manufacturing companies provides a benchmark against which all other multivariate studies can be measured. The Altman model is a linear combination of five variables, and records a 95% classification accuracy of failed/non-failed companies:

$$Z = 1.2X_1 + 1.4X_2 + 3.3X_3 + 0.6X_4 + 1.0X_5,$$

where

$$X_1 = \frac{\text{Current assets - current liabilities}}{\text{Total assets}},$$

$$X_2 = \frac{\text{Retained earnings}}{\text{Total assets}},$$

$$X_3 = \frac{\text{Earnings before interest and tax}}{\text{Total assets}},$$

$$X_4 = \frac{\text{Market value of preferred and common equity}}{\text{Book value of total liabilities}},$$

$$X_5 = \frac{\text{Sales}}{\text{Total assets}},$$

and a Z-score below 1.8 corresponds with a company considered to be a 'prime candidate for bankruptcy'. The lower the Z-score, the higher the perceived probability of failure.

In the UK the Taffler (1983) model, detailed in Chapter 2, is the most widely exposed failure prediction model and the one which has been subject to the most extensive testing. In many other countries, the shortage of failed cases and their distribution across many industries has caused problems of much greater severity than those experienced in the UK and USA. Nevertheless, a number of other studies have used publicly available accounting information, with varying degrees of success, to predict failure.

To date, economic theory has played a negligible part in the development of failure prediction models. Given the absence of a substantial theoretical underpinning, most research studies have been exploratory, trying to establish the model, method, variables and firms which give the best predictions. Research to date has demonstrated that the classification performance of predictive models is not highly sensitive to the mathematical relationship chosen or the statistical method employed. Linear additive models based on linear discriminant analysis are the simplest to construct and interpret, and their outcomes are not dissimilar to any comparable model.

Corporate turnaround

Existing failure prediction models are only *predictive* in the sense that they identify those companies currently trading which have financial profiles similar to previous failures. Without verification over an extensive time period they are *classification* rather than *predictive* models. As with all similar models the 'distressed' set will overpredict failure, in that it will also contain some companies who effect recoveries and some who will be taken over before they are allowed to fail. Some of the 'distressed' set of companies might eventually effect a financial recovery if they were to implement appropriate turnaround strategies. This provides a positive angle for early warning models in that it identifies some cases in need of remedial action. From a strategic perspective it might also help to associate the achievement of 'recovered' status with the implementation of key management actions. Slatter (1984: 105) identifies a number of generic recovery strategies that might be adopted, depending on the cause of the 'distressed' state. He specifies seven major causes of decline and potential failure:

- poor management;
- inadequate financial control;
- high cost structure;
- lack of marketing effort;
- competitive weaknesses;
- financial policy;
- ill-advised acquisitions and projects.

Each of these is associated with a particular set of generic recovery strategies:

- Poor management is associated with autocratic leadership, an ineffective board, the neglect of core businesses and lack of management depth. Appropriate remedial action would require new blood in the management team, organizational change and decentralization.
- Inadequate financial control is associated with a poorly designed accounting system, misuse of information, the distortion of costs through misallocation of overheads and an organizational structure which hinders rather than facilitates control. This would be improved by new management and decentralization if accompanied by tighter financial controls.
- High cost structure is associated with operational inefficiencies, competitor control of raw materials and proprietary knowledge, low scale economies and high labour costs. Cost reduction strategies and a revised product-market focus are appropriate for recovery. Cost reduction strategies would include those directed towards: raw material costs, aimed at improved buying practices, better utilization and the possible substitution of materials; unit labour costs, aimed at increasing productivity and reducing headcount; and overhead costs, targeting manufacturing, marketing and distribution.
- Lack of marketing effort is associated with inadequate or inflexible response to changing patterns of demand and product obsolescence. Improved marketing pursues a revenue-generating strategy embracing changed prices, more selling effort, rationalizing of the product line, focused promotion, and a closer focus on customer needs.

- Competitive weakness is reflected by lack of strength in both price and product competition and an absent product-market focus. A reliance on old products will be apparent, with inadequate differentiation and no new product ideas on the horizon. Cost, marketing and product weaknesses must be addressed, with growth via acquisition considered as a means of overcoming deficiencies in the product-market area.
- Financial policy weakness is characterized by high debt–equity ratios, expensive sources of funding and conservative financial policies. A new financial strategy will likely include debt restructuring and revenue-generating policies.
- Failed acquisitions are characterized by the purchase of losers at a price which is set too high. Poor post-acquisition management often results in a quick resale. Ill-advised big projects, which threaten the company's survival, are associated with start-up difficulties, the loss of major contracts and the underestimation of capital requirements and market entry costs.

Asset reduction is the most appropriate recovery strategy in the circumstances, embracing:

- reducing fixed assets, through divesting operating units and specific assets, management buyouts and sale and leaseback arrangements;
- reducing working capital, through extending creditors and reducing both inventories and debtors – this would include cancelling orders, returning goods, the sale of surplus raw materials, tighter credit and possibly factoring arrangements for debtors.

The extent to which these strategies are appropriate will also be determined by the severity of the crisis and peculiar industry characteristics. Where short-term survival is threatened we might anticipate a recovery strategy comprising four strands:

- cash generation
- asset reduction;
- debt restructuring; and
- very tight financial control, embracing cash management, cost reduction, product refocus and improved marketing.

RISK MEASUREMENT

Traditional approaches to cash-flow evaluation, such as the measurement of capital expenditures, place far too much emphasis on expected returns and far too little on the potential risks incurred. Spreadsheet software has facilitated the use of sensitivity analysis to the extent that no project appraisal is complete without its consideration. However, an awareness of the impact of realistic variations on outcome is not enough; we should pay more attention to the risk element in any venture, appropriately quantified, in order to provide improved decision support.

Most accounting textbooks emphasize discounted cash flow, payback, internal rate of return and net present value as appraisal tools. Arguably, these are all concerned with quantifying the returns from the project and not the risk. (The payback period might additionally be viewed as a measure of risk since it indicates the time taken to recover sums invested.)

The survey evidence discussed in Chapter 2 suggests that strategic factors – rather than discounted cash-flow results – are of increasing importance in determining capital expenditure decisions; similarly, the survey evidence discussed in Chapter 7 suggests that managers would like a more detailed analysis of risk levels prior to decision-making.

Too often the income or cost savings employed are point estimates which are, at best, educated guesses, at worst crystal-ball gazing. Alternative scenarios are frequently ignored, and the probability of alternative outcomes rarely quantified. Incorporating a range of realistic cash-flow outcomes will at least generate a better idea of what might happen, replacing a single point estimate with a best–worst range. Spreadsheet software is well equipped to accomplish such a task, and to go further in generating a distribution of outcomes where we have an idea of the likelihood of alternative scenarios.

Where probabilities can be estimated, a full-blown distribution of outcomes can be produced, so that risk management becomes an essential part of the evaluation.

Figure 9.1 demonstrates the ideal circumstances, with each level of potential returns linked to a specified degree of likelihood so that it is possible to evaluate quantitatively the level of risk associated with a particular project. Such an ideal picture can only be generated when the likelihood of alternative cash flows can be estimated accurately. But even if such accuracy is not possible – and in practice it rarely will be – the ability to state that one outcome is more likely than another is important. Such weightings could then be included in an analysis of the risk of a project.

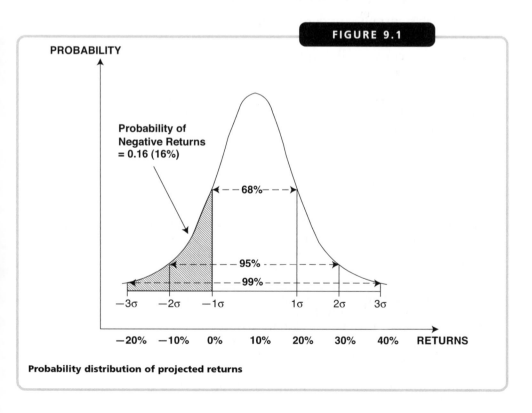

FIGURE 9.1

Probability distribution of projected returns

Project evaluation pitfalls

Any appraisal of the quality of investment decisions should address the way in which the decisions have been taken as well as their consequences. This would include the following stages:

- Project generation: which projects are put forward for examination?
- Cash flows: how and by whom are these estimated?
- Analysis: what methods and assumptions are employed?
- Selection: importance of financials/non-financials in project choice?
- Authorization: documentation of monitoring process for project implementation?
- Evaluation: do the project outcomes match/exceed expectations?

A post-audit investigation can potentially have a significant impact on the manner in which future appraisals are conducted. If it is viewed as a learning experience, seeking improvement opportunities, rather than as a witch-hunt of those who have made errors, then real bottom-line benefits are achievable.

Problems with implementing post-audit schemes range across the whole gamut of which? where? how? and by whom? Big companies may be able to audit internally, others may need to employ consultants. Either way, the continued co-operation of those individuals involved in implementing the project is essential. Any breach of confidence or finger-pointing will reduce the levels of active co-operation and, potentially, destroy the learning opportunities. The post-audit could extend over:

- all projects currently underperforming;
- all projects implemented (underperforming or not);
- all projects considered (implemented or not); and
- a sample of any of the above.

The post-audit case study (Alumina PLC) discussed in Chapter 4 demonstrates the potential for devious managerial action which can both mask underperformance and aid the pursuit of a personal agenda.

RISK ANALYSIS

The focus on returns frequently causes the assessment of the risk attaching to a project to be neglected. Managerial decision-making requires information on both risks and projected returns to be available. Risk assessment should, at the very least, incorporate an examination of the likelihood and outcomes of the best and worst scenarios.

It might be argued that cash-flow projections are only estimates, so that the probabilities attaching to such estimates can only be figments of the imagination! But if we have evidence to suggest that one outcome is more likely than another then that is useful, and potentially significant, information that can be incorporated into the analysis with probability weightings of, say, 0.55 and 0.45 respectively. Probability estimates for alternative outcomes can be combined through decision trees to give an indication of the distribution of possibilities.

Consider a simple numerical example in the form of a company, Cable Technology, which is heavily dependent on export markets and with sales revenues highly susceptible to variations in economic factors, particularly exchange rates, interest rates and the rate of price inflation. It sources much of its raw material requirements overseas too, so that its import prices can vary wildly. It exercises a tight control over those costs under direct control, particularly labour costs. Forecasts of price and wage-cost inflation are an important part of Cable Technology's planning and budgeting process and it relies heavily on estimates from the Marketing Department.

Current estimates suggest that the rate of price inflation will lie between 6% and 9% over the next quarter, with 7% the most likely figure, with a 40 per cent chance. There is a 30 per cent chance of it being 8%, 20 per cent of it being 9% and only 10 per cent of it being as low as 6%. The rate of wage-cost inflation is reckoned to be 1% or 1.5% higher than the corresponding rate of price inflation. For the two lower rates of price inflation there is a 40 per cent chance of a 1% difference, a 60 per cent chance of a 1.5% difference. For the two higher rates of price inflation there is thought to be a 70 per cent chance of a 1% difference and only a 30 per cent chance of a 1.5% difference. If the expected rate of wage-cost inflation exceeds 8.5% or the chances of a blow-out to a figure greater than 9.5% exceed a 10 per cent chance, then Cable Technology institutes further short-term cost-cutting measures.

The rates of price and wage-cast inflation, together with their respective probabilities, can be represented in the form of a decision-tree structure. The rates of wage-cost inflation are conditional on a predetermined rate of price inflation and the associated conditional probabilities measure the coincidence of two separate events. The joint probability of a particular rate of wage inflation is, therefore, the product of two separate probabilities: that for a particular rate of price inflation, and the subsequent conditional probability. These are detailed in Figure 9.2.

Weighted arithmetic means reveal an expected rate of price inflation of 7.6%, and an expected rate of wage inflation of 8.825%. The latter figure marginally exceeds Cable Technology's target figure of 8.5%. Reference to the distribution of rates of wage-cost inflation in the final column of Figure 9.2 indicates a 20 per cent chance (i.e., 0.14 + 0.06) of a rate greater than or equal to 10%. The likelihood of a rate in excess of 9.5 per cent is, therefore, well beyond Cable Technology's acceptable levels. Both of these outcomes will trigger increased cost-cutting activity.

In practice decision-tree structures can be much larger than those in Figure 9.2 – both longer (representing more separate outcomes identified) and wider (with additional dependent outcomes and more probabilities). In theory there is no limit to the number of conditional probabilities that might be considered jointly. When all outcomes, and their distribution, have been determined a thorough spreadsheet-based sensitivity analysis might be conducted to evaluate the significance of any probability assumptions. Brewer et al. (1993) discuss the use of 'fuzzy logic' which adds a new dimension to the spreadsheet-based appraisal of risk by incorporating uncertainty into each of the cells of the analysis. Although helpful in situations where we are short of data, some decision-tree models may quickly become very complicated, and simulation methods or Monte Carlo methods may be preferred.

The simulation method might be used in our Cable Technology case to predict the likely rate of wage-cost inflation in a particular period.

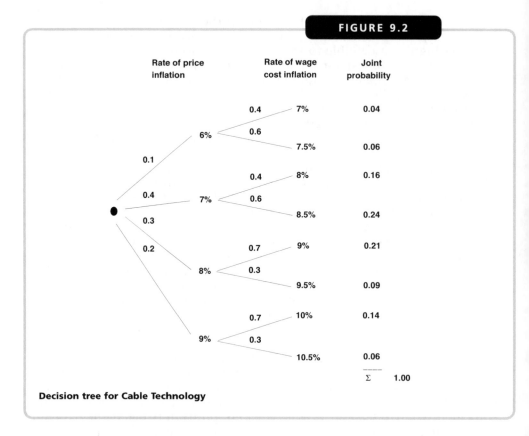

FIGURE 9.2

Rate of price inflation	Rate of wage cost inflation	Joint probability

Decision tree for Cable Technology

Economic estimates reveal that the rate of price inflation will be 6% (with a probability of 0.1), 7% (with a probability of 0.4), 8% (with a probability of 0.3), or 9% (with a probability of 0.2).

The simplest method of simulating observations involves making no assumptions about the *actual* distribution of the price inflation variable. The probabilities provided are accepted as fact, and no possibilities outside the 6–9% range are considered. Random numbers from a two-digit range 00 to 99 are assigned to the variable values in accordance with the stated probability. For example, price inflation of 6% has a 0.1 (i.e., one in ten) probability. Ten of the one hundred random numbers are, therefore, allocated to this possibility (i.e., 00 to 09).

The complete allocation would be:

Price inflation (%)	Probability	Random (no. range)
6	0.1	00–09
7	0.4	10–49
8	0.3	50–79
9	0.2	80–99

The appropriate random number range is simple to derive and corresponds exactly with the probabilities provided. Thus, the generation of a random number equal to 23, say, from tables or from a random number generator would select 7% as the corresponding value for inflation. This value can then be treated as a representative observation in any further analysis. Given a rate of price inflation of 7%, the corresponding rate of wage inflation will be either 8% or 8.5%. A second random number generation allows this selection to be made in accordance with the respective probabilities of 0.4 and 0.6:

Price inflation (%)	Wage-cost inflation (%)	Random no. range
	8	00–39
7		
	8.5	40–99

Successive random numbers of 23 and 31, say, would, therefore, select a price inflation of 7% and a wage-cost inflation of 8%. If price inflation is not a relevant variable for further analysis and forecasting we could go straight to wage-cost inflation by directing attention to the right-hand column of Figure 9.2. A random number range in accord with the stated conditional probabilities allows the selection of a single rate:

Rate of wage-cost inflation (%)	Probability	Random no. range
7	0.04	00–03
7.5	0.06	04–09
8	0.16	10–25
8.5	0.24	26–49
9	0.21	50–70
9.5	0.09	71–79
10	0.14	80–93
10.5	0.06	94–99

A single random number of, say, 67 would then select a 9% rate of wage cost inflation.

Alternatively, we might assume that the 'rate of price inflation' is actually distributed normally, with our estimates representing sample observations from a normal population. Then we can use the calculated sample mean and standard deviation to smooth out the discontinuities of the estimated pattern and provide a normal distribution with the following ranges of values and associated probabilities:

INF % (X)	PROB (P)	PX	$X - \bar{X}$	$P(X - \bar{X})^2$
6	0.1	0.6	−1.6	0.0256
7	0.4	2.8	−0.6	0.1440
8	0.3	2.4	0.4	0.0480
9	0.2	1.8	1.4	0.3920
		7.6		0.6096

The mean is thus

$$X = \Sigma PX = 7.6\%$$

and the standard deviation

$$S = \sqrt{P(X - \bar{X})^2} = \sqrt{0.6096} = 0.78076\%.$$

Here the normal distribution ordinate $Z = (X - \bar{X})/S$ within the distribution of values, and associated normal probabilities can be established by calculating $Z = (X - 7.6)/0.78076$ for different class boundaries. These are detailed in Table 9.1.

The normal curve area is derived from tables of the normal distribution, and the difference in these values provides the probability of an observation occurring between the respective class boundaries. This probability establishes the range of random numbers to be selected from the two-digit random number range 00–99.

Thus the probability of an observation in the range 7.75 to 8.25 is 0.22, equivalent to 22 of the 100 random numbers, from 58 to 79 inclusive.

If any of these random numbers is chosen in the simulation it will generate a value of 8% for 'price inflation'. Other random numbers will generate different values, directly in accordance with their relative probability. Similar distributions, and corresponding sets of random numbers, for each variable in any analysis allow all combinations to be considered and a distribution of overall outcomes produced. This method might, therefore, be applied to the rate of wage-cost inflation too by using the data of Figure 9.2 as the basis for the construction of the normal distribution.

Now the foregoing may sound very theoretical and devoid of practical application, but let us return to our earlier point about matching method with data. Suppose we are in a start-up situation, with a new venture for which we have little guidance on outcomes. We need to make forecasts of

TABLE 9.1

Normal distribution simulation

Mid point	Class boundaries	Z Ordinate	Normal Curve Area	Z probability	Random Number Range
	5.25	−3.01	0.49869		
5.5				0.01	00
	5.75	−2.37	0.49111		
6				0.03	01–03
	6.25	−1.73	0.45818		
6.5				0.10	04–13
	6.75	−1.09	0.36214		
7				0.19	14–32
	7.25	−0.45	0.17364		
7.5				0.25	33–57
	7.75	0.19	0.07535		
8				0.22	58–79
	8.25	0.83	0.29673		
8.5				0.13	80–92
	8.75	1.47	0.42922		
9				0.05	93–97
	9.25	2.11	0.48257		
9.5				0.02	98–99
	9.75	2.75	0.49702		
				Sum 1.00	

costs and revenues so that we can budget. The information available may be confined to the views of others, and to the outcomes of other similar ventures. All we have, then, are educated guesses for forecasts, but that is better than nothing at all, if it allows us to project a range of outcomes, so that an analysis of possible risks and returns can be conducted. The next section details just such a case, which is concerned with the potential risks and returns of an investment opportunity. It combines probabilistic risk estimates, via decision trees or simulation methods, through traditional spreadsheet methods, to allow the development of a risk profile.

CASE STUDY

Casual Fashions: A risk analysis case study

Casual Fashions is a hypothetical national retail chain considering an expansion in the number of its outlets by moving into the Meadowhall shopping centre in Sheffield. It is conducting a full project appraisal, covering estimates of sales, costs, profits and movements in the economy. The market research team has established the likelihood of alternative trading patterns in order to generate decision trees and facilitate a simulation study. They have estimated the number of visitors to the centre, the proportion likely to enter the new shop and the spending patterns within the shop; all have been allocated probabilities over a realistic range. Their aim is to produce a probability distribution for projected sales in the first year of operations. They believe that annual sales will initially be in the range £3 million to £48 million, with mean value of £15.6 million. Their analysis reveals that the distribution of outcomes is not symmetrical, but skewed significantly, as illustrated by Figure 9.3.

FIGURE 9.3

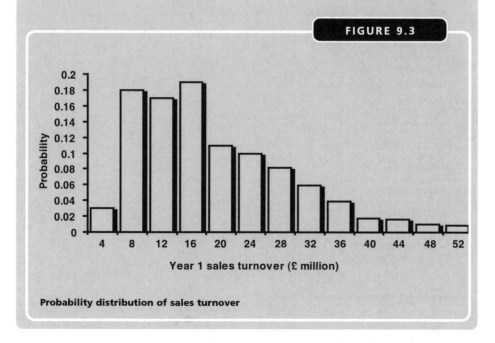

Year 1 sales turnover (£ million)

Probability distribution of sales turnover

CASE STUDY (cont.)

Cost projections allow the group's management accountant to construct a spreadsheet in the form shown in Figure 9.4 in order to calculate profit, tax liabilities, cash flows and discounted present values. Fundamental to the spreadsheet is the projected year 1 sales figure, the variation of which has already been established in Figure 9.3. By substituting sales figures into the spreadsheet, internal rates of return (IRR) can be generated for each level of activity. By directing the output to a graphics package, the management accountant can produce a scatter diagram of the type shown in Figure 9.5, mapping IRR against year 1 sales. From this we know that the mean sales level (£15.6 million) in the first year of trading will correspond with an IRR of around 22%, marginally in excess of the group's 18% cost of capital hurdle for new investment projects.

The common axes in Figures 9.3 and 9.5 (relating to sales turnover in the first year of operations) allows the data from the two to be combined in order to graph probability against IRR. The resulting diagram, detailed in Figure 9.6, gives the required

FIGURE 9.4

Profit statement (£ million)	Year 0	Year 1	Year 2	Year 3	Year 4	Year 5
Sales	0	15.6	20.7	24.4	28.9	32.3
less cost of goods sold						
Opening stock						
plus purchases						
less closing stock						
Gross profit						
less other expenses						
Lease expense						
Staffing costs						
Stockholding costs						
Depreciation on maintenance costs						
Depreciation on start-up costs						
Net profit (loss) before tax						
Income tax payable						
Net profit after tax						
Carried forward tax loss						
Cashflow statement (£ million)						
Cash inflows						
Sales						
less cash outflows						
Sales						
lesscash outflows						
Purchases						
Lease payments						
Staffing costs						
Stockholding costs						
Starf-up costs						
Maintenance costs						
Income tax paid	2.31					
Net cash flows	22.1					
Net present value @ 15%						
Internal rate of return (%)						

Spreadsheet for cashflow analysis

CASE STUDY (cont.)

FIGURE 9.5

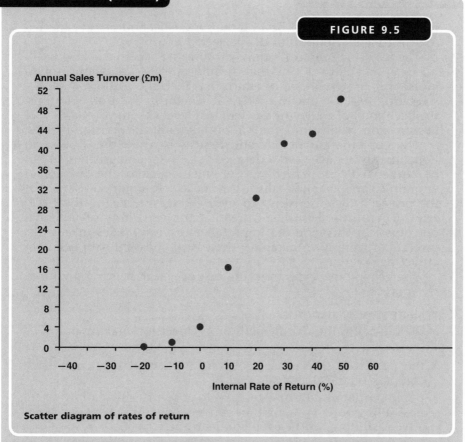

Scatter diagram of rates of return

FIGURE 9.6

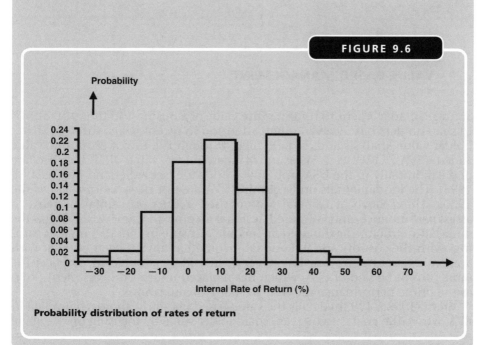

Probability distribution of rates of return

indication of risk. It goes beyond the spreadsheet output of expected returns to a distribution of the projected returns.

The results are not uniformly encouraging. There is a 15% likelihood (a probability of 0.15) that the project will actually lose money. Worse still, the likelihood of returns less than the cost of capital is a staggering 49%. Despite the potential benefits in the form of returns, the likelihood of achieving the required level of returns is almost as likely as not – vitally important information for the decision-makers.

The combination of risk and returns is, therefore, not at all hopeful at this stage, and a detailed sensitivity analysis has still to be conducted! In particular, we must consider the impact of economic variables and realistic time delays. It is quite possible that the project will be sensitive to such changes, reducing the likely rates of return and further increasing the variability of potential outcomes. In this case the importance of year 1 sales makes this project particularly vulnerable if there is any possibility of delays in attracting revenue.

The general messages from the case are clear. It is essential that we appreciate:

- alternative scenarios;
- the impact of the risk element on the decision-making process;
- the sensitivity of outcomes to realistic variations;
- the power of spreadsheet software in conducting a relatively complex financial analysis; and
- the potential pitfalls of internal rate of return calculation where misleading outcomes might be generated by the existence of negative cash flows in the evaluation stream.

VALUE-BASED MANAGEMENT

Strategic management to optimize the value of a business in terms of returns to shareholders has received much attention in recent years, through shareholder value analysis and, in particular, through the use of economic value added (EVA).[1] EVA is a measure of shareholder value that has become popular, initially in the USA, and now worldwide (see Adler and McClelland, 1995). The fundamentals underpinning EVA are not new. As long ago as the 1920s, Alfred Sloan at General Motors used 'return on capital' systems to assess performance, and GEC used 'residual income' in the 1930s. EVA has the same basic structure as the residual income measure in that it compares earnings with the cost of capital. Residual income has always been popular with academic accountants, but has never been widely adopted in practice; the same cannot be said of EVA, which has replaced return on investment (ROI) as the prime performance measure in many organizations.

Stern (1993a, 1993b) details the value-based planning approach implicit in EVA, where the goal is to increase shareholder value by focusing on the share price. If the goal of the firm is 'growth' then an emphasis on size and market share may cause the return on capital to be inadequate to compensate shareholders for the risks they are taking; share prices will fall as a result. EVA attempts to align the interests of managers and shareholders by managing physical and human assets to yield optimum returns. The implications are:

- performance measurement in terms of changes in shareholder value; and
- managerial incentive schemes which link salaries and bonuses to operational performance, via shareholder value.

A number of authors (e.g., Tully, 1993; Walbert, 1993; McConville, 1994) emphasize the use of EVA as a performance yardstick of widespread application within organizations, embracing acquisition and investment decisions as well as employee compensation schemes.

The supposed advantages of EVA are as follows:

- There are no artificial upper or lower bounds to bonus earning capacity, and so none of the earnings smoothing and associated manipulation of the kind reported by Healy (1985).
- It provides a clear and unambiguous earnings goal (i.e., share price improvement) rather than one which is artificially or politically derived through the negotiation of interested parties (e.g., beating budgeted or target performance levels).
- Some portion of 'earned' bonuses may not be awarded immediately, but deferred to ensure that increases in EVA achieved are not just 'one-offs' but can be sustained in the medium term.
- A 'golden handcuffs' clause may be introduced to prevent executive resignations without the loss of accumulated deferred bonus earnings.

Shareholders view incentive schemes expressed in such terms as pursuing interests congruent with their own, so it is not surprising that the introduction of an EVA-based compensation scheme induces an immediate increase in share prices. Shareholders clearly expect more of the same.

Whereas residual income is defined as profit (before tax) minus cost of assets (as a percentage of assets employed), EVA takes an economic income approach:

$$\text{EVA} = \text{Accounting income} - \text{Cost of capital.}$$

It moves towards a cash base by adjusting traditional accounting income for the impact of those accounting policies which do not have a cash effect, but which do influence accounting income. This means reversing the impact of many accounting standards in the calculation phase.

The notional percentage interest term of the residual income calculation is replaced by the weighted cost of capital (WACC) to reflect both the cost of equity, the cost of debt and the relativities between the two. The overall EVA calculation, therefore, provides a direct measure of shareholder value of potential benefit for measuring firm performance.

Tully (1993) details the calculation of EVA for two US companies (see Table 9.2): the goal is a positive EVA outcome, one which indicates that the operation is creating wealth through the efficient management of capital. In the case of Anheuser-Busch, for example, WACC is calculated as

$$0.67 \times 14.3\% + 0.33 \times 5.2\% = 11.3\%,$$

TABLE 9.2

Calculation of EVA for two companies

	Anheuser-Busch	Spiegel
Operating profit (£m)	1,756	188
Tax payable (£m)	617	69
Profit after tax (£m)	1,139	119
Cost of equity	14.3%	18.3%
Cost of debt	5.2%	6.8%
Equity weighting	67%	37%
Debt weighting	33%	63%
Weighted average cost of capital	11.3%	11.1%
Total capital (£m)	8,000	1,600
Cost of capital (£m)	904	178
Economic value added (£m)	+235	−59

the cost of capital is

$$11.3\% \times £8000m = £904m,$$

and then the cost of capital is subtracted from profit after tax to give

$$EVA = 1139 - 904 = £235m.$$

Good performance, a positive EVA outcome, therefore equates with 'beating the cost of capital', rather than 'beating budget' or achieving positive operating earnings. EVA may be raised by:

- earning more profit from less capital – by cutting costs and withdrawing capital from activities in which costs exceed returns; and
- investing in high-return projects – by achieving growth through investment where returns exceed costs.

Neither of these recommendations is at all startling. Like residual income, EVA will tend to penalize:

- companies with good future prospects which are not necessarily reflected in one year's cash flows;
- asset-intensive companies;
- companies expanding aggressively through an acquisitions strategy;
- resource-rich companies, notably those in extractive industries, oil and gas and mineral exploration.

The complexity in the calculation of an apparently simple measure like EVA lies in the specification of its components – 'accounting income' and 'cost of capital'.

The EVA approach to performance measurement relies on cash flows, and requires adjustments to be made to historic cost accounting numbers derived from the profit and loss account and the balance sheet. These adjustments eliminate (or at least alleviate) the effect of alternative accounting opinions, as reflected by accounting standards so that the profit and loss account approximates cash revenues and expenses and the balance sheet approximates the actual cash invested. The clearest impact is apparent in, for example, the depreciation of investments against expected future cash flows and the capitalization of research and development expenditures which are then expensed over the lives of successful projects.

Adjustments to accounting numbers have to be considered in a number of areas, including:

- provisions;
- advance revenues;
- research and development costs;
- reserves;
- depreciation;
- extraordinary losses and gains;
- leases;
- goodwill;
- deferred tax.

Provisions about payments or write-offs may be so conservative as to understate both the profits and assets of the business. A reversal of these provisions may give a more accurate indication of the cash costs of these expenses and better reflect their timing and certainty. In practice, provisions for employee entitlements, warranty claims, inventory diminution and doubtful debts would all be reversed because of the conservative guess-work they embrace.

Advance payments (e.g., premiums, fees, subscriptions and progress payments) may be received from customers well before accounting standards permit them to be recognized as revenues in the profit and loss account. The recognition of such as revenue as and when it is received more accurately reflects the timing of cash flows.

Research and development (R&D) costs may be accounted for in a number of alternative ways as permitted by accounting standards, normally either as 'full costs' (all R&D expensed in the year in which it occurs) or 'successful efforts' (unsuccessful R&D expensed and successful R&D amortized over the length of the project). Value-based adjustments demand consistency and require all R&D expenditures and exploration costs (both successful and unsuccessful) to be capitalized and written off over the life of successful research and development.

Reserves attributable to asset revaluations and foreign exchange fluctuations are reversed and deducted from capital. Asset revaluations have no impact on cash flows, and deductions from capital associated with their reversal give a more accurate indication of the cash cost of the assets. Some assumptions may be necessary to accommodate asset revaluations that have been made in previous time periods. Changes in the value of foreign-held assets and liabilities similarly have no impact on cash flows until those assets are realized.

Depreciation charges over the useful life of the asset are permitted. Although depreciation is not a cash item, it does reflect that assets (and the cash flows generated by these assets) have a finite life. Long-life assets or those where the length of life is uncertain remain undepreciated.

Extraordinary, non-recurring and abnormal losses are added to capital on an after-tax basis; such gains on the same basis are deducted from capital to reflect a 'full cost' (rather than 'successful efforts') approach.

Leases are all treated in a similar manner (i.e., existing operating leases are treated in the same way as finance leases). Operating leases are thus defined as non-cancellable leases to separate the performance of the company from its means of finance and to eliminate the erroneous distinction between 'rent' and 'buy' in the accounts. This may necessitate some discount rate assumptions to perform present value calculations.

Goodwill amortization is reversed from the profit and loss account and added back to capital to remove erroneous assumptions about the lives of assets and businesses.

Deferred tax provisions in the tax charge of the profit and loss account mean that the latter does not give an accurate indication of the actual tax paid in cash by a business. Again, timing differences cause the problem, this time a variation between the recognition for accounting purposes and assessment for income tax purposes. In practice many of these deferred tax provisions will be associated with differences between 'useful life' and 'taxation' depreciation on fixed assets. The adjustment requires future tax benefits to be netted off the provision for deferred tax and the net increase (or decrease) in deferred tax provision to be deducted from (or added to) the taxation charge in the profit and loss account.

Despite these adjustments EVA remains a historic cost measure since it does not incorporate market value assessments. The subjectivity of the revaluation of non-traded assets and the non-trivial costs of continual revaluation drive this decision. However, we must not confuse the motivation of improved performance with purely financial issues. For example, accounting manipulations (e.g., asset revaluations) might be employed in a strategic manner to ensure that debt covenants are satisfied and that the company is portrayed in a favourable light by statutory financial reporting obligations.

The need for consistency in the adjustments made to accounting income is paramount if comparability is to be reliable. Estimates of the cost of equity, the cost of debt and of the relativities between the two in the WACC must also be reliable, because the EVA outcome is potentially sensitive to errors in this area.

EVA undeniably ignores the non-financial factors which drive a business, using a measure which is essentially short-term and based on historic costs. Its strength is its unerring focus on increasing market value as a goal pursued by shareholders, and whose interests can be aligned with management.

Where the goal is to increase shareholder value by focusing on the share price, the targets for attention are corporate goals which may not be in the interests of shareholders; thus if 'growth' is the stated goal of the firm, but the emphasis on size and market share causes the return on capital to be inadequate to compensate shareholders for the risks they are taking, then the share price will fall. Shareholder value analysis attempts to reorient goals so that the interests of managers and shareholders are aligned; the implications of such an approach are that management performance is measured in terms of changes in shareholder value, and that managerial incentive schemes will link salaries and bonuses to operational performance via shareholder value. Shareholders apparently view such incentive schemes as consistent with their own interests, in that they are likely to reduce short-term management manipulation and encourage the pursuit of long-term share price growth. Dunlap (1996) details how such a philosophy can be fundamental to the achievement of strategic goals.

Dunlap is infamous for his work in turning around troubled enterprises worldwide. These firms, which include American Can, Cavenham Forest Industries, Australian Consolidated Press Holdings, Scott Paper and

Sunbeam, have been restructured at great speed, refocused on what they do best, and redirected to protect and enhance shareholder value. The strategy adopted by Dunlap in pursuing shareholder value is described by his 'Ten Commandments' for a smart approach to business:

1 Business is simple and needs to follow four simple rules:
   - Get the right management team – as small as is feasible.
   - Cut costs to improve the profit and loss account.
   - Focus on the core business and dispose of non-core assets to improve the balance sheet.
   - Get a real strategy – one which requires setting a few major attainable goals and tenaciously pursuing them.

2 Squeeze corporate headquarters to eliminate perks and retrench high-priced but unproductive management. Top of the list for elimination are company cars (for all but salespeople), subscriptions to trade journals and associations, and charitable donations. By eliminating the excess baggage, which might be brands, suppliers, inventory or working capital, and which is neither adding value nor producing profit, a slimmer more efficient operation results. He cites his rule of 55 (1996: 59) as a suitable starting point for such action:
   - 50% of a company's products typically generate only 5% of their revenues and profits;
   - 50% of a company's suppliers provide only 5% of their purchased goods and services.

3 Focus on shareholder value in order to align the interests of the board of directors with those of the shareholders. Dunlap decries recent moves to emphasize 'stakeholder interests' on the grounds that they are impossible to measure, and recommends a focus on share price because that can. He recommends director compensation in the form of share equity and cites studies by Elson in the USA (Dunlap, 1996: 226) which show that those companies whose directors hold few shares have poorer corporate performance, together with chief executives who are more likely to be overpaid. He is adamant in the view that 'shareholders own the company; they take all the risks' and that, therefore, the company's top priority is towards the shareholder, rather than towards customers or employees.

4 Develop a marketing strategy to achieve 20% earnings growth, 20% return on sales and 20% sales growth. The approach to marketing is entirely consistent with the 'First Commandment' in that it depends on building the right team, tenacity in pursuing difficult goals and the establishment of strong monitoring and control systems.

5 Link employee incentives directly to corporate performance in the pursuit of goal congruency. Dunlap cites a study showing that 73% of US companies that lost money still incentivized their chief executives; he asks why. He asks the same question again with respect to the abject failure of boards of directors to fire underperforming chief executives. Both questions are in some respects rhetorical in that he supplies the reason in terms of the personal interrelationships between board members and the existence of a 'club' mentality which often precludes such behaviour. He demands that executive compensation be tied to shareholder value.

6 Use consultants sparingly, because most of them will only tell you what you want to hear.

7 Reward leadership and outstanding performance at every level. Ideally these rewards will be in the form of shares (not share options) to encourage congruent behaviour from management at all levels.

8 Put your money where your reputation is. The adoption of the 'shareholder value' message at board level should establish a transparent process for the development of an objective compensation programme, with targets set for director share ownership.

9 Be outrageous, but be prepared to take responsibility and criticism for actions. Dunlap has always been outspoken, and makes no secret of the fact that he has become a multimillionaire by investing heavily in the companies that he has successfully turned around.

10 Remember you are not in business to be liked. He suggests that 'if you want a friend, get a dog' (1996: xii). He has two!

Approaches to business, such as that proposed by Al Dunlap, show that the longer-term interests of shareholders and management can be aligned and that 'shareholder value' can assume a fundamental role in the strategic management of a business.

SUMMARY

This final chapter is concerned with developing measures of performance in areas of extreme uncertainty – even embracing speculation on performance levels for activities that have not yet commenced. The forecasting of cash flows is an essential activity for budgeting, project appraisal, investment decisions and value-based management, among others, so the emphasis accorded to forecasting here is wholly appropriate. We recognize that forecasts will not always be accurate, indeed that recognition is more important than accuracy itself. A sensitivity analysis of alternative assumptions and an analysis of the risk associated with variations in outcome will yield a realistic picture of alternative scenarios – and dictate appropriate management action.

NOTE

1 EVA is a registered trademark of Stern Stewart & Co. Ltd.

References

Abdeen, A.M. and Haight, T.G. (2002) 'A fresh look at economic value added: Empirical study of the Fortune 500 companies', *Journal of Applied Business Research*, 18(2): 27–36.

Adler, R. and McClelland, L. (1995) 'EVA: Re-inventing the wheel', *Chartered Accountants Journal* (NZ), May: 35–9.

Agarwal, V. and Taffler, R.J. (2003) 'The distress factor effect in equity returns: Market mispricing or omitted variable?'. Working Paper, Cranfield University School of Management.

Albrecht, K. (1988) *At America's Service: How Corporations Can Revolutionize the Way They Treat Their Customers*. Homewood, IL: Dow Jones-Irwin.

Albrecht, K. and Zemke, R. (1985) *Service America! Doing Business in the New Economy*. Homewood, IL: Irwin.

Aldrich, H.E. (1979) *Organizations and Environments*. Englewood Cliffs, NJ: Prentice Hall.

Altman, E.I. (1968) 'Financial ratios, discriminant analysis and the prediction of corporate bankruptcy', *Journal of Finance*, 23: 589–609.

Altman, E.I., Haldeman, R.G. and Narayanan, P. (1977) 'Zeta analysis: A new model to identify bankruptcy risk of corporations', *Journal of Banking and Finance*, June: 29–54.

Altman, E.I., Marco, G. and Varetto, F. (1994) 'Corporate distress diagnosis: Comparisons using linear discriminant analysis and neural networks (the Italian experience)', *Journal of Banking and Finance*, 18(3): 505–29.

Ambrosini, V. (2002) 'Resource based view of the firm', in M. Jenkins and V. Ambrosini, *Strategic Management: A Multi-perspective Approach*, 2nd edn. Basingstoke: Palgrave.

Amir, E. and Lev, B. (1996) 'Value relevance of non-financial information: The wireless communications industry', *Journal of Accounting and Economics*, 22(1–3): 3–30.

Amit, R. and Schoemaker, P.J.H. (1993) 'Strategic assets and organizational rent', *Strategic Management Journal*, 14(1): 33–46.

Anandarajan, A. and Christopher, M. (1987) 'A mission approach to customer profitability analysis', *International Journal of Physical Distribution and Materials Management*, 17(7): 55–68.

Anderson, E.W. and Sullivan, M. (1993) 'The antecedents and consequences of customer satisfaction for firms', *Marketing Science*, 12(Spring): 125–43.

Anderson, E.W., Fornell, C. and Lehmann, D.R. (1994) 'Customer satisfaction, market share, and profitability: Findings from Sweden', *Journal of Marketing*, 58(3): 53–67.

Andrews, K.R. (1971) *The Concept of Corporate Strategy*. Homewood, IL: Irwin.

Anthony, R.N. (1965) *Planning and Control Systems: A Framework for Analysis*. Boston: Harvard University Press.

Anthony, R.N., Dearden, J. and Govindarajan, V. (1992) *Management Control Systems*, 7th edn. Boston: Irwin.

Anthony, R.N., Hawkins, D.F. and Merchant, K.A. (2003) *Accounting: Text and Cases*, 11th edn. New York: McGraw-Hill.

Argenti, J. (1976) *Corporate Collapse*. London: McGraw-Hill.

Ashton, R.H. (1976) 'The robustness of linear models for decision making', *Omega*, 14(5): 609–15.

Askarany, D. and Smith, M. (2004) 'The Diffusion of Management Accounting Change', *British Accounting Association Annual Conference*, York, April.

Atkinson, A.A., Banker, R.D., Kaplan, R.S., and Young S.M. (1995) *Management Accounting*. Englewood Cliffs, NJ: Prentice Hall.

Atkinson, A.A., Balakrishnan, R., Booth, P., Cote, J.N., Groot, T., Malmi, T., Roberts, H., Uliana, E. and Wu, A. (1997a) 'New directions in management accounting research', *Journal of Management Accounting Research*, 9: 79–108.

Atkinson, A.A., Waterhouse, J.H. and Wells, R.B. (1997b) 'A stakeholder approach to strategic performance measurement', *Sloan Management Review*, 38(3): 25–37.

Australian Bureau of Statistics (2002) *Non-profit Institutions Satellite Account, Australian National Accounts 1999/2000*. Cat. No. 5256.0. Canberra: ABS.

Ax, C. and Bjornenak, T. (2000) 'The bundling and diffusion of management accounting innovations – the case of the balanced scorecard in Scandinavia'. Paper presented to the 23rd Annual Congress of the European Accounting Association, Munich, April.

Banker, R.D., Potter, G. and Srinivasan, D. (2000) 'An empirical investigation of an incentive plan that includes nonfinancial performance measures', *Accounting Review*, 75(1): 65–92.

Barber, L. (2003) *Benchmarking Graduate Retention*. Brighton: Institute for Employment Studies.

Barney, J. (1991) 'Firm resources and sustained competitive advantage', *Journal of Management*, 19(1): 99–120.

Barth, M.E. and McNicholls, M.F. (1994) 'Estimation and market valuation of environmental liabilities relating to superfund sites', *Journal of Accounting Research*, 32(Supplement): 179–219.

Bayne, C.K., Beauchamp, J.J., Kane, V.E. and McCabe, G.P. (1983) 'Assessment of Fisher and logistic linear and quadratic discriminant models', *Computational Statistics and Data Analysis*, 1: 257–73.

Bayon, T., Bauer, H. and Gutsche, J. (2002) 'Customer equity marketing', *European Management Journal*, 20(3): 213–22.

Becker, B. and Huselid, M. (1998) 'High performance work systems and firm performance: A synthesis of research and managerial implications', *Research in Personnel and Human Resources Management*, 16: 53–101.

Behin, B. and Riley, R. (1999) 'Using nonfinancial information to predict financial performance: The case of the US airline industry', *Journal of Accounting, Auditing and Finance*, 14: 29–56.

Beischel, M.E. and Smith, K.R. (1991) 'Linking the shop floor to the top floor: Here's a framework for measuring manufacturing performance', *Management Accounting* (US), October: 25–9.

Bellis-Jones, R. (1989) 'Customer profitability analysis', *Management Accounting*, 67(2): 26–8.

Berger, P.D., Bolton, R.N., Bowman, D., Briggs, E., Kumar, V., Parasuraman, A. and Terry, C. (2002) 'Marketing actions and the value of customer assets: A framework for customer asset management', *Journal of Service Research*, 5(August): 39–54.

Bitner, M.J., Faranda, W.T., Hubbert, A.R., and Zeithaml, V. (1997) 'Customer contributions and roles in service delivery', *International Journal of Service Industry Management*, 8(3): 193–206.

Blackstone, J.H. (2001) 'Theory of constraints – a status report', *International Journal of Production Research*, 39(6): 1053–80.

Blanchard, P. (1997) 'Doing business in cyberspace', *Charter*, December: 42–3.

Blattberg, R.C. and Deighton, J. (1996) 'Manage marketing by the customer equity test', *Harvard Business Review*, 74(July–Aug.): 136–44.

Blattberg, R.C., Getz, G. and Thomas, J.S. (2001) *Customer Equity-Building and Managing Relationships as Valuable Assets*. Cambridge, MA: Harvard Business School Press.

Booth, R. (1995) 'Simple as ABC: Process mapping', *Management Accounting*, 73(3): 32.

Boring, E. (1930) 'A new ambiguous figure', *American Journal of Psychology*, July: 444.

Box, G.E.P. and Jenkins, G.M. (1976) *Time Series Analysis: Forecasting and Control*. San Francisco: Holden Day.

Brewer, P.C., Gatian, A.W. and Reeve, J.M. (1993) 'Managing uncertainty', *Management Accounting* (US), October: 39–45.

Bromwich, M. and Bhimani, A. (1989) *Management Accounting: Evolution Not Revolution*. London: CIMA.

Burrell, G. and Morgan, G. (1979) *Sociological Paradigms and Organizational Analysis: Elements of the Sociology of Corporate Life*. London: Heinemann.

Buzby, C.M., Gerstenfeld, A., Voss, L.E. and Zeng, A.Z. (2002) 'Using lean principles to streamline the quotation process: A case study', *Industrial Management and Data Systems*, 9: 513–20.

Cameron, K.S. and Whetten, D.A. (eds) (1983) *Organisational Effectiveness: A Comparison of Multiple Models*. New York: Academic Press.

Carlzon, J. (1987) *Moments of Truth: New strategies for Today's Customer Driven Economy*. Cambridge, MA: Ballinger.

Carter, C.R. and Hendrick, T.E. (1997) 'Organizational determinants of time-based strategies and tactics', *International Journal of Physical Distribution and Logistics Management*, 27(8): 445–58.

Chan, Y.L. and Lynn, B.E. (1993) 'Organizational effectiveness and competitive analysis: An analytic framework', *Advances in Management*, 2: 85–108.

Chen, Y.N. and Kleiner, B.H. (2001) 'New developments in creating cycle time reduction', *Management Research News*, 24(3–4): 17–21.

Chenhall, R.H. (2003) 'Management control systems design within its organisational context: findings from contingency-based research and directions for the future', *Accounting, Organizations and Society*, 28(2–3): 127–68.

Chenhall, R.H. and Langfield-Smith, K. (1998) 'Adoption and benefits of management accounting practices: An Australian study', *Management Accounting Research*, 9: 1–19.

Clarke, F.L., Dean, G.W. and Oliver, K.G. (1997) *Corporate Collapse: Regulatory Accounting and Ethical Failure*. Melbourne: Cambridge University Press.

Coase, R. (1937) 'The Nature of the Firm', *Economica*, 4: 331–51.

Collins, J. and Porras, J. (1994) *Built to Last: Successful Habits of Visionary Companies*. New York: HarperCollins.

Collins, R. and Green, R. (1982) 'Statistical methods for bankruptcy prediction', *Journal of Economics and Business*, 34: 349–54.

Collis, D.J. and Montgomery, C.A. (1998) *Corporate Strategy: A Resource Based Approach*. Boston: Irwin McGraw-Hill.

Connolly, T. and Ashworth, G. (1994) 'Managing customers for profit', *Management Accounting*, 72(4): 34–9.

Cooper, R. (1985) *Camelback Communications Inc*. Harvard Business School Case.

Cooper, R. and Kaplan, R. (1988) 'How cost accounting distorts product costs', *Management Accounting* (US), April: 20–7.

Cooper, R. and Kaplan, R.S. (1991) *The Design of Cost Management Systems*. Englewood Cliffs, NJ: Prentice Hall.

Cooper, R. and Kaplan, R.S. (1992) 'Profit priorities from activity-based costing', *Harvard Business Review*, 70(May–June): 130–5.

Cooper, R.G. (1985) 'Selecting winning new product projects: Using the New Prod system', *Journal of Product Innovation Management*, 2: 34–44.

Coughlan, P. and Darlington, J. (1993) 'As fast as the slowest operation: The theory of constraints', *Management Accounting*, 71(June): 14–17.

Covin, J.G. (1991) 'Entrepreneurial versus conservative firms: A comparison of strategies and performance', *Journal of Management Studies*, 28: 439–62.

Cullen J., Broadbent, J.M. and Gray, I.H. (1994) *Management Accounting Control Systems: Practical Elements*. London: CIMA.

Darlington, J., Innes, J., Mitchell, F. and Woodward, F. (1992) 'Throughput accounting: The Garrett Automotive experience', *Management Accounting*, 70(June): 32–38.

De Bono, E. (1970) *Lateral Thinking: A Textbook of Creativity*. London: Penguin.

De Bono, E. (1992) *Serious Creativity*. Glasgow: HarperCollins.

Delbecq, A.L. and Van de Ven, A.H. (1971) 'A group process model for problem identification and program planning', *Journal of Applied Behavioural Sciences*, 7(4): 466–91.

Deming, W.E. (1986) *Out of the Crisis: Quality Productivity and Competitive Position*. Cambridge: Cambridge University Press.

Dierickx, I. and Cool, K. (1990) *A Resource Based Perspective on Competitive Strategy*. INSEAD, September.

Dorsch, M.J. and Carlson, L. (1996) 'A transaction approach to understanding and managing customer equity', *Journal of Business Research*, 35(3): 253–64.

Dorsch, M.J., Carlson, L., Raymond, M.A., and Ranson, R. (2001) 'Customer equity management and strategic choices for sales managers', *Journal of Personal Selling & Sales Management*, 21(2): 157–66.

Doyle, P. (2000) 'Value-based marketing', *Journal of Strategic Marketing*, 8: 299–311.

Dunlap, A.J. (1996) *Mean Business*. Singapore: Butterworth-Heinemann Asia.

Easton, G. and Jarrell, S. (1998) 'The effects of total quality management on corporate performance: An empirical investigation', *Journal of Business*, 7(1): 253–307.

Einhorn, H. and Hogarth, R. (1986) 'Judging probable cause', *Psychological Bulletin*, 99: 3–19.

Eisenberg, H. (1997) 'Re-engineering and dumbsizing: Mismanagement of the knowledge resource', *Quality Progress*, May: 57–64.

Epstein, M. and Manzoni, J.F. (1997) 'The balanced scorecard and tableau de bord: Translating strategy into action', *Management Accounting* (US), August: 28–36.

Eskildson, L. (1995) 'TQM's role in corporate success: Analyzing the evidence', *National Productivity Review*, 14(4): 25–38.

Farslo, F., Degel, J. and Degne, J. (2000) 'Economic value added (EVA) and stock returns', *The Financier*, 7: 115–18.

Forbes, D.P. (1998) 'Measuring the unmeasurable: Empirical studies of nonprofit organization effectiveness from 1977 to 1997', *Nonprofit and Voluntary Sector Quarterly*, 27(2): 183–202.

Fornell, C. (1992) 'A national customer satisfaction barometer: The Swedish experience', *Journal of Marketing*, 56(1): 6–22.

Fornell, C. (2000) 'Customer satisfaction, capital efficiency, and shareholder value'. Working paper, Michigan University.

Foster, G. and Gupta, M. (1999) 'The customer profitability implications of customer satisfaction'. Working Paper, Stanford University.

Foster, G. and Young, M. (1997) 'Frontiers of management accounting research', *Journal of Management Accounting Research*, 9: 63–79.

Foster, G., Gupta, M. and Sjoblom, L. (1996) 'Customer profitability analysis: Challenges and new directions', *Journal of Cost Management*, 10(1): 5–7.

Fox, L. (2004) *Enron: The Rise and Fall*. New York: Wiley.

Frydman, H., Altman, E.I. and Kao, D.G. (1985) 'Introducing recursive partitioning for financial classification: The case of financial distress', *Journal of Finance*, 40(1): 269–291.

Gantt, H.L. (1994) 'The relation between production and costs', *Journal of Cost Management*, 8(1): 4–11 (first published 1915).

Garland, R. (2002) 'What influences customer profitability? Service–profit chain: Non-financial drivers of customer profitability in personal retail banking', *Journal of Targeting, Measurement and Analysis for Marketing*, 10(3): 233–48.

Ghosh, D. and Lusch, R.F. (2000) 'Outcome effect, controllability and performance evaluation of managers: Some field evidence from multi-outlet businesses', *Accounting, Organizations and Society*, 25: 411–25.

Gibson, W. (1998) 'Laughing all the way to the databank', *Charter Business Software Guide*: 18–19.

Goldratt, E.M. and Cox, J. (1986) *The Goal*. New York: North River Press.

Goold, M. and Campbell, A. (1987) *Strategies and Styles: The Role of the Centre in Managing Diversified Corporations*. Oxford: Blackwell.

Gosling, D.H. (1988) 'Measuring the performance of divisional cost centres', *CMA Magazine*, July/August: 30–3.

Gosselin, M. (1997) 'The effect of strategy and organizational structure on the adoption and implementation of activity based costing', *Accounting, Organizations and Society*, 22: 105–22.

Grant, R.B. (1991) 'A resource based theory of competitive advantage: Implications for strategy formulation', *California Management Review*, 33(3): 114–35.

Griffiths, I. (1986) *Creative Accounting: How to Make Your Profits What You Want Them to Be*. London: Firethorn Press.

Gurau, G. and Ranchhod, A. (2002) 'Measuring customer satisfaction: A platform for calculating, predicting and increasing customer profitability', *Journal of Targeting, Measurement and Analysis for Marketing*, 10(3): 203–17.

Hair, J.F., Anderson, R.E., Tatham, R.L. and Black, W.C. (1998). *Multivariate Data Analysis*, 5th edn. Upper Saddle River, NJ: Prentice Hall.

Hamel, G. and Pralahad, C.K. (1994) *Competing for the Future*. Boston: Harvard Business School Press.

Hamer, M. (1983) 'Failure prediction: Sensitivity of classification accuracy to alternative statistical methods and variable sets', *Journal of Accounting & Public Policy*, 2: 289–307.

Hammer, M. and Champy, J. (1993) *Re-engineering the Corporation: A Manifesto for Business Revolution*. New York: HarperCollins.

Hammer, M. and Stanton, S.A. (1995) *The Re-engineering Revolution*. New York: Harper Business.

Handa, V. and Adas, A. (1996) 'Predicting the level of organizational effectiveness: A methodology for the construction firm', *Construction Management and Economics*, 14: 341–52.

Harari, O. (1997) 'Ten reasons TQM doesn't work', *Management Review*, 86(1): 38–44.

Hart, A. and Smith, M. (1998) 'Customer profitability audit in the Australian banking sector', *Managerial Auditing Journal*, 13(7): 411–18.

Harvey-Jones, J. (1992) *Troubleshooter 2*. London: BBC Books.

Harvey-Jones, J. and Massey, A. (1990) *Troubleshooter*. London: BBC Books.

Hayes, R. and Abernethy, W. (1980) 'Managing our way to economic decline', *Harvard Business Review*, 58(4): 67–77.

Healy, P.M. (1985) 'The effect of bonus schemes on accounting decisions', *Journal of Accounting and Economics*, 7: 85–107.

Hellier, P., Geuersen, G.M., Carr, R.A. and Rickard, J.A. (2003) 'Customer repurchase intention: A general structural equation model', *European Journal of Marketing*, 37(11–12): 1762–1802.

Henderson, B. (1970) 'The product portfolio', *Perspectives*, no. 66. Boston: Boston Consulting Group.

Heskett, J.L., Jones, T.O., Sasser, W.E. and Schlesinger, L.A. (1994) 'Putting the service–profit chain to work', *Harvard Business Review*, 72(2): 164–70.

Hiromoto, T. (1988) 'Another hidden edge – Japanese management accounting', *Harvard Business Review*, 66(4): 22–6.

Hogan, J.E., Lehmann, D.R., Merino, M. Srivastava, R.K., Thomas, J.S. and Verhoef, P.C. (2002) 'Linking customer assets to financial performance', *Journal of Service Research*, 5(1): 26–38.

Holder, W.W. (1987) 'The not-for-profit organization financial reporting entity: An exploratory study of current practice', *Financial Accountability and Management*, 3: 311–30.

Hopwood, A.G. (1976) *Accounting and Human Behaviour*. Englewood Cliffs, NJ: Prentice Hall.

Horngren C.T., Foster, G. and Datar, S.M. (1994) *Cost Accounting: A Managerial Emphasis*, 8th edn. Englewood Cliffs, NJ: Prentice Hall.

Houghton, K.A. and Smith, M. (1991) 'Loan risk and the anticipation of corporate distress: West Australian evidence', in K. Davis and I. Harper (eds), *Risk Management in Financial Institutions*. Sydney: Allen & Unwin.

Howell, R. and Soucy, S. (1990) 'Customer profitability: As critical as product profitability', *Management Accounting (US)*, October: 43–7.

Hughes, K.E. (2000) 'The value relevance of nonfinancial measures of air pollution in the electric utility industry', *Accounting Review*, 75(2): 209–28.

Hunt, S.D. and Morgan, R.M. (1995) 'The comparative advantage theory of competition', *Journal of Marketing*, 59(2): 1–16.

Huselid, M. (1995) 'The impact of human resource management practices on turnover, productivity and corporate financial performance', *Academy of Management Journal*, 38: 635–72.

Innes, J. and Mitchell, F. (1995) 'A survey of activity based costing in the UK's largest companies', *Management Accounting Research*, 6(2): 137–53.

Institute of Chartered Accountants in England and Wales (2002) *Guide to Professional Ethics*. London: ICAEW.

Institute of Chartered Accountants in England and Wales (1993) *Internal Control and Financial Reporting Draft Guidelines for Directors of Listed Companies*. London: ICAEW.

Ittner, C.D. and Larcker, D.F. (1998a) 'Are nonfinancial measures leading indicators of financial performance? An analysis of customer satisfaction', *Journal of Accounting Research*, 36: 1–35.

Ittner, C.D. and Larcker, D.F. (1998b) 'Innovations in performance measurement: Trends and research implications', *Journal of Management Accounting Research*, 10: 205–39.

Ittner, C.D. and Larcker, D.F. (2001) 'Assessing empirical research in managerial accounting: A value-based management perspective', *Journal of Accounting and Economics*, 32: 349–410.

Ittner, C.D., Larcker, D.F. and Meyer, M.W. (2003a) 'Subjectivity and the weighting of performance measures: Evidence from the balanced scorecard', *Accounting Review*, 78(3): 725–58.

Ittner, C.D., Larcker, D.F. and Randall, T. (2003b) 'Performance implications of strategic performance measurement in financial services firms', *Accounting, Organizations and Society*, 28: 715–41.

Jain, D. and Singh, S.S. (2002) 'Customer lifetime value research in marketing: A review and future directions', *Journal of Interactive Marketing*, 16(Spring): 34–46.

Jazayeri, M. and Cuthbert, P. (2004) 'Research in management accounting: What needs to be researched'. Paper presented to the *British Accounting Association Annual Conference*, York, April.

Johnson, H.T. and Kaplan, R.S. (1987) *Relevance Lost: The Rise and Fall of Management Accounting*. Boston: Harvard Business School Press.

Jones, T.O. and Sasser, W.E. (1995) 'Why satisfied customers defect', *Harvard Business Review*, 73(Nov.–Dec.): 88–99.

Kahnemann, D. and Tversky, A. (1972) 'Subjective probability: A judgement of representativeness', *Cognitive Psychology*, July: 430–54.

Kahneman, D. and Tversky, A. (1979) 'Prospect Theory', *Econometrica*, 47(2): 263–92.

Kale, S.H. (2003) 'CRM in gaming: It's no crapshoot', *UNLV Gaming Research & Review Journal*, 7(2): 43–54.

Kaplan, R.S. (1984) 'The evolution of management accounting', *Accounting Review*, 59(3): 390–418.

Kaplan, R.S. (1992) 'In defense of activity based cost management', *Management Accounting* (US), November: 58–63.

Kaplan, R.S. and Norton, D.P. (1992) 'The balanced scorecard-measures that drive performance', *Harvard Business Review*, 70(Jan.–Feb.): 71–9.

Kaplan, R.S. and Norton, D.P. (1993) 'Putting the balanced scorecard to work', *Harvard Business Review*, 71(Sept.–Oct.): 134–47.

Kaplan, R.S. and Norton, D.P. (1996) 'Using the balanced scorecard as a strategic management system', *Harvard Business Review*, 74(Jan.–Feb.): 75–85.

Kaplan, R.S. and Norton, D.P. (2004) 'Strategy Maps', *Strategic Finance*, March: 27–35.

Kato, Y., Boer, G. and Chow, C.W. (1995) 'Target costing: An integrative management process', 9(1): 39–51.

Keeley, M. (1978) 'A social justice approach to organizational evaluation', *Administrative Science Quarterly*, 22: 272–92.

Kennedy, T. and Affleck-Graves, J. (2001) 'The impact of activity-based costing techniques on firm performance', *Journal of Management Accounting Research*, 13: 19–45.

King, M., Lapsley, I., Mitchell, F. and Moyes, J. (1994) *Activity Based Costing in Hospitals*. London: CIMA.

Kotler, P. (1994) *Marketing Management – Analysis, Planning, Implementation and Control*, 8th edn. Englewood Cliffs, NJ: Prentice Hall.

Kotter, J. and Heskett, J. (1992) *Corporate Culture and Performance*. Indianapolis: MacMillan.

Kraft, K.L., Jauch, L.R. and Boatwright, E.W. (1996) 'Assessing organizational effectiveness in the service sector', *Journal of Professional Services Marketing*, 14(1): 101–16.

Lennox, C. (1999) 'Identifying failing companies: A re-evaluation of the logit, probit and DA approaches', *Journal of Economics and Business*, 51: 347–64.

Lewy, C. and du Mee, L. (1998) 'The ten commandments of balanced scorecard implementation', *Management Control and Accounting*, April: 34–6.

Linstone, H.A. (2002) 'Eight Basic Pitfalls', in H.A. Linstone, and M. Turoff, (eds), *The Delphi Method: Techniques and Applications*. New York: New Jersey Institute of Technology, pp. 559–71.

Linstone, H.A. and Turoff, M. (2002) *The Delphi Method: Techniques and Applications*. New York: New Jersey Institute of Technology.

Lo, A.W. (1986) 'Logit versus discriminant analysis', *Journal of Econometrics*, 31: 151–78.

Lothian, N. (1987) *Measuring Corporate Performance: A Guide to Non-financial Indicators*, London: CIMA.

Lusch, R.F. and Harvey, M.G. (1994) 'The case for an off-balance-sheet controller', *Sloan Management Review*, 35(2): 101–6.

Mabberly, J. (1992) *Activity Based Costing in Financial Institutions*. London: Financial Times Pitman.

MacCrimmon, K.R. and Wehrung, D.A. (1986) *Taking Risks*. New York: Free Press.

Malina, M.A. and Selto, F.H. (2001) 'Communicating and controlling strategy: An empirical study on the effectiveness of the balanced scorecard', *Journal of Management Accounting Research*, 13: 47–90.

Maltz, A.C., Shenhar, A.J. and Reilly, R.R., (2003) 'Beyond the balanced scorecard: Refining the search for organizational success measures', *Long Range Planning*, 36: 187–204.

McConville, D.J. (1994) 'All about EVA', *Industry Work*, 18 April: 55–8.

McIlhattan, R.D. (1987) 'How cost management systems can support the JIT philosophy', *Management Accounting* (US), September: 20–6.

McKim, B. (2002) 'The difference between CRM and database marketing', *Journal of Database Marketing*, 9(4): 371–5.

McLeay, S. and Omar, A. (2000) 'The sensitivity of prediction models to the non-normality of bounded and unbounded financial ratios', *British Accounting Review*, 32: 213–30.

McNair, C.J. and Leibfried, K.H.J. (1993) *Benchmarking: Adding Distinctive Value to Every Aspect of Your Business*. New York: Harper Business.

Merchant, K.A. (1981) 'The design of the corporate budgeting system: Influences on managerial behaviour and performance', *Accounting Review*, 56(4): 813–29.

Merchant, K.A. and Van der Stede, W.A. (2003) *Management Control Systems: Performance Measurement, Evaluation and Incentives*. London: Financial Times Prentice Hall.

Miles, R.W. and Snow, C.C. (1978) *Organizational Strategy, Structure and Process*. New York: McGraw-Hill.

Miller, D. and Friesen, P.H. (1982) 'Innovation in conservative and entrepreneurial firms: Two models of strategic momentum', *Strategic Management Journal*, 3: 311–28.

Mintzberg, H. (1978) 'Patterns in strategy formulation', *Management Science*, 24: 934–48.

Morris, R.D. (1998) 'Forecasting bankruptcy: How useful are failure prediction models?', *Management Accounting*, 76(5): 22–4.

Mumford, E. and Hendricks, R. (1996) 'Business process re-engineering RIP', *People Management*, May: 22–9.

Neely, A., Adams, C. and Kennerley, M. (2003) *The Performance Prism: The Scorecard for Measuring and Managing Stakeholder Relationships*. London: Financial Times Prentice Hall.

Ness, J.A. and Cucuzza, T.G. (1995) 'Tapping the full potential of ABC', *Harvard Business Review*, 95: 130–8.

Nord, W.R. (1983) 'A political-economic perspective on organizational effectiveness', in K.S. Cameron and D.A. Whetton (eds), *Organizational Effectiveness: A Comparison of Multiple Models*. New York: Academic Press.

Norreklit, H. (2000) 'The balance on the balanced scorecard – a critical analysis of some of its assumptions', *Management Accounting Research*, 11: 65–88.

O'Donoghue, F. (1997) 'Back to the future', *Charter*, October: 46–7.

Ohlson, J.A. (1980) 'Financial ratios and the probabilistic prediction of bankruptcy', *Journal of Accounting Research*, 18(1): 109–31.

Otley, D.T. (1999) 'Performance management: A framework for management control systems research', *Management Accounting Research*, 10: 363–82.

Otley, D.T. (2001) 'Extending the boundaries of management accounting: Developing systems for performance management', *British Accounting Review*, 33: 243–61.

Ouchi, W.G. (1977) 'The relationship between organisational structure and organisational control', *Administrative Science Quarterly*, 22: 95–113.

Ouchi, W.G. (1979) 'A conceptual framework for the design of organisational control mechanisms', *Management Science*, 25(9): 833–49.

Pacey, J.W. and Pham, T.M. (1990) 'The predictiveness of bankruptcy models: Methodological problems and evidence', *Australian Journal of Management*, 15(2): 315–38.

Parasuraman, A., Zeithmal, V.A. and Berry, L.L. (1988) 'SERVQUAL: A multiple item scale for measuring customer perceptions of service quality', *Journal of Retailing*, 64(Spring): 12–40.

Parker, L.D. (2001) 'Reactive planning in a Christian bureaucracy', *Management Accounting Research*, 12: 321–56.

Penrose, E.T. (1959) *The Theory of the Growth of the Firm*. London: Blackwell.

Perera, S., Harrison, G. and Poole, M. (1997) 'Customer-focused manufacturing strategy and the use of operations-based non-financial performance measures: A research note', *Accounting, Organizations and Society*, 22(6): 557–72.

Peteraf, M. (1993) 'The cornerstones of competitive advantage: A resource based view', *Strategic Management Journal*, 14(3): 179–91.

Pfeffer, J. and Salancik, G. (1978) *The External Control of Organizations: A Resource Dependence Approach*. New York: Harper & Row.

Porter, M.E. (1980) *Competitive Strategy: Techniques for Analyzing Industries and competitors*. New York: Free Press.

Porter, M.E. (1985) *Competitive Advantage: Creating and Sustaining Superior Performance*. New York: Free Press.

Porter, M.E. (1990) *The Competitive Advantage of Nations*. New York: Free Press.

Porter, M.E. (1996) 'What is strategy?', *Harvard Business Review*, 74(6): 79–91.

Prahalad, C.K. and Hamel, G. (1990) The core competence of the corporation', *Harvard Business Review*, 68(May–June): 79–91.

Puxty A.G. (1993) *The Social and Organisation Context of Management Accounting*. London: CIMA.

Quinn, J.B. (1980) *Strategies for Change: Logical Incrementalism*. Homewood, IL: Irwin.

Ramesh, R. and Woods, R. (1996) 'Car giants profit more from less', *Sunday Times*, (26 October): 15.

Rappaport, A. (1986) *Creating Shareholder Value*. NewYork: Free Press.

Reichheld, F.F. and Sasser, W.E. (1990) 'Zero defections: quality comes to services', *Harvard Business Review*, 68(Sept.–Oct.): 105–11.

Reinartz, W. and Kumar, V. (2000) 'On the profitability of long-life customers in a noncontractual setting: An empirical investigation and implications for marketing', *Journal of Marketing*, 64(4): 17–35.

Reinartz, W. and Kumar, V. (2002) 'The mismanagement of customer loyalty', *Harvard Business Review*, 80(July–Aug.): 86–94.

Rigby, D.K., Reichheld, F.F. and Schefter, P. (2002) 'Avoid the four perils of CRM', *Harvard Business Review*, 80(Feb.): 101–109.

Rogers, E.M. (1995) *Diffusion of Innovation*, New York: Free Press.

Roslender, R. (1992) *Sociological Perspectives on Modern Accountancy*. London: Routledge.

Rumelt, R.P. (1991) 'How much does industry matter?', *Strategic Management Journal*, 12(3): 167–85.

Said, A.A., HassabElnaby, H.R. and Weir, B. (2003) 'An empirical investigation of the performance consequences of nonfinancial measures', *Journal of Management Accounting Research*, 15: 193–223.

Sakurai, M. (1989) 'Target costing and how to use it', *Journal of Cost Management*, Summer: 39–50.

Salamon, L.M. and Wojciech, S. (2001) 'Volunteering in cross-national perspective: Evidence from 24 countries'. Working Papers of the Johns Hopkins Comparative Nonprofit Sector Project, no. 40, Johns Hopkins Center for Civil Society Studies, Baltimore, MD.

Sawhill, J. and Williamson, D. (2001) 'The erosion of the competitive advantage of strategic planning: A configuration theory and resources based view', *McKinsey Quarterly*, no. 2: 96–107.

Scapens, R.W. and Bromwich, M. (2001) 'Management accounting research: The first decade', *Management Accounting Research*, 12(2): 245–54.

Scharitzer, D. and Kollarits, H.C. (2000) 'Satisfied customers: profitable customer relationships pharmaceutical marketing: how pharmaceutical sales representatives can achieve economic success through relationship management with settled general practitioners—an empirical study', *Total Quality Management*, 11(7): 955–65.

Schmalensee, R. (1985) 'Do markets differ much?', *American Economic Review*, 75: 341–51.

Selznick, P. (1957) *Leadership in Administration: A Sociological Interpretation*. New York: Harper & Row.

Senge, P. (1990) 'The leader's new work: Building learning organizations', *Sloan Management Review*, Fall: 7–23.

Shanahan, Y.P. (2002) 'A contingent examination of strategy-cost system alignment: Customer retention and customer profitability analysis'. Paper presented to the 25th Annual Congress of the European Accounting Association, Copenhagen, April.

Shank J.K. and Govindarajan, V. (1992) 'Strategic cost management: The value chain perspective', *Journal of Management Accounting Research*, 4: 179–97.

Shapiro, B.P., Rangan, V.K., Moriarty, R.T. and Ross, E.B. (1987) 'Managing customers for profit (not sales)', *Harvard Business Review*, 65(5): 101–108.

Shenhar, A.J. and Dvir, D. (1996) 'Long term success dimensions in technology-based organizations', in G.H. Gaynor (ed.), *Handbook of Technology Management*. New York: McGraw-Hill.

Sheth, J.N. and Sharma, A. (2001) 'Efficacy of financial measures of marketing: It depends on markets and marketing strategies', *Journal of Targeting*, 9(4): 341–56.

Shields, M.D. (1997) 'Research in management accounting by North Americans in the 1990s', *Journal of Management Accounting Research*, 9: 3–61.

Shields, M.D. and Young, S.M. (1989) 'A behavorial model for implementing cost management systems', *Journal of Cost Management*, 3(1): 13–28.

Siew, K.S. and Boon, S.N. (1996) 'The impacts of business process re-engineering on organizational controls', *International Journal of Project Management*, 14(6): 341–8.

Slatter, S. (1984) *Corporate Recovery: A Guide to Turnaround Management*. London: Penguin.

Smith, M. (1990) 'The rise and rise of the NFI', *Management Accounting*, 68(May): 24–6.

Smith, M. (1993) 'Customer profitability analysis revisited', *Management Accounting*, 71(8): 26–8.

Smith, M. (1997) *Strategic Management Accounting: Issues and Cases*, 2nd edn. Sydney: Butterworth. Sydney.

Smith, M. (1998) 'Measuring organisational effectiveness', *Management Accounting*, 76(9): 34–6.

Smith, M. (2003) *Research Methods in Accounting*. London: Sage.

Smith, M. and Dikolli, S. (1991) 'The demystification of the acronym in management accounting', *Accounting Forum*, 15(2): 97–114.

Smith, M. and Dikolli, S. (1995) 'Customer profitability analysis: An activity based costing approach', *Managerial Auditing Journal*, 10(7): 3–7.

Smith, M. and Graves, C. (2005) 'Corporate turnaround and financial distress', *Managerial Auditing Journal* (in press).

Smith, M. and Gunalan, S. (1996) 'The identification of recovery candidates among financially distressed companies', *Accountability and Performance*, 2(2): 69–92.

Smith, M., Kestel, J.M. and Robinson, S.P. (2001) 'Economic recession, corporate distress and income increasing accounting policy choice', *Accounting Forum*, 25(4): 334–52.

Smith, M., Ahmad, S.A. and Thahear, A.S.M. (2004) 'Modelling PN4 Classification among Malaysian Listed Companies', *Asian Review of Accounting*, December.

Smith, T. (1992) *Accounting for Growth: Stripping the Camouflage from Company Accounts*. London: Century Books.

Soderlund, M. and Vilgon, M. (1999) 'Customer satisfaction and links to customer profitability: An empirical examination of the association between attitudes and behavior'. SSE/EFI Working Papers Series in Business Administration no. 1999: 1, January.

Sparling, D. and Turvey, C.G. (2003) 'Further thoughts on the relationship between economic value added and stock market performance', *Agribusiness* 19(2): 255–67.

Srivastava, R.K., Shervani, T.A. and Fahey, L. (1998) 'Market-based assets and shareholder value: A framework for analysis', *Journal of Marketing*, 62(1): 2–18.

Srivastava, R.K., Shervani, T.A. and Fahey, L. (1999) 'Marketing, business processes, and shareholder value: An organizationally embedded view of marketing activities and the discipline of marketing', *Journal of Marketing*, 63(4): 168–80.

Stalk, G., Evans, P. and Shulman, E. (1992) 'Competing on capabilities: The new rules of corporate strategy', *Harvard Business Review*, 70(March–April): 57–69.

Stern, J. (1993a) 'Value and people management', *Corporate Finance*, July.

Stern, J. (1993b) 'EVA share options that maximise value', *Corporate Finance*, August.

Stern, J.M., Stewart, G.G. and Chew, D.H. (1996) 'EVA: An integrated financial management system', *European Financial Management*, 2(2): 223–45.

Taffler, R.J. (1982) 'Forecasting company failure in the UK using discriminant analysis and financial ratio data', *Journal of the Royal Statistical Society, Series A*, 145(3).

Taffler, R.J. (1983) 'The assessment of company solvency and performance using a statistical model: A comparative UK-based study', *Accounting and Business Research*, 13(52): 295–308.

Taffler, R.J., and Abassi, B. (1984) 'Country risk: A model for predicting debt servicing problems in developing countries', *Journal of the Royal Statistical Society, Series A*, 147(4): 541–68.

Tanaka, T. (1993) 'Target costing at Toyota', *Journal of Cost Management*, 7(1): 4–11.

Taylor, F.W. (1947) *The Principles of Scientific Management*. London: Harper & Row (first published 1911).

Thorngate, W. (1980) 'Efficient decision heuristics', *Behavioral Science*, May: 219–25.

Tully, S. (1993) 'The Real Key to Creating Value', *Fortune*, 20 September.

Tversky, A. and Kahneman, D. (1974) 'Judgment under uncertainty: Heuristics and biases', *Science*, 185: 1124–31.

Walbert, L. (1993) 'America's best wealth creators', *Fortune*, 20 December.

Waldersee, R. and Sheather, S. (1996) 'The effect of strategy type on strategy implementation actions', *Human Relations*, 49(1): 105–22.

Waldron, D. and Galloway, D. (1988) 'Throughput accounting: Ranking products profitably', *Management Accounting*, 66(Dec.): 34–5.

Wallin, K. (2004) 'Help IMA lead the profession', *Strategic Finance*, March: 6.

Ward, K. (1992) *Strategic Management Accounting*. Oxford: Butterworth-Heinemann.

Ward, K. and Ryals, L. (2001) 'Latest thinking on attaching a financial value to marketing strategy: Through brands to valuing relationships', *Journal of Targeting*, 9(4): 327–40.

Weick, K.E. and Daft, R.L. (1983) 'The effectiveness of interpretation systems', in K.S. Cameron and D.A. Whetton (eds), *Organizational Effectiveness: A Comparison of Multiple Models*. New York: Academic Press.

Wernerfelt, B. (1984) 'A resource based view of the firm', *Strategic Management Journal*, 5: 171–80.

Wheelen, T.L. and Hunger, J.D. (2004) *Strategic Management and Business Policy*, 9th edn. Upper Saddle River, NJ: Prentice Hall.

Whitt, S.Y. and Whitt, J.D. (1988) 'What professional services firms can learn from manufacturing', *Management Accounting* (US), November: 39–42.

Williams, J. and Ashford, J.K. (1994) *Management Accounting Control Systems: Knowledge*. London: CIMA.

Williams, K., Haslam, C., Williams, J., Abe, M., Aida, T. and Mitsui, I. (1995) 'Management accounting: The Western problematic against the Japanese application', in A.J. Berry, J. Broadbent and D. Otley, (eds), *Management Control: Theories Issues and Practices*. London: Macmillan.

Wilson, A. (2002) 'Attitudes towards customer satisfaction measurement in the retail sector', *International Journal of Market Research*, 44(2): 213–23.

Wooten, T.C., Coker, J.W. and Elmore, R.C. (2003) 'Financial control in religious organisations: A status report', *Nonprofit Management & Leadership*, 13(4): 343–65.

Zajac, E.J. and Bazerman, M.H. (1991) 'Blind spots in industry and competior analysis', *Academy of Management Review*, 16: 37–56.

Zavgren, C.V. (1985) 'Assessing the vulnerability of failure of American industrial firms: A logistic analysis', *Journal of Business Finance and Accounting*, 12(1): 19–45.

Index

Added to a page number 'f' denotes a figure and 't' denotes a table.